DESERT VICTORY

DESERT VICTORY

The War for Kuwait

NORMAN FRIEDMAN

NAVAL INSTITUTE PRESS
Annapolis, Maryland

Library of Congress Cataloging-in-Publication Data

Friedman, Norman, 1946–
    Desert victory : the war for Kuwait / Norman Friedman.
        p.   cm.
    Includes bibliographical references and index.
    ISBN 1-55750-254-4 (alk. paper). — ISBN 1-55750-255-2 (pbk. :
alk. paper)
    1. Persian Gulf War, 1991.   I. Title.
DS79.72.F75   1991
956.704′3—dc20   91-21088
                                                             CIP

Printed in the United States of America on acid-free paper ∞

9 8 7 6 5 4 3 2
First printing

Contents

Acknowledgments

I WOULD LIKE TO thank Tom Epley, Paul Wilderson, and Fred Rainbow of the U.S. Naval Institute for having suggested this book. Mary Lou Kenney, my editor, greatly expedited its production, cheerfully accepting and digesting extensive changes to the text as fuller information became available. Linda Cullen obtained most of the photographs; she and Fred Rainbow culled a considerable pile of material for the set from which the illustrations were chosen. Deborah Farrell arranged for the production of the maps, drawn by William Clipson. Susan Sweeney prepared the index. I am indebted to the entire Naval Institute book production staff, and particularly to Pam Schnitter and John Cronin, for an extraordinarily quick passage from manuscript to finished book.

This book could not have been written without considerable assistance, both from friends and from the office of the Chief of Information of the U.S. Navy. I am particularly grateful to Stewart Slade of Forecast International, Steve Zaloga, Kernan Chaisson of Forecast International, Eric Grove, Lon Nordeen of McDonnell Douglas, A. D. Baker III, editor of *Combat Fleets*, Michael Pocalyko, Daniel A. David, David Steigman of *Navy Times*, David Isby, K. N. Rausch, Paul van Riper, Mac Greeley of the Naval Institute, Antony Preston, editor of *Naval Forces* and of the invaluable NAVINT biweekly newsletter, Lyle Bien, John Miller of the Naval Institute, Robert F. Dunn, John Gresham, William Lipsmeyer, Steve Ramsdell, and Joseph Stanik. All helped make this book more accurate. Whatever errors remain are, of course, my own responsibility. I would like to emphasize that the views stated in this book are entirely my own, and should not be considered those of anyone assisting me or of the U.S. Navy or the U.S. Defense Department.

Most important of all, I would like to thank my wife, Rhea, for her love and her support, including invaluable editorial advice, and for her encouragement during a very hectic project.

DESERT VICTORY

Introduction

AT MIDNIGHT ON 15 January 1991 the United Nations' ultimatum to Iraq ran out. Saddam Hussein had refused to leave Kuwait; he would have to be thrown out. The United Nations had now officially sanctioned force, and the United States and its coalition allies had built up the wherewithal to exert that force. Still, no one really knew whether it would be used. War seemed impossible. Through the next day, there was a nervous pause as last-minute peace feelers ran their course at the United Nations. Some imagined that this ultimatum would merely be replaced by another. After all, the deadline had come and gone without immediate military action. One reporter said that a Saudi prince had assured him that a deal was in the works: there would be no war. War was, after all, too frightening for its potential to destabilize the whole region.

These were all fantasies. The outbreak of war had been delayed only because the advantages of an initial air strike on a moonless night were far too great to forego. It appears that the United States had miscalculated at almost the last minute by defining the ultimatum in terms of New York, rather than local Middle Eastern, time; by midnight in New York the sun was already up in Iraq and Kuwait. Perhaps there was some hope that Saddam Hussein would make the first overt move, and thus relieve the coalition forces from whatever onus was involved in attacking first (after, of course, Saddam's own initial attack the previous August). In any case, the choice of interpretation meant that the attack had to be set for the night after the ultimatum ran out, the 16th.

All through the day of the 16th, airplanes in Saudi Arabia and the Gulf states, and on board carriers in the Persian Gulf and the Red Sea, were armed and checked. They began taking off about midnight, local time. By 2:30 A.M. Baghdad was being bombed. This was no gradually escalating phased attack as in Vietnam. In that war the U.S. government spent seven years debating the wisdom of "going downtown" to bomb Hanoi. It never was willing to hit the ultimate "downtown" target, the seat of the North Vietnamese government. This time the attackers leveled Saddam's palace, the centerpiece of downtown Baghdad, on the first night. They also destroyed most of his national air-defense system, so that they could return the next day and the next night, and for more than forty more days and nights. The war began as it would continue, with very heavy, virtually unrestrained, attacks. The coalition meant to win as clearly and as quickly as possible.

For many, the strike on Baghdad (and the other concurrent air strikes throughout Iraq and Kuwait) marked the beginning of the war for Kuwait, the war which ended with the victorious coalition's call for a cease-fire about six weeks later. More properly, the war began on another night, about five months earlier, when Saddam's tanks rolled over the Kuwaiti border, on 2 August 1990. It included a lengthy naval blockade. This book tells the story of that war, from Saddam's triumph in Kuwait to his military defeat.

The outcome of the war seemed astonishing. Until January 1991 Iraq had generally been considered the dominant military power in the region, abundantly supplied with every kind of modern hardware. Yet its fall was precipitous and remarkable, too, in how small a price the Iraqis were able to exact from their attackers.

This victory can be ascribed both to U.S. prowess and to Saddam Hussein's ineptitude. It is important that we be able to distinguish the two and not ascribe our success exclusively to the methods and weapons used against Iraq. In some cases we may even have triumphed despite self-imposed limitations.

Stunning victory tends to blind the victor to the lessons worth learning. Victims tend to do better. In this case, the lessons may well be learned by other Third World countries, which may find themselves in positions not too different from Iraq's in the near future. After all, the Third World combines U.S. vital interests with disastrous forms of political instability. The victory over Iraq will, one hopes, discourage other Third World leaders from lethal adventures like Saddam's. However, it seems utopian to imagine that the United States will not soon once more find itself in combat (or, at least, threatening combat) in some part of the Third World.

None of this is to diminish the scale of the American achievement. The dimensions of the victory were literally unimagined prewar. For example, fewer Americans died in the war than had died accidentally in Saudi Arabia beforehand. It was actually safer to be in combat on the ground in Kuwait or Iraq than to walk some parts of major American cities. Few readers will forget that, at almost every juncture, U.S. officials from President Bush on down, cautioned against undue optimism. Yet the unpleasant surprises, so feared, never materialized.

This book, then, attempts to understand the background and the course of the war. The account of the course of the war is based on interviews with a variety of observers, official and unofficial, both in Washington and abroad, and on a reading of contemporary press accounts. Although much detailed information has yet to be released, and much remains to be said, it appears that the war can be understood well enough for lessons to be drawn. The main area of uncertainty, which time is unlikely to dispel, is in Iraqi thinking. In addition, because the coalition never occupied much of Iraq, it is impossible to be sure of the extent to which the air campaign damaged particular Iraqi targets. That issue, which is by no means insignificant, will be addressed in the body of the book.

The war was fought in a climate of intensified interservice rivalry due to a declining U.S. defense budget. The rivalry is an inescapable consequence of shrinking overall resources, and it recalls past episodes such as the bloody air force–navy battle of 1949. This episode is somewhat different in that U.S. high command relationships were radically revised after the passage of the Goldwater-Nichols Act in 1987. In some ways the effect of the Act is to favor an air force/army concept of operations and to militate against classical naval ideas. The war against Iraq naturally becomes a test of the new arrangements. We must determine whether success in this particular war occurred because of the new arrangements or despite them. For example, it may have been much more important that President Bush decided both to apply maximum force and to keep official Washington out of the war than that Central Command subordinated the naval air force in the Gulf to the local air force general. This sort of question is significant because it is most unlikely that any future conflict in the Third World will repeat the favorable circumstances encountered this time.

This book focuses on the overall logic of the war; some details of forces, their structure, their equipment, and their tactics have been relegated to appendices. The course of the war was very much determined by the relationship between Saddam Hussein's political system and what turned out to be his fatally flawed military machine. Perhaps the most interesting lesson of the war is that the sort of conventional analysis used to project Iraqi performance failed to take into account the structural problems inherent in Saddam's Iraq. Because Saddam's system shares important features with those of many other Third World states, such insights may well have implications for the conduct of future conflict, both within the Third World and between the United States and possible Third World enemies. Without considering the peculiar effects of the Iraqi political system, it would not have been possible to imagine the outcome of the war, with its extraordinarily low casualty rate. The United States very nearly decided not to fight precisely because this particular factor had not been understood.[1]

This is not a new problem, and understanding local conditions does not always make for confidence. For example, many historians of the Vietnam War have suggested that the United States ultimately failed because its government never understood the depth of motivation of the North Vietnamese enemy. In that case, better understanding might have deterred us, or it might have encouraged us to use much more extreme measures earlier on. It certainly would not have supported us in the escalatory strategy we used.

In the present case, lack of understanding (and, surely, the sad experience of Vietnam) made for what turned out to be undue caution. The common thread is that the character of a potential enemy's society and his political system are at least as important, in determining military success or failure, as whatever hard data can be accumulated on his weapons. It may be that this lesson has been missed in the past because in the two world wars (when the basic techniques were worked out) the United States Army largely fought societies not too different from itself. For those societies, it was relatively easy to project factors such as motivation, so such projections were never terribly explicit. In the case of the one major exception, Japan, it was indeed difficult to estimate just what it would take to convince the enemy to surrender. Just how difficult is shown by the continuing debate as to whether the atomic bombs were necessary. Although there is reason to wonder whether, after 1945, the Soviet Union would also have presented problems due to its dissimilarity to Western societies, fortunately our projections of Soviet behavior have not been put to the test.

In the case of Iraq, moreover, our adversary may well have turned our usual attention to the objective measures of military power against us, by building up a grossly overblown picture of his arsenal. He had an important advantage which will likely be shared by other potential Third World antagonists. Despite the excellence of our intelligence collection systems, they tend to be focused on the most threatening potential adversary, the Soviet Union. Although it is easy to say that many Third World countries are potential enemies, their number is far too large for any single country to attract much attention before a crisis bursts. When the crisis occurs, therefore, many national decisions are based largely on the sort of unclassified data that appear in standard military references and journals. Even after the crisis has begun and collection systems have been refocused on the potential enemy, the interpretation of the data they collect depends critically on the context already built up. Unless intelligence agencies have been very active beforehand it is probably difficult for them to assemble a detailed picture of local politics and society.[2]

Thus whatever the local government manages to feed the media, particularly the specialist media, can have disproportionate impact. Saddam Hussein seems to have understood this point particularly well. Unless we comprehend just what he was trying to do, and how close he came to success in that effort, we will have missed much of the import of our experience. It was, of course, our good fortune that Saddam was much less adept at warfare than at prewar propaganda.

More generally, the experience in Iraq and Kuwait seems to illustrate the limitations of the main thrust of modern U.S. intelligence, which relies on concrete data collected largely from space and which has largely dispensed with human intelligence.[3] Space-based assets can see what is there at a particular moment, but they cannot see where it is going (they only see the ground at substantial intervals), and they certainly cannot give direct insight into why it is doing something. The rundown under President Jimmy Carter, which eliminated most U.S. human intelligence assets, also eliminated many of the ground-based listening stations in favor of space-based electronic surveillance. That, too, proved unfortunate; listening resources (mainly aircraft) had to be rebuilt at great cost to support the war in Iraq and Kuwait.

Whatever the level of intelligence resources available, it is already quite clear that the United States forces were unable to know with any certainty when, for example, the Iraqis had abandoned serious efforts at air defense. As a consequence, a substantial fraction of all air-attack assets had to be devoted to insurance against some resurrection of the Iraqi air-defense system long after it had ceased to be a threat. Similarly, the space-based assets are much better equipped to count vehicles than to count troops. It seems now to be accepted that U.S. estimates of the number of soldiers in Kuwait were much too high. In neither case was the error particularly deadly, but that was only because the miscalculation was always in a conservative direction, and because the coalition forces never really found themselves hard-pressed. In different circumstances, overestimates on this scale would have made offensive operations impossible, because too many forces would have been diverted against what turned out to be non-threats.

1

Background to War: Saddam Hussein and His Iraq

THE CHARACTER OF modern Iraq and of its ruler shaped the war and opened important opportunities to the allied coalition. Like most of the other Middle Eastern states, Iraq was created as part of the World War I peace settlement. The borders drawn at that time crossed ethnic boundaries and guaranteed that, for many years at least, none of the countries thus created would achieve full internal unity (that is, a strong sense of psychological nationhood). The two important exceptions are Egypt and Iran (Persia).

The case of Iraq was paradoxical in that Baghdad and the area around it were a vital center of classical Islamic culture in the Middle Ages, a time in which the Islamic world was far in advance of the European world. Thus, to at least some Iraqis, Iraq is the source of Arabic culture. However, the historical reality is that the high culture of Baghdad was wiped out by Mongol invasion. Ultimately the area now constituting Iraq was won by the Ottoman Empire (Turkey), which held it until the British conquered the region in 1917.[1] By that time there were three quite distinct ethnic groups, occupying virtually separate regions: the Kurds in the north, the Sunni Arabs in the area around Baghdad, and the Shi'ite Arabs in the south. There were also a variety of other groups, such as the Assyrians, a Christian sect.[2] The Sunnis, a minority, were the main Ottoman administrative class and formed whatever urban elite that existed. The Shi'ites' main centers were the southern holy cities of Karbala and Najaf; they had little interest in, or loyalty to, the Ottoman government in Baghdad.

Modern Iraq has a Shi'ite majority (currently about 55 percent of the population) living in the southern half of the country, down to the Iranian and Saudi borders, and a large Kurdish minority (about 20 percent) in the north (including the oil area around Mosul and Kirkuk). To the extent that Iraqis have a national identity, it is probably concentrated in the Arab Sunni Muslims living around the upper Euphrates River, from the Syrian border to the west of Baghdad, and along the upper Tigris between Samarra and Mosul.[3] The country is ruled by the Sunni minority. However, as the Iran-Iraq War showed, the Shi'ites consider themselves distinct from their religious (but not ethnic) brethren in Iran.[4]

Oil makes these distinctions more important. The Kurdish area in the north contains the largest oil fields, around such cities as Mosul and Kirkuk. For example, Kirkuk alone accounted for 26 percent of Iraqi oil production before the Iran-Iraq War. This area, which accounts for abut 60 percent of Iraqi oil production, exports its oil largely by pipeline through Turkey. Because it was distant from the fighting with Iran, it was developed further during the Iran-Iraq War. This is the area which Britain, then the mandatory power controlling Iraq, defended against Turkey in the early 1920s. The other major oil area, in the Shi'ite south, accounts for about 30 percent of total production. The main field, Rumaila, crosses the Kuwaiti border. In fact, one of the prewar Iraqi claims was that Kuwait was illegally poaching on the Iraqi side of the border. In March 1991 there were serious suggestions that the entire field be awarded to Kuwait as reparations. The remaining 10 percent of Iraqi production is in small fields within the Sunni area.

From the beginning of the post-Ottoman Iraqi state in 1920, the Sunnis controlled the government, and the Kurds and the Shi'ites revolted against them. The Kurds wanted independence

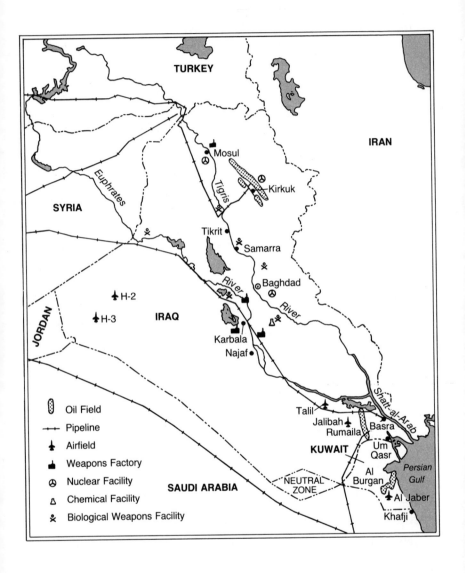

on ethnic lines (they are non-Arab Sunnis); the Shi'ites wanted independence on religious lines. Although the Shi'ites were eventually suppressed, they always presented a threat to the central Sunni group. Restiveness among the Shi'ites increased after the triumph of militant Shi'ism in Iran in 1979, and Saddam justified his attack on Iran the following year partly in terms of the need to protect Iraq (that is, Sunni dominance) against that force. Similarly, much of modern Iraqi history is the story of attempts to suppress Kurdish nationalism. After the Iraqi defeat, both the Kurds and the Shi'ites rebelled.

Iraq is hardly unique in having been concocted of different regions containing a variety of ethnic groups which have no natural connection except through the central government claiming sovereignty over them.

Virtually all governments in the area have to contend with three quite different forces. One is loyalty to tribe or ethnic or religious minority. An example would be Kurdish nationalism within Iraq. A second force is a sense of pan-Arab or pan-Islamic sentiment (which are not the same, since by no means are all Muslims also Arabs). The third is a nascent sense of nationhood (the colonial powers' concoctions take on a life of their own), which the local rulers may or may not consider a positive development.[5]

Before the invasion of Kuwait, the politics of the Arab countries were much affected by the image of a potentially unified Arab nation.[6] Arab unity, and concomitant rejection of the West, was often presented as an alternative to a disunity that could be blamed for the many economic and social problems of the Arab world. The call to unity enjoyed great force because so few of the populations of individual countries of the region have a real sense of nationhood. Loyalty is much more often to family and tribe. Without a strong sense of nationhood, governments find themselves appealing to the supposed (and largely illusory) desire for overall unity, for a return to what are presented as the glorious days of the briefly unified Muslim world of the Middle Ages. The main modern candidates for the centers of that world have generally been Cairo, Baghdad, and, to a lesser extent, Damascus. The

Egyptian version of pan-Arabism, as espoused by Gamal Nasser, was discredited by the military disaster of 1967. From then on, the main functioning pan-Arab movement was ba'athism in Syria and Iraq, with some minor competition from Muammar Qadaffi's Libya.

Saddam Hussein's attraction as an aggressive pan-Arabist based in one of the traditional centers of the Arab world was particularly strong after Egypt had explicitly retreated from pan-Arabism by making peace with Israel and through rapprochement with the ultimate non-Arab power, the United States. Syria lost its pan-Arab status by backing non-Arab Iran in the Iran-Iraq War.

Virtually every head of state had to fear that Saddam would turn local success in Kuwait into a pan-Arab movement whose adherents would try to overthrow him so as to join Saddam's pan-Arab state. Saddam could easily argue that his success in a war to unite the Arab world gave him more legitimacy than the hereditary rulers of the Gulf states. It was probably indicative that Iraqi soldiers in Khafji said that they were "with Saddam, for Arabism."[7] In none of the countries of the area does the head of state enjoy sufficient popular support (let alone the support of something like an election) to ensure his survival in such circumstances.

Arab nationalism coexists with a wider hope for Muslim unity.[8] Like Christianity, Islam is a proselytizing religion. Many of its adherents are well aware that it once controlled much of Europe, and there is a strong lingering resentment of the defeat of Islam by the West over the past two centuries. The modern Arab world is being badly torn by the stresses of modernization, and many see this stress (which afflicts every modernizing society) as the result of yet another surrender to the infidel West. The struggle with the infidel can have strong emotional resonance, particularly in those societies that have been least successful in modernizing. It is terribly easy to blame economic failure on the infidel and to turn more strongly toward Islam (and against the West). The richer oil states have experienced less of this stress.

Saddam sought to use the old battle cry of the struggle against the infidel in order to mobilize the largely poor Arab world against the coalition that formed against him. His claim carried considerable irony, in that he ran a secular state (his foreign minister, Tariq Azziz, is a Christian). However, to the extent that it was believed, it held particular peril for the Saudi government, the keeper of Islam's holiest site, Mecca.[9] Saddam hoped that, by reaching over the heads of their governments, he could draw strength from the entire Arab world. Whether or not that was a realistic threat, it was a major consideration for those in the West who, while abhorring Saddam's invasion of Kuwait, still wanted to be able to do business in the Arab world. Thus Saddam's strategy was potentially quite deterring. Saddam's pan-Arab propaganda was also often interpreted to mean that he would be able to mobilize terrorism throughout the Arab world and, by extension, throughout the West.[10]

Since 1968, Iraq has been ruled by the Ba'ath party, which overthrew an earlier military dictatorship. Ba'athism was conceived in the late 1930s by Michel Aflaq and Salah Bitar, fellow students at the Sorbonne from 1928 to 1932. At this time Arab nationalism was already a strong force, and there was much admiration for fascism and nazism—that is, for totalitarian and semisocialist ideologies. The Soviets were promoting communism as a means of attacking the West in what would now be called the Third World. The Ba'ath was one of a variety of totalitarian anti-Communist parties formed in the Arab world in the late 1930s. Like communism, it was a conspiratorial minority party organized in cells. In theory, the system of cells in any one country built up to a regional command council, which was subordinate to a "national" (that is, pan-Arab) council designed ultimately to rule the Arab world. Aflaq's 1943 manifesto recalls earlier Nazi rhetoric in its emphasis on a Leader who would embody the mystical spirit of the Arab nation (that is, in a combination of blood and culture) and whose legitimacy would not be decided on the basis of any sort of popular vote.

Thus ba'athism is a nominally pan-Arabist and socialist totalitarian ideology much of whose appeal is for the ejection of the West (and Israel) from the Arab world. Depending on which writer one reads, it is either a cynical device for maintaining power in any one Arab country (in this case, in both Syria and Iraq) or a movement with potential appeal throughout the Arab world and thus specifically opposed to local nationalism.[11]

As a nominally pan-Arab movement, the Ba'ath party could hope to disregard internal ethnic disunity, much as the "internationalist" Soviet Communist party could hope to overcome national divisions within the Soviet Union. The reality, of course, is that, as in the case of the Soviet Union, one national group is dominant. In this case it is the minority Sunnis.[12] Pan-Arabism had another effect on the Ba'ath party itself. The party's ideology led it to imagine that it could attract all Arabs, including ethnic minorities in other countries, under its wing. This miscalculation seems to have been a major cause of the war between Iraq and Iran.[13]

From the beginning, the main natural enemies of the Ba'ath in Iraq were the Communists (the alternative secret government) and, once power was seized, the army. The Ba'ath first seized power in February 1963 by dominating the governing council installed by an Iraqi Army coup. Its success inspired Syrian Ba'athists in their own coup the following month. However, the Ba'ath attempt to push the army entirely out of power failed, and in November an army countercoup succeeded. One lesson of that failure was that disunity within the party had provided the essential opportunities for its enemies.[14]

In 1966, after having had an extended period in prison to ponder such points, Saddam Hussein was appointed security chief of the Ba'ath party, charged with creating a police force for internal control.[15] After the Ba'ath won again in 1968 this internal control mechanism in turn became the Iraqi secret police force. As its chief, Saddam became the second most powerful man in the country, deputy chairman of the Revolutionary Command Council.

The Iraqi Ba'athists depended on terror, apparently to a degree extraordinary even in the Third World, to maintain their position. In a manner reminiscent of Stalin, they used fabricated plots to justify mass executions and torture. They knew that they could be ousted only by coup, that is, only by conspiracy, and therefore their primary concern was to eliminate all possible internal threats. For those outside the inner circle, the effect was not unlike Stalin's series of purges. Throughout, Saddam played Beria to his older cousin's Stalin. Fortunately for him, his older cousin, the head of state, Gen. Ahmad Hassan al-Bakr, was not particularly paranoid and made no serious attempt to undercut him. Then, in 1979, Iraqi Shi'ites became restive as their faith triumphed in Iran. President al-Bakr wanted to temporize with Shi'ites within the party. Characteristically, his security chief, Saddam Hussein, argued against any compromise. An army-Shi'ite coup seemed quite possible.[16] Saddam Hussein managed to convince President al-Bakr to resign.

He then purged the party. At an extraordinary party meeting on 22 July 1979, the Shi'ite secretary of the Revolutionary Command Council read the usual fabricated confession as a preamble to his own execution; other senior party members were simply ordered out and shot. The main potential rivals, a senior general and the deputy prime minister, had already been killed. One estimate is that 500 senior members were dead by 1 August, including a third of the ruling Revolutionary Command Council.

To ensure against further problems, Saddam created a Stalin-like personality cult combining adulation with abject fear. Quite aside from positive measures such as the prominent display of his picture and endless mentions of his name in the Iraqi media, Saddam made it a capital crime to insult him in any way. It is difficult to distinguish between acts and the legend of ferocity that Saddam built up, but the record is quite gruesome. For example, early in the Iran-Iraq War, it became clear that the Iranians would settle if only Saddam (who had ordered several important Shi'ite clerics killed) would step down. Saddam called for a show of hands within the Revolutionary Command Council. He asked those who had agreed that he should step down to go outside, and shot them. To Saddam, disloyalty included any sort of criticism. Critics, even those within the inner circle, had to be silenced lest they taint his image.

Unfortunately Saddam had little of the experience he needed for wartime leadership. Apart from a few years of exile in Egypt, he had spent no time outside Iraq. His image of the West seems to have been a series of disconnected caricatures. Iraqi diplomats, who may well have had a clearer idea of Western realities, had little desire to face the consequences of disagreement.[17] Nor had Saddam any military experience or training, a lack which showed in the vulnerability built into the defense of Kuwait. All of his real experience was concentrated on the one vital task of remaining in power by dealing with current or potential domestic rivals.

Saddam's type of state, in which power is largely secured by the fear of the inhabitants, is ultimately brittle. It is vulnerable to military defeat or other disaster because the central government cannot tolerate the sort of demonstrably competent leadership (for example, in the army), needed to deal with a severe crisis such as the Iran-Iraq War. Not only can the regime not fully reward competence displayed at a high level; often it will prefer mediocrity. Indeed, Saddam was careful to dispose of any particularly popular figure who might form the basis of an opposition movement. For example, in the fall of 1989 the war minister, who had directed the final successful offensive against Iran, was killed in a staged helicopter accident.

Saddam did not merely suspect disloyalty; he expected it, and made what seem grotesque efforts to insure against it. For example, the border positions in Kuwait were backed by fortifications intended to prevent troops from fleeing. Deserters said that they had been told their positions were surrounded by mine fields. Special squads, probably drawn from Saddam's elite force, the Republican Guard, were assigned to kill deserters and to prevent units from surrendering. It appears that the wartime disposition of the Republican Guard divisions north of Kuwait was designed at least in part to preclude retreat by the regular units closer to the likely front in Kuwait.[18]

Like many other Third World rulers, Saddam has obtained consent of the governed in three ways. The first method is coercion by secret police. Such police break up nascent opposition. In the case of Iraq they went further, intimidating those merely neutral toward the regime and its personality cult. A second method is to blame external enemies for any problems the state cannot easily solve. In Iraq, as in much of the Middle East, the primary external enemy has been Israel (cynics would say much more as a slogan than as an understood reality). Real enemies were generally coupled with Israel in Iraq rhetoric (a particularly bizarre pairing when applied to Iran). A third tactic is to reward its citizenry as well as it can. Despite the regime's overwhelming police power, it apparently was not too sure that the public left at home during the Iran-Iraq War would tolerate much privation. The practice of reward required the Iraqi government to borrow much more than otherwise might have been required to fight the war, since internal development could not be stopped to finance the war. In much the same way the early and complete looting of Kuwait provided rewards to the Iraqi public. The theory seems to have been that as long as the public received some benefits it would passively accept the regime, including the regime's need for troops.

Ultimately the survival of the regime depends on the confidence of the members of its security apparatus. If they lose faith, the regime may quickly be destroyed. The weekend after the defeat of the Iraqi Army by the coalition, security units in Basra watched passively while Iraqis demonstrated against Saddam, an act which was theoretically punishable by death. At least some of them were presumably more afraid of the vengeance of a future regime than of the commands of the current one. Similarly, toward the end of the Kuwait war, the efforts of Iraqi censors in Baghdad became noticeably less apparent in Western television reports from that city. The censors, representing the Iraqi security forces, seemed to be losing morale. They must have been aware that too many Iraqi citizens could contrast the local media with foreign sources of information such as the BBC and the Voice of America, not to mention with the evidence of their own eyes and ears that enemy aircraft could operate so freely over Baghdad itself.

Once in power, Saddam substantially expanded his personal bodyguard formation, the Republican Guard, into a special internal security brigade.[19] He needed loyalty, not merely to the Ba'ath party but, much more, to himself. His choice was to recruit only members of his extended family or, at the most distant, those from his native village, Tikrit (they would think of themselves almost as blood relatives). This applied both to his bodyguard and to his inner cabinet.[20] Ultimately the Republican Guard had a wider role in relation to the Iraqi Army itself.

The main threat to Ba'ath control was always the army, which had overthrown several previous Iraqi governments. The Ba'ath solution was twofold: a separate, politically based Popular Army was built up, and Ba'ath commissars, largely patterned on the Soviet model, were placed within the regular army to insure the loyalty of its officers. Moreover, many Ba'ath officials took over military ranks and perquisites so as to improve political control of the army. The Iraqi Army officer corps was heavily purged both before and during the war.[21] As in the pre-1941 Soviet Union, such practices did not make for much professionalism.[22]

The new Ba'ath party Popular Army received the best weapons. In 1980 it had about 150,000 active armed members (total membership may have been 250,000), up from 75,000 in the prewar period.[23] The goal was 275,000 to 325,000 members by about 1981. The Popular Army was responsible for rear-area (that is, strategic) air defense and civil defense. A few brigades were formed to fight at the front. These units, whose officers had been chosen entirely for their political loyalty, were ineffective and actually represented areas of weakness in the Iraqi front. In 1982 the Popular Army officers were purged and the combat brigades subordinated to the regular army.[24]

Thus the first Ba'ath attempt at forming a parallel army as an anticoup force largely failed. Saddam's next attempt was to build a new elite force out of his Republican Guard Brigade. Again the objective was to combine total political loyalty to the regime with the best available weapons. To pursue the natural analogy with Nazi practices, the Republican Guard is reminiscent of the early military wing of the SS, which was Hitler's personal bodyguard unit. The expansion of the Republican Guard to an elite fighting force certainly recalls the creation of the Waffen SS, though the result was much less impressive. The use of Republican Guard cadres to preclude mass surrenders by threatening to shoot soldiers certainly parallels the SS role. There are, of course, differences of degree; a British analyst observed that Saddam and his government resembled the Nazis "but without their human warmth."

The Guard brigade and Iraqi special forces were badly damaged when they were used at Khorramshahr in October 1980. However, the Guard was subsequently enlarged. By late 1982 there were three brigades (two armored, one mechanized infantry). After another failure (the February 1986 attempt to capture the Fao Peninsula), Saddam Hussein decided to build up an armored assault force. It had to be separate from the regular army because regular armored units could not be trusted to avoid coups. The Guard, with its loyal officer corps, was the obvious choice. The survivors of the original three brigades were used as a cadre from which sixteen new brigades were formed. By late 1986 the Guard fielded three armored, one mechanized, and one commando brigades. Five Guard brigades fought at Basra, where the last major Iranian offensive failed.

The Guard was then expanded again as a tank-heavy assault force; by the end of the war in 1988 reports described twenty-eight to thirty-four separate brigades. The new Guard divisions were formed in 1987, partly by recruiting college students (the Iraqi universities were ordered closed in the fall of 1987). These students, who had been exempt from the draft before, knew that the alternative was the regular army and trench warfare. The Guard divisions thus concentrated the best available men. However, because their officers were chosen for political loyalty rather than competence, these formations never performed any better than the better regular army divisions. That is not uncommon with special army formations designed primarily to protect a regime.

Loyalty was bought in a variety of ways. The Guards were paid better than regular troops, were better fed, and received the best equipment. Guard units were withdrawn from combat after 30 percent losses; regular divisions had to remain in combat until they had sustained 50 percent losses. It seems likely that the choice of the Guard to invade Kuwait was actually a reward: they got the first opportunity to loot.

Saddam seems to have believed that however much he paid, only blood ties could bring positive loyalty (other inducements could only buy a more passive and uncertain loyalty). Given his own motivation to seize and maintain power, he probably could not believe that any material inducement could compete with the army's natural appetite for power. Thus in the Iran-Iraq War he tended to shun the aggressive armored tactics that would have required (and developed) the sort of tank commanders who might later have been interested in overthrowing him (and who so frequently run coups in the Third World). He found static tactics, and the kind of forces (such as combat engineers) used to fight a static war, much less threatening internally.

Ultimately, the Guard was not expendable because it was the regime's ultimate protection against coup or uprising. Thus, whatever the state of their equipment, the Guards in the Kuwait theater were in what Saddam considered the safest position, across the Iraqi border. There they were well positioned to cut off any retreat by the regular army units Saddam expected actually to fight for Kuwait. If any confirmation of the Guard's role was needed, it was provided in the uprising in Basra immediately after the war: the Republican Guard fought the Iraqi Army. It can even be argued that the course of the war strengthened Saddam's hand, in that the regular Iraqi Army was badly punished, whereas the Guard divisions were partly saved by the timing (which some would now call premature) of the cease-fire. Thus the immediate postwar balance between the strength of the Guard and the strength of the regular army was actually tilted in the direction of the Guard.

Expansion of the Republican Guard continued after the end of the Iran-Iraq War, with a further considerable expansion announced in 1990 (but probably not implemented at all). It seems likely, then, that Saddam Hussein planned to make the Guard his main army force. It is not clear how he expected to maintain loyalty in so diluted a force. For more details of Guard strength and organization, see Appendix A.

Even though it was the bulwark of the regime, the Guard itself had to be tightly controlled. In particular, Guard units almost certainly could not act without specific orders from Saddam Hussein himself. Thus the general breakdown in communications within Iraq late in the Kuwait war tended to paralyze the surviving Guard units outside the battle zone. At first the Guard merely watched demonstrations form. Saddam was unable to order them to intervene. Within a few days, however, they were enthusiastically massacring demonstrators. Communication with the leader had been restored.

Similar considerations apply to the Iraqi Army. Saddam did not want it to show initiative, because that initiative could easily be applied to the task of overthrowing him. He wanted it not to act *except* at his behest, and that meant that most of the time it was effectively powerless. At best, even with communications undamaged, Saddam would be unable to manipulate his forces against a rapidly moving threat. With communications in disarray, his army was virtually paralyzed.

The intimate connection between political reliability and avoiding initiative is not unique to Iraq. Saddam's regime is merely an extreme example. The system of positive and highly centralized control from the top, which is adopted for political insurance (against coups), is characteristic of the Soviets and of current or past client states such as Cuba, Ethiopia, North Korea, and Syria. The defeat of Iraq, then, which is attributable in large part to paralysis due to near decapitation, must be an unpleasant object lesson for the others.

The creation of large elite units like the Guard creates its own problems. No society, especially no developing one, has an inexhaustible supply of potential junior officers or good noncommissioned officers or even of moderately educated individuals who can make useful technicians and equipment operators. Normally they leaven formations and educate those around them. Drawn off into special units, they leave the other formations with fewer human resources. The process also creates resentments. The Germans encountered exactly this problem when, during World War I, they created special storm troop units out of their regular army. The storm troops performed excellently, but to many observers the effect was largely to demoralize what was left of the regular army. Iraq experienced this problem twice over. First, many of the college students and other educated individuals ended up in Guard units. Second, in the latter stages of the Iran-Iraq War, the regular army infantry units were combed for better personnel, who were formed into special forces units quite analogous to the German storm troops (see Appendix A for details).

The resulting lack of human resources showed particularly clearly in the Iraqi armored force. Effective armored combat places particular strains on junior officers and senior noncommissioned officers commanding platoons and companies. Whatever the state of overall command and control, much depends on how well these junior officers can think for themselves. That much is true of ground combat, but tank warfare also demands an unusually high percentage of mechanically competent personnel. Even the best tanks break down, but a good crew can often easily fix them. Without the expertise, however, large armored forces cannot be really effective, and often cannot move at all. One indication of the Iraqi problem was that during the armored thrust at the end of the Iran-Iraq War the Guards tanks operated in brigades, not armored divisions. The appropriate conclusion seems to have been that they lacked the ability to field and operate larger formations, whatever the number of tanks Saddam had bought. Certainly the large armored units encountered in the final battle, which were at least nominally intact at that point, fought ineffectively. Their problems cannot all have been a consequence of poor materiel.

Anticoup considerations probably explain the performance of the Iraqi Air Force. Third World air forces always have the potential to execute coups, since they can destroy the national leadership by air attack.[25] Unlike an army, an air force generally cannot be checkmated by the creation of a rival air force. One solution is to make it an elite force, ensuring loyalty through rewards. The alternative, which seems to have been Saddam's preference, is to hold down the air force's real capability. Despite considerable numerical superiority, the Iraqi Air Force made only a very poor showing against Iran. Reportedly, during the war it had to depend heavily on foreign pilots for Exocet and other missile (for example

AS-30L) attacks. That was very reasonable in Saddam's terms, since the missiles would also have been usable against his own government.

Saddam took additional insurance against any air force–led coup. He built a complex of heavily reinforced, deeply buried bunkers, proof against any conventional air-delivered weapon, to protect himself, his senior governmental officials, and the Republican Guard command structure (which would be used to prevent any army or air force coup attempt).[26] This bunker program was also one reason the coalition never had a very realistic chance of killing Saddam Hussein.

As in any other Soviet client state, the air force was responsible for national air defense. However, its control system could also be used to command a coup. The command centers were hardened against air attack, but they were all built above ground, so that they were vulnerable to attack by security forces armed with weapons such as tanks. Moreover, it appears that key points were guarded against air attack weapons controlled by a parallel defense force, initially drawn from the Popular Army and ultimately from the Republican Guard. These units had French Rolands and Crotales rather than the Soviet-supplied weapons of the Iraqi Air Force and the regular army.

That is not to say that the Iraqi Air Force was left altogether unprotected. The Ba'ath party was always alive to the possibility of surprise attack, as most stunningly demonstrated by the Israelis against the Egyptian Air Force in 1967. Hard shelters were therefore built in large numbers, to shield the aircraft against just such an attack. Many had a suggestive feature: a bomb or blast wall in front of their entrance. The wall did provide useful protection, but it also blocked that entrance so that an airplane in the shelter could not scramble. Indeed, a tank could easily destroy the airplane in its shelter long before the airplane could be laboriously brought out. By way of contrast, both NATO and the Warsaw Pact, the other major aircraft shelter builders, studiously avoided any obstruction to quick take-off. It is difficult to avoid the conclusion that Saddam and his party were more concerned with the possibility of an air force–run coup than with problems of actual warfare against an external enemy.

Ba'ath Iraq faced a number of external threats. Both it and Ba'ath Syria naturally had pretensions to lead the entire Arab world, and neither was particularly eager to share leadership. Thus Ba'athist Iraq faced permanent enmity on the part of Ba'athist Syria, whether or not it was particularly realistic for either to imagine that it could unite any more of the Arab world. Inherent Syrian enmity (which could also be traced back to Iraq's earlier attempts to head a Fertile Crescent Federation) would have important effects on the course of both the Iran-Iraq War and the Kuwait war that followed. The enmity between Arabs (Iraqis) and Persians (Iranians) long antedates this century.[27] In addition, Turkey never quite accepted the loss of the Ottoman province of Mosul.[28]

Internally, the most prominent problem has been Kurdish nationalism, which had been strong at the birth of modern Iraq. Through the whole prewar history of the Ba'ath regime, the Iraqi government was at war with its large Kurdish minority, which wanted independence.[29] Iran generally supported the Kurds as a way of applying pressure to Iraq in a long-standing dispute over the Shatt-al-Arab, the waterway from the main Iraqi port of Basra to the Persian Gulf. In 1975 Iraq acceded to Iranian demands in return for the withdrawal of Iranian support of the Kurds, after which the Kurds were massacred. However, there were always enough left to threaten an explosion should the regime be weakened in some way, for example, during the Iran-Iraq War (the Kurds became particularly active after 1984). At the end of the war, Iraqi forces again massacred the Kurds, this time using poison gas.

The recent failure of Iraqi arms seems to have been foreshadowed by the poor performance of the Iraqi Army against the Kurds during the revolt of the 1970s, even when the Kurds made the classic error of establishing liberated zones and thus tied their forces to defending those zones. The Iraqis were unable to dislodge them, and Kurdish resistance was successful until the Iraqi deal with Iran cut their supplies of weapons. Even then they managed a fighting withdrawal to sanctuaries in Turkey (after which the Turks themselves became nervous, since they, too, had a large Kurdish minority). Contemporary observers found Iraqi military incompetence in the Kurdish war quite extraordinary.

Saddam's primary emphasis on internal rather than external security determined much of his military strategy and also much of the Iraqi command and control structure. Military strategy tended toward static tactics because more mobile ones required forward commanders with great initiative, and because such men could easily turn on the regime. In a larger sense, Saddam preferred to avoid leaving much initiative to his forward commanders, for fear that they would fall into the habit of thinking and acting independently. He always sought direct control of military operations. Despite his inexperience, he exerted just such power for the first half of the Iran-Iraq War. It was only after a series of disasters that he was willing to delegate at all, and subsequently the Iraqis began to do better. Even then, he seems to have wanted veto power over the offensive plans drawn up at the end of the war. They seem to have been set-piece plans with little allowance for tactical choice once battle had begun. They succeeded in 1988 largely because by that time the Iranians opposing them had been exhausted, and also because of the sheer weight of Iraqi materiel. It seems likely that this sort of rigid planning was practical largely because Iraq had been provided with excellent tactical intelligence, for example, satellite photography. Moreover, by the end of the war, the Iranians were no longer capable of flexible and connected large-scale operations. They had suffered too badly.

Saddam was probably much encouraged in his ultimate attack on Kuwait by the support he had enjoyed from both the West and the conservative Arab states (particularly, ironically, Kuwait and Saudi Arabia) during the war with Iran. He seems not to have realized the extent to which this support represented a choice of a lesser over a greater evil. Prewar Iraq was a Soviet client state, and in addition it posed the threat of Ba'athist subversion. These threats, however, were dwarfed by the sort of militantly anti-Western pan-Islamism espoused by the Iranian revolutionaries from 1979 on. The new Iranian regime greatly exceeded Iraq in enmity toward the West, and its particular brand of religious fervor seemed to have a very good chance of spreading well beyond Iranian borders, for example, into Saudi Arabia. On several occasions Iranian pilgrims tried to seize religious shrines, such as the Grand Mosque, in the holiest Saudi city, Mecca.

Western policy was consistent. The Gulf represents so great a proportion of the world's oil reserves that the West, for which oil is so vital, cannot cheerfully acquiesce in its control by a hostile power. In 1980, that meant opposing Iran, because Iran had so excellent a chance of consolidating power in the region. There was very little question that the Iranian government was hostile. Saddam Hussein's Iraq could not have been much better liked, but it was the sole military barrier to Iranian success. The West had to back Iraq, not so much in hopes of ensuring Saddam's own success as in hopes of precluding a devastating Iranian victory or, indeed, of precluding any decisive victory by either side. It was not that Saddam's Western backers wanted the long exhausting war to continue; they would have been much happier had the war not broken out in the first place.

Saddam's surprise was that precisely the same policy required the West to oppose him once he had declared his own aggressive intent by overrunning Kuwait. He had no clear vision of the West. After all, none of his diplomats, who could have supplied that vision, was willing to incur his displeasure by disagreeing with him. Thus the roots of the war in Kuwait lay in Saddam's rule by terror.

Wartime Western support of Iraq was both financial and directly military. The financial aid allowed Saddam to buy a wide variety of weapons, some of them from such new Third World suppliers as China and Brazil. Military aid ultimately included the intelligence data on which the final, successful, Iraqi offensives were based. France, in particular, provided modern air-to-surface missiles, such as Exocet and the laser-guided AS-30L (which was first used in combat during the Iran-Iraq War). All of this was in addition to massive shipments from Iraq's former patron, the Soviet Union.[30] The Gulf states, particularly Kuwait and Saudi Arabia, granted large loans and transferred weapons to Iraq during the war.

It is not clear whether the Western tilt toward Iraq included a conscious willingness to accept Saddam's use of chemical weapons (gas). Certainly he was able to acquire factories to manufacture mustard and nerve gases, mainly from Germany. Certainly, too, both Britain and the United States refrained from protesting very strongly either at the exports or at Iraqi use of gas against Iranians, even though such action was contrary to treaties dating back to 1925 (and even though both countries were fearful that the Soviets planned to use large numbers of chemical weapons in wartime). Similarly, the West did not seek to stop Saddam's program to develop a series of long-range ballistic missiles derived from the Soviet Scud (and, apparently, supported largely by German experts). In general, the wartime view seems to have been that, as bad as Saddam might be, the alternative, a Gulf theocracy ruled from Teheran, was much worse.

The great question in 1989–90 was whether almost a decade of Western military assistance, which had been crucial to his survival, had caused Saddam Hussein to moderate his extreme stated (but apparently unrealistic) goals. It was widely argued that Western support had weaned Saddam away from his close prewar relationship with the Soviets, particularly since the Soviets were also supplying Iran during the war. Saddam did not change his Ba'athist rhetoric, but that stance was not so different from the position anywhere else in the Arab world as to cause much alarm.

The growing view that Saddam had become trustworthy was particularly appealing because, with the war over, a relatively populous and advanced Iraq was an attractive trading partner. It produced very little of what it needed, but had abundant supplies of oil, and thus an assured income. Once the Iran-Iraq War ended, it seemed likely that Iraqi energies would turn to reconstruction. Numerous Western visitors hoped that, by flattering Saddam Hussein, they could extract the sort of commercial deals that seemed inevitable. Saddam himself seems to have concluded that the flattery showed the weakness and decadence of a greedy West interested only in taking his money.

By early 1990 the United States government certainly shared the view that Saddam could be a moderating factor in the Persian Gulf region, a postwar balance to the religious fervor of the Iranian government. In consequence, it tended to doubt that Saddam would attempt any fresh adventures. It seemed perfectly reasonable, in the early summer of 1990, that he would use some threats to pressure neighbors such as Kuwait into concessions, and the U.S. government saw little point in interfering. Unfortunately, Saddam's view of the United States and its goals differed radically from Washington's perspective. Thus he saw the U.S. ambassador's bland statement, made late in July, that the United States did not care to interfere in inter-Arab disagreements, as approval of the invasion he was already preparing.

In fact nothing had changed. In 1990 Saddam Hussein was still the same brutal but inept aggressor that he had been a decade earlier. He had learned little if anything, and he still considered the threat or reality of military action much the best way of securing his goals. His own character, and that of his regime, would shape the political and military course of events culminating in the disaster of February 1991.

In August 1990 Iraq had been at peace, at least nominally, for only about two years. The very long war with Iran had left the country deep in debt, both to the Western powers and to the wealthier Arab states, mainly Kuwait and Saudi Arabia. Although Iraq had gained some Iranian territory in the war, it had not obtained thereby any additional sources of revenue, such as further oil production. The war had also left Saddam Hussein in possession of a very large and well-armed army. The victory over Iran in 1988 had been relatively ambiguous, seen by many as the result of mutual exhaustion rather than of clear defeat. It was widely believed outside Iraq that both countries would be spending the next decade rebuilding, using their large oil revenues to pay for the cost of reconstruction and to service their extensive war debts.

Iraq was also left somewhat insecure. It had gained some Iranian territory, but only at the expense of increased Iranian hostility. There was every reason to suspect that Iran would reopen the war once it had healed its deep wounds, and it was so much larger that the ultimate prospect cannot have been attractive. In the north, the Kurdish minority within Iraq, badly bloodied by Saddam's attacks, remained restive. Saddam also faced the permanent hostility of Syria, which had backed Iran during the long war. None of these problems was particularly pressing, but all required Iraq to maintain substantial permanent garrisons of troops outside the Gulf area. These commitments absorbed much of the Iraqi standing army.

The protracted Iran-Iraq War cannot have ended, then, to Saddam Hussein's total satisfaction. He enjoyed absolute power largely through the efficiency of his secret police (one account of the Ba'ath regime is called *Republic of Fear*), but by late in the war there was a very evident sense of war-weariness, and Iraqi tactics were reportedly shaped by a reluctance, on the part of the troops themselves, to accept heavy casualties. During the war, Saddam used the funds he borrowed both for weapons and for continued development within Iraq; presumably he hoped that by doing so he could avoid popular discontent with a costly war. The end result, however, was a heavy postwar debt burden amounting to about $80 billion. Given the unsatisfactory end of the war, any postwar austerity program (which would normally have been required to pay off the debt as well as to finance postwar reconstruction) would have made for further political strain.

Initially, Saddam hoped to solve his problem by selling oil, but the end of the war inevitably increased world oil production (at least partly because Iran had much the same idea), and prices fell. Saddam's next thought seems to have been to use the army he still retained both to cancel a large part of the debt and to extort further funds.[31]

It appears in retrospect that Saddam's campaign, which ultimately led to war, began in February 1990, with appeals to the "Arab masses" and with increased posturing against Israel and the United States.[32] The object seems to have been to demonstrate strength that the Gulf states, including Saudi Arabia, could not resist, both militarily and in a direct political appeal to elements of their populations.[33] Meanwhile he demanded money: at the 12

February 1990 meeting of the Arab Cooperation Council (Iraq, Jordan, Yemen, and Egypt) he reportedly said that he needed $30 billion in fresh money, presumably from Kuwait and Saudi Arabia. He also reportedly said that if he was not given it, he knew how to take it. The campaign of extortion had begun.

It seems likely that Saddam was aware that extortion might lead to war. Reportedly in April he offered to return some Iranian territory and prisoners in order to settle differences permanently—in other words, to prepare for other military options. [34]

In May, at the Arab League meeting in Baghdad, Saddam demanded that Kuwait pay him $27 billion. Late in June, as a preparation for the annual OPEC meeting, a senior Iraqi official toured the Gulf to press for lower production quotas (that is, for better prices for Iraqi oil). At this time Kuwait and the United Arab Emirates (UAE) were both producing well over their OPEC quotas, so they were particular targets for such pressure. The Iraqi official also demanded that each of the Gulf states pay Iraq $10 billion, going so far as to produce a list of Kuwaiti assets to show that the country could afford to pay.

In mid-July Saddam publicly threatened military action if the overproduction problem was not resolved. [35] He privately continued to demand money, and the Kuwaitis soon concluded that the public statements cloaked much more. Iraq moved 30,000 troops to the border, but the U.S. interpreted this as saber-rattling. It seemed inconceivable that Iraq would invade its small neighbor. To help stabilize the situation, the U.S. Navy held joint maneuvers with UAE warships in the Gulf. However, the U.S. issued mixed signals. It reiterated that coercion was unacceptable, but also reminded the world that there was no U.S. treaty with Kuwait. Saddam called the U.S. ambassador, April C. Glaspie, to an audience on 25 July; it was the first time he had seen her since her arrival in 1988.

Saddam apparently said that he desperately needed the cash. Ambassador Glaspie was apparently at pains to soothe a prickly Saddam, assuring him that the United States sought his friendship (there was a dispute over a Voice of America attack on him) and did not wish to interfere in Arab-Arab disputes, such as the border dispute with Kuwait. She told him that the United States would not brook armed attack on Kuwait, and he assured her (as he assured the Egyptians and the Saudis at the same time) that he had no intention of attacking. Again, it appears that the State Department could not imagine that Saddam would behave as he did. It interpreted his troop concentration on the Kuwaiti border as bluster, not as preparation for an invasion.[36] At a final Iraqi-Kuwaiti meeting in Saudi Arabia on 31 July, the Iraqis demanded $10 billion plus some territory and drilling rights. The Kuwaitis asked for time to think about the demands, but the Iraqis withdrew. It now seems likely that the purpose of this final meeting was to distract the Kuwaitis from the final preparations for invasion.

Saddam invaded at 2 A.M. (local time) on 2 August. He was, in effect, a debtor canceling his debt by robbing the bank.

Saddam has been described as an unsuccessful brinksman, a man willing to drive to the brink of a situation but utterly unable to recognize the point of no return. In 1979, he incorrectly assumed that Iran was disintegrating to the point of vulnerability to a quick attack. The thrust toward Abadan failed, and Saddam's assumption that ethnic Arabs in the area would rally to him instead of remaining loyal to Iran proved incorrect. It would be unfair to say that Saddam was solely responsible for beginning the war (Ayatollah Khomeini, who bore a grudge because Saddam had ejected him from Iraq, tried to foment a rising among Iraqi Shi'ites), and the basic problem of Iranian-Iraqi enmity had very long standing. However, at least in the recent past it had generally led only to sporadic small-scale fighting. After 1979 Saddam was unable to withdraw from combat, and the war continued for a painful decade. The Kuwait war seems to have been a repetition of failed brinksmanship.

In both cases, the problem was that, once he had taken a position, Saddam refused to back down. In the case of Iran, he almost deliberately constructed a situation in which his enemy could not tolerate his survival. In Kuwait, he quickly decided that retreat was intolerable, and even the most abject offers of a way out failed. His own "peace offer" was really an attempt to elevate the seizure of Kuwait to a grandiose attempt to solve all the regional problems in the Arabs' favor, and it seems to have been intended only as rhetoric. In both cases, Saddam may literally have been unable to imagine the possibility of later disaster.

2

The Invasion

KUWAIT IS essentially a seaport with some inland oil fields. It is slightly smaller than New Jersey. The country has no great strategic depth and is virtually impossible to defend for long against a determined attack. There is no natural barrier to the north, on the Iraqi side, or to the south, on the Saudi side. Two roads cross the Saudi border, a major one almost on the coast, and a track about 50 miles inland. The coastal road is particularly important because it runs through an otherwise largely impassable marshland. The sandy area to its west is too soft for many vehicles during the hot summer months, but the winter rains leave it hard enough for wheeled as well as tracked vehicles. Further west, still along the border, is a virtually impassable sandy area. The Kuwaiti-Iraqi border to the west of Kuwait is defined largely by a wide wadi (depression), the Wadi al-Batin, running north-northeast. Dry in summer, it is filled by winter rain and thus forms a natural (if limited) barrier along the country's western border. Although tracked vehicles can cross the border along most of its length, wheeled traffic is largely limited to the two main roads, which meet at Kuwait City. The inland track, which crosses at the kink in the Kuwaiti-Saudi border, is the shortest inland route between Saudi Arabia and Kuwait City. The Iraqis considered it a natural coalition invasion route into Kuwait. Several large oil fields lie between the Saudi border and Kuwait City itself, in effect blocking any northward route to the city between the coastal road and the inland track.

The Kuwaiti-Saudi border itself is marked by a low sand mound (a berm) inside the Saudi border. This is the mound through which the coalition invading force cut, and which was seen on U.S. television.

Kuwait Bay is the largest harbor along the southern Gulf coast. Two large islands lie offshore: Bubiyan, in the north, near the Iraqi border, and Faylakah, further offshore and further south. There are also numerous smaller uninhabited islands and off-shore oil rigs.

In July 1990 no one seems really to have expected Iraq to attack, whatever its posturing across the border. Saddam's choice of timing had two apparent advantages. First, it came when the Kuwaiti government was least alert and when many of its senior officials were on vacation abroad, hence not available for instant reaction. Second, it came at a time when it would be particularly difficult for any counterattack force to conduct military operations. The intense heat saps energies. Moreover, Saddam could always threaten to use gas weapons, as indeed he had done both against the Iranians and against his own Kurdish citizens. The clothing used to protect against gas is almost unwearable in the hot months.

Both advantages carried their own disadvantages. Kuwait officials out of the country on 2 August quickly formed an effective government in exile (Saddam apparently thought that he could seize the emir and thus preclude such a development). As for foreign attack, Saddam seemingly grossly overestimated the speed of the coalition buildup. The timing actually worked against him, because coalition forces whose buildup began in August were not ready for action until winter, when it was actually much easier for them to fight.

The invasion was mounted by three Republican Guard divisions (two armored, the Medina and Hammurabi, and one mechanized, the Tawakalna). One raced down the coastal road to Kuwait City, another was assigned to seize the inland oil fields, and the third was assigned to secure the Saudi border. As insurance

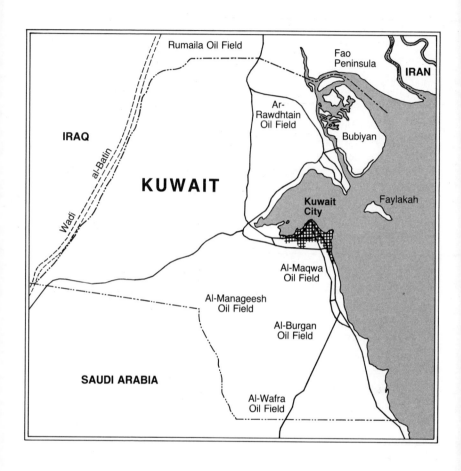

against any possible counterattack by the Saudis, the Iraqis activated their national air-defense system.[1]

The Kuwaitis' first warning of the invasion came when a Kuwaiti balloon- (aerostat) borne radar detected large numbers of vehicles approaching at night, along the road from the north. The warning sufficed to allow the emir to escape, although the Iraqis came close to catching him with a helicopter assault from the Gulf. Warning was not sufficient to bring much of the Kuwaiti Army out of its barracks, although those who could fought hard, and the royal palace fell only after extensive shelling.

The Kuwaiti Air Force A-4Kus managed to keep operating for three days despite the loss of their base. They used a road alongside the base as a runway, shuttling fuel and ammunition from the base buildings as required, always under Iraqi artillery fire. This performance, so different from that of the Iraqi Air Force a few months later, ended only when fuel and ammunition ran out; the aircraft withdrew to Saudi Arabia.

Many army units unable to respond to the alarm fought a small-unit war for a few days before heading south. The Kuwaiti Chieftain tanks fought until they exhausted their ammunition. Some units were able to conduct organized resistance for up to a week. Other army units stayed behind to become the kernel of the Kuwaiti resistance movement.

Two fast-attack boats of the Kuwaiti Navy managed to escape, at least one of them firing at Iraqi tanks. Iraq seized the rest of the small Kuwaiti fleet, as well as some Western-supplied equipment, such as Hawk defensive missile batteries.[2]

The effect of the escape of the Kuwaiti government, and particularly of the emir, was to make it impossible for Saddam to resolve the episode neatly. Saddam was unable to substitute any puppet regime of his own to legitimize the seizure. The Kuwaiti government in exile called publicly on the world to reverse the Iraqi aggression, and a resistance organization was built up inside the country. Because of its obvious legitimacy, the government in exile was able to draw on the large bank accounts transferred electronically out of the country just before Kuwait City fell. Saddam did seize whatever cash was physically in the country, and his troops enthusiastically looted, to the point of eating most of the animals in the Kuwait Zoo. There was apparently no official attempt to reconcile ordinary Kuwaitis to the new Iraqi government. Accounts of Iraqi atrocities were later used to justify the U.N.–sponsored resolution to eject Iraq from Kuwait by force. Kuwait was so rich that there was still enough for heavy looting to continue through the period of Iraqi occupation and the January-February war. An Iraqi column destroyed by U.S. aircraft as it tried to flee Kuwait City at the very end of the war was filled with looted goods, to the point that its smashed remains smelled heavily of stolen perfume.

Certainly it had been clear by July 1990 that Kuwaiti-Iraqi relations were in crisis. However, neither that information nor the concrete intelligence of an Iraqi military concentration on the border necessarily sufficed to demonstrate to the U.S. government that the invasion of Kuwait was imminent. U.S. resources are finite, and false alarms are quite common, particularly in a Third World whose governments much prefer posturing to decisive but risky action. In this case, the U.S. government literally could not believe that Iraq, which it considered to have joined the ranks of reasonable states (due to Western support during the Iran-Iraq War), would misbehave so badly. Saddam Hussein could not possibly be the thug he actually was.

Although governments do their best to collect information—intelligence—their fate depends on how well they interpret that information. Frequent false alarms do not help, because each wastes scarce resources and casts suspicion on the underlying intelligence. Of course ignoring a real emergency can be fatal. A large literature supports the theory that missed warnings make surprise attacks possible, and one key is the sheer frequency of false alarms.[3]

Good interpretation of intelligence demands thorough knowledge not only of a country's concrete resources, but also of its leaders' motives and thought processes. Even information gained by intercepting communications rarely gives an unambiguous warning. However, long-term knowledge of communications patterns can help. All of this means that the U.S. intelligence community is much more capable of interpreting, say, Soviet indications, than of understanding, let alone interpreting, what it can learn in any particular Third World country. The reason is that the Third World is quite varied, and there can never be sufficient resources to cover much of it in any detail on a permanent basis.

In this case, the State Department's unwillingness to believe that military force arrayed on the border might be more than a signal was clearly an important factor in missing the warning signs.[4] However, it seems unlikely that we can hope for much better warning performance in most areas of the Third World, no matter how clear-headed we are about local aggressiveness.

Thus it is probably realistic to accept that many Third World developments, some of them rather important to the United States, are fundamentally difficult to predict. If the United States is to retain the ability to intervene in some crises abroad, then the question will be the one posed by the Kuwait war: To what extent can we maintain forces in position against a sufficient range of possibilities? There are no reliable crystal balls, and the great bulk of reasonable warnings are false alarms. The lesson for the future is probably that, as in Kuwait, reliance will have to be placed on sufficient mobile forces (which will necessarily usually mean the U.S. Navy and Marine Corps) to contain aggression while the less mobile, ground-based forces based in the United States can be built up for some sort of counteraction.

There was no immediate military obstacle to a continued Iraqi push into Saudi Arabia. Indeed, there were definite intelligence indications that Saddam planned to continue. It now appears that Saddam expected ultimately to seize and dismember Saudi Arabia as well as the small Gulf states such as Bahrain and Qatar. Reportedly it was very widely believed that he planned to drive to a line at least south of Dhahran, so that he could seize the Saudi oil and ports. This intelligence helped convince the Saudis to invite U.S. ground and ground-based air forces into their country, a step they had studiously avoided during the Iran-Iraq War.

That Saddam could not immediately go farther was largely his own fault. His logistics were insufficient to support any further offensive; fuel and munitions had to be shifted from within Iraq.

His armored units suffered considerable breakdowns during the advance into Kuwait. A short time after Kuwait had been seized, Saddam announced that most of these forces were withdrawing. Contemporary news films showed tanks being loaded on board transporters for the journey back to Iraq. What the narrators did not say was that these were tanks that had broken down en route, and that they were being returned to Iraq for repair. Saddam would have had to bring up fresh armored forces to press farther south. At least as importantly, his troops paused to loot Kuwait. They could not reorganize and push south until they had been sated.[5]

Whatever Saddam's ultimate plans, he lacked a sufficiently organized army in Kuwait to press south against organized resistance. The means to mount just such a resistance began to appear in Saudi Arabia during the week after the invasion of Kuwait. Thus the two to seven days bought by Kuwaiti organized resistance transformed the situation from one in which even the disorganized Iraqi force might merely have drifted south to one in which it would have had to fight. Saddam had to defer whatever plans he had for Saudi Arabia.

As the allied force built up in Saudi Arabia, Saddam had to face a real military threat against his own position in Kuwait. The force that had seized the emirate was not sufficient for that. Saddam's solution was to make peace with Iran, returning both the territory and all the prisoners he had taken during the long Iran-Iraq War. That, in turn, made it more difficult for him to disgorge Kuwait. He had already thrown away territory won at enormous expense, a sacrifice that could be justified only if it brought something better: Kuwait. To lose Kuwait, too, and to do so without a fight, would have marked Saddam as a loser. Humiliation on that scale would quite possibly have been lethal.

It is by no means clear that Saddam ever made this equation explicitly; it is, however, implicit in the political system within which he operates. The difference between Saddam and, say, Nasser is that he has tended to take bigger risks and thus to risk much bigger disasters. Nasser was much better at cutting his losses at the point at which he could still survive politically. Nasser was also luckier than Saddam: he had a patron, the Soviet Union, which could and would intervene to protect him from ultimate disaster. Saddam in 1990 was particularly unlucky in that his main former patron, again the Soviet Union, was unwilling to do much to help him.

3

Forming the Coalition

SADDAM PRESUMABLY intended the invasion not only to seize Kuwait, but also to intimidate his other major Arab creditors, the Saudis and the small but rich states along the southern shore of the Persian Gulf. Before the seizure, he did not enjoy much in the way of military respect. The Iraqi Army performed poorly against Israel in 1973 and against the Kurds in 1975. Almost a decade of war with a prostrate Iran had failed to produce any decisive result. Now, however, it seemed that Saddam the boaster was also Saddam the successful invader. Apparently he intended to use the big arsenal he had amassed during the war with Iran to seize, or at least to dominate, the Persian Gulf.

In addition to conventional weapons, Saddam had begun to acquire advanced weapons during the Iran-Iraq War, initially gas and Scud ballistic missiles. He had an ongoing nuclear weapons program, despite the setback caused by Israeli destruction of one of his reactors in 1981. Such weapons could be operated by small numbers of skilled soldiers. The overall quality of the mass Iraqi Army, therefore, had little bearing on the possible use of advanced weapons. Saddam had already resorted to use of both mustard and nerve gases against Iranian troops and then against his own rebellious Kurdish citizens. An arms show staged in Baghdad in 1989 had emphasized this threat. Saddam displayed a variety of supposedly Iraqi-developed missiles and other hardware, claiming that he had an independent ability to develop the new technology.

Saddam also maintained that his new missiles could deliver gas against Israel. This claim was important in his campaign to separate the rich Gulf states from their U.S. protector. As the only Arab ruler who could (at least in theory) attack Israel so decisively, Saddam could say that any attack on him was also an attack on the Arabs' main hope of destroying their central enemy. After all, a series of disastrous wars had shown that the other Arab forces, armed with conventional aircraft and with armor, could not succeed.

One probably unintended effect of Saddam's well-publicized unconventional weapons program was the increasing feeling on the part of several countries that he had to be dealt with before his programs could mature. President Bush repeatedly said that the United States had to act because Iraq might be as little as a year away from possessing an atomic bomb. He was ridiculed at the time, but evidence collected during the war (largely during the initial air strikes) apparently indicated that Iraq was no more than twelve to eighteen months from having its first atomic bomb. Matters were indeed at a dangerous pass.[1]

For their part, the major Western powers could not accept Saddam's coercion. The fate of the Gulf was much too important for that, as demonstrated during the Iran-Iraq War. Both the United States and Britain had long maintained forces in and around the Persian Gulf. For example, as a long-term friend of Kuwait, Britain stopped a threatened Iraqi invasion in 1961. Although British forces formally withdrew from the Gulf ("East of Suez") in 1968, British influence survived—for example, in the form of army officers seconded under contract to the local armies. The U.S. Navy has operated a permanent Middle East Force based in Bahrain since 1949, and Saudi Arabia is a de facto ally. Both the United States and Britain maintained substantial naval patrols throughout the Iran-Iraq War, and some of the ships involved were still on station when Iraq invaded Kuwait in 1990.

The United States in particular had substantially upgraded its commitment in 1979, when President Carter explicitly labeled the Gulf an area of vital interest. He ordered the formation of a new Rapid Deployment Force, primarily to intervene against any Soviet drive south through Iran or Pakistan to the war waters of the Gulf. President Carter's fear was that the Soviets, blocked from any direct advance through Europe, would see seizure or intimidation of the oil states of the Gulf as an ideal alternative way of controlling the industrial West.

At the time, some commentators suggested that Carter was really setting up a force that could fight to seize Middle Eastern oil, implying that U.S. troops would die for the big oil companies. The same charge was raised in 1990. The reality, as the president saw it, was rather different. The threat was that someone else would fight to seize oil, not just for profit but as a way of gaining control of the industrial West, which could not survive without vast quantities of imported oil.

It might be argued that whoever controls a massive pool of oil still has to sell it, so consumers will merely be paying one seller rather than another. That was, after all, the effect of oil nationalization in the Middle East. That is not, however, true of every possible owner of the oil fields. Some might be much more interested in a political agenda than in cash profits; they might concentrate on the political gains achievable through extortion of the Western oil-consuming powers. This sort of description seemed to apply to the Soviets in 1979, to the Iranians after that, and also to Saddam. Even were Saddam not to invade Saudi Arabia at once, he would surely be able to control that country by intimidation.

At the very least, Saddam could impoverish the West. Much worse, his control over oil production could be used to force whatever concessions he wanted, since nothing forced him actually to produce and sell the oil he controlled. Given Saddam's earlier behavior, it was virtually certain that he would try to use that leverage to obtain the means for further military action, not least for the destruction of Israel. It followed that acquiescence in Saddam Hussein's seizure of Kuwait would almost certainly lead to a later, and much nastier, war. Saddam's appetite seemed bottom-less; ultimately he would demand what he could not be given.

It did not matter that the United States bought most of its imported oil from outside the Gulf. World oil production is shared among all consumers. Any massive cut in one producing area forces the consumers to share out the remaining production. Thus all importers are deeply affected by the fate of any single major producing area. The Gulf accounts for more than half of known world oil reserves, exercising a dominant effect on the world oil market.

For the United States, the Rapid Deployment Joint Task Force (RDJTF), the forerunner of the Central Command (CentCom) which fought the war for Kuwait, was a new sort of military organization. None of the local countries of the Gulf area would accept U.S. ground or ground-based air forces on a permanent basis. Nor could the United States, which already maintained substantial garrisons in Europe and in the Far East, afford to keep large forces permanently in or near the region even were bases offered. It just did not have enough forces that could be spared from other commitments. Forces not permanently assigned to Europe or the Far East had to be available to meet a wide variety of possible crises throughout the world, not only in the Gulf area. The same units had to be available to reinforce those already forward-deployed abroad. The situation was further complicated in that any movement of large ground forces involved not only troops (who could be flown in) but also masses of vehicles and materiel, which really could go only by sea—and which might, therefore, take quite some time to arrive.

For war in Europe, the solution was to mix permanently forward-deployed units with prepositioned equipment and stores (POMCUS, prepositioned materiel configured to unit sets) that could be matched up with units whose men would be brought in by air in an emergency. The difference between POMCUS and the usual stockpiles of spare vehicles and spare ammunition was that it was set up for immediate issue to troops coming in by air. It helped immeasurably that a large infrastructure of air and ground bases already existed in Western Europe, including massive quantities of spare parts and maintenance shops and equipment. It helped most of all that the European forces were designed with a single well-defined contingency, a Soviet ground thrust into Western Europe, in mind.

The situation in the Gulf area was much more difficult. Whatever the president's views, it was never entirely clear to what type of crisis the RDJTF would be responding, or, for that matter, which countries in the area might admit RDJTF forces in the event of any particular crisis. Soon after the force was established, it was apparent that Iran itself, one of the countries the force had been designed to defend, was more of a local threat than the Soviets (who were badly stalled in Afghanistan). The force's overall role just could not easily be defined prior to the crisis to which it was responding. The solution was to establish the RDJTF as a planning staff that could, in wartime, call upon deployable navy, air force, marine, and army resources. Prepositioning on the ground was out of the question. Even had any of the local countries agreed to accept prepositioned stocks, the force staff could never be sure that that country was anywhere near the combat zone. On the other hand, without some prepositioning the U.S. ground troops could not hope to react very rapidly to a crisis, since only troops and light vehicles could quickly be flown in.

In this case the solution was to preposition some equipment on board merchant ships, some of them held near Diego Garcia in the Indian Ocean. The closest equivalent to POMCUS was the squadron of Maritime Prepositioning Ships (MPS) supporting a Marine Expeditionary Brigade (MEB). The army and air force maintained their immediate support equipment on board Afloat Prepositioning Ships (APS) off Diego Garcia.

U.S. concern for the stability of the Persian Gulf and Southwest Asia long survived the end of the Carter administration. Much of the APS and MPS fleet was built up under the Reagan administration. In 1983 the RDJTF was upgraded to a specified and unified command (a CINC), Central Command (CentCom). CentCom planned and commanded the coalition forces that fought the Kuwait war.

Despite the existence of CentCom, the United States was not willing by itself to expel Saddam from his new possession. Throughout the Arab world, distaste for Saddam's aggression existed side by side with strong resentment for more than a century of what was seen as Western dominance. Any Western country directly attacking an Arab country risked inflaming that feeling. Saddam might well be defeated, but the resulting popular explosion could bring about the effect he had sought, expelling the West from the vital oil resource. In this sense military success might well bring political disaster.

However, Saddam's invasion of Kuwait directly threatened the Gulf states. Saddam's justification, that Kuwait itself was no more than an artifice of the colonialist West, was potentially devastating to most Third World countries. Apart from being untrue (as a state, Kuwait long preceded the formation of Iraq), much the same could be said of most Third World states. Moreover, unprovoked aggression like Saddam's has been quite rare since World War II. Countries have often attempted to seize disputed territory, but they have generally tried to avoid the appearance of simply swallowing others unprovoked.[2]

Saddam also argued that the seizure of Kuwait was a form of social justice, a seizure of unjustified wealth on the behalf of the mass of impoverished Arabs. This argument carried further threats to wealthy Gulf states such as Saudi Arabia. Like them, Kuwait relied heavily on non-Kuwaitis, such as Palestinians and Pakistanis, to operate the oil fields and to perform other essential labor, both skilled and unskilled. Citizens enjoyed the fruits of enormous oil revenue; the noncitizens were well paid, but many of them had to resent the special status of the citizens. Saddam's cry for the downfall of the wealthy, for the justice due the impoverished, could, therefore, be translated throughout the Gulf as a call for the overthrow of the established governments by the temporary, immigrant workers, and particularly by the Palestinians.[3]

This was not a new or surprising threat. It was well known that states such as Kuwait and Saudi Arabia subsidized the Palestine Liberation Organization (PLO) and its more radical offshoots largely to avoid internal subversion. During the war, Palestinians in Saudi Arabia repeatedly voiced their support for Saddam, and several Arab foreigners were executed after trying to ambush a bus carrying U.S. troops. By midwar both the Saudis and the Kuwaiti government in exile were considering plans to limit the number of postwar foreign workers.

Virtually from the beginning, Saddam questioned the legitimacy of any rulers opposed to him, calling for their assassination. Saddam equated legitimacy with pan-Arabism. In the absence of almost any other inherent justification, such as a sense of distinct nationhood (that is, broad-based political unity), it was very difficult for any local ruler, particularly an obviously pro-Western one, to deal with that sort of argument.

None of the Gulf states, not even Saudi Arabia, had anything remotely like the firepower or military experience required to stop, let alone defeat, Saddam Hussein. However, his pretensions made it particularly difficult for the states he threatened to collaborate with the Western nations, whose firepower and advanced military technology were needed to win. The old call for Muslims to unite against the infidel, the historic invader, was always present just below the surface of the situation.

The Gulf states were not unaware of the problem. All had considerable resources, but very limited populations. None was willing to militarize to the point of real military safety. They tried rapid-deployment and cooperative solutions. In the mid-1970s the Saudi government financed a Pakistani division and air units on the understanding that they would be deployed to protect Saudi Arabia in an emergency (equipment for their use was stockpiled in Saudi Arabia).[4] This arrangement lapsed after 1979, when Pakistan found itself menaced by large Soviet forces in Afghanistan and thus could no longer imagine deploying a large part of its own army and air force. Moreover, from 1980 on there was escalating tension with India over Punjab and Kashmir. Pakistan did send small forces to Saudi Arabia in 1990, but they were nothing like what had been envisaged in the past.[5] Thus the beginning of the Iran-Iraq War made it painfully obvious that outside assistance, however well arranged, might not always be forthcoming.[6] The

Gulf states (Kuwait, Saudi Arabia, Bahrain, Qatar, the UAE, and Oman) formed a Gulf Co-Operation Council (GCC) in May 1981 to improve their security against the threat of the Iran-Iraq War. The GCC was necessary because the smaller states could not in themselves develop viable air and naval defenses. It also supported a small rapid deployment force. The GCC was the major channel for Kuwaiti aid to Iraq during the Iran-Iraq War.

The United Nations provided a remarkably apt solution to the Gulf states' problem. Both the Western powers and many Arab governments could condemn the seizure of Kuwait within its wider ambit, without forming an explicit coalition. The United States, the only global power capable of mounting the sort of assault required, was the core of the implicit coalition that formed, but the Arab governments were able to join without subordinating themselves explicitly to the most prominent of the infidel powers. Thus formed, the coalition was even able to withstand Saddam's frequent charge that his Arab enemies were standing, in effect, alongside their worst hereditary enemy, Israel, the ally of the United States.[7]

The resort to the United Nations also made it possible for the Soviet Union to support the anti-Iraq coalition without any explicit connection to the United States. As the Iraqis' main arms supplier, the Soviet Union was potentially a valuable ally. Ultimately the Soviets would supply some key details of Iraqi defenses. Perhaps much more importantly, they would withdraw technicians without whom much of the Iraqi defensive system could not function.

The United States had not experienced true coalition diplomacy and warfare since World War II. It demanded a high order of diplomatic skill. Whatever the balance of contributions to the overall power of the coalition, Washington could never appear to be forcing its partners. Yet the U.S. government always knew that the decisive action which so frightened the coalition partners was exactly what was required to deal with Iraq. Saddam was ever aware of opportunities to split the coalition, and his charge was always much the same: the Arab coalition partners were acquiescing in a projected or actual massacre of the faithful orchestrated by the greatest of the infidel powers. Through the war, his missile attacks on Israel were designed to demonstrate that his Arab enemies were, in effect, Israeli collaborators. For its part, the U.S. government always had to fear that any Israeli retaliation would cause the Arab members of the coalition to bolt for fear that Saddam's charge would stick.

The coalition also eventually included most of the NATO powers. Here, too, the situation was delicate. Given the long British commitment to the Gulf, the British government of Margaret Thatcher generally shared the U.S. view of Saddam and of the likely need to defeat him by direct military action. The other European governments were far less enthusiastic. All had disagreed with earlier aggressive U.S. interventions in the Arab world, such as the air strikes on Tripoli in 1986. As major Iraqi trading partners (and creditors) many of them saw the invasion of Kuwait in less decisive terms. All feared that Saddam would be able to rouse the Arab world to expel any Western country that actively helped attack an Arab state. Postwar trade, particularly military trade, would become impossible. In 1990, Jean-Pierre Chevenement, the French minister of defense, was particularly aware of this possibility. During the Iran-Iraq War he had founded the Franco-Iraqi Friendship Society—the principal military trading contact with Saddam Hussein's government.[8]

Saddam also managed to attract a sort of following among Europeans cool to the United States and therefore to the U.S.–sponsored resistance to the Iraqi attack. This sort of reflexive anti–U.S. sentiment extended all the way across the European political spectrum, although it was sometimes cloaked in more conventional political terms (for example, that Saddam deserved support as a modern socialist attacking absolutist monarchies). It was encouraged by a sort of isolationism that set in among many Europeans, particularly Germans, as the Soviet position in Eastern Europe (against which the United States had provided a vital counterweight) seemed to collapse. It was easy for many to see the United States as a classical Western bully in the Arab world. Apologists for Saddam called for an "Arab solution" to the problem, one excluding the Western powers, which were the only ones powerful enough to deal militarily with Saddam.

For all of these reasons, it was extremely important that the opposition to Saddam Hussein, both in peace and eventually in war, be sponsored not by the United States, and not by Saudi Arabia, but by the United Nations. There was a good reason why the vast majority of members, many of whom might have been considered Saddam's natural allies against the West, agreed to resolution after resolution demanding that Iraq withdraw from Kuwait and, after reports of looting, that Iraq pay appropriate reparations. To the extent that the invasion of Kuwait was accepted by the international community, virtually all the states of the Third World, who were the vast majority of the members of the United Nations, were open to destruction by larger neighbors. Saddam's refusal to heed any of these resolutions made it possible for the coalition partners to press ahead with the crucial resolutions authorizing military action.

Unfortunately for Saddam Hussein, he invaded Kuwait at just the moment when the decline of the cold war freed the United Nations to do the peacekeeping or policing job for which it had been created in 1945. The Soviets, who in earlier times would surely have vetoed the U.S.–sponsored resolutions, this time supported them. The Soviet Union badly needed Western cooperation in its reconstruction, and its strategy was a combination of military/political disengagement (to save money and to release needed resources) and attempts to gain Western economic support. The Soviets therefore badly wanted to show that they were responsible members of the community of nations. They could not be seen as brooking aggression, particularly aggression for which no obvious justification had been advanced. The Chinese, who might have vetoed the resolutions on the grounds that they represented an assault on the Third World, were inclined to support the United States, at least partly because they were more interested in resuming U.S. economic ties than in fomenting world disorder. For both, the key development was the decline of militant ideology.[9]

That is not to suggest that Saddam was entirely without allies.

He enjoyed help on two distinct levels. On one, the governmental level, Saddam could expect several countries to oppose any anti-Iraqi coalition led by the United States. Some had their own territorial ambitions, and disliked the precedent the coalition would be setting. Prominent in this group were Cuba, Libya, and India. Yemen acted as an Iraqi client state, possibly spurred by promises of booty in Saudi Arabia or among the smaller Gulf states. The Saudis eventually ejected Yemenis from their country and had to station forces (most likely those contributed by Pakistan) on the Yemeni border to preclude the formation of a second front.

On a second level, Saddam sought to exploit the anger of many Arabs. For years, their governments had skirted trouble by telling them that their poverty and other problems could be blamed on an external enemy, usually either the United States or Israel or some combination of the two. Now Saddam, the ruler of a relatively rich state (impoverished only by his own war) appealed to the poor to fight the rich. He also sought to exploit the charge that the coalition members were, in effect, collaborating with Israel.[10]

Saddam's two themes came together in Jordan. A majority of its inhabitants are Palestinian refugees who support any attempt to destroy Israel. The Jordanian government, nominally pro-Western, became very friendly to its powerful neighbor, Iraq, during the Iran-Iraq War. Now it could not retreat. The Palestinians, or at least the PLO, supported Saddam's war as their great hope for the liberation of their lost homeland. Iraq was Jordan's main trading partner, so any U.N.–mandated sanctions against it would hurt the country very badly, increasing unrest. Normally Jordanian politics was dominated by the tension between the Jordanian (mainly Bedouin) citizenry and the Palestinians. On the war issue, King Hussein was able to achieve unified support by siding strongly with Iraq. During the runup to the war he repeatedly cautioned that war would bring disaster. He literally could not win. A coalition victory would enrage much of his population, while at the same time cutting off the vital aid previously provided by the Saudis and Kuwaitis. Whatever the king's position during the war, the resulting mob would surely destroy him. An Iraqi victory would destroy the king's freedom of action; his country would be reduced to an Iraqi protectorate. The king could only hope that there would be no war at all. Given that Saddam clearly was unwilling to retreat, the king was forced to hope that the coalition would back down. It was his scientists who most strongly advanced the "nuclear winter" theory concerning Saddam's threat to burn the Kuwaiti oil wells.[11] It may not have been coincidental that a U.S. gossip columnist wrote shortly before the war that King Hussein's queen, who had been born in the United States, was quietly buying an estate in Florida. Given the context, the estate looked very much like a potential future home in exile.

Jordan was particularly valuable to Saddam. As long as the border was open, Iraq could not be cut off from external supplies without cutting off a neutral country, Jordan, as well. Jordan could also supply valuable military support. For example, through late 1990 Jordanian RF-5 fighters flew reconnaissance along the Saudi border, looking into areas in which any allied invasion force had to mass. Because they were neutral aircraft beyond Saudi airspace, they could not legitimately be intercepted, even in the event that rules of engagement allowed operations against Iraqi aircraft.

Reportedly Saddam sought to ensure Jordanian support by promising to grant King Hussein the throne of Medina, the portion of what is now Saudi Arabia from which the Saudi royal family drove his great grandfather in 1924.[12] In any case, Saddam's particular appeal to the Palestinians virtually ensured that Jordan would support him. To make sure of that support, Saddam had two senior PLO officers, who did not fancy his chances, killed. The projected carve-up of Saudi Arabia apparently also included territory for Saddam's other major regional ally, Yemen; presumably Iraq would have taken the coastal strip including major oil fields.

In effect there were two coalitions, the inner group which actually fought Iraq, and the outer group at the United Nations that passed resolution after resolution. The outer group (particularly the Soviets and the Chinese) tended to limit coalition war aims to the restoration of Kuwait (and the payment of reparations). It was not at all willing to contemplate the destruction either of Iraq as a state or of Saddam Hussein himself. Just as the precedent of the invasion of Kuwait was unacceptable, it was frightening to imagine the United Nations granting the United States and its coalition partners the license to destroy any other member country.

The members of the fighting coalition had a much more comprehensive goal: they wanted to rid the region of Saddam Hussein and to disarm Iraq, either completely or at least completely enough to deny Saddam's successors any grandiose options. They tended to gloss over the difference between the explicit war aim and the vital implicit one by saying that Saddam would surely not long survive the destruction of his army, or that the Iraqi people (that is, the Iraqi governing elite) could avoid much unpleasantness (and, after the war, perhaps some indemnities) by eliminating Saddam.

This was, and is, a real problem. The United Nations by its nature tends to avoid clear-cut military results such as the total defeat of a member state. In this case, for example, Saddam Hussein did not have to endure the humiliation of a military victory parade through the streets of Baghdad. He could proclaim that (despite the clear evidence to the contrary) his forces had won. He could, apparently, retain the loyalty of substantial Republican Guard units. A week after the end of the war, the U.S. government found itself threatening to bomb Republican Guard units that tried to suppress the internal rebellion by using poison gas. The terms of the temporary cease-fire (signed early in March 1991) forbade Saddam from using fixed-wing aircraft at all (U.S. F-15s shot down two that did fly), and that prohibition was widely read as an attempt to keep Saddam from crushing the rebellions. However, the temporary cease-fire terms did not prohibit use of helicopters (the Iraqis apparently said they were needed to maintain communications in a country whose bridges had largely been destroyed). General Schwarzkopf later said that he had been "suckered," that it was this gap in the terms of the temporary cease-fire that permitted Saddam's Republican Guard to crush the Kurdish and Shi'ite risings. In any case, such prohibitions were as far as the United States could go in restraining Saddam's remaining security forces within Iraq. They may not have been anything like sufficient.[13]

In a speech in March 1991, President Bush said that he would probably have gone into the Gulf with or without United Nations sanction: "I might have said, to hell with them—it's right and wrong, it's good and evil, he's evil, our cause is right—and, without the United Nations, sent a considerable force to help." The Saudis would surely have fought anyway, since they faced Iraqi invasion. Syria would probably have adopted a stance of unfriendly neutrality toward Iraq. Perhaps the most important issue would have been whether the Soviets would have continued their own support of Iraq, including the provision of technicians, spare parts, and probably satellite intelligence. It is not clear whether the United States would have been so willing to bomb Baghdad had large numbers of Soviet technicians been there, or had Soviet transports been actively using the Baghdad airport.

As it was, as the war proceeded the Soviets made several attempts to gain credibility in the Arab world by brokering a cease-fire well short of coalition goals. The United States could not really afford to brush off these attempts for fear of damaging a valuable relationship, yet it also could not afford to accept them. The most frightening was the last-minute approach, which the Iraqis seemed to accept, for a pull-out from Kuwait. This deal would have allowed Saddam to salvage his army intact. The U.S. reaction was to substitute an alternative offer (described as no more than a restatement of the United Nations conditions, but embodying a short deadline).

The main Arab coalition partners (Egypt, Saudi Arabia, and Syria) had all been reluctant to invade Iraq proper, and they all balked at a ground attack when it seemed that Saddam would pull out in any case within a week or so (albeit with his forces intact). President Bush obtained an agreement by promising to end the campaign as soon as all Iraqi troops were out of Kuwait. As a consequence, he ordered a unilateral suspension of offensive operations on the evening of 27 February. At that time U.S. tanks were mustering to attack surviving Republican Guards. They stood down, and the Guard units lived to put down the postwar anti-Saddam rebellion. It is also likely that considerations of coalition warfare precluded any U.S. push to Baghdad.

One further point is worth making. The United States led the coalition forces in the field, but many of the members could not join on that basis. The Arab League sent troops who fought under Arab command (a concept never fully defined). Because the Gulf is outside the NATO area of operations, the joint command arrangements developed for NATO were irrelevant, and individual governments made their own arrangements. For example, at one point the French Army unit was abruptly withdrawn from the front line facing Kuwait. There was some limited attempt to group forces under the Western European Union (WEU), but the key to command unity seems to have been the British decision, very early in the crisis, to send forces to the Gulf to work with the U.S. forces being deployed. Thus the two largest non-Arab forces in the Gulf were under joint control.[14] Ultimately usable coalition command arrangements were worked out, and their success is probably largely attributable to President Bush's efforts. Such issues are typical of coalition warfare; they are not aberrations explainable only in terms of Middle Eastern illogic. The ultimate victory of the coalition was very much President Bush's victory in the difficult diplomacy that held it together.

This is not a new idea, but it has been a long time since the United States fought a true coalition war (World War II). NATO is indeed a coalition, but it has been built up into a robust and virtually permanent structure. That robustness in turn can be traced to the members' acceptance of a single type of military threat, posed by the Soviet Union, which has been so great that they have had few difficulties in rationalizing their responses. Even so, most observers of NATO have been impressed by the stresses as much as by the successes. A coalition like the one created to fight in Kuwait is infinitely less robust.

The Kuwait situation may be typical of the future, in a political sense. If it has any reality at all, the "new world order" sought by President Bush is a prescription for future coalition efforts. The president clearly hopes that aggression will be countered in a multinational way, through the United Nations. Whether or not that is a realistic expectation, any analysis of the Kuwait war must take into account the looseness and potential instability of wartime coalitions, particularly those under stress as they enter combat.

Coalition warfare is difficult at best and nearly impossible at worst. Military logic often will have little relevance when coalition politics intrudes. Even though the United States supplied the great bulk of the forces in this case, it could not totally dominate the outcome. In particular, members of the coalition undoubtedly differed in the extent to which they wanted a particularly clear-cut conclusion to the war.

The U.S. view at the end of the war seems to have been that it would be best for Iraq to be very clearly defeated and for internal groups, such as the Kurds, to win partial or total independence. Other coalition partners cannot have been willing to accept any such clear-cut result. For example, both Turkey and Iran have substantial Kurdish minorities of their own. Any great Kurdish victory in Iraq would make their own Kurds restive at best; in recent years both countries have put down Kurdish risings in their own territory. The Kuwaitis and Saudis (and probably residents of the other Gulf states, and possibly even the Egyptians) would have feared any triumph by the Shi'ites in the south of Iraq, since that triumph would have carried much the same liabilities as an Iranian triumph in the recent war against Iraq itself. They wanted the Sunni regime to remain in power in Iraq. In a larger sense, they probably argued that any concession to national identity in postwar Iraq would carry enormous dangers for every other regime in the area. The State Department would have echoed these sentiments. It surely also argued that the elimination of Iraq as a state would leave a power vacuum for Syria (by no means a permanently friendly state) and Iran to fill. A close observer of the U.S. official reactions to the Kurdish and Shi'ite risings after the end of the Kuwait war would notice a perceptible shift from tacit support to neutrality permitting Saddam to win. That shift almost certainly derived from a cooler calculation of coalition interests.

Historically, the United States seems to fight best when it goes to war against a clearly evil enemy. The abstract national interest does not generally suffice to cement a domestic coalition in favor of war. In this respect, U.S. entry into World War I is probably the closest equivalent to the Kuwait war. Before April 1917, a large segment of the U.S. population found it extremely difficult to imagine going to war to support corrupt monarchies, particularly czarist Russia. In the move toward war, the complexities of international politics had to be largely submerged in favor of a view in which the kaiser and Germany represented evil incarnate, and the allies represented freedom, that is, the basic (but largely unexpressed) U.S. ideology of democratic self-determination. President Wilson found himself caught between the realities of coalition requirements and his own national ideology. The other coalition partners did not really want the map of Europe reshaped by nationalism. Each of them was to some extent heir to a poly-national country and empire, and nationalism (self-determination) was ultimately quite frightening. Yet the allies badly needed the United States. President Wilson was, therefore, able to insist that the postwar settlement satisfy the U.S. view that nationalities should be able to determine their own futures. Incidentally, that settlement very nearly created a Kurdish state.

What President Wilson did not appreciate was the destructive potential of nationalism. After all, it was a Serbian nationalist who touched off the war by shooting Archduke Francis Ferdinand at Sarajevo. This time, the coalition partners were in a much better position to limit any U.S. idealism. Unlike President Wilson, President Bush had no illusions about a postwar U.S. retreat into isolation. Moreover, he was much more sophisticated about the dangers of local nationalism; he knew a lot more about the more dismal aspects of local history.

Even so, the idealism inherent in U.S. politics was an important aspect of the situation. An essential element of the process of domestic coalition-building was the widespread publicity given Saddam Hussein's cruelty. He was presented, quite properly, as Hitler in a new guise. After the war it was clearly somewhat embarrassing to be allied with Syria, whose dictator, Hafez Assad, can easily be presented as Saddam's moral equivalent (the alliance with Stalin in World War II carried much the same problems, but at the time Stalin had more enthusiastic admirers in the West).

U.S. idealism explains the widely stated hope that success in this war would somehow resolve the long-standing problems of the Middle East as a whole, particularly the Israeli-Arab dispute. Unfortunately, at least as of April 1991 any such solution seemed as far away as before. The issues involved are just too complex, and, many would say, the Israeli scapegoat is just too valuable for most of the governments in the region to abandon it. Wars tend to solve military problems, like Saddam's aggressively oriented army. Larger political-social problems can be solved by occupation and by the forcible reorientation of a society (as in, say, Germany after 1945), but none of the coalition partners would have accepted any such solution for Iraq (or, more properly, none would have agreed to any particular such solution).[15] Real coalitions almost never make for clear-cut actions beyond military victory, because their members generally have rather different ideas of just what those solutions should achieve.

None of this made the war any less worthwhile. Saddam Hussein had to be stopped because he, much more than any other local leader, was willing and able to throttle the West's access to the most vital world resource. He, much more than any other local leader, was willing and able to crush all of his neighbors. The West, led by the United States, had to act in Kuwait and Saudi Arabia because no other country in the world would have believed its guarantees of protection had it not fought in the Third World area it had so long and so loudly labeled as essential to its existence. Moreover, the war's stunning demonstration of U.S. (and other Western) resolve and competence will almost certainly greatly reduce the number and scale of challenges to that resolve over the next decade or so. It is no small thing to fight to make the world a much safer place, even if parts of it do not become materially more civilized.

4

The Embargo

FOR THE UNITED STATES and the coalition it built, the issue in August 1990 was how to confront the Iraqi attack. The only option for an immediate military response was an air strike, executed either by carrier aircraft or by long-range, land-based bombers. Both alternatives were quite limited. Iraq is a large country and had not been studied in great detail as a potential enemy. There was, therefore, no available information on which air targets might be so critical that their destruction would stop (or even slow) the Iraqi military machine. There was no particularly good reason to imagine that a few hundred or even a few thousand tons of bombs, however well placed, would end the problem. There was every reason to expect that any U.S.–sponsored air attack would give Saddam Hussein sufficient rationale for invading Saudi Arabia. The United States would then still be faced with a ground war, but one that would begin sooner, allowing little time for preparation.

That was, after all, the case in the war the United States and its coalition partners actually fought the following year. The bombing campaign eliminated much of Saddam Hussein's war machine, but much of it was directed at eliminating his overall threat to the region, for example in the form of chemical and biological weapons and his nuclear industry. Such attacks, had

they been executed in August 1990, would certainly have punished him, but they could not have stopped his advancing army.
The experience of war was that a protracted air campaign (which
could not have been mounted instantly in August 1990) did badly
punish the Iraqi Army, but that army could be defeated only by
coalition ground forces. Those forces would inevitably take some
time to build up.

These arguments applied to both potential instruments of U.S.
air attack, long-range bombers (probably flying from the United
States) and carriers off the coast. In either case, it would have
taken a careful and shrewd study of Iraq to determine what small
group of targets, if any, should have been destroyed to achieve
decisive results. Direct attack on an advancing Iraqi Army would
have required far more aerial firepower than either the long-range
bombers or carrier attack aircraft could have mustered at the
time, simply because no single strike could destroy very many of
the advancing vehicles. A large army might include, for example,
thousands of tanks. The only sort of bomb that could be sure of
stopping an invasion on that scale would be nuclear, but nuclear
weapons were clearly inappropriate in this case.[1]

The carriers would have been best placed for sustained air bombardment of moving Iraqi army forces, because they could have
come within an hour or two of the targets, and because they carry
their own reconnaissance aircraft and can therefore plan strikes
on the spot. However, their dozens of attack aircraft probably
could not have destroyed enough Iraqi vehicles quickly enough
to have stopped a determined push. Moreover, the total bomb
tonnage available to each carrier, about 2,000 tons, probably
would not have sufficed in itself (after these weapons had been
expended, the carrier would have had to withdraw periodically
for replenishment). Long-range bombers, such as B-52s, flying
from the United States could have dropped large tonnages, but
they were ill-suited to attacks on moving formations, because
their targets are generally chosen and briefed before they take off.
The round-trip to the United States is about 26 hours, and very
early in the crisis there was no assurance that any ally would have
provided basing closer in. In both cases, the likelihood is that,

had Saddam Hussein kept going, air attacks by carrier aircraft would have been used to slow his advance while a defended perimeter, analogous to the Pusan Perimeter in Korea in 1950, was built up as the basis for an eventual counteroffensive.

There could be little hope that any quick air strikes on Iraq would necessarily cause Saddam to disgorge Kuwait. The presence of clearly visible carriers could help deter him from further operations, but actually to have used their aircraft for attacks on Iraq would have had little more than symbolic effect. Such attacks might well have been disastrous.

That is not to deny the value of air strikes in a more deterrent situation, as in Libya in 1986. In that case, the main effect of a limited strike was to demonstrate graphically that Colonel Qadaffi's air defenses could not possibly protect him against something nastier. He got the hint and desisted from terrorist acts. Actual coercion by air strike is a different proposition. It was quite clear that Saddam Hussein would not cheerfully withdraw from Kuwait. It was even possible that he so identified the success of his operation with his own prestige that he would consider any withdrawal suicidal.

More generally, the question was whether Saddam could be deflected from his course by an immediate threat of air attack, or whether something much more costly was needed. Ironically, just this question had been hotly debated in the U.S. government during 1990. The question at the time was how the United States might best project its power abroad. Projection includes both peacetime persuasion (such as whatever might have been done to convince Saddam to back down before attacking Kuwait) and the use of actual force once that persuasion has failed. In the case of Kuwait, one object of persuasion was to convince Saddam Hussein not to try to seize Saudi Arabia after he had conquered Kuwait.

Much of the time, the United States would prefer not to resort to armed force at all. It is far better to exert influence quietly, not least because that allows foreign nations to agree to be influenced without losing face. The navy argued that such influence is best exerted by forces that can stay within range of a foreign country without that country's (or anyone else's) consent. Naval forces are clearly the main case in point. Long-range airplanes, such as B-52s, can fly from the United States, but they make little impression unless they do so to drop bombs. If persuasion must be by latent threat rather than by actual armed action, then only a force floating offshore seems effective. In the case of Saudi Arabia, it can be argued that a very manifest U.S. ability to strike at Iraq (from the sea) whether or not the Saudis agreed to a local U.S. presence convinced the Saudis that there was little point in bending to Iraqi pressure. After all, in places like Libya the United States had demonstrated quite clearly that its carriers could and would bomb recalcitrant states. Clearly a very long-range, land-based bomber can also deliver bombs without local consent (albeit with the consent of the states it flies over, and usually by using tankers based in foreign countries), but as far as persuasion is concerned it is more a case of "out of sight, out of mind." Ships are both visible and independent.

Moreover, the threat entailed by aircraft depends on the potential victim's belief that they can in fact do him fatal damage (remember that presence more often means threat than execution). Before the war began, Iraq was credited with a very effective air-defense system. A threat must be seen to be believed, but no one imagined that the bombers could fly over Baghdad unmolested (it took an imaginative, large-scale attack to make that possible in January 1991). Saddam surely believed that his large investment in national air defense had bought him some immunity from just such a threat. It is most unlikely, therefore, that the mere threat of air attack would have sufficed to eject him from Kuwait, particularly since he was so very aware of the possibly fatal effects of bowing to that pressure. Once the war began, of course, the big bombers could have very real effects, but that was a different issue.[2]

One argument raised in 1990 was that AWACS, the E-3 early-warning airplane, provided a new kind of presence. There was little question that such an airplane, flying near a potential aggressor's territory, could detect and track his forces. Often they could also intercept the communications that would signal his intent.

The air force argued that in 1980 the presence of AWACS aircraft over Western Europe had deterred the Soviets from invading Poland to crush the Solidarity movement. The Soviets would have been too aware of the consequences of U.S. knowledge (obtained via AWACS) of their preparations. Unfortunately, that persuasive effect required considerable sophistication on the part of the Soviets, as well as belief that, once AWACS detected their operations, real consequences would follow. Unfortunately, not all governments are entirely aware of what AWACS radar or electronic monitoring (ESM) coverage entails. That coverage is invisible. Certainly, Saddam himself could never have been described as particularly sophisticated, and his disastrous command and control arrangements seem to argue quite the opposite.

Moreover, AWACS represented a potential military threat to an aggressor only if other forces were available to act on the information it could provide. Only aircraft could have responded instantly, and to do so they had to be quite close to the targets. Those available just lacked the ability to destroy Iraq or an advancing Iraqi Army. Saudi AWACS aircraft flying in August 1990 almost certainly detected the signs of the Iraqi invasion, but Saddam Hussein seems not to have been unduly bothered by the possibility that such information would escape. He could have been deterred only by some force capable of doing him immediate and obvious harm.

Finally, AWACS aircraft have only a limited range. Their presence therefore depends upon the willingness of some other government to support U.S. presence actively and openly. That willingness varies from country to country, but it certainly cannot be assumed in advance.

The other form of presence considered within the U.S. government was troops in nearby countries. There is no question but that such troops can exert enormous influence, but there is also no question but that governments think long and hard before they accept a substantial foreign presence on the ground. Moreover, because troops require vast amounts of materiel for their support (even if they merely threaten and do not actually fight), any substantial deployment is slow and cumbersome. The lengthy course of the Desert Shield buildup was a good demonstration (and, by previous standards, it was startlingly fast).

Desert Shield was also a good example of the problems that local governments encounter when they are offered troops. The Saudis were initially quite reluctant to accept a large U.S. ground force. Almost certainly they feared that Saddam would use the mere presence of so many infidels so close to the holiest sites in Islam as an argument that the Saudi royal family was no longer fit to act as custodian for those places, and therefore as a lever to overthrow the Saudi government. The Saudis were willing to take the chance only if they could be convinced that it was worthwhile, and that the United States would indeed do something about Saddam. It was probably extremely helpful that the Saudis could point to the presence of U.S. carriers offshore as proof that the anti-Iraqi forces would be in the region whether or not they consented to the presence of U.S. and other non-Muslim ground forces. In any case, it would have been most unlikely for any state in the region to have accepted those same troops before the crisis became very overt, as insurance against crisis. Once the crisis was past, moreover, the United States had to be quick to assure the local governments that it would withdraw its troops in favor of naval forces.

The other quick military options that immediately come to mind are amphibious assault and air landing. Neither could be considered realistic, given the sheer size of Iraqi forces and the necessarily limited strength of transportable Marine or airborne assault units.[3]

Thus there was no realistic chance of immediate effective military action, either by the United States or by any other nation. Yet, something had to be done immediately in order to dispute Saddam's right to what he began to call his nineteenth province. Any later military operation to liberate Kuwait would have seemed, to most of the world, a separate act of aggression. Given Saddam's strong propaganda machine, some such perception, particularly in the Arab world, was inescapable. However, early action could help maintain the momentum, the perception that it was directly connected to Iraqi aggression. Moreover, if that action was carefully chosen, it would seem proportionate, even moderate.

The only immediately available option was to institute economic sanctions, which could be visibly supported by naval interdiction. The two are linked but distinct. The economic sanctions included a refusal, adhered to by most countries, to buy Iraqi oil. That cut off Saddam's main source of income. He had gained some cash when seizing Kuwait, although the Kuwaitis had managed to transfer most of their holdings abroad (the government in exile was thus able to finance itself, and even to contribute substantial funds to support the allied war effort).

Similarly, the U.N. called upon its members to cease trading with Iraq. Given Iraq's dependence on imports, this latter condition was a severe economic hardship for many nations. In theory, however, the shortage of cash would ultimately damage Iraq more, since even suppliers willing to dodge the sanctions might find the absence of Iraqi cash unappealing. One of the more spectacular effects of sanctions was to strand most of the Iraqi MiG-21s in Yugoslavia, where they were being repaired.[4]

The embargo presumably motivated Saddam Hussein's 1 September decision to ration food, including bread, within Iraq (rationing was tightened on 14 September). He was clearly affected by it, and on 10 September he offered free oil to any developing country which sent ships to run the blockade to pick it up. He got no takers.[5] On 19 October Iraq announced gasoline rationing, due to a shortage of ether and other chemicals needed for refining (however, this unpopular form of rationing was abandoned on 28 October).

The embargo could not, of course, be complete. Even had all the states of the region wished to enforce it fully, the long land borders with Iran and Jordan were ideal for smuggling. Libya and probably others were quite willing to break the U.N.–declared embargo by air. However, neither by smuggling overland nor by the air bridge could Iraq obtain very large quantities of materiel. Before the war, Iraq had been notorious for doing maintenance "by DHL," that is, by ordering spares to be shipped via air courier as they were needed, presumably generally for spot payment. The likely effect of the embargo, then, was to reduce sharply the supply of spare parts for many Iraqi weapons. To avoid losing all effectiveness, the Iraqis would have had to cut their operating tempo, which in this case meant their training tempo. Five months of inactivity before the air campaign began cannot have helped. These factors may help explain the nearly total failure of Iraqi air defenses after 16 January.[6]

Overall, these effects are difficult to evaluate. Some of those who claimed, before the war, that Iraqi military capability was being drastically reduced may also have hoped to avoid military action altogether; many wanted the sanctions to go on for much longer. Those who, like the Israelis, claimed that the embargo was having little effect included some who were more interested in permanently removing the Iraqi military threat to the region. The Kuwaitis pointed out that the main effect of the embargo was to motivate the Iraqis to loot Kuwait more enthusiastically, and that economic pressure would never force them out.

Peacetime blockades and sanctions have a poor record of success. Supporters of full reliance on sanctions, as a sort of humane means of applying pressure, argued that the case of Iraq was special, since turning off the oil would also turn off virtually all of the regime's foreign exchange income. However, it must have been obvious to any observer that, should Saddam survive, he would eventually regain his oil income. The canny supplier willing to take a small economic risk could lend him money at high interest in the expectation that within a few years the international community would tire of the exercise. It seemed virtually inevitable that countries badly damaged by the enforced cutoff of trade with Iraq would eventually disown any sanctions. Thus it was unlikely that the sanctions would ever force Saddam out of Kuwait, let alone that they would last for much more than a few months. By mid-January 1991 they had probably done all that could have been expected of them.

Perhaps the greatest value of the blockade/sanction was that it maintained pressure on Iraq while the military coalition was assembled, and while land, air, and sea forces were amassed in Saudi Arabia. Initially the presence of those forces helped protect the Saudis against further Iraqi pressure, which would have been designed to force the Saudis to demand that the sanctions be revoked. Saddam seems to have discounted the possibility that the land forces growing in Saudi Arabia were something more, that they were the beginning of a force that would ultimately eject him. That possibility seemed so obvious in August and September 1990 that it was surprising at the time that Saddam did not begin a further war with a spoiling attack on the small forces in place.

The answer is probably to be found in Saddam's view of the United States, the leader of the coalition pressing him to disgorge Kuwait. Certainly the United States and its allies were building the necessary capability, but Saddam seems to have dismissed that as an empty threat; he felt that the United States lacked the necessary will. He seems to have considered the buildup largely a gesture to placate the Saudis rather than the beginning of an assault force. The buildup would certainly block his further advance, but surely it would only be temporary. He did fortify Kuwait, probably mainly in order to deter the allies from any quick cheap counterstroke.

Saddam seems also to have grossly overestimated the rate at which U.S. forces brought into Saudi Arabia could develop combat potential; he seems not to have understood in the least the extent of the logistical effort described in the next chapter. Thus he may never have been aware of what others saw as an obvious opportunity to push on into Saudi Arabia after U.S. troops had begun landing in that country but before they could effectively resist him. This lost opportunity has now been so well publicized that it is difficult to imagine a future Saddam foregoing a parallel opportunity.

In August only the United States and Britain had substantial naval forces in or near the Persian Gulf: eight U.S. ships of the Joint Task Force Middle East (including a cruiser, a destroyer, and five frigates, led by the flagship *La Salle*) were already in the Gulf. Britain had an Armilla Patrol (HMS *York*, two frigates, HMS *Battleaxe* and HMS *Jupiter*, and the supply ship *Orangeleaf*). The frigates were recalled from Mombasa and Penang. France had a frigate (*Protet*, to be joined by *Commandante*

Ducuing) on station, and the Soviets had a Udaloy-class destroyer. In addition, the United States had carrier battle groups in the Indian Ocean (*Independence* group) and in the eastern Mediterranean (*Eisenhower* group), with an additional carrier battle group en route to the Mediterranean (*Saratoga* group) to relieve the *Eisenhower* group. The initial decision was to retain the Mediterranean group on station, passing it through the Suez Canal into the Red Sea. The battleship *Wisconsin* and an amphibious ready group were also deployed to the area.

These forces were initially assigned to enforce the sanctions by interdiction. The carriers and the battleship were also an initial holding force to deter any further Iraqi aggression. The interdiction began as an Anglo–U.S. operation. The U.N. Security Council soon approved it. Other nations, including the Soviet Union, eventually contributed warships to a multinational blockade force operating in both the Persian Gulf and the Red Sea. For some of the navies, this was the first major modern out-of-area deployment.[7]

Geography simplified interception; sea traffic to or from Iraq must pass through either the Persian Gulf or the Red Sea (via Aqaba in Jordan). The Persian Gulf choke point is the Strait of Hormuz; the Red Sea choke point is the Strait of Tiran. Both are well outside Iraqi tactical aircraft range. In fact surveillance had to begin well away from the choke points, to give the interception forces time to reach ships and to board them. Moreover, ships sometimes refused to stop and had to be pursued; that pursuit had to be far enough from Iraqi waters to prevent a ship from reaching sanctuary. In addition, surveillance had to extend into the direction of Iraq, because the embargo covered trade *from* that country as well as shipping *to* it. Thus the operating area of the multinational force extended well into both the Persian Gulf and the Red Sea, as well as far out into the Arabian Sea.

The embargo involved a considerable technical problem. The interception area was quite large and involved numerous merchant ships, not all of which were going anywhere near the ports in question. The interception force itself was relatively small, so that its ships had to be used economically. All merchant ships in a large area, then, had to be tracked and identified, and interception force ships had to be assigned to check the ones that counted. This problem was not too different from that of tracking large numbers of ships for engagement by long-range, antiship missiles, a problem that had exercised the U.S. Navy since the introduction of the Tomahawk antiship missile about a decade earlier. The U.S. solution was ultimately to combine all available (and often disparate) sources of information, relying on a computer to make sense of the mix. The alternative, to buy specialized sensors that would constantly scan the sea surface, had been rejected as far too expensive. The embargo demonstrated that the U.S. choice had been correct. Computer terminals for the system were quickly distributed to the coalition ships enforcing the embargo. A P-3C modified specifically to identify ships (under a program called Outlaw Hunter) proved particularly successful.[8]

Although the interception was not in itself an act of war (as defined by the United Nations), the blocking force always had to reckon with the possibility of a surprise attack. The suddenness of the attack on the USS *Stark* (by an Iraqi Mirage firing Exocets) in 1987 had made a strong impression on many navies. As a result, many of the ships were provided with hastily added antiair weapons. (These emergency improvements are described in Appendix C.)

The U.S. ships carried four-man Coast Guard Law Enforcement Detachments (LEDets), who were especially valuable for their knowledge of international and maritime law, shipping procedures, and shipboard documents. This pattern had been developed for the Coast Guard/Navy drug interdiction operation in and around the Caribbean approaches to the United States.

Interceptions, initially by U.S. ships, began on 17 August 1990 with the USS *John I. Hall* in the Red Sea (the Iraqi tanker *Al Fao*) and with the USS *England* in the Persian Gulf (the northbound *Al Abid* and *Al Byaa*). The other navies soon joined, and by late 1990 about 30 percent of all boardings were being conducted by the other navies.

By the time of the initial cease-fire, nearly 7,000 ships had been intercepted, and 30 to 40 ships were being checked daily. Many were only interrogated by bridge-to-bridge radio, but about 1,000 had been boarded, and 5 to 10 were being boarded daily. It was estimated that the oil embargo as applied to tankers (that is, not including the effect of closed pipelines) was costing Iraq $30 million per day, about half its total oil revenue.

Iraq tried to resist. Some ships refused to stop; at one point Saddam Hussein publicly ordered Iraqi captains not to stop on pain of death. In some cases ships had to be boarded by armed parties, often ten-person Marine Corps special-operations teams, landed by helicopter. Some Iraqi captains continued on course even after shots had been fired across their bows, in the knowledge that the allied navies were most reluctant actually to disable their ships. For example, on 28 October 1990 an Iraqi tanker, *Amuriyah*, was spotted by the Australian frigate *Darwin*. She was soon joined by the USS *Reasoner*, a frigate, and the USS *Ogden*, an amphibious ship (typically carrying a Marine special-operations team), and by the British frigate HMS *Brazen*. The Iraqi captain initially refused to answer his bridge-to-bridge radio at all, then tried to stall (he wanted two to three hours to contact the ship's owners before allowing the boarding party aboard). He was given fifteen minutes, but did not slow, even with HMAS *Darwin* running across his bows. Warning shots and low-level passes by F-14s and F/A-18s also had no effect. Then the USS *Ogden* launched a helicopter gunship (AH-1W) to provide cover while a second helicopter brought the Marines aboard the tanker. They took control, stopped the ship, and allowed the boarding party to come aboard. After all this, they found no prohibited cargo, and the ship was allowed to proceed.

The Iraqi goal seems to have been to create an embarrassing incident in which the coalition would have been shown to have used excessive force against a clearly innocent target. The high point of this effort was probably the *Ibn Khaldoon* incident (26 December). This "peace ship" had been chartered by the "Arab Women's Union," and was carrying a large number of female peace activists.[9] Again the Iraqis' purpose seems to have been embarrassment. The unarmed Iraqi sailors lunged for the boarding party's guns and had to be beaten off. The ship's manifest showed milk and medicine for Iraqi children. However, she was actually carrying large quantities of contraband: rice, milk, sugar, and cooking oil. The object of the exercise seems to have been to provoke obvious brutality by American and Australian sailors. The boarding was filmed. The Iraqis interspersed real footage with doctored photographs of women in the hospital (clearly implying they had been victimized by the boarders). This film was shown in Yemen and possibly in other Arab countries in hopes of breaking the coalition. The tactic failed, and a second projected "peace ship" was canceled.

Iraq also tried the classic evasive tactic, sending contraband via a neutral port, Aqaba. Because goods destined for use by neutral Jordan would have to be passed, ships headed for Aqaba had to be boarded and their cargo manifests checked.[10] There was little point in trying to run the blockade directly into Iraq or occupied Kuwait. Thus about 93 percent of all boardings were in the Red Sea.

The Iraqis also continued to try classic blockade-running tactics, such as using deceptive markings to hide their ships' identities, using false names on bridge-to-bridge radio, and hiding contraband. Toward the beginning of the Kuwait war, their ships' masters were being described as more and more belligerent.[11]

Naval interdiction continued through and beyond the war, since it was applied not only to force Iraq out of Kuwait (which the war accomplished) but also to force it to pay full reparations (which had not been accomplished at the time of writing).

Appendix C lists warships from outside the Gulf that participated in the embargo and in the subsequent war.

5

The Buildup

IT WAS SOON obvious that ejecting Iraq forcibly from Kuwait would require a massive military operation, which could not be mounted instantly. In August 1990 the U.S. made a threefold plan. First, Central Command (CentCom) was to be activated. Second, it would be provided with substantial forces, built up as quickly as possible to preclude any further Iraqi advance while pressure was applied both diplomatically and through the U.N.–approved sanctions. And finally, CentCom would begin to plan operations to be mounted in the event Saddam had to be ejected by force at a later date. None of this meant that the U.S. government had definitely decided on war. Rather, the military option had to be prepared for because there was no reason to be certain that anything short of force would suffice. Indeed, there was excellent reason to believe that as of August there was no political consensus for war. That came only later.[1]

The U.S. buildup was code-named Desert Shield, to emphasize that it shielded Saudi Arabia from further attack. It was paralleled by a major British deployment (Operation Granby), a French deployment (Operation Daguet), substantial Egyptian and Syrian deployments, and by smaller units contributed by other nations.

CentCom typified the increasingly "joint" character of U.S. command and control, and its performance during the early crisis and subsequent war will no doubt be used as evidence of the concept's usefulness. Evaluation is complicated by the fact that the U.S. force turned out to be so overwhelming, and so overwhelmingly successful that even less than efficient command would quite possibly have been effective. Efficiency is really tested only when resources are thin or when the enemy pushes the pace.

In the current organization, the chain of command runs from the president down to the secretary of defense and then to the chairman of the Joint Chiefs of Staff, in this case Gen. Colin Powell. The other members of the Joint Chiefs, such as the chief of staff of the army and the chief of naval operations, are responsible for raising forces and, largely, for selecting senior commanders, but they do not themselves have any part in the chain of command. Actual operations are the province of the commanders-in-chief of the specified and unified commands (the CINCs). The local CINC, in this case Gen. H. Norman Schwarzkopf, has under him component commanders from the different service branches.[2] In this case they were AFCENT (air force), ARCENT (army), MARCENT (marines), NAVCENT (navy), and SOCCENT (special operations forces).

Entire component headquarters organizations were moved into place: Ninth Air Force (Lt. Gen. Charles Horner) for AFCENT, Third Army (Lt. Gen. John Yeosock) for ARCENT, I Marine Expeditionary Force (Lt. Gen. Walter Boomer) for MARCENT, and Seventh Fleet (Vice Adm. Henry Mauz, later Vice Adm. S. Arthur, aboard the USS *Blue Ridge*) for NAVCENT. These officers and the headquarters groups they direct do not automatically command the forces assigned to them. The CINCs are free to organize their forces as they like. In this case, General Schwarzkopf appointed an air force general (General Horner) as commander of his unified air component, a post designated JFACC (joint force air component commander). JFACC was responsible for all air missions. However, its main product, the ATO (air tasking order), the mechanism of control, was primarily oriented toward the strategic air war against fixed targets in Iraq. The ATO was not really well adapted to close air support or to the unpredictable air operations involved in the sea areas flanking Saudi Arabia and the Kuwait theater of operations. This issue will be discussed in greater detail in the chapter on the air campaign.

The CINC organization has evolved and strengthened since World War II, and it has always been somewhat controversial. The rationale for having a single CINC with the power to direct all the forces under him to cooperate is that it is more efficient. In theory, the CINC system replaces one marked by a long and unhappy history of interservice bickering. The question is whether interservice rivalry has been primarily a source of inefficiency or, rather, a means by which the country gets the most out of its necessarily disparate forces. The navy has long argued that ground-based air and ground forces have enough in common that they have a common point of view, but that naval forces are fundamentally different. That is, true jointness, which would mean a really successful combination of land (including land-based air) and naval forces requires commanders of each to reach agreements. Jointness achieved by dictum will tend to be inefficient. The fundamental differences in philosophy and practice between sea-based and ground-based services derive not from tradition or other superficial factors, but from real physical differences in the areas in which they operate. Disagreement is inevitable when the services must work together, but that is not necessarily the same as inefficiency. The navy would argue that jointness is best achieved much as a pluralistic United States achieves consensus. An army commander trying to use naval assets, or for that matter a navy CINC trying to use ground assets, will find it difficult to take the peculiar characteristics and potential of the other service into account. The more dictatorial his power, the less he will feel inclined to listen to advice from representatives of the other services.

In a larger sense, the choice has been to stifle dissent in the name of eliminating interservice rivalry, on the ground that dictated decisions are necessarily most efficient. That certainly has not been the case in the larger civilian world. Dictatorships have often been touted as more efficient. However, bereft of internal critics, they have more often failed just because, with dissent stifled, they also lost the ability to tell when their policies were misguided. It seems very likely that the United States succeeded in World War II largely because its policies were derived from a variety of voices, freely expressed. Each of the services made its case passionately; advocates of each alternative policy undoubtedly blamed the others for pigheadedness due to blind tradition. The reality was much more positive.

The United States already has a potential center of military power in the person of the secretary of defense. Secretaries differ in their personalities and in the extent to which they seek to dominate the services, but the different services have always retained separate lines of communication with the president in the persons of their chiefs. Now unification has gone much further. In 1987 Congress passed the Goldwater-Nichols Act. It strengthened the organization of the Joint Chiefs of Staff (JCS); officers must now spend considerable time on joint staffs before achieving senior command.[3] The bill also gave the chairman of the Joint Chiefs a sole line of communication up to the president via the secretary of defense. In the past, the chairman had been obliged by law to communicate differing views to the president. Now he communicates only his own view, even if that view differs from that of the majority of the service chiefs. Now there are two centers of military power, and the single chairman will often be far more powerful than the civilian secretary. That is not an arrangement well suited to accommodating a plurality of views. It is also an uncomfortable position for the chairman, who now has a far more executive position than in the past.

This possibility was realized at the end of the Kuwait war. The president decided to cease offensive action after 100 hours. It turned out that reports of the destruction of enemy forces had been somewhat too rosy. The local commander, General Schwarzkopf, later reported that he had recommended continuing the battle (presumably after the president had spoken). He sent his suggestion up the chain of command. It was rejected, with the unfortunate consequence that the surviving Iraqi army forces were able to massacre those rebelling against Saddam. In the subsequent search for blame, it was suggested that the chairman of the Joint Chiefs, Gen. Colin Powell, had taken it upon himself to block General Schwarzkopf's suggestion. A less executive chief might have let the political authority, the president, decide.

The navy largely lost its argument in 1987 due to intense pressure for greater centralization and coordination. That was for the most part an argument about U.S. strategy in the theater of greatest concern, Europe. The army and air force argued that the navy was insufficiently involved, that it was too interested in fighting its own sort of war rather than supporting them in combat. They saw the emerging Maritime Strategy as proof of their contention that the navy was uninterested in their concerns (many in the navy translated these arguments as anger at their own success in reversing a long-term downward trend in naval funding).

For reasons that are difficult to understand, neither ground service appreciated that they could not live, let alone fight, for long unless the navy managed to beat off the Soviet threat to sea communications. The navy's view was that the only effective means of defeating this Soviet threat was early attacks on the Soviet fleet. That, in turn, required the sort of carrier-heavy fleet the Maritime Strategy demanded. Once the Soviet fleet had been destroyed, the navy would have been free to perform exactly the sort of direct support the army and the air force wanted.[4] This problem of communication is recalled by the air force's tendency, during and after the Kuwait war, to class the navy's attacks on Iraqi missile boats as "support," in much the same category as its own transport operations, rather than as strikes on Iraqi offensive forces. Yet the navy's rollback of the Iraqi Navy was as necessary to its offensive attacks against Iraqi land forces as was the air force's rollback of Iraqi air defenses.

The mechanism for assuring coordination (or, in the naval view, for eliminating dissent) was the strengthened JCS organization, which would have more operational and planning control over the deployed forces. The more operational JCS had to have a single executive chief.

Proponents of the stronger JCS generally pointed to the Soviet

General Staff (which is nominally an all-service organization) as a model for future U.S. practice; many also considered the old German General Staff a good model. There was little question that the Germans had been quite effective tactically, but the navy argued that in both world wars their General Staff had failed ultimately, largely because, as an army organization, it had been unable to understand the threat of power projected overseas by the United States. As for the Soviets, whatever the pan-service character of their General Staff, it was clearly mainly an army organization designed for a limited range of contingencies. The United States is the only really global power, and consequently it must deal with a much wider range of possibilities. The navy argued that greater plurality makes for better awareness of just that range.

More generally, the navy argued that cooperation enforced by a chairman of the JCS and then by a local CINC would often mean misuse of naval forces, simply because commanders steeped in the facts of ground combat would not appreciate what those forces could contribute. This argument is too often corrupted as fear that a limited naval contribution would translate into bad publicity and thus into postwar cuts in naval forces.

None of this is to deny that interservice rivalry exists. To some extent competition is a healthy way of causing the different services to do their best. However, enforced jointness seems to be a poor way of taming that competitiveness. Nor is it clear that every U.S. operation requires the participation of all the services. For example, excessive attention to jointness has often been cited as a reason for the failure of the U.S. hostage rescue operation in Iran in 1980. Many within the navy felt that air force F-111s were included in the 1986 raid on Tripoli only to satisfy jointness.[5]

Central Command occupied a peculiar position among the CINCs in that it was inherently the most joint of all: it could not function without considerable infusions from all the services. Each of the other CINCs, though nominally commanding components from all the services, is naturally dominated by one service or another. CINCLANT, for example, is the mainly naval organization responsible for operations in the Atlantic. Because it was designed to fight a largely ground-based war against the Warsaw Pact, CINCEUR is dominated by the army and air force (the question of which service dominates depends on the details of U.S. strategy for this sort of war). Through the 1980s, the navy argued strongly that the entire geographically oriented CINC system was obsolescent because it did not allow for the sort of operational flexibility that U.S. circumstances demanded.

The issue is really one of mobility. Ground forces are tied to specific ground areas; their commanders naturally think in terms of defending those areas. Naval commanders, whose forces are not so tied, tend to think in less geographically oriented terms. To some, the navy's Maritime Strategy, which encompassed attacks all around the Eurasian land mass, harkened back to the classical British maritime-oriented strategy. Facing a French juggernaut on the European continent, the British chose to back a variety of local allies, but always to withdraw to the sea when any of them did poorly. Because they could always cut their losses, the British emerged from a series of world wars with the French in a dominant economic position. Their policy was not really one of exploitation: the temporary allies had quite good reasons of their own for fighting the French. What was special about the British was that, as long as the French were only a land power, they could never end the war they were fighting, so ultimately they were defeated. From a British point of view, the best strategy was one in which British interests were put well ahead of the interests of temporary coalition partners. Once they abandoned that maritime-oriented strategy in 1914, the British were tied down to a continental meat grinder and, it would seem, were irreparably damaged.

The British strategy of the Napoleonic Wars clearly went far beyond what the U.S. Navy was espousing nearly two centuries later, but both share an unwillingness to make or maintain permanent continental commitments. Both share a strong suspicion that such commitments represent the wrong balance to accept in coalition warfare, a potentially excessive national sacrifice for coalition partners. Such a strategy has no place for a CINCEUR, because no CINCEUR will cheerfully abandon the Europe he is tasked to defend. Similarly, it has little room for separate permanent fleets because forces must be free to swing back and forth as they are needed. The naval argument is that the enemy power is the ultimate target, and that any land areas lost along the way will be recovered when that enemy is defeated. In the recent war, it turned out that the road to Kuwait City ran through the ruins of Baghdad. Some might argue that the U.S. government stopped far short of ultimate victory in order to satisfy the coalition partners, but there was no question of going in the other direction, making excessive sacrifices just because they would benefit the allies. The balance between national and coalition interests is perhaps the most difficult issue in any form of coalition warfare, and the troubled history of NATO strategy exemplifies it.

Quite aside from a fundamental and instinctive difference in outlook, ground and naval forces differ in their approach to war. Again, that is a consequence of the facts of physics. A small piece of ground will support massive forces, but they, in turn, require large dumps of fuel, ammunition, and spare parts. These forces also tend to be quite massive, and they have to operate close together for maximum efficiency. Television viewers will remember the sight of vast numbers of tanks and other vehicles crossing the border into Iraq as VII Corps attacked. Coordination of those vast numbers has to be positive and direct, and it must come from above. A subordinate commander who shows too much initiative can upset an operational plan just as badly as one who hangs too far back. What counts is that every unit commander, at every level, conforms to the same detailed plan. That is not a cultural preference: it is an operational necessity. The U.S. Army and Air Force share these characteristics with other ground-based services abroad.

For example, U.S. Air Force strike tactics (as used in the Kuwait war) emphasize large numbers of airplanes, often from different squadrons or wings, all crossing the target area in a short time. To orchestrate such an attack, the air force uses computerized planning, and successful execution demands a high degree of discipline. The attack can be ruined as much by a particularly aggressive pilot as by a timid one.[6]

Naval forces are, by their nature, quite different. They are mobile on an enormous scale, but that mobility is bought by constructing relatively large and expensive ships too costly to build in enormous numbers. Tactics and strategy must exploit mobility: often, naval forces influence events ashore simply because they present so broad a range of threats. In doing so they tie down large numbers of the opposing ground forces (exemplified in this situation by the ten Iraqi divisions along the coast kept in place by a single marine amphibious unit). Similarly, a single carrier striking group can attack widely scattered points ashore in quick succession. Forces are sufficiently dispersed that individuality is not merely valued but essential. Rigid planning is virtually impossible because it cannot take account of accidents of weather and enemy action; the sea environment is fluid. Long-haul communications cannot be trusted in wartime. One classic formulation is that the army (or air force) writes the book describing exactly how a job is to be done; the navy book lists what *cannot* be done (the rest is up to the doer).

The geography ashore often determines what ground forces can do; one hears that "geography is destiny." Because the sea is largely trackless, it imposes far fewer limitations. As a result, large-scale maneuvering is more commonly a feature of naval warfare. That, in turn, makes reconnaissance, particularly self-contained reconnaissance, and deception more important features of sea than of land warfare. In this particular case, the flatness of the terrain opened up an unusually broad range of alternatives for the allied ground forces, to the extent that the campaign in southern Iraq was likened to a naval operation. Even so, its progress was far more shaped by logistics (for example, by the need to build up large dumps of ammunition and supplies) than a naval operation would be, and the length of the fast armored thrust was far shorter than the distance naval forces might normally travel in a few days at sea.

Air forces are clearly more mobile than their ground counterparts, but they are limited by their ties to a fixed base, usually within a few hundred miles of their operations. Without the mass of material at the base, they cannot function for any great length of time. With it, they can develop great combat power. No air force planner can ever forget either the mobile reach of the airplanes or the immobility of the base or bases on which they depend—or, for that matter, the logistical chain (in this case, a seaborne chain) on which both depend. The situation is fundamentally different for an aircraft carrier commander, whose base is itself mobile (a carrier can cover about a thousand miles a day), and can be operated quite independently for about a week at a time.

One peculiarity of the difference between navy and ground forces experience is in a perception of the meaning of rear (that is, safe) versus forward areas. Because mobility on the ground is limited in its reach, a ground commander will instinctively divide the world into a forward combat zone and a safe rear zone, where supplies can be built up with limited protection. Any enemy force cutting through to the rear area (as in the German blitzkriegs) can have a devastating effect. If an enemy has this capability, the consequent need to defend the rear area (for example, against air attack) sharply reduces the combat power available farther forward.

The plan to fight a nonlinear war—that is, a war without well-defined forward and rear areas, was a considerable innovation for the U.S. Army. Even so, neither the U.S. Army nor the U.S. Air Force seemed to show much expectation that areas far to the rear, such as maintenance bases and ammunition dumps, would be bombed. To the extent that there is an accepted air threat, it was met largely by a small number of defensive fighters.

The naval situation is radically different. There are safe rear areas, but they are hundreds or thousands of miles from a combat zone. The enemy enjoys the same seaborne mobility as does the United States, and whatever is not defended may well be attacked. Much effort must therefore go into protection. Because all naval forces are few in number, however, such protection may translate into the elimination of the threat and thus will also have an offensive character. Alternatively, it may be possible to eliminate the enemy's threat by forcing him to attack a particularly well-defended naval force, and that elimination may be decisive. Such decisions also happen on land, but they are less likely simply because the sheer numbers are so much greater. More generally, the relation between offense and defense is very different for naval forces than for land forces. Moreover, because naval forces are so limited in numbers, they tend to be more multipurpose than those ashore, and distinctions like offensive versus defensive are often less than meaningful.[7]

No one service is better or worse than another, but they are different, not only in appearance but also in deeper ways. It is extremely rare for a ground-based officer to grasp the considerations of naval forces in any instinctive way, and vice versa.[8] The navy's argument, historically, has been that the country gets the most out of its disparate forces when neither expects the other to operate in its fashion. Cooperation is the key to success, but it cannot easily be enforced. That view may well be a product of classic naval operating practice. The army and air force perspective has been that any sort of cooperation can and should be enforced from above. After all, that is how they themselves operate.

In the past, and indeed even in this crisis, the military situation has been simplified for the United States by the presence of a large overseas base structure and massive ground forces forward-deployed to meet a perceived Soviet threat. If the immediate Soviet threat is really declining, then the base structure abroad will inevitably shrink. In some cases, such as this one, our friends will be more than happy to cooperate, and their bases will support us. However, it would seem unwise to assume that such a best case will always apply. We will have to fall back on those resources that are inherently mobile (so that they cover the widest possible range of scenarios) and that are fully under U.S. control.

Basing has two complementary aspects. One is to provide facilities to support the forces that will actually fight in the combat zone. In this case, for example, it was fortunate that the Saudis had already built up a series of large air bases that the air force's F-15s and F-16s could utilize. The other, and less obvious, aspect is to support the flow of troops and materiel into that combat zone. For example, an F-15 flying from the United States to Saudi

Arabia must be refueled seven times during its fifteen-hour flight. The tankers supplying the fuel need their own bases, and the use of those bases requires local consent. Similarly, aircraft need overflight permission, particularly when they are flying combat missions. In this war France permitted B-52s based in England to fly through its airspace, and also supported their operations with tankers.[9]

There is no particularly good reason to imagine that the United States will always enjoy this type of cooperation. We can probably hope to use local base facilities (if the enemy has not been sensible enough to destroy them first), but history suggests that support agreement will be much more difficult to achieve. For example, in 1973 the NATO allies were less than enthusiastic about U.S. support of Israel. They banned use of their bases to support the U.S. aerial resupply effort. As a consequence, airplanes flying from the United States had to take a more circuitous path, and they could not carry much in the way of payloads. U.S. carriers provided some vital refueling support.

Margaret Thatcher, who as British prime minister committed her country's forces to the Kuwait buildup, later remarked that such participation would have been impossible (or, at the least, greatly delayed) had the European Community grown (as many expect it will) toward political unification. Mrs. Thatcher, who should know, expects that any such entity will be inward-looking, protectionist, and, in effect, isolationist. There are already some pointers in that direction. Once the war in the Gulf had ended, several of the European powers proposed that U.S. naval command be superseded by operation under the aegis of the Western European Union (WEU). They had already operated that way during the Iran-Iraq War. The WEU is sometimes advertised as a potential European counterweight to American influence within NATO.

It follows that in situations in which considerable local support is denied, we must rely heavily on naval forces to project power. The laws of physics dictate that only ships can easily carry heavy weights (such as large numbers of aircraft) over long distances at reasonable speed. It is certainly true that aircraft can fly from the

United States to deliver limited numbers of bombs anywhere in the world. However, in most cases (as in this one) the point of quick intervention is to be able to pose an immediate and credible threat rather than to do actual (and necessarily limited) damage. A few bombers could do much more if they delivered nuclear bombs, but that option has long been foreclosed, and is unlikely to be reopened.

All mobile forces are inherently limited because they must carry their resources with them. But a ship at sea differs from an airplane in the air because it can remain on station; it can threaten as well as strike. The airplane can orbit, but only for a limited period, and to maintain even one airplane permanently on orbit over any distant point is prohibitively expensive. In the case of an aircraft carrier, the number of strike aircraft is limited (though large), and, moreover, the carrier cannot remain in combat for much more than five to seven days before exhausting stocks of weapons and fuel. Similar considerations (in this case, thirty days' supplies) apply to a Marine Expeditionary Brigade (MEB) supported by maritime prepositioning ships. Sustained combat, even by limited forces, consumes vast amounts of materiel, and those amounts require fixed dumps, which in turn have to be built up. [10]

The only really mobile military resources available to the United States in the Kuwait war were the aircraft carriers already near the Persian Gulf and the marines whose equipment and logistical back-up were aboard ships at Diego Garcia and at Guam. These elements could block any further advance into Saudi Arabia until heavier forces arrived. It took about five months to build up those heavier forces. In order to preserve the valuable sustained capability against the possibility of an Iraqi attack, the two carriers brought into the area (one from the Mediterranean into the Red Sea, one from the Indian Ocean to the mouth of the Persian Gulf) drastically reduced their operating tempo. Even though land-based aircraft were rapidly flown to Saudi Arabia, the carriers on station probably accounted for the bulk of available air power in the theater until late fall 1990.

It is easy to view the heavier forces, the ground-based aircraft and the army, as instrumental in winning the war. But it is clear that that would be simplistic. Without the instant availability of the maritime forces there would have been no five-month buildup, no military option. The Iraqi force in Kuwait would surely have been sufficient to pressure Saudi Arabia to preclude any use of its territory to launch a counterattack.

Just before the crisis began, the United States had a total of fourteen deployable carriers, one of them forward-deployed in Japan. Continued forward-deployment requires not one ship but three: one on station, one working up or steaming home, and one refitting. Typically the United States tries to maintain two carriers in the Mediterranean, one or two in the Far East, and one in the Indian Ocean. The Indian Ocean deployment is particularly expensive because a carrier is counted as on station only after she comes within a fairly restricted area of the North Arabian Sea. Steaming time there, from either the East Coast or the Far East, is considerable; thus it requires about five (rather than three) carriers to maintain a continuous presence in the Indian Ocean.

The permanent Indian Ocean carrier deployment was dropped in February 1990 due to the end of the Iran-Iraq War, in favor of occasional deployments (a one- to two-week swing into the Arabian Sea on every second or third deployment) from the Seventh Fleet. As the crisis in the Gulf built up through July 1990, the carrier USS *Independence*, which was making just such an occasional deployment, was retained in the Arabian Sea. She was, therefore, available when Iraq invaded Kuwait in August 1990. To the extent that postwar U.S. policy will depend upon a permanent seaborne presence in the area, it seems likely that once again the United States will have to station a carrier battle group permanently in the northern Arabian Sea, with all the problems that entails for total carrier force numbers.[11]

It is entirely possible that early in the crisis the Saudi government might have been sufficiently intimidated by Saddam Hussein that it would not have agreed to any U.S. assistance. The carriers were sovereign U.S. territory. The Saudis could benefit from their presence without having to make a positive, and possibly politically difficult, decision to seek or accept U.S. support. Once the carriers were there, they provided enough cover that the Saudis could disregard Saddam's attempt to intimidate them. The carriers, representing a fully independent U.S. national capability, were the crucial factor without which the buildup, let alone the intervention, would have been impossible.

The initial naval response was by the two forward-deployed fleets, the Sixth (Mediterranean) and the Seventh (Far East, including the Indian Ocean). In addition to having a carrier near the crisis area, each fleet also had an amphibious ready group. In the buildup, Atlantic Fleet ships generally transited the Suez Canal to the Red Sea; Pacific Fleet ships generally came on station in the North Arabian Sea and the Gulf of Oman, with access to the Persian Gulf. The most important exception was the *Theodore Roosevelt* battle group, from the Atlantic Fleet, which steamed directly into the Persian Gulf.

When the crisis began, the closest carrier was the USS *Independence*, on station in the Arabian Sea. She moved toward Oman. The carrier *Dwight D. Eisenhower* was operating in the Mediterranean. She moved east, to within strike range of western Iraq, and then passed through the Suez Canal into the Red Sea. Soon both ships were within striking range of the Saudi-Kuwaiti border. They were on station three days before any ground force or land-based air force deployments began. In August, the *Saratoga* battle group and the battleship *Wisconsin* with her surface action group left Norfolk to join the ships in the Red Sea, to increase carrier strength in the area to three full battle groups.

In September, the *Midway* battle group left Japan for the Arabian Sea to double the carrier presence there. In addition, the battleship *Missouri* deployed to the Persian Gulf, so that by late fall each sea flank included both two carrier battle groups and a battleship-centered surface action group carrying Tomahawk cruise missiles as well as 16-inch guns for shore bombardment.

Until late in the fall, the carriers in the Red Sea and the Arabian Sea probably accounted for the bulk of available U.S. ready tactical air power in the region. They were the airborne shield that protected Saudi Arabia. The battleships' 16-inch guns were effective against the sort of shore defenses the Iraqis erected along the Kuwaiti coast; their presence was, in effect, a prerequisite for an amphibious assault. They also carried Tomahawks (and fired the initial rounds, once the war began). The battleships had been brought into service in the early 1980s precisely to relieve pressure on carrier deployments.

Aircraft flying from the carriers in the Arabian Sea (Gulf of Oman) to the Saudi-Kuwaiti border were almost at the limit of their striking range. However, for the most part before the war began the carriers stayed out of the more constricted waters of the Persian Gulf (from 2 to 6 October the USS *Independence* demonstrated that she could operate successfully in the Gulf). Until hostilities had begun, there was little reason for carriers to spend much time in the confined waters of the Persian Gulf. There they faced a variety of hazards, both shallows and floating mines. The hazards could not have kept them out of the Gulf in an emergency (the carriers ran in when war broke out), but there was little point in risking any damage before hostilities could begin.[12]

By mid-August the *Eisenhower* had nearly completed her scheduled deployment. She and her battle group were relieved by the *John F. Kennedy* battle group from the Atlantic Fleet. Similarly, the *Independence* battle group was relieved by the *Ranger* battle group in January 1991.

After President Bush announced a doubling of the U.S. commitment on 8 November, two more carrier battle groups deployed to the area: the *America* to the Red Sea and the *Ranger* to the North Arabian Sea (with access to the Persian Gulf proper). When the war began, the naval force was boosted to full six-carrier strength by the *Theodore Roosevelt* battle group, which arrived in the Persian Gulf on 21 January.

As soon as the emergency began, the air force started to prepare some of its tactical aircraft to fly directly to the Gulf. The aircraft can deploy very quickly as long as they can be tanked in flight and have prepared bases at which to land. Deploying squadrons are accompanied by transports carrying war reserve spares kits (WRSK kits, which include some "suitcase"-size test equipment) and support personnel. In this case, the air force maintained an afloat prepositioning ship (APS) at Diego Garcia loaded with bombs and with some vital spares. True sustained mobility, however, was limited. The air force could not easily transport its base maintenance organization (it relies on centralized intermediate-level maintenance at the wing level, whereas the navy is more decentralized and does more at the squadron or carrier level). WRSK kits could last only so long before the effects of a long line of supply became evident. Thus any deployed units that must remain in place for very long (as was the case in the Gulf) eventually require large tonnages of supporting maintenance equipment and spare parts. They were brought by sea and by C-5 transport. In the case of the Gulf, moreover, the environment, with its savage dust storms, could greatly reduce the time allowable between major overhauls. Fortunately war broke out before any of the deployed airplanes required depot-level work. Even so, the readiness levels of the airplanes suffered from the severity of the Saudi environment (particularly its dust storms).[13]

Because its aircraft can fly very rapidly between prepared bases, the air force deployment structure is relatively flexible. For example, the air force could deploy large numbers of tactical aircraft from Europe to Saudi Arabia without losing the capability to move them rapidly back to Europe in the event of an emergency. Its situation was therefore rather different from that of the army, for which major deployments were relatively permanent. This flexibility, however, required that masses of weapons and spare parts be predeployed. Hence the importance of the air force's APS ship at Diego Garcia.

In 1990 the air force maintained a total of thirty-six tactical wings divided between Europe (USAFE), the Pacific (PACAF), and the United States (Tactical Air Command).[14] Wings are the normal self-contained administrative units; typically the air force operates one wing per base. The squadron (typically three per wing) is the tactical unit. Because it is smaller, it is easier to move. The initial deployments to Saudi Arabia, then, were squadron by squadron, most of them directly from the United States. Once sufficient base facilities had been built up, entire wings could deploy. Details of deployment to Saudi Arabia and the Gulf area are given in Appendix B.

By 24 August 1990 the air force had 222 F-15C, F-15E, F-16, F-4G, F-111, F-117, A-10, and B-52 aircraft in and around Saudi Arabia. When first-phase deployment was completed on 2 September, the air force had 400 combat and 200 support aircraft in place. Depending on how strength is measured, the air force component at that time was equivalent to four to six aircraft carrier wings (the forty-eight F-15C interceptors were roughly equivalent to two carriers' worth of F-14A interceptors). These bare figures do not show the extent to which deployed spares and munitions could support sustained operations.

Given the range of its aircraft, some parts of the air force could strike Iraq from outside the Gulf proper, albeit at a price in payload. B-52s were deployed to Britain, to Spain, and to Diego Garcia (some also operated from Saudi Arabia itself in wartime). Some were supported by tankers flying from France. Once Turkish permission was secured, F-111s could attack western Iraq from NATO bases there (which had long been prepared to support them). Because these bases were within range of Iraqi forces, however, their use demanded special efforts (mainly by other NATO powers) to assure their defense.[15]

Perhaps jet fuel was the greatest single limitation in air force deployment. Saudi Arabia has no jet fuel refining capacity of its own. Fuel had to be brought by tanker from Singapore (liquids were by far the largest item in CentCom logistics).

The only mobile ground units capable of immediate sustained operations were marines whose equipment was aboard two squadrons of preloaded Maritime Prepositioning Ships (MPS) at Diego Garcia and Guam. Each squadron carried equipment, ammunition, and supplies sufficient to support a Marine Expeditionary Brigade (MEB) in combat for thirty days. The marines themselves (the 1st MEB from Hawaii and the 7th MEB from California) and their light equipment were flown into Saudi Arabia. Because the MPSs were preloaded with combat requirements in mind, the marines were able to stand up their brigades quickly. The 7th MEB left California on 12 August and it began to arrive at Al Jubail on the 14th. MPS Squadron 2 sailed from Diego Garcia on 8 August and arrived on the 15th. The marines of the 7th MEB were in place near the Saudi border and ready for combat on the 20th. As of 25 August, the brigade had 15,248 marines, 123 tanks, 425 artillery pieces, and 124 aircraft in place, having deployed over 12,000 nautical miles. The deployment required 259 MAC (Military Airlift Command) sorties and the five MPSs.

It is difficult to extend the extremely valuable MPS capability to larger ground units. Any unit using such a ship must buy—and maintain and upgrade—at least a double set of equipment, one for normal deployments and training, and one afloat on board the MPS squadron at sea. It must expect, too, to deploy its troops by air carrying virtually none of its equipment, trusting the MPSs to turn up as and when needed, at a usable port. These considerations made the MPS concept initially controversial within the Marine Corps itself, and they probably preclude its extension to, say, an army mechanized division. Moreover, true strategic mobility requires not a single set of MPSs, but several such squadrons predeployed within quick steaming distance of the several likely Third World crisis areas. In the case of the marines, that capability was obtained by buying three MPS squadrons and setting up a flexible basing and maintenance arrangement.

The MEB's aircraft included F/A-18 fighter-bombers, AV-8Bs for close air support, heavy A-6E attack bombers, EA-6B jammers, attack helicopters (AH-1Ws), and transport helicopters (CH-46s for medium lift and CH-53s for heavy lift). All could operate either from shore bases or from ships (usually amphibious carriers [LPH, LHA, and LHD] for the AV-8Bs and the helicopters). The deployed 3d Marine Air Wing strength is listed in Appendix B. Ultimately this "heavy" wing accounted for fully 86 percent of the total combat air strength of the Marine Corps.

While the first two MEBs were "marrying up" with their heavy equipment in Saudi Arabia, an amphibious task force built on Amphibious Group 2 (including three helicopter carriers) brought the 4th MEB, along with additional support elements, from the East Coast of the United States into the Persian Gulf. The 4th MEB remained afloat as a potential amphibious force. It was soon joined by one of two Seventh Fleet (Pacific) amphibious ready groups from the Philippines (carrying the embarked 13th

Marine Expeditionary Unit [MEU]). It, too, remained afloat. This amphibious task force began rehearsal landings, beginning with a night amphibious raid exercise, "Sea Soldier," in which the 13th MEU landed over the beach and the 4th MEB followed, both by helicopter and surface craft. Later the 4th and 5th MEBs (see below) and the 13th MEU staged a series of large-scale and attention-getting landing exercises. Ultimately, with two amphibious ready groups and two full amphibious groups in the Gulf, CentCom had the ability to make a full MEF-sized amphibious landing.

Other marines were brought in to fill out the two MEBs into a full division/air wing team, the I MEF (Marine Expeditionary Force). The MEF was initially joined by the British 7th Armoured Brigade. When that unit was withdrawn just before 15 January to merge into the British 1st Armoured Division, it was replaced by the 1st Brigade of the U.S. 2d Armored Division, which fought with the I MEF as it advanced toward Kuwait City. Through the first phase of Desert Shield, the I MEF accounted for about half the U.S. combat troops in Saudi Arabia. See Appendix A for details of MEF/MEB equipment and organization. Suffice it to say here that these organizations do not correspond precisely to army units with similar designations (brigade, regiment, division). An MEB is closer in total strength to an army division than to an army brigade, although it lacks the armor of current army heavy divisions (hence the reinforcing armor brigade).

The I MEF was one of the three active-duty marine division/ wing task forces. At the beginning of the crisis, two of the three MEFs were assigned to the United States, the third forming a strategic reserve for the Far East (mainly Korea). That formulation understates the extent of smaller marine deployments. For example, just before the crisis began, the corps' main active overseas deployments were a major exercise (by the 13th MEU) in the Philippines (which was beset by a guerrilla war) and the force (the 22d MEU) afloat off Liberia, evacuating Americans and other foreign nationals caught by the civil war there. Even the units assigned to the Gulf were needed elsewhere. Early in January 1991 ships and marines had to be detached to the south to rescue the ambassador and other U.S. citizens from Mogadishu, Somalia.

A second MEF (2d Marine Division/Air Wing) was brought into Saudi Arabia as part of the second-phase buildup ordered on 8 November. In addition, a second afloat MEB (the 5th, from San Diego, on board Amphibious Group 3) was brought into the Gulf. This time reservists (from the 4th Marine Division and its air wing) were called up. Only one MPS squadron (on the East Coast) remained, so most of the deployment had to be supported by conventional cargo ships. Most of the force was flown in from Cherry Point and Camp Lejeune on the East Coast.

The only other highly mobile (in a strategic sense) ground forces available to the United States were the two army airborne divisions, the 82d and the 101st. They carried some of their vehicles, including Sheridan light tanks, with them by air. However, the limitations inherent in air transport left them with little capability for sustained combat. That was consistent with their assigned role: the airborne troops were intended to jump over an enemy's lines to seize ground in his rear, holding that ground until a heavier, more self-sustaining force moving overland could link up with them. In Saudi Arabia, neither airborne unit could face sustained operations until much of its materiel had arrived by sea.

In August 1990 U.S. forces were designed to fight "one and a half" wars, a somewhat misleading formulation. The "one" war was the big war against the Soviets, which absorbed large forward-deployed forces. The big war was imagined as a surprise attack by the Soviets. Their thrust would have to be absorbed by troops already in place. War in Korea would be a miniature version of this big war, the main difference being greater reliance on troops shipped in and on naval aircraft operating from carriers offshore. In each case, however, the threat tied down substantial U.S. forces. Heavy ground forces, which have limited inherent mobility, were distributed to meet the requirements of the "one" war. Substantial forces (two armored corps and supporting troops) were forward-deployed in Europe and in South Korea, where they would probably have to fight with little or no strategic warning.

They could be reinforced by further forces based in the United States. The logistical problem was the same as that faced by the forces built up in the Gulf: men and women could fly across the world in less than a day, but not the mountain of materiel they needed to fight. In the case of Europe, the solution was to maintain the mountain locally, so that troops flown in could be matched up with their predeployed materiel.[16]

Success depended on how well those forces could fight in place and, to a lesser extent, on how quickly U.S. troops could be flown in to mate up with their predeployed equipment. Such wars were always envisaged as intensive but brief, most likely ending in threats of nuclear escalation.

In August 1990 the two big armored corps (V and VII) were forward-deployed in Europe, assigned to NATO (and not withdrawable without NATO assent). Each had an armored cavalry regiment to scout for it, with three more divisions and corps-level assets (principally a combat aviation group, two or three brigades of corps artillery, and an engineer brigade). Total strength in Europe, then, included two armored cavalry regiments (the 2d and 11th), three armored divisions (the 1st, 2d, and 3d, the 2d forward-deployed in central Germany), and three mechanized infantry divisions (the 1st, 3d, and 8th, the 1st forward-deployed). An additional infantry division (the 2d) was in South Korea, with another (the 25th) in Hawaii in support.

The "half" war was the lesser war (much less than half as violent as a big central war against the Soviets) in some Third World country. In the case of the Gulf, the United States could not predeploy either troops or materiel. Among other things, it was never so clear, before the August crisis, just how or when the United States might find itself acting in the region. For example, many of the pre-1990 scenarios were concerned with protecting Iran or Pakistan from a Soviet thrust south. It was clear only that the Gulf was a volatile area, and that it was vital to U.S. and other Western interests. The solution adopted, then, was to form a planning staff, Central Command (Centcom).[17]

MPSs were deployed to support marines who would hold until heavier forces could be deployed. A carrier in the Indian Ocean provided CentCom's early tactical air assets. CentCom's concept of operations was that the prepositioned MEBs would arrive first, to hold ground until a lightweight army corps (the XVIII Airborne Corps) could be built up. It would consist of the two quick-deployment lightweight divisions (the 82d and 101st) and the 24th Mechanized Infantry from the United States. In fact in this case the marines stayed in Saudi Arabia and built up their own strength to something close to corps level. All of these units could move their fighting vehicles and support equipment relatively quickly, but they could not sustain operations for very long without massive infusions of materiel: food, ammunition, spare parts. In the end, fully 95 percent of what CentCom needed came by sea.[18]

The Gulf was not the only contingency area. Many marines, for example, were on board the ships of the ready amphibious groups forward-deployed in the Mediterranean and in the Far East. The quick-response army units, the two airborne divisions, were held back in the United States, and had most recently fought in Grenada and Panama.

Ground forces in the continental United States were largely a "swing" reserve, available either to reinforce the forward-deployed units, or to deploy to fight the "half" war. In a large "half" war, it was always assumed that the relatively mobile marine expeditionary brigades would go in first to hold off early attacks. They had enough ammunition and other materiel to fight for thirty days, and it was assumed that some army divisions could be brought into combat within the first thirty to sixty days to relieve or to supplement them.

The lengthy time intervals were imposed by the need to move most ammunition and other essentials by sea. Troops could move by air, in this war generally by chartered commercial airliner, but without their heavy equipment and ammunition they would arrive essentially as armed tourists.

In August 1990 the heavy U.S.–based "swing" force consisted of four mechanized infantry divisions (the 1st, 4th, 5th, and 24th), an armored division (the 2d), and an armored cavalry division (the 1st).[19] Some of the units in the United States could not fight without contributions from the National Guard or the Army Reserve, an intentional practice (the use of the "total force") intended to make maximum use of available limited manpower.[20] The 24th Mechanized Infantry Division had been specially selected for rapid sea deployment, using fast sealift ships kept at ninety-six-hour notice in U.S. ports. It was, therefore, earmarked for early deployment to Saudi Arabia. The other heavy U.S.–based divisions were inherently less mobile. The initial deployment involved one of them (the 1st Armored Cavalry), which arrived between sixty and seventy-eight days after mobilization. Another U.S.–based division (the 1st Mechanized Infantry) was ultimately deployed to Saudi Arabia (in the augmentation announced 8 November).

Through late 1990 ground force deployments to the Gulf were limited to the fire brigade (marines and 82d and 101st divisions), the 24th Mechanized Infantry Division "swing" unit based in the United States, the 1st Armored Cavalry Division from the United States, and the 3d Armored Cavalry Regiment from the United States. They amounted to the full army "half" war capability.

As the force approved in August was built up in Saudi Arabia, the U.S. government had to decide on any further deployment. Since the deployment already under way fully taxed available transportation, no decision really had to be made until early November. While the buildup proceeded, the Iraqi force in Kuwait doubled or tripled, presumably in response. That foreclosed any immediate allied offensive option, and it also suggested that Saddam Hussein might have hopes of a further offensive of his own.

About 6 November 1990, then, President Bush made the momentous decision to move one of the two heavy armored corps from Europe to Saudi Arabia. At the least, the new force would match the Iraqi buildup. However, it had a wider significance. Until that point, virtually all U.S. ground forces in the theater had been drawn from what amounted to the contingency reserve. Much of the force added after 6 November came from resources that in the past had been held back for other purposes. At least in theory, these forces could not be held in Saudi Arabia indefinitely. Many saw the November choice, then, as a choice for offensive action. Some critics went so far as to charge that the administration deliberately waited until after the November U.S. election to announce the additions (the administration response was that the timetable was dictated by shipping considerations).

The heavy European-based VII Corps took some considerable time to move to the Gulf. It would have taken a long time to move back to Europe in an emergency, so the movement was possible only because the Soviet threat to NATO had been so substantially reduced by Mikhail Gorbachev. This, then, was one of Mr. Gorbachev's several major contributions to the war. At the time, given estimates of Iraqi strength in Kuwait, it seemed that victory would have been impossible without the presence of the heavy European units (later lower estimates of Iraqi strength make this less obvious). As it was, VII Corps made the decisive deep stroke against the Iraqis. None of the units already on the ground could have made the same sort of attack. By August 1990 the U.S. government had already planned major withdrawals from the NATO force, so it was not difficult to imagine moving some of those forces into the Gulf area. With the VII Corps, the army moved the U.S.–based 1st Mechanized Infantry Division into Saudi Arabia.

On the other hand, ground forces could not be drawn from the Pacific. Enmity between North and South Korea actually increased through 1990. The North Koreans may have seen the U.S. naval deployment to the Gulf as an opportunity for them, and that possibility made it particularly important for the United States and its coalition partners to resolve the situation as rapidly as possible.

The United States was the main, but hardly the sole, contributor of ground forces to the Gulf coalition. The second largest Western contributor, Britain, also was able to deploy substantial forces otherwise committed to NATO. The French division was part of the French rapid-deployment force, which was intended partly for operations outside Europe and thus corresponded partly to the U.S. "swing" force. Egypt and Syria both contributed substantial army units. These deployments involved substantial shipping, most of it commercial. The effect of using commercial cargo ships rather than the fast Ro-Ros (roll-on, roll-off) used by some of the U.S. units was to stretch out shipping times. There were also many smaller deployments, both from within the Arabian peninsula (for example, by Qatar and by free Kuwaiti forces) and from a wide variety of other countries. For example, some members of a contingent of Afghan Mujahideen guerrillas were the first troops to enter Kuwait City. Other countries sent troops to Saudi Arabia for defensive but not offensive operations (Bangladesh, Bahrain, Morocco, Niger, Pakistan, and Senegal). Czechoslovakia contributed a 200-man chemical decontamination unit, in which it took great pride (as the first Czech operation since 1945 outside Soviet control). Poland contributed a hospital ship and a salvage tug. For details of the ground and air units contributed to Desert Shield/Desert Storm, see Appendices A and B.

Overall, the pattern of Desert Shield, the buildup and protection of Saudi Arabia, actually followed in outline much of the thinking of the Maritime Strategy developed during the previous decade but largely discredited later on. The reason is that the Maritime Strategy was an expression of classic and enduring naval principles rather than a transitory expression of contemporary political ideas.

Then as now, the threat was a land power seeking to invade a friendly area. Then as now, it would take significant land forces to stop or reverse the invasion. In the case of Europe, it had to be accepted that much of the large allied ground force initially present in the theater would be wiped out in the first battles. In Saudi Arabia there was no large land force, with its logistical base of munitions, fuel, and spares, in the first place. In each case, although troops and airplanes could be flown in, the mountain of ammunition and other necessities, which made those individuals into a fighting force, could not. That also applied to heavy vehicles, such as tanks.

The Maritime Strategy argued that U.S. and allied maritime forces could provide essential assistance to ground operations in several ways. They could force an enemy to spread out his defenses, because he could not accurately predict where a naval air or amphibious blow might fall. That would reduce the load on the ground forces themselves (in Desert Storm, this flexibility

was used to tie down large Iraqi forces along the Kuwaiti coast).
Because naval forces could maneuver freely, they might also be
well placed to interdict enemy forces heading toward the battle
zone, but out of range of local land-based aircraft. They could
provide essential cover to the ground forces while early losses
were made good. Finally, they could cover the seaborne movement of essential materiel, without which the ground war could
not be fought at all.

In the Saudi case, initial cover, provided by the carriers and
then by the marines, made possible a buildup on the ground.
Without that cover, the army and air force units flown into Saudi
Arabia would have been terribly vulnerable to any determined
Iraqi attack. That vulnerability almost certainly lasted through
the late fall of 1990. It is not that the army and air forces are
inherently weak, but rather that they are very large, and that their
innate logistical support is necessarily more ponderous than that
of the marines or the seaborne navy.

Throughout the crisis, the United States probably benefited
enormously from Saddam Hussein's caricature picture of the
world; he may well have imagined that all of these units represented an immediate, rather than a potential, threat virtually as
soon as they arrived. An enemy even vaguely familiar with the
facts of logistics would have realized otherwise.[21]

The classic way to support an operation like the buildup in
Saudi Arabia is by chartered commercial shipping. Unfortunately
in 1990 the United States lacked any substantial merchant fleet.
For some years it had been recognized that a national emergency
deployment would require large numbers of merchant ships.
From World War II on, a reserve merchant fleet was built up. It
was mobilized for both Korea and Vietnam, but by the 1970s the
ships, mostly built during World War II, were no longer viable.
As long as the only important contingency was a NATO war, this
situation seemed acceptable: materiel would be carried by ships
of the other NATO allies, and even by important Asian allies such
as Korea and Japan. However, the situation changed radically
with acceptance of the CentCom mission in Southwest Asia.
There the United States might well have to build up forces on its

own. Allies might even deny it the use of their ships. After all, the NATO allies' record of assistance in U.S. military operations in the Middle East was less than encouraging.

The Defense Department therefore became interested in what it called strategic sealift (as opposed to the specialized tactical, that is, amphibious lift built to support the marines). This $7 billion effort began in 1984.[22] The strategic sealift force includes active, ready, and standby ships. The active force consists of thirteen specially configured maritime prepositioning ships in the three squadrons (based at Diego Garcia, Guam, and on the U.S. East Coast), each supporting a MEF, and eleven Afloat Prepositioning Squadron (APS) ships. All are continuously manned by merchant crews, and each MPS squadron has a navy commander and staff. The MPSs are preloaded and forward-deployed. The APS ships, which do not form an administrative squadron, are intended to support the army and air force. Those at Diego Garcia on the eve of the crisis were two tankers (for water and for fuel), four lighter-aboard-ship (LASH) ships, two break-bulk cargo ships (one carrying equipment), and one float-on float-off (Flo-Flo) ship loaded with small harbor craft and barges. An eleventh ship, carrying air force munitions, operated in the Mediterranean. Two of the LASH ships carried air force ammunition. One carried a containerized 500-bed field hospital (to be offloaded and set up ashore). Like the MPS squadron, the APS ships were conceived to unload at unimproved ports. Much of their capability was not needed in Saudi Arabia.

The ready force, in U.S. ports with nucleus crews, consists of a squadron of eight fast sealift ships (FSS, organized as Fast Sealift Squadron One, sufficient to carry the equipment for a full heavy division), two hospital ships (AH), and two Marine Corps aviation support ships (T-AVB). The FSS are ready at four days' notice, the hospital ships at five days' notice. The FSSs are not preloaded, so the four days' readiness is somewhat deceptive, in that it takes additional time to assemble and load a division's worth of materiel.

Then there is a Ready Reserve Force (RRF) consisting of ninety-four purchased modern merchant ships (as of 1 January 1990) upgraded to U.S. standards and modified for military lift. This group includes crane ships to provide an independent capability to unload containers in unequipped ports. These ships were bought during the 1980s on the soft world shipping market. The RRF is held at ten- to twenty-day readiness. The RRF is part of a larger National Defense Reserve Fleet (NDRF) consisting mainly of merchant ships turned in to the Maritime Administration by their owners, and retained against larger emergencies. Some of the better of these ships are expected ultimately to be upgraded to RRF status. About 130 NDRF (non-RRF) ships are still in reasonably good condition for activation, but they could not have been readied in time for this crisis. Some of the NDRF ships date back to World War II. As of 1990, the RRF was scheduled to expand to 142 ships by FY94.

The MPSs were extremely successful. The first ships, from Diego Garcia, arrived on 15 August. Not only did they suffice to support an airlifted MEB, but some of their tanks were lent to the army units airlifted into Saudi Arabia to provide them with early capability. The FSSs were ordered activated on 7 August, and the first of them arrived in Savannah for loading on 11 August. She sailed on the 14th and arrived in Saudi Arabia on the 27th, covering 8,700 nautical miles at an average of 27 knots. It took six more FSSs and three commercial ships to complete the division lift on 13 September, twelve days behind schedule.[23]

The next phase of the sealift was to activate RRF ships and to charter merchant ships to fill the gaps in the RRF fleet. There was a particularly urgent need for Ro-Ros and LASH ships, which were not well represented in either the U.S.–flag or the RRF fleets.[24] Of 173 ships in the original deployment (completed 5 December 1990), 49 were foreign-flag ships (28 percent; but only 15 percent of total U.S. cargo tonnage was carried by foreign-flag ships). Foreign-flag shipping was more significant in the second phase of the buildup (it carried 22 percent of cargo tonnage), in which most of the cargo came from Europe (8 million square feet of equipment, compared to 5 million square feet from the United States). The problem was that cargo was not available in the European ports early enough. Ships arriving there had to wait so long that they could not make multiple trips to Saudi Arabia before the war began on 16 January. Thus it took more ships to make a given total number of trips to Saudi Arabia, and more foreign ships had to be chartered. During the second buildup phase, too, the third MPS squadron was used to deliver a third Marine Corps MEB to Saudi Arabia on 13 December.

Sealift carried 95 percent of everything CentCom needed to live and to fight. It triumphed in Desert Shield/Desert Storm. However, these operations revealed problems suggestive of possible future failure. Without a viable merchant fleet, the United States cannot maintain the reserve merchant mariners needed to crew whatever ships it buys or charters. Without a viable merchant fleet, too, the United States is unlikely to be able to maintain the shipbuilding and ship repair industries without which the largest government-owned fleet cannot be maintained.

The other NATO nations have seen their own once-large merchant fleets decline. The British drew the conclusion from their Saudi experience that such decline was unacceptable. Their solution is an unusual tax incentive, announced in March 1991 as part of the official budget. Once at sea on an ocean voyage, sailors will not be liable for any British taxes. Nor will their employers. The effect is probably to double real wages for British merchant seamen while drastically reducing their expenses to deep sea shipowners (the measure cannot help the collapsing fishing and coastal shipping industries).[25]

In the United States, there has been much talk of government-sponsored fast sealift construction. The Marine Corps MPSs are much admired because they allowed the marines to form combat formations (MEBs) virtually immediately upon arrival. To make similar provision for even a single heavy (armored or mechanized) army division (as is now being proposed) would be almost impossible, because the division is so much larger than the MEBs and because combat-loading (as on board the MPS ships) is so much less efficient, in loading terms, than is conventional high-density loading.

The larger issue is whether the U.S. government should buy large numbers of merchant ships specifically to support some future version of Desert Shield. The ships would have to be laid up awaiting the emergency, and the crew to operate them would have to be supported on some reserve basis. Without a viable U.S. merchant fleet, they would have no civilian jobs similar to their reserve roles. That contrasts with the situation in airlift. Most U.S. military airlift is performed by reservists drawn from the civilian airline industry. Emergency capacity is provided by civilian airliners of the Civil Reserve Air Fleet (CRAF) and by chartering civilian airliners. There is no vast fleet of idle government-owned airliners waiting for an emergency.

In the case of ships, the argument is that voyages are so long that the civilian shipping industry could not readily divert any large fraction of its strength to meet an emergency. Airliners can be diverted much more quickly, particularly if, as in this case, the emergency itself drastically reduces the civilian demand for seats. That argument does not in itself invalidate the reasoning that it is uneconomical for the U.S. government to maintain a capacity that could pay at least partly for itself. It may well be that the government can call on only a fraction of the overall shipping fleet instantly, but in any case the rest of the fleet is valuable insurance against losses. That Saddam Hussein made no real effort to intercept or destroy the shipping supporting Desert Shield and the subsequent war should not blind us to the very real possibility of such attacks in a future crisis.

Much of the shipping supporting Desert Shield had to pass through the Mediterranean and then through the Suez Canal. In the Mediterranean, Libya supported Iraq, at least verbally. There was a real possibility that this support could have become much more concrete. Coalition warships, such as the light battle group built around HMS *Ark Royal*, had to operate in the Mediterranean to deter any such action. After all, the Libyans had once gone so far as to fire a Scud missile at an Italian island on which the U.S. Navy had an installation.

The canal itself had to be a very attractive target. Large demonstrations showed clearly that many Egyptians disagreed with their president's policy of supporting the coalition. It would not have taken very much effort for some of them to have fired short-range missiles, such as rocket-propelled grenades, at the warships and merchantmen passing through the canal. It would also have been quite possible to mine either the canal or its Mediterranean approaches. In 1984 a Libyan Ro-Ro ship mined portions of the Red Sea. The Germans operated a mine countermeasures squadron to protect the Mediterranean entrance to the canal. Egypt is prohibited by treaty from barring passage through the canal to any nation. That led to some extreme measures. In one case, a ship carrying munitions had a Libyan officer. The ship had to be unloaded, and her munitions shipped by land to the Red Sea terminus of the canal. Presumably without munitions aboard she could not easily have been scuttled in the canal.

As for the far terminus of the support effort, Saudi Arabia presented an unusual situation. Because the country imports virtually everything it uses, it has extraordinarily good port facilities.[26] It seems unlikely that this good fortune will be repeated in any future version of Desert Shield (in which case facilities would have to be seized or created). Nor will it necessarily be the case that future intervention will occur before a prospective aggressor manages to destroy port facilities and local airfields. Saudi Arabia has excellent examples of both, but they are few, and a more farsighted man than Saddam Hussein would probably have been able to put them out of action. In that case early U.S. intervention would have been limited to the carriers and, possibly, the MPS-supported MEBs. Quite possibly the amphibious ready group marines would have had to seize beachheads or ports for the MPSs. These lessons will no doubt be learned by observers of Desert Shield who do not wish to suffer Saddam's fate.

Despite the existence of the port facilities, there was still a fair chance that Saddam Hussein would have been able to prevent the U.S. buildup. Prewar Saudi Arabia had a large foreign population, including many Palestinians and Yemenis at least nominally sympathetic to Saddam Hussein. Some of them could hope to disrupt port facilities. In addition, there were rumors that Saddam had bought midget submarines, divers from which could attack merchant ships entering port or at dock. Such threats were not fantasies; during the Vietnam War the Viet Cong repeatedly attacked and even sank ships in the long channel leading to Saigon. Port security was a major enterprise.

In this case, Bahrain, Ad Dammam, and Al Jubail all had to be protected. The U.S. Coast Guard activated Port Security Units from its Ninth District (HQ, Cleveland), who worked with U.S. mobile inshore underwater warfare (MIUW) units, also reservists. In each port, the MIUW unit maintained sensors in the water and surveillance radar feeding a command van, which might occupy an offshore barge or a pierhead. Those inside the van kept a plot of movements into and around the port and sent out some of the coast guard unit's six 22-foot Boston Whaler boats to investigate. Typical targets were divers, dhows, and unidentified merchant ships. The units also provided security for ships as they entered port. Typically they worked with local coast guard officers responsible for communications, fishery law enforcement, and identification checks. Each of the three mixed navy–coast guard units had about 220 personnel (100 coast guard).[27]

The outcome of Desert Shield provided the coalition with the option to attack Saddam Hussein, but it was by no means obvious that the option would be exercised. It seems likely that through much of the fall of 1990 Saddam still believed that he would not have to face combat, and that only a preemptive attack on his part could have caused problems. His forces were careful to avoid contact with the allies, and there were only a few incidents of aircraft even approaching the Kuwaiti-Saudi or Iraqi-Saudi borders. Saddam's air force generally refrained even from reconnaissance flights, leaving that task to Jordanian RF-5s flying along the border with Saudi Arabia. Many in the media were surprised that hostile forces eyeball to eyeball did not quickly fall into combat.

Beside his acquisition of military technology, Saddam tried more spectacular threats based on the oil facilities he had seized in Kuwait. Wells would be fired and oil spilled into the ecologically delicate Persian Gulf. A variety of scientists, many of them politically allied with Iraq (or against Western military intervention, which was not the same thing) were willing to state that either action would be disastrous on a global scale. For example, they suggested that the oil fires would produce results comparable to those adduced for nuclear winter.

Finally, Saddam gathered several prominent terrorists to Baghdad, the obvious message being that, whatever it might do militarily, the West would suffer badly. This threat was convincing, because so many of the worst terrorist atrocities had originated in the Middle East. Perhaps its main consequence was a collapse of international air travel after war broke out. This was the one case in which personal jitters could be effective. It could not, however, have much effect on the coalition governments.

6

The Fortification of Kuwait

THE IRAQI Republican Guard divisions that seized Kuwait were withdrawn after looting it. Regular Iraqi army units were rapidly brought into the country to secure the border against what Saddam Hussein feared might be a quick counterattack. It is instructive that, lacking any understanding of U.S. logistics, he seems to have feared or believed that the United States could build up quickly to offensive power on the ground.[1] To preclude that attack, Saddam exercised two parallel strategies. One was the conventional military choice: he fortified the Kuwaiti-Saudi border and the Kuwaiti coast. The other was psychological: he sought to create sufficient fear of the cost of attacking him that the United States, the core of the coalition, would shrink from doing so. The two campaigns were interconnected in that it would be expensive to liberate Kuwait only to the extent that the country had been sufficiently fortified.

Saddam apparently believed that the United States would shrink from serious military sacrifice, that it was soft and decadent despite its apparent economic and military strength. He was impressed by what he saw as U.S. weakness in withdrawing from Vietnam after losing 50,000 troops. He may have been aware of the numerous post-Vietnam claims, in the United States, that foreign war would be impossible in the future. He certainly noted the weak reaction to the attack on the USS *Stark* by one of his aircraft. He interpreted Washington's unwillingness to become involved in local bargaining (just before the invasion) as acquiescence to his power. Senators flattering him to gain trade deals seemed, to Saddam, to be confirming his bloated self-image, and their own weakness. To some extent, this misinterpretation, which was the basis of the war, was likely due to Saddam's limited experience of the world outside Iraq. Like dictators before him facing U.S. wrath, Saddam may have been impressed by apparent U.S. weakness. Used to constancy in the characters of other countries, these rulers find it difficult to imagine the sort of sudden hardening of commitment common in U.S. history.

Saddam seems to have expected the United States to feint and threaten, but then to withdraw under pressure, under the cover of some face-saving formula (the withdrawal from Beirut after 241 marines had been killed was officially a "strategic redeployment"). He recalled the failure of Desert One, the botched rescue of the Iranian hostages. The U.S. attack on Grenada seemed to show that the United States would fight only easy wars; after all, it did not tackle Fidel Castro. Saddam's belief may explain his series of threats (for example, "you will swim in your own blood") during the tense buildup in the fall of 1990.

Saddam seems to have used Western defense journalists to spread the word that his army, even if it was primitive, could enforce terrible attrition on enemy troops. For example, elaborate drawings of typical Iraqi fortifications in Kuwait were widely published. Considerable publicity was given to reports that Iraq had effective chemical and biological weapons, and that they would be delivered against troops caught in the fortifications. By the end of 1990, Saddam was predicting huge U.S. casualties—to buy which he was willing to lose as many as 2 million Iraqi lives. Few asked whether the Iraqis in question would be quite as willing as Saddam to make this sacrifice. Only in retrospect does the question seem so obvious.

Saddam's initial triumph was the postwar (1989) Baghdad military exhibition, featuring numerous new missiles described as fruits of Iraqi industry. Most Western observers failed to notice how many of them were standard Soviet-supplied weapons with vital portions removed to change their appearance (and, incidentally, to render them nonfunctional). Others seem to have been repainted Western equipment, such as an Italian-made Mirach reconnaissance drone labeled a cruise missile.

The limited information released about the Iran-Iraq War made for little public understanding of the sophistication (or lack of same) of Saddam's systems. That left most observers, including many who should have known better, focusing on the weapons themselves. They were impressive, at least on paper. Saddam was particularly well endowed with artillery and with its extension, rockets and missiles—a natural concentration for any Soviet client. For example, Saddam had financed the Canadian artillery genius, Dr. Gerald Bull, the inventor of modern base-bleed shells and of the new generation of long-range guns bought by, among others, Austria, China, South Africa, and Spain. In theory, they greatly outranged comparable coalition weapons.[2] Much publicity was also given to supposed clandestine Iraqi arms purchases, such as fuel-air and cluster bomb technology.[3] Iraq also possessed Scud missiles and locally developed longer-range derivatives.

Many more detailed reports later proved to have been complete fabrications. Despite detailed accounts of massive upgrading of armored vehicles, the tanks caught and killed in Iraq and Kuwait were almost all garden-variety. The new naval mines so publicized at the 1989 Baghdad show were not found in the waters of the Gulf, although quite real ones made in Iraq (but using Soviet components) were.

Saddam seems never to have entertained the thought that this sort of publicity might suggest that his military was too powerful to be permitted to expand unchecked. Yet that was one of the major arguments later used to justify the attack on Kuwait, to the extent that virtually disarming Iraq became a primary coalition objective. Saddam's combination of aggressiveness and weapons of mass destruction seemed particularly intolerable. Once war began, then, these weapons and the industrial base erected to support them became primary coalition targets.

There is no question that Saddam did want new technology,

and that he would willingly pay the price for it. For example, he invested heavily in nuclear, biological, and chemical weapons technology. He did pay Dr. Bull to develop some sort of very long-range gun, possibly for satellite launching (Bull had worked on a similar project for the U.S. Army in the 1960s). The question is, rather, what Saddam got for his money, and to what extent he knowingly embellished his position for deterrent value. It seems in retrospect that the Baghdad show and also such announced projects as the Adnan early warning airplane were much more for show than for reality, and that Western observers, at least those speaking and writing in public, were largely taken in. Saddam thus may only have been part of a long tradition of Third World military high technology projects that turned out to be largely for show. Examples would include the Egyptian jet fighter and long-range missile projects of the 1950s and 1960s. Enough Third World projects of this sort have been real (for example, India) that it is not enough to dismiss them out of hand. Saddam presumably banked on that ambiguity.

Moreover, in some cases Iraq possessed interesting bits of military technology that had *not* been publicized prewar and that, properly employed, might have been quite nasty surprises. For example, at Khafji it had both Dutch-supplied night vision equipment and a simple FLIR jammer. The U.S. forces relied very heavily on FLIRs for night vision and even for vision through smoke and heavy dust on a daytime battlefield. The Iraqi jammers might conceivably have nullified that advantage. Iraq also had a jammer for the coalition's TOW antitank missile, again a key weapon in the war that followed. Neither countermeasure was particularly effectively used, but both had much more potential for causing the coalition severe losses than the nonweapons so ostentatiously shown in 1989. The key reason neither was effective was probably abysmally poor overall Iraqi military performance at the personnel and unit command level, a factor none of the prewar assessors seems to have taken into account.

Western observers knew little of the state or quality of Iraqi personnel. The elite Republican Guard divisions received considerable publicity, but the Iraqi army was typically described merely as battle-hardened, battle-experienced. Few if any noticed that battle-hardened often means battle-weary.[4] Press accounts suggesting that, by the end of the Iran-Iraq War, Iraqi commanders had been most reluctant to try any tactics promising losses were largely forgotten. Similarly, it was very difficult for observers, including those in Western intelligence, to estimate the competency of the Iraqi technical arms, including the air force.

The published accounts of Iraqi military prowess had real consequences. In the fall of 1990 several civilian analysts produced estimates of the likely course of events should the United States and its coalition partners attack the Iraqi forces in Kuwait. Their work was necessarily based on unclassified data, that is, on exactly those publications susceptible to Saddam's propaganda campaign. During the congressional debate on adopting military measures to force Iraq out of Kuwait, the recurrent theme of opponents of such measures was the expected heavy toll of American lives. Yet the war proved that Iraqi capability was ludicrously poor. To some extent poor Iraqi performance was a direct consequence of the overwhelmingly good U.S. tactics and technology, a disparity that would have been difficult to estimate before the war.

That still leaves some important questions. It may be that our technique for predicting the effect of combat depends too heavily on raw data (for example, numbers of tanks) and takes too little account of determining factors such as competence and command and control. It is important not to take an enemy's capability too lightly in formulating battle plans, but what turned out to be unrealistically high estimates of U.S. battle casualties were nearly self-deterring. The civilian estimators generally applied widely accepted techniques, and few of their source data were really controversial. It is likely, therefore, that their military counterparts came to much the same conclusions. None of this is to suggest that U.S. forces will always triumph at minimal cost, but rather that the reasons for this particular victory could have a valuable lesson to teach.

It may be that the Western powers, having backed Saddam during the Iran-Iraq War, could not admit that his forces had been less than competent, even in their triumph in 1988. The evidence was certainly there, in more than a decade of military disaster: against the Israelis, against the Kurds, against the Iranians during much of the war. All of these cases had been well documented.[5]

The Iraqi combat engineers were considered experienced and were generally highly rated. Much of their good performance could be traced to Saddam's willingness to promote competent engineer officers, a practice that could be contrasted with his unwillingness to promote or even to tolerate aggressive tank leaders and his apparent preference for a relatively incompetent air force. As has been suggested earlier, this preference probably derived from his overriding consideration: prevention of a military coup against him.[6]

The fortification of Kuwait generally followed the pattern developed during the Iran-Iraq War, consisting of a fairly deep barrier backed by artillery and mobile reserves. Clearly there was insufficient time for the entire Kuwaiti frontier to be fortified. Saddam had to guess which routes potential invaders might take. He (or his field commanders) seems to have assumed that any attack from the south would come either up the coastal road or along the track from the west, at the point on the frontier closest to Kuwait City. It seems to have been assumed that no potential invader would cross the border between the two roads, because in this direction extensive oil fields largely shielded Kuwait City from the south. It probably seemed obvious that the problems of fighting in or around an oil field, with all the cover that it offered a defender, and with all its immense hazards, would deter any attacker bent on crossing it. On the frontier, then, Iraqi attention focused on two relatively narrow areas.

The other major perceived threat was a seaborne attack, north or south of Kuwait City. Great attention went into coastal fortifications, including the reinforcement of every coastal structure the Iraqis could find. They were well aware that the United States had large Marine Corps forces afloat off their coast, and they could not imagine that these forces would not be used.

These themes were found expressed on an Iraqi commander's

sand table captured in Kuwait City. No other attack routes seem to have been considered very seriously. Iraqi military dispositions consisted of reserves in the Wadi al-Batin (to deal with a thrust along the inland track) and other reserves in central Kuwait (to deal with the coastal assault or with the attack up the coastal road). Six divisions were ultimately dug in along the coast.

From Saddam Hussein's point of view, the only problem was that fortification would take time, during which the Americans might be able to make a lightning strike. He seems to have been particularly impressed with the threat of a Marine Corps amphibious assault.

Saddam therefore needed some form of cover during what he saw as a period of special vulnerability. His choice was to take Western hostages. On 15 August all Westerners in Kuwait were ordered to report to three hotels for relocation to strategic military and civilian sites throughout Iraq. Many were wise enough to go underground, and roundups continued through the fall. Those who escaped over the Saudi border provided the first accounts of the destruction of Kuwait by the Iraqi occupying force.

Saddam Hussein offered to free his hostages if President Bush would withdraw from Saudi Arabia and cancel the embargo. By the 20th of August, Iraq was announcing that adult male hostages had been moved to potential targets to act as human shields. Women and children were kept in Baghdad. Throughout the fall, a series of Western elder statesmen and peace activists visited Baghdad to negotiate for the release of groups of hostages. Presumably Saddam Hussein considered it unlikely that the United States would strike while these negotiations were in progress. Moreover, selected releases of small groups of Europeans or Japanese could make for stresses within the coalition, since each release seemed to indicate that the coalition member involved had made some sort of private deal with Iraq.

Saddam clearly hoped that what seemed like proof of private deals would make the Western coalition members distrust each other. He seems to have had hopes of a different effect on the Arab members of the coalition. He wanted to demonstrate to the Arab world that the coalition was a fiction; that, in fact, it was the creature of the two imperialist powers, the United States and Britain. To the extent that virtually all of the other coalition members seemed to be willing to make deals, Saddam could argue that he was really fighting only the United States and its own main ally, Great Britain (which he could characterize as the colonial power that had created the unnatural Kuwaiti state in the first place). This was a shrewd strategy; the Arab states found it much easier to fight within a broad coalition than to declare themselves U.S. allies. Saddam clearly hoped that popular Arab revulsion for the United States, the perceived friend of Israel, would then force Arab members out of the coalition.

This was not altogether a matter of cynical manipulation of the facts. The United States really was the mainspring of the coalition, and the next largest Western contributor was Great Britain. It was reasonable for Saddam to imagine that, as long as U.S. and British hostages remained at the strategic sites, neither country would be willing to attack (there is, however, good evidence that neither was nearly as deterred as Saddam imagined).

For Arab cultural reasons, the human shields had to be adult males (that is, potential warriors). Thus Saddam found it easy to announce, at the end of August, that he would release women, children, and sick adult men. It is not clear whether he ever expected the United States to give in so as to get the hostages back; they seem to have been more a matter of strategic cover while Kuwait was fortified. Saddam Hussein said as much when he announced the release of the remaining hostages on 6 December.

Throughout the fall of 1990, there was speculation that the Western powers might attempt a hostage rescue, or a rescue of the diplomats trapped in Kuwait. For example, on 1 September the Saudi defense minister, Prince Sultan bin Abdul-Aziz, stated that his country would not be used as a theater of offensive action, for example, a hostage rescue. At this time there was still widespread expectation that eventually some deal would be worked out, and therefore that the hostage-taking was the main issue. President Bush seems to have recognized from the beginning that it was no more than a distraction. It was also apparently accepted from the first by the administration that the hostages, spread out through Iraq, could not be rescued by any reasonable military action. All plans for military action, if it were to be taken, envisaged the liberation of Kuwait, not merely of the Western hostages. President Bush had learned President Carter's hard lesson: concentration on hostages would make the administration itself hostage to Saddam, and thus would prevent serious contemplation of more fruitful initiatives.

The Iraqi combat engineers used the time bought by the hostage-taking to good effect. Their fortifications consisted of a sand ridge (a berm) backed by an antitank ditch (which could be filled with burning oil), a belt of barbed wire, and extensive mine fields (it was estimated before the war that Iraq had laid between 500,000 and 2.5 million mines on the Kuwaiti border with Saudi Arabia). Dug in well behind the berm and the other obstacles were tanks, infantry, and long-range artillery in triangular strong points (that is, strong points without any exposed rear, so that they could keep fighting even as an assault force passed by). In theory, an attacking enemy would be slowed down while penetrating the berm and the other obstacles. Caught there, it could easily be engaged by long-range Iraqi artillery firing, among other things, chemical shells. Reportedly there were three such belts, although it is not at all clear that the inner ones were continuous. There was never much question but that such fortifications could be breached, but most Western experts estimated that assaults would be expensive. Saddam believed that such estimates would be quite deterring; he was fond of saying that U.S. society could not accept a battle that might cost it 10,000 dead.

The apparent strength of the Iraqi position in Kuwait masked considerable weakness. It was certainly true that an allied force caught in or just beyond the berm could be destroyed by fixed Iraqi artillery (which outranged the allied guns), but it was also true that, given the primitive command and control arrangements, the guns could not react quickly to engage a fast-moving force. Zeroed on particular points along the defensive belt, they could not engage targets well beyond, in Saudi Arabia, that the Iraqis had failed to locate because they had no sensing system.

These points were probably suspected but not definitely known to the coalition planners.

The border defenses had another disastrous defect. They had virtually no air defense. The Iraqis had had no experience of serious air attack during the Iran-Iraq War, because the Iranian revolution had destroyed most of the old Imperial Iranian Air Force. For reasons difficult to imagine, Saddam Hussein seems to have assumed that his national air defense would largely preclude air attacks on the soldiers in Kuwait, and that their own organic air defenses (largely hand-held missiles) would suffice beyond that.

Finally, and probably worst of all, for all the effort put into protecting the border with Saudi Arabia, nothing had been done about the Saudi-Iraqi border to the west of Kuwait and little had been done about the Iraqi border with Kuwait. Western Kuwait was, in effect, an open door, and the Republican Guard between Kuwait and the Euphrates River had an open flank and rear. General Schwarzkopf would eventually win the war largely by using just that open door into southern Iraq, and he must have been at least slightly nervous that it had been left open as a temptation into some terrible surprise.

As the coalition began to mass forces in Saudi Arabia, more capable Iraqi units were brought into Kuwait. The invasion was mounted by 100,000 troops and 300 tanks. In mid-August, it was estimated that there were 120,000 Iraqi troops in Kuwait, with another 50,000 en route (to match the coalition buildup in Saudi Arabia). At this time Saddam Hussein apparently feared that he would also be facing a thrust from Turkey; reportedly he built up his forces on the Turkish border. These forces would also be needed to put down any Kurdish rising touched off by Iraqi military difficulties in the south. At the beginning of September 1990, the United States estimated that there were about 150,000 Iraqi troops in Kuwait supported by another 115,000 in southern Iraq, with a total of 1,500 tanks, 1,200 armored personnel carriers, and 800 artillery pieces in the region. During the second week in September, 95,000 troops and 600 tanks were added, and the United States estimated that about 40 percent of the force in the region belonged to the Republican Guard.

Iraqi troops in Kuwait in mid-September reportedly amounted to ten divisions: three armored, two mechanized, four infantry, and one special forces. Republican Guard units were being extracted from Kuwait to form a tactical reserve, and also as a direct screen around Baghdad (and a strategic reserve).

At this point substantial Iraqi forces were still tied down on the Iranian border. Saddam Hussein made strenuous efforts to free them up by surrendering the expensive territory gained during the long Iran-Iraq War. On 15 August he offered to withdraw from the Shatt-al-Arab, and on the 18th Iraqi troops began to dismantle their field fortifications there under white flags. Iraq returned most (but not all) of the Iranian prisoners it had held since the 1988 cease-fire (thus exacerbating Iranian sensitivities). However, on 10 September the two countries resumed diplomatic relations. Saddam would later frequently hint that Iran was willing to take joint action with him against the infidels in the Gulf, but there was little or no evidence of such action. The main effect of the Iraqi withdrawal from the Iranian border was to release five divisions for service in Kuwait, with three infantry divisions moved to each of the Syrian and Turkish frontiers.[7] This amounted to about half the force on the Iranian border. By this time Syria had massed about 50,000 of its own troops on its border with Iraq, partly in response to pro-Iraqi disturbances created by Saddam to prevent Syria from sending troops to Saudi Arabia.

By the end of September, the U.S. government credited the Iraqi force in Kuwait with 360,000 men, 2,800 tanks, 1,800 armored personnel carriers, and 1,450 artillery pieces, presumably including the units transferred from the Iranian front. By the first week in October, the official total was 430,000 troops, 3,500 tanks, 2,500 armored personnel carriers, and 1,700 artillery pieces. These figures include both Kuwait proper and southern Iraq, the future Kuwait theater of operations (KTO). Three Iraqi army corps (the 2d, 3rd, and 7th) were stationed in the future KTO. The Republican Guard, the protectors of the regime, were further back, along the Kuwaiti border with Iraq. They were the ultimate mobile reserve.[8]

At the same time, Iraqi forces near the Turkish border were

built up to about 250,000 men, and Scud missiles were moved to within range of the Incirlik air base, which the United States hoped to use in the event of war. The Scuds, which were well publicized, were intended as a deterrent to Turkish permission for U.S. use of the base in a non-NATO role. The Turks in turn asked their NATO allies to provide air protection.[9]

By early November, the Iraqi forces in the KTO were credited with more than 400,000 troops, 3,500 tanks, and 2,500 artillery pieces; elements of twenty-five divisions (controlled by four corps headquarters) were said to be present. A tactical reserve had been built up astride the Wadi al-Batin on the Iraqi-Kuwaiti border. The buildup continued through the month, so that by mid-November the Iraqi army in the KTO was credited with 425,000 men and 3,700 tanks. Revised U.S. estimates released early in December showed 450,000 men and 3,600 tanks. In midmonth the Iraqis were credited with 480,000 men and 4,000 tanks (plus 2,500 APCs and 2,700 artillery pieces). At this time Iraq was thought to have twenty-eight to twenty-nine divisions in the KTO (3d and 4th Corps), with fourteen to fifteen in Kuwait proper, presumably exclusive of the Republican Guard. When the war began in January, the Iraqi Army in the KTO was estimated at 530,000 men, about 4,300 tanks, 2,700 armored fighting vehicles, and 3,000 artillery pieces. This increase was partly a result of a reassessment of the intelligence interpretation process.

All of the Iraqi figures are approximate, but the trends illustrated are clear. Most likely the estimates were constructed as Iraqi unit headquarters were identified (for example, from their signal traffic) in the KTO. Later it would be suggested that all of the estimates were far too high, that Iraq never had more than about 300,000 troops in Kuwait and nearby Iraq proper. Appendix A gives nominal unit troop strengths, but with the strong caveat that Third World armies like Iraq's often do not fill out their nominal tables of organization. The lesson is probably that it is extremely difficult to count men and vehicles on this scale, whereas unit-counting is a well-developed art.[10]

7

Military Considerations

FOR THE UNITED STATES Army, the war for Kuwait raised a very important question. This was the first major U.S. ground war since Vietnam (Grenada and Panama were clearly minor actions). U.S. naval air forces and naval forces had demonstrated their capabilities both in the Persian Gulf and off Libya. The U.S. Air Force had shown its own capability when participating in the Libyan raid. But Saddam Hussein was certainly right when he said that the U.S. Army had not fought a hard war since Vietnam. Worse, many Americans subscribed to the view that the peacetime army was entirely too cocksure. In the past, American armies had very often lost the first battle (and so learned respect for their opponents) before going on to win the war. This time, with a relatively small volunteer army and with no draft to make up for early losses, the army had to fight like a force of veterans from the beginning. After all, it would be up against Iraqis who, whatever their level of competence, had actually been in large battles.

Vietnam provided no real precedent, since it had been a protracted guerrilla war with few large battles. This time, the enemy would be a regular army. The situation recalled Korea, where an enemy offensive struck a force of U.S. volunteer soldiers. Their relatively poor initial performance had often been cited by opponents of the volunteer army concept. Many had argued that the

United States had adopted a volunteer army only because the social effects of the draft had proven so disastrous in Vietnam.

But this time there were some major differences. The least-known was that the U.S. Army had made an enormous investment in a National Training Center (NTC) in the Mojave Desert. There its troops could fight mock battles against an opposing force permanently based at the NTC. New technology, in the form of lasers whose hits could be automatically scored and tabulated, made these battles quite realistic. The opposition force tended to win. The army did lose its first battle, over and over again, but only against its own opposition force. It came to Saudi Arabia chastened, as previous American armies had been chastened by their early failures, and well aware of what it had to do. Thus, in enormous contrast to previous wars, the U.S. Army which came to Saudi Arabia in 1990–91 was already somewhat battle-hardened and battle-wise. It proved remarkably effective when the time came to fight.

The second major difference was that this time the enemy force enjoyed no sanctuary. In Korea, a paramount U.S. political decision had been not to attack across the Yalu River into China. The North Koreans could withdraw into China, and they could be sure of their supply lines across the Yalu. Even when the Chinese entered the war, U.S. policy did not change, because it was more important to avoid escalation than to end the war decisively. Similarly, the North Vietnamese enjoyed a variety of sanctuaries, both inside their country and along their supply lines, throughout the Vietnam War. In both cases, the sanctuary was granted because the local enemy had a major foreign ally or allies, and because the United States could not afford to be sucked into an open-ended war in a peripheral area (as would have been the case had the sanctuary been violated). In this case Iraq had no major friends, and the wind-down of the Cold War limited the extent of any other U.S. commitments. The United States could easily withdraw substantial forces from Europe, though not from the Pacific (the Korean situation was not affected by the rapprochement with the Soviets).

Several factors strongly affected the timing of any coalition plan for attack. One was the rate at which coalition forces could be built up and then acclimatized to the desert. The first buildup was completed late in 1990, so (had Saddam Hussein not made his own buildup) an attack might have been mounted about December. The second buildup was completed as the attack proceeded, about January. The timetable may also have been affected by fears that a runaway Soviet General Staff would try to reinforce Saddam Hussein and thus preclude a coalition attack.[1]

The weather also imposed a timetable. In theory, modern military forces can fight in almost any weather. However, warfare is more difficult in the hot, dry summer. As mentioned earlier, the clothing needed to protect against chemical or biological warfare is nearly unwearable in the summer. Cooler weather generally arrives in the Gulf in late November and lasts through much of March. However, at the beginning and end of the cool season (but not between) there are severe dust storms, which can damage electro-optical sensors and also some equipment, such as helicopter rotor blades. The sensors and the attack helicopters provided the coalition force with much of its crucial technological advantage. Thus the combination of cool weather and relative freedom from dust storms provided the coalition force with a short window of opportunity between late December and late February or early March.

Religious considerations also imposed a sort of timetable. It was widely suspected that the Arab coalition partners would be inclined toward a truce during the month-long holiday of Ramadan, which would begin on 17 March. Saddam might well have exploited such a hiatus to regroup. It might even have been politically impossible to resume offensive operations after a Ramadan truce. Many in the U.S. military remembered how the North Vietnamese had used a series of truces to recover from the effects of U.S. offensives. Truces during the Iran-Iraq War had had much the same effect. Even were no truce to be agreed during Ramadan, the Saudis would want to permit Muslim pilgrims to arrive for the annual visit to Mecca, the Haj, in June. That would be very difficult if hostilities were still in train at the time.

The war against Iraq illustrated (and tested) the central concepts of ground warfare that have been developed in this century. Iraq found itself using much the concepts of World War I when it fought Iran through a lengthy stalemate. Three years later, Iraq's enemies used the solutions developed specifically to avoid a World War I–like stalemate (albeit in dramatically more modern form) to defeat it. In so doing they added another chapter to the long debate over just what those solutions should have been.

Like World War I, the Iran-Iraq War was largely a victory of the static defense over moving offensive forces. In each case, the offensive side tried to break through a defensive line. It could generally pour enough concentrated fire into a limited length of defensive line to make a breach. However, in each case the defender could move his own forces quickly enough to seal the breach before much of the attacking force could get very far beyond it. In the Iran-Iraq War, the Iranian attackers were generally light infantry on foot. They were very brave, but they were unable to get far before mechanized Iraqi forces, held in reserve to the rear of the fortified front line, crushed them. In some cases, as in World War I, the infantry themselves could not even get to the Iraqi line because they were wiped out by machine guns and even by exotica such as electrified lines in marshland they had to cross.

In each case, the crucial factor was the relative mobility of attacker and defender. In World War I, for example, the attacker moved on foot. The defender could move troops by train, at least up to just behind the front. He could therefore concentrate large forces very quickly, whereas the attacker could only penetrate at walking pace, if that. There was also a crucial difference in the sort of firepower available to attacker and defender. The attackers could not carry heavy weapons with them. They therefore had to rely on indirect-fire weapons (artillery) fixed behind their own lines and firing on preplanned targets. Typically an attacking infantry force marched behind a barrage creeping ahead at a preplanned rate. Because the advancing troops generally could not communicate with the guns (they lacked radios and their unreeling field telephone lines often broke), that artillery could not take account of surprises, whether good or bad: it could not concentrate on stubborn enemy strong points, nor could it press ahead to take advantage of sudden enemy weakness. Typically assaults had to be planned to reach prearranged objective lines. After a halt, the artillery fire for the next push forward could be planned. By way of contrast, the defenders had direct-fire weapons (mainly machine guns), which could shift their fire to take account of exactly what was happening. The machine gunners could be forced to take cover during a bombardment, but they generally survived to emerge and wipe out the advancing infantry. However, the key point was that, whatever the infantry could do, they could not do it very quickly, and the enemy could always recover.[2]

The Iranians' situation was not too different from that of French or British troops going "over the top" in World War I. They had some mobile radios, but they were still on foot, and the Iraqis were a good deal more mobile than the Germans had been in World War I. Their vehicles could deliver troops directly to the front. The Iranians expended vast numbers of highly motivated light infantry in attacks on the trenches the Iraqis learned to build. Their breakthroughs bought them very little, and a series of "final offensives" reminiscent of the futile "final push" characteristic of World War I thinking brought them little gain.

Saddam Hussein seems to have concluded that a sufficiently strong and deep front line could generally stall an attacker long enough for his artillery and other weapons to break up the attack. His own reserves, outside enemy artillery range to the rear, could be relied upon to complete the job. This was much the conclusion the French Army drew from its World War I experience.

By late 1987 it seemed likely that the Iranians would collapse of their own exhaustion, but that did not happen. The Iraqis themselves were not terribly enthusiastic about mounting an offensive. In 1988, however, supported by considerable intelligence (reportedly including U.S. satellite data) they were able to plan a small set-piece armored offensive. This attack seemed to prove that Iraq had graduated beyond the sort of crippling warfare it had experienced during most of the Iran-Iraq War. It was executed by Republican Guard armored brigades. The reality was likely less impressive. The Guard units followed preset battle plans, with little room for maneuver to accommodate changed circumstances. Iraq succeeded largely, then, because its plan was limited in scope and was based on excellent tactical intelligence.[3] Saddam himself seems not to have considered his 1988 victory a disproof of his belief in a primarily defensive approach to future war, as reflected in his dispositions in and around Kuwait.

The 1988 offensive was by no means decisive on any strategic scale. It did not, for example, threaten Teheran. Iraq was not even able to capture the main Iranian oil-producing area around Abadan. As in 1918, both sides had such strategic depth, and their defenses were so successful, that neither had much chance of capturing a target the fall of which would automatically end the war. Moreover, as casualties (and exhaustion) mounted on each side, it became more and more difficult for either government to seek any kind of peace. In the case of World War I, the key was psychological: when the Allies, reinforced by large fresh forces from the United States, counterattacked after the big German offensive, Gen. Erich Ludendorff, chief of the German General Staff (and de facto German dictator), cracked. The German army and the German public had held on mainly because they had believed in ultimate victory. Once Ludendorff admitted that he was losing, the sacrifices taken for granted a few days earlier could no longer be extracted. Even though Ludendorff reversed himself within a few days (and even though he realized that a deliberate retreat might well save the German position), the damage was done and surrender soon followed. The result, incidentally, was that the army felt that it had never really been defeated, but rather that it had been betrayed by the politicians. Hence the bitterness later exploited by Hitler.

Similarly, by 1988 both combatants in the Iran-Iraq War had been exhausted. In this case the key was an external force, the United States. The Iranians could not admit that their hereditary enemies, the Iraqis, had bested them. However, when the "great Satan" demonstrated gross technological superiority (and ruthlessness) when the U.S. cruiser *Vincennes* shot down an Iranian airliner, they could tell themselves that they were facing larger and more overwhelming forces. Suddenly it was honorable to cease hostilities, at least for the present. As in World War I, military events relatively minor in themselves forced governments to acknowledge that they had long since passed beyond the point of national exhaustion.

Both World War I and the Iran-Iraq War showed, then, that countries could absorb surprisingly heavy losses without capitulating. The fundamental lesson was that it was very difficult to end a war with such a country. The U.S. approach in the Gulf was an interesting attempt to solve this problem. Once the Iraqi Army had been ejected from Kuwait, the United States announced a unilateral cessation of offensive action. U.S. and other coalition forces would defend themselves, but surviving Iraqis were permitted to withdraw intact from the edges of the battle area. Saddam Hussein did not have to make a humiliating capitulation (he did have to accept the U.N. terms). The Iraqis were offered a cease-fire, which required some negotiation, and ultimately the war was concluded with a U.N.–imposed permanent cease-fire. The final terms were indeed humiliating, but they probably cannot be enforced unless Iraq is occupied. That is unlikely. The U.S. solution, then, was to quit as soon as the essential explicit object of the war had been attained, rather than to seek some more decisive ending. Iraqi endurance in the Iran-Iraq War probably had some major role in this decision. The alternative, to force total capitulation by taking Baghdad itself, was certainly practicable, but it would have been quite expensive and might well have been unpalatable to the U.S. allies. There may also have been some hope that a quick and apparently clean end to the war would preclude any Iraqi attempt at vengeance by terrorism.

Saddam Hussein seems to have drawn the lesson from his war with Iran that his country had the endurance and the capacity to fight another war of exhaustion, and he seems tacitly to have assumed that he could force any enemy to accept just those terms. He seems to have been altogether unaware that virtually all of Western military development after 1918 (the fruits of which he faced in 1991) was intended specifically to avoid the sort of bloodletting that the stalemate of 1914–18 had produced. Happily ignorant of more than seven decades of work and war outside the Persian Gulf, Saddam could confidently face his prospective Western enemies, sure that none of them would accept the sort of casualties, or indeed the sort of indecisiveness, characteristic of the Iran-Iraq War. He was doing no more than repeating what so many had said after 1918: that the meat-grinder war had made war itself obsolete, that no civilized nation would ever willingly face it.

After 1918, the main Western countries sought to return to more universal concepts of military operations. In effect, land warfare is always a contest between moving forces seeking either to seize territory or to encircle and thus break up their enemies, and static forces seeking to defend their ground. The main variation on this theme is that the moving force sometimes seizes some strategic point that the defender must try to recapture (sometimes destroying itself in the process). For example, General Schwarzkopf's strategy called for the coalition army to occupy ground between the Iraqi Army in Kuwait and its supply lines back up to Basra and Baghdad. Whatever the strength of its fortifications inside Kuwait and southern Iraq, that army could not tolerate a large enemy force cutting it off; it had to come out and fight.

The great question, then, was how to overcome the strength of a defensive line. Three solutions were devised: a means of smashing through the line (armor), a means of passing over it (air attack), and a means of getting around its flanks (airborne and amphibious assault). All were used very successfully in World War II and all contributed to the victory in and around Kuwait.

The original idea of armored vehicles was to provide advancing infantry with their own supporting machine guns and artillery. Moving with the infantry, tanks could directly engage enemy machine guns. The infantry would not have to stop to wait for preplanned fire; they could just keep moving. This is much the sort of attack that succeeded in 1918, and it is the sort of attack Saddam himself launched successfully in 1988. It could break the defense more satisfactorily, but it could not penetrate deeply enough to secure decisive results. By 1918, however, advocates of tank warfare hoped for something much more spectacular. If really fast tanks were used, they could outrun any attempt to close the breach.

A moving column of fast tanks would travel far too quickly to be supported by fixed artillery, but tactical aircraft could make up for much of that. A mobile force can encircle an enemy; it can fight a war without a single well-defined front. It can tear up an enemy's unprotected rear areas. The complete destruction of enemy forces can indeed be decisive, particularly if the enemy has no hope of replacing them. That was the war-ending blow the coalition used in 1991. Similarly, a really deep thrust can carry the offensive all the way to the enemy's capital, and literally force surrender. This threat was held out but not really used in 1991.

Some of the early armor enthusiasts believed that tanks could replace virtually all other elements of a ground army. It turned out that, although tanks could move through and smash open an enemy defensive line, they could not themselves hold ground (at least not if they were to remain mobile). For that, they must be accompanied by mobile infantry who can dismount to hold the territory into which they have been brought. Such mechanized infantry generally ride tracked armored personnel carriers. They are essential not only to hold ground but also to prevent enemy infantry from using their own short-range, antitank rockets. Tank assaults are, therefore, usually preceded by an initial bombardment (by artillery and air attack, as in Kuwait) which helps reduce antitank fire. The tanks are generally accompanied through the enemy defense by foot infantry who clear out dug-in enemy soldiers.[4]

In 1939 and 1940 the Germans convincingly demonstrated what a fast-moving armored and mechanized infantry force could do. General Schwarzkopf repeated the lesson in 1991. In each case, the only really effective defense would have been an attack against the flanks of the moving force, cutting it off from its sources of supply and then encircling it. In 1991 General Schwarzkopf took elaborate measures to protect the flanks of the fast-moving VII Corps from just such attacks.

Both in France in 1940 and in Iraq and Kuwait in 1991, mobility bought the attacker a crucial advantage over a more numerous but essentially immobile enemy. Classical combat theories demand large numerical advantages for victory, such as 3:1 for an assault. Because an armored force can move very quickly, it can concentrate great power on a short portion of the enemy's line. Once loose behind that line, he can attack elements of the enemy force in succession before they can coalesce into something powerful enough to stop the advance. If the force moves fast enough, the enemy can never concentrate at all. He really has only two ways to solve the problem: withdraw so far (to regroup) that he escapes the fast pace of the armored thrust entirely, or make his own counterthrust. In the Gulf, Saddam's attempts to obtain a cease-fire and withdraw his troops in good order from Kuwait can be read as an attempt to reform outside of the battle area and thus to stave off military disaster.

General Schwarzkopf's successful offensive in the Gulf war was an application of the U.S. post-1945 solution to the threat of a Soviet armored thrust into Western Europe: AirLand Battle. In the 1980s the U.S. Army planned to do what France should have done in 1940: mount a strong offensive into the enemy's own rear, where he would be most vulnerable. The only important difference from AirLand Battle doctrine was that in Europe the U.S. Army planned not a pure offensive but rather a counterattack (beginning as the enemy attack began, not after it had stalled, as previous planners had imagined). Nor did U.S. thinking in a NATO context encompass smashing through an enemy defensive position.

AirLand Battle was devised in the early 1980s when U.S. planners admitted that NATO's thin defensive line could not possibly contain an attack by an enormously mobile modern armored army (a point Saddam Hussein might have learned to his profit). NATO found itself in a dilemma: to defend in depth would be to sacrifice virtually all of Germany (and to plan to do so would be politically unacceptable). Yet to drive east at the outbreak of war seemed so offensive as to threaten and perhaps provoke the Soviets. The U.S. view was that nothing could provoke the offensive-minded Soviets, and that once a central European war had begun, politically based limits on maneuver could not but be counterproductive. By 1991, the United States, but not its allies, had wholeheartedly accepted AirLand Battle. That proved a most fortunate decision; much of the low cost of the ground phase of the war can be attributed to the sheer speed and depth of the U.S. advance. That speed was attained because the U.S. Army had equipped itself specifically to execute an AirLand Battle offensive.

Saddam Hussein apparently imagined that a U.N. force dedicated merely to liberating Kuwait would not dare go anywhere else (that is, into Iraq proper). In effect that echoed European NATO doubts that it would be proper to save Western Europe by invading Eastern Europe, as AirLand Battle demanded. Some U.S. commentators had much the same view. General Schwarzkopf, a long-time practitioner of AirLand Battle, knew that he needed battle space and that the issue was winning, not just staying within Kuwaiti frontiers. Moreover, by attacking through Iraq beyond the fortified zone, General Schwarzkopf was able to capitalize on the mobility and endurance of his force.

Although armored forces could certainly break an enemy's line, they still might have to fight grinding battles, particularly against other tanks. The great question since 1918 has been whether air attack offers a much simpler and cheaper alternative. In its simplest form, as proposed by such advocates as Brig. Gen. William ("Billy") Mitchell, the idea is that airplanes can reach the strategic objective, the enemy's industrial heart and his capital, directly. After all, surely the ultimate objective of the meat grinder on the ground is to penetrate that far, and it is far simpler for airplanes to do so. Airplanes also offer the greatest leverage for technological superiority.

In its purest form, as advocated by the Italian Gen. Giulio Douhet, the theory of strategic airpower holds that a direct attack on the enemy's population can so discredit an enemy government that the people themselves will revolt and thus end the war very quickly and at minimum human cost. One early adherent, the British Air Marshal Sir Hew "Boom" Trenchard, almost eliminated British defensive fighters in the 1920s on the ground that they detracted from resources to be spent on long-range bombers.

World War II showed that this pure strategic air-power theory was deficient. Bombing of civilians tended to reinforce their will to resist, because it never hurt them badly enough to demoralize them completely. In the case of the Kuwait war, there was no question of direct attack on the Iraqi population: neither the United States nor its coalition partners was willing to risk the general outcry that would cause. There was, rather, a hope that a graphic demonstration of Saddam's inability to protect his population from such embarrassments as the loss of power and even of sewage services would undermine such popular support as he retained. By the end of the war, some residents of Baghdad had indeed been emboldened to demonstrate against Saddam (acts nominally punishable by death). However, there was little to suggest that the popular point of view would have much effect on a regime supported by efficient secret police. It may have been much more significant that U.S. aircraft successfully attacked Ba'ath party bunkers, suggesting to those around Saddam that they could indeed be killed by his policies. It is too early (in April 1991) to judge whether these hints were effective.

The nascent Royal Air Force argued, too, that bombing could cause native troops to surrender, so that portions of the British Empire could be policed without recourse to expensive ground troops. Trenchard put his theory to the test in, of all places, Iraq, which was then a British Mandate under the League of Nations. Tribesmen bombed for the first time did indeed scatter when the airplanes arrived, and tribes did seem to prefer to behave rather than risk air attack. However, they were never really pacified. Eventually they learned that air attack was a limited instrument. Half a century later the Soviets would learn in Afghanistan that Trenchard's ideas were more hopeful theory than reality. Aircraft could kill quite efficiently, but the enemy troops, in this case the Muslim guerrillas, were never quite wiped out.

In this war, air attacks certainly badly damaged the Iraqi Army, though it will never be clear just how badly. The Iraqis had antiaircraft weapons, and, like the Afghans, some of them stood and fought, though without much impact on the air offensive (see the list of coalition air losses in Appendix E). Certainly, too, many of them preferred desertion to continued very heavy pounding. The combination of direct destruction and a high desertion rate (some of it also due to the cutoff of supplies as aircraft cut internal Iraqi communications) certainly made General Schwarzkopf's job far easier. It is also quite possible that the need to dig in against air attack precluded the Iraqis from any sort of effective counterattack, as it would have been difficult for their troops to dig out quickly enough. There seems little reason to expect, however, that the Iraqi Army as a whole would have surrendered to air attack alone. It would have continued to suffer, but it was learning that no level of attack could have killed it off altogether.

Strategic air attacks of the classic kind advocated after World War I began at the outbreak of the Kuwait war. They had a special role, one not envisaged in earlier wars. In the case of Kuwait, part of the coalition objective was to destroy Iraq's ability to attack its neighbors, particularly with weapons of mass destruction. Generally, to neutralize such a capability requires the physical occupation of the facilities, and their destruction in detail by troops. In this case, however, political factors made it virtually impossible for coalition troops to penetrate very deep into Iraq. The only available weapon was attack from the air, classic strategic bombing. Strategic bombing (in the sense of attacks far behind the battle zone) was also used to destroy Iraqi facilities relevant to the war effort in the south, such as railways and bridges. This campaign is described in detail in Chapter Nine.

Advocates of classic strategic bombing always hoped that the attacks in themselves would bring down the enemy, that a government faced with the potential for unacceptable damage would prefer surrender. That never really worked, probably because many of the target governments considered the consequences of surrender worse than bombing. In Saddam's case, he very likely assumed that he would be killed (by his own officers) in the event he surrendered, or even retreated. After all, he had shown no particular concern for a terrible casualty rate in the Iran-Iraq War. Thus the strategic air campaign this time demonstrated only that large-scale air attack could do devastating damage, but (as in the past) it could not in itself have great political effect.

The one great historical counterexample seemed to be Vietnam in 1972. In that case, many of the most important targets were off limits (for political purposes) through much of the war. Advocates of strategic air attack pointed out that, once those targets (many of them "downtown," as in downtown Baghdad) were brought under attack (mainly in the Christmas bombings of Hanoi in 1972), the enemy became quite interested in reaching an accommodation. However, this was still an ambiguous case. By late 1972 the North Vietnamese had been stretched to the limit by their failed ground attacks on the south. Their offensive strategy had failed, largely because of U.S. resistance on the ground and in the air, both direct and in support of the South Vietnamese. However, they were also aware that the United States was willing to withdraw its own troops altogether if only a politically acceptable settlement could be reached. They could, therefore, accept a settlement that gave them time to regroup. Meanwhile, their own political offensive within the United States was succeeding, so they could expect that U.S. forces would not return when, as was inevitable, they mounted a fresh ground offensive. The successful resistance of the spring of 1972, then, might well have been a last gasp rather than an indication of things to come. This judgement was borne out in the successful Vietnamese offensive of 1975. The lesson of the Vietnam bombings, then, seems to have been that air attacks could force an enemy, already badly damaged and very tired, to accept relatively indecisive terms. It could not produce outright surrender (which the United States could not demand in 1973).

Congressman Les Aspin of the House Armed Services Committee made the strategic attack argument most strongly during the approach to war in the fall of 1990. He thought that air attacks could themselves end the war in three weeks at the cost of fewer than a hundred American lives. He was right about the numbers, and only slightly wrong about the time, but his argument proved defective. He probably greatly overestimated the effect on Saddam Hussein of severe damage to Iraq (a quick postwar estimate of the cost to repair that country is about $1 trillion). Aspin had been a Defense Department systems analyst, and he had dealt for years in estimates of relative damage and system capability. Most likely his belief that damage alone would suffice can be traced to that concentration, which was not too different in kind from the intelligence analysts' fascination with the numerical strength of the Iraqi forces. Saddam himself probably saw matters quite differently. He may even have imagined that it would be glorious just to hold onto Kuwait despite the best efforts of the U.S.-led coalition (as it was in fact portrayed by Radio Baghdad), and that glory might have been the beginning of a sweep through the Arab world. Given an efficient and brutal secret police, Saddam never really feared the sort of popular reaction that proponents of strategic bombing expected.

There was always some question as to just how effective strategic bombing could be. In World War II, it was discovered that many factories that had been heavily bombed (and that appeared totally destroyed in strike photographs) had nevertheless returned to production within a few days. It also turned out that quite small details determined just how effective such attacks could be. After the war, for example, Albert Speer, who had been in charge of German war production, said that the big factories in the Ruhr had finally stopped because of damage to their internal transportation systems, not because of overall bomb damage. Actual occupation by allied troops was often necessary to stop production. Speer even suggested that, shorn of many of their amusements (which had been destroyed by bombing), some Germans actually worked harder than they had before, so that in some sectors of the economy production rose during the big bombing campaigns.

The allied strategic bombing campaign had proven far more expensive than prewar air advocates had imagined. Enemy air defenses exacted a terrible toll. The bomber force, with its stringent requirements for highly trained men, killed far too many of its own. The airplanes themselves were expensive to make, in terms of other, alternative weapons that might have been made in their place. Those airplanes (or at least the resources to build them) had been diverted from such mundane but productive tasks as close air support of the advancing troops and support of the convoys carrying the materiel needed to fight the war. The issue was so controversial that the U.S. government conducted a detailed survey of the results of bombing, the U.S. Strategic Bombing Survey. Its results were depressing. Bombing had been useful, but the appearance of the damage it had done had much exceeded the reality. It was by no means clear that the terrible damage done directly to Germany had materially hastened its collapse, either militarily or from a governmental point of view.

After World War II, then, there was no question but that airplanes were an essential element of military power. However, it was by no means certain that the air effort should be concentrated in strategic, as opposed to tactical, aircraft. This question was quickly resolved at the time in favor of the strategic bombers, but that was only because the new nuclear weapons promised the sort of mass destruction that conventional bombers had failed to deliver during the war. The question was reopened in 1950, when it became clear that nuclear weapons could not be used in the new sort of limited war, Korea. In this sense the Kuwait war was another limited, that is, nonnuclear, conflict. In fact, the role of strategic bombing was probably far greater in Kuwait than in the past, simply because the physical destruction of certain key strategic targets, which was a basic war aim, could not have been accomplished in any other way within the political limits imposed by the war.

The great question remained. Strategic bombing was clearly the province of a separate air force.[5] History demonstrated, moreover, that separate air forces tended to prefer strategic bombing or deep air attack to providing tactical services. For example, the U.S. Air Force was created in 1947 largely because the combination of apparently successful strategic air attacks on Germany and Japan and the advent of the atomic bomb suggested that strategic air attack could usefully replace other forms of warfare. An important factor at this time was that, as in the period after 1918, it appeared that strategic nuclear bombing would be far less expensive than any other form of warfare. World War II had not been a meat grinder like its predecessor, but it had been far from inexpensive. Early postwar estimates of what it would cost to deal with a large Soviet army were terrifying. By about 1949 the U.S.

government was wholeheartedly accepting the strategic air power argument because it believed that it could not afford to maintain conventional forces during a protracted cold war.

The nuclear weapons were intended to deter the Soviets from possible adventures in Eurasia. The outbreak of war in Korea in 1950 clearly demonstrated that deterrence had its limits. The air power debate was reopened. By this time the army had been shorn of any tactical air force, and the separate air force, badly battered by budget limitations, had decided to concentrate on what it considered the most important aspect of air power, strategic attack. In Korea, it discovered once again that strategic bombing without nuclear weapons had definite limitations. North Korea was terribly punished, but that did not induce surrender. Inattention to tactical air power proved embarrassing, although it was largely overcome.

Ever since the formation of the U.S. Air Force there has been a three-way struggle for control of U.S. aircraft. Advocates of pure air power have argued for a single service to control all of the aircraft on the ground that all are amenable to a common tactical concept. That would mean the abolition of separate U.S. naval and Marine Corps air arms. In the Gulf war, the apparent success of a single air operations command, which controlled all of the major tactical aircraft in the theater, was cited by those who still advocate this idea.

The navy has argued that aircraft should be considered more in tactical terms, and operated by those they support on the surface of the earth. The navy and marines have retained their own aircraft on this basis. The army, which needed aircraft for much the same purpose as the marines (close air support), tried several times after 1947 to obtain its own tactical air arm. Eventually the air force agreed that the army could operate helicopters but not fixed-wing tactical aircraft. That agreement was the origin of the current large army attack-helicopter force, which performed so well in Kuwait. The agreement has never really been accepted by the army, and recently Congress demanded that air force A-10s (which are used for close air support) be handed over to the army and to the marines.

The air force itself still clearly prefers deep strikes to support near the battle itself, even in a purely tactical situation. For example, air force F-16s were used to attack Iraqi vehicles well beyond the battle line. They could not be used closer to friendly vehicles for fear of hitting them (they lacked the sort of target recognition devices that task required). Lantirn night targeting pods, which were essential for many tactical missions, were not available in numbers during the war because their development had a much lower priority than that of strategic bombers, even after the decline of the Soviet threat rather reduced the strategic threat. The air force did contribute A-10s, but as of 1991 it planned to discard them as soon as possible. Close air support, the main marine air mission, was not even part of the carefully integrated Air Tasking Order (ATO) with which the air force ran much of the Desert Storm air war (the ATO system was not really adapted to close air support). Because the ATO computers generated the statistics on sortie rates and usages, they automatically downgraded purely tactical operations. Because those using the statistics did not realize the details of ATO function, these statistics became yet another shot in the tactical versus strategic air war.

The lesson of the seven decades since 1918 seems to have been that, like the tank, the bomber could be terribly destructive but it could not hold and seize territory by itself. Unless it dropped a nuclear weapon, an airplane could damage an enemy, but often that had to be a prelude to ground assault. The question in the Kuwait war will probably always be whether the bombing made the ground assault so easy that it should be credited with the lion's share of the victory. It is probably fairer to say that the ground forces still had to fight hard, and that they were so competent that they made it look easy.

One other more recent air-power idea deserves mention here. During the 1970s, U.S. nuclear strategists became increasingly skeptical that the mere threat of damage to the Soviet Union's economy or to its population would suffice to deter Soviet leaders. After all, their forebears had been quite willing to kill millions of Soviet citizens for little reason other than to enforce their will. One alternative raised at the time was to threaten those leaders directly. Presumably an essentially selfish leadership would care only about a direct threat to its existence. It was fairly clear that no precision bombardment could be aimed at the regime's essential prop, its secret police, whereas it might well be possible to destroy the bunkers in which the Soviet leaders themselves would shelter. Proposals for decapitation strikes became a feature of U.S. strategic doctrine (the question was always whether a decapitated Soviet Union, like a headless chicken, would flail about in nuclear fashion, rather than quietly succumb; that is, whether decapitation could, in fact, end a war). Decapitation had the enormous appeal of being morally much more attractive than killing numerous Soviet citizens who had had little to do with the decision to go to war in the first place.

This thinking had an echo in the approach to war in the Persian Gulf. If anything, Saddam Hussein was far more self-centered than any Soviet leader. In September, the air force chief of staff, Gen. Michael Dugan, unwisely told a reporter that the war could quickly be won by attacking Saddam directly: "we know where he is, and where his mistress is, and where his family is, and we can get them." Unfortunately his remarks were anathema (and literally illegal), because the U.S. government is unwilling to announce a plan to kill a foreign head of state. Nor could the U.S. government have been sure in which of the many deep bunkers in Baghdad Saddam lurked at any particular time. It was certainly never clear that anyone knew exactly where he was (that is, in which room of which building, as opposed to, somewhere in Baghdad). U.S. knowledge would probably have sufficed had the instrument of attack been a nuclear warhead, but conventional bombs are quite limited in their effects. Perhaps saddest of all, no existing weapon could have dug Saddam out of one of his deep bunkers. Only quite late in the war did the air force order the development of a special, heavy, guided bomb specifically designed to destroy deep bunkers. Developed in a record twenty-two days (from order to use), it was dropped by an F-111 on a Ba'ath bunker on the last morning of the war. That attack almost certainly was partly intended as a message to Saddam, that he could indeed be killed. In that sense, General Dugan, who was fired for his excessively candid remarks in September, was vindicated half a year later.

General Dugan had made the case for the totally surgical use of air power. During the development of the F-117A "stealth fighter" (actually a light bomber), the air force had reportedly become extremely interested in its potential for discrete political attacks, such as the sort the general was proposing. It was never clear that this idea made very much sense. As in the case of the Soviet Union, actually resorting to (as opposed to threatening) decapitation was never clearly the best option. If the country was not badly damaged, then the destruction of Saddam himself might well leave some equally unpleasant successor in office. It was by no means clear that the successor's first act would be to surrender Kuwait.

Bombers and tanks represented physical means of smashing through or over the enemy's deep defenses. After World War I there was also intense interest in somehow evading those defenses by outflanking them. That generally meant an amphibious or airborne assault. After all, by the end of 1914 the line of trenches ran across Europe from Switzerland (whose neutrality seemed sacrosanct) to the sea. It was quite obvious that a successful amphibious assault could have turned the Germans' flank. The technology did not yet exist, but it was developed, largely in the United States, between 1918 and 1941.[6] Although few World War II amphibious operations were flanking attacks in the sense envisaged in 1918, the modern U.S. Marine Corps concept of deep amphibious attack has much of the deep flanking attack about it. The great advantage of an amphibious attack is that the attacker has so many alternatives (the enemy's entire coastline) that a concentrated defense becomes extremely costly. World War II experience showed that unless an attacker was destroyed before he could land or at the very point of landing, he generally could not be defeated. Because modern amphibious forces can attack almost anywhere along a coast (they are much less restricted in their choice of beach than their World War II forebears), they can tie down defending forces all along a coastline.[7]

Kuwait presented much the sort of opportunity perceived but

missed in 1918. The Iraqi fortifications on the Saudi border could clearly be outflanked from the sea. In fact the captured sand table in Kuwait City showed that the Iraqis feared an amphibious assault either north or south of the city. As might have been expected, the Iraqi defense against such an attack tied down considerable resources that could not be employed elsewhere. In this particular case the defending divisions concentrated on coastal defense to the exclusion of defense against the attack that actually came up from the south.

Airborne attack was the other outflanking technique developed after 1918. Initially, advocates of strategic bombing thought of paratroops as the air equivalent of the mechanized troops that should accompany tanks, the means of holding ground whose defenders the strike arm had destroyed. In fact it turned out that the paratroops could never carry enough to hold out for long against really determined opposition. Airplanes just could not transport enough, particularly enough heavy weapons. For example, the U.S. 82d Airborne Division operates the only U.S. light tank, because its tank must be air-transportable. These forces were, however, very valuable because they could move deep into an enemy's territory and hold on long enough for ground forces to link up with and relieve them. For example, units could be moved by air to seize key road junctions.

Airborne assault had a mixed record in World War II. Units could and did seize key points, but usually they could not survive unless the associated ground units arrived in time (the "bridge too far" at Arnhem was the most celebrated example of a bold but failed airborne assault). Postwar, the helicopter offered the possibility of moving a large unit very quickly into an enemy's rear, and helicopter gunships could provide a useful degree of support even against his tanks. Helicopter-borne units, moreover, could operate in more or less roadless areas, such as in Vietnam. Similarly, a form of helicopter assault is part of the overall technique of amphibious attack. As in Vietnam, it has the virtue of quickly moving troops and light equipment over a trackless beach. As in conventional ground operations, the inserted force has to wait for heavier equipment to arrive over land, in this case from landing craft or amphibious vehicles.

The key virtue that helicopter assault offered General Schwarzkopf in Iraq was speed: only the fastest-moving force could reach and cut the key road leading out of southern Iraq.

As the later chapters show, the success in Kuwait and southern Iraq was a combination of virtually all the military ideas developed after 1918 to solve the central problem of World War I, the paralysis imposed by a combination of effective defenses and a relatively immobile offense. It would be difficult to isolate any one decisive contributor to the overall victory. The United States has been unusually successful in melding together quite disparate military traditions in its different forces. That is true jointness. It is not as clear that the form of jointness used in the Persian Gulf, as mandated by current law, caused the success or whether true jointness was achieved despite the law.

The actual course of the war was shaped in part by the administration's perception that a ground assault would probably be quite bloody. Although few in the administration thought it likely that Iraq would withdraw under bombing pressure alone, it was politically impossible for the government not to give the air offensive a chance. As noted above, the air offensive was essential in any case as a means of achieving important coalition goals not otherwise practicable. Destroying the Iraqi national air-defense system was an inescapable prerequisite to those key attacks. It was therefore impossible for the war *not* to open with heavy air attacks. It may also have been the case that the air assets required for any early ground campaign could not have been spared from the essential early strategic and defense-suppression attacks.

The war inevitably fell into two distinct stages, a pure air offensive followed by a ground campaign. Inevitably, too, this strategy carried political dangers. Once the air offensive had begun and was running smoothly, with a low rate of losses, many both within the United States and abroad took the position that it should be allowed to continue indefinitely even though it had not met the objective of ejecting Saddam from Kuwait. In this bizarre line of thought a ground offensive would be considered a further and unwarranted escalation.

It seems unlikely that Central Command ever considered the air war alone a likely war-winner. Instead, the successful air offensive opened up the Iraqi Army to the disaster imposed by coalition ground forces. The ground forces and their associated tactical aircraft actually destroyed the Iraqi Army, forcing the Iraqi government to accept the terms ending the war. This defeat also opened access to Baghdad, the seizure of which would presumably have been an alternative way to force an end to the war. In both cases, the mix of strategies developed since 1918 worked to achieve a decisive defeat over an army still thinking in the terms of 1918, albeit with much more modern weapons.

The sequence of U.S. actions looked like the sort of escalation attempted unsuccessfully in Vietnam, but the Bush administration had something very different in mind. A Vietnam-like strategy of gradual escalation would have presented Saddam Hussein with a series of steps, each inflicting a degree of pain and offering an implicit threat that worse was to come. In theory, at some point the threat would be so frightening (given the demonstrated pain) that he would give in. Such a scenario probably works only if the object of the escalation finds the pain much worse than the consequence of giving in. The administration probably concluded quite early that Saddam was entirely unwilling to withdraw, that he equated withdrawal with his own end. That may not have been terribly rational on his part, but it called for a campaign to destroy him (or at least his armed forces) rather than one merely to convince him.

The choice, then, was to apply pressure in stages, as the means of that application became available during the buildup, but also to use each stage as preparation for the next. Because each step was so clearly distinct, Mr. Hussein was publicly offered the chance to stop the process each time a later stage was reached (blockade to air offensive, air offensive to ground offensive).[8] However, the administration seems not to have been particularly surprised when its offers were rejected. The administration did have to accept the inherent danger that political forces beyond its control would prevent it from each of the two key escalations (to the air war and then to the ground war), but it was able to overcome that problem. The alternative, to have done virtually nothing until enough forces had been built up, would have destroyed all of the momentum in the anti-Saddam coalition.

Another important and public difference from Vietnam was that the U.S. government refused to grant Saddam Hussein any sanctuary. The attack on his presidential palace on the opening night of the war was both an essential blow to Iraqi command and control and an announcement that the errors of the Vietnam War air campaign would not be repeated. Attackers would "go downtown" throughout the war, and Saddam knew from the beginning that he was a potential target. Thus there was never any real sense that the war was a confined operation with limited and perhaps obscure ends. Saddam was the enemy, and the United States and its allies intended to win quickly and overwhelmingly.

In fact, of course, there were restrictions. The war was a coalition affair, and the U.S. officers directing it were always well aware of the sensitivities of their partners. In particular, they took special pains to distinguish Saddam and his government from the populace at large, and thus to avoid attacks on civilians. That was not always possible, if only because bombs could not always fall directly on their intended targets, and it is not clear to what extent civilians in the Arab world believed it. Saddam himself took pains during the war to display what he described as civilian damage due to indiscriminate bombing. Many of those watching were unaware that much of the damage could be attributed to Iraq's own spent antiaircraft projectiles falling back to earth, a common problem in other wars.

Even so, within a short time it was clear to the Iraqi government that efforts would be made to avoid attacking civilians. That led the Iraqis to hide some of their command structure and also some of their military resources around schools, mosques, and archaeological sites. In most cases that rendered them safe.[9]

Finally, George Bush was careful to avoid managing the conduct of the war from Washington. He confined himself to some of the fundamental decisions, such as the decision to use armed force in the first place to liberate Kuwait, and to the diplomacy required to maintain the allied coalition. This was hardly a trivial issue, and it was deftly handled. Much of Saddam Hussein's effort went into attacking the coalition and trying to isolate the United States, so that even military victory would be worthless.

Micromanagement of operations had contributed to disaster in Vietnam, and both the president and his military aides were well aware of that. The decision actually went further. The Washington military establishment was not permitted to control the war in any detail, to the extent that many in Washington were irked that they had little or no input into military operations. One consequence was that the war could be conducted virtually without the leakage generally associated with Washington. To the extent that victory depended on a successful deception operation, that had to be extremely important.

As commander in chief, President Bush was, of course, ultimately responsible for the course of the war. The choice to avoid any interference with General Schwarzkopf's operational planning cannot, therefore, have been altogether easy; presidents have always been tempted to affect operational decisions. Indeed, modern communications make that temptation, if anything, much stronger. President Bush was, then, making a courageous decision, since he knew that in the end he would be held responsible for any military disaster.

There is always a strong temptation for the Washington military and political establishment to try to control forces in the field; the same might be said of any other capital at war. Modern telecommunications give the illusion that those in a war room in the Pentagon have very nearly the same information as a commander thousands of miles away. Whatever the information it receives, however, the war room has a very different perspective, much of it shaped by domestic politics, and by local (often nonmilitary) views of the conduct of the war. In the past, the argument for noninterference (or at least for minimized interference) has been that the leader on the spot can best see what is going on. However, modern sensors, such as reconnaissance satellites, often provide the war room with better, or at least with different, information from what is easily available in the field. The war room's temptations thus grow. President Bush and his chief of staff, Gen. Colin Powell, made a fundamental decision, that the perspective of the man on the spot, General Schwarzkopf, was what mattered. Washington would provide whatever support it could, including intelligence, but it would not tell him how to fight. General Schwarzkopf's brilliant success would seem to show that this was exactly the right balance. Critics of Washington and its meddling in previous wars now have a case to prove that they were right.

It is only fair to say that international conditions made it much easier for the president and his advisors to relax the tight control of the past. Until about 1950, Washington generally tried to control actions in the field out of the natural temptation it shared with all other governments. Once the Soviets had nuclear weapons, however, there was a growing perception that minor errors committed by junior officers in the field could touch off a nuclear war by accident. The perception was probably more self-serving than accurate, but it grew through the 1960s and 1970s, to the point where in at least one crisis Washington was dictating rudder orders to the Sixth Fleet. This perception also fueled large investments in communications, culminating in WWMCCS, the worldwide military command and control system, the means by which Washington could, in theory, exercise detailed control of operating forces. By the 1980s, however, there was a growing perception that the nuclear balance was fairly stable, and that even quite considerable blunders were unlikely to destroy the world. President Reagan was able to reverse previous practice. For example, in 1981 navy F-14s engaged Libyan aircraft in the Gulf of Sidra. The president quite publicly said that he did not mind being informed of the incident only after it had happened. His presidency also included two examples of disastrous interference from higher echelons: the failure to provide adequate security to the marines in Beirut in 1983, and the flawed raid on the Bekaa Valley. The raids on Tripoli in 1986 and the successful operations in the Persian Gulf in 1987 probably mark the beginning of reduced interference from the top.

The British experience in the Falklands in 1982 may also have been relevant. It was certainly widely discussed at the time. The forces in combat were largely allowed to follow their own military logic. As vice president at the time, much involved in the decisions to support Britain so fully, President Bush in particular would have been fully sensitive to the way in which the Falklands war was managed.

8

Seizing Air Control

ONCE IT WAS clear that Saddam would neither withdraw nor begin a war himself, the only acceptable measure was an ultimatum: the U.N. authorized the use of force unless Iraq satisfied the series of resolutions, primarily calling for unconditional withdrawal and for reparations. It was fairly certain that Saddam would not accept any such demand, since doing so would amount to accepting defeat and, in his view, oblivion. It was more surprising that he rejected a series of last-minute, face-saving offers. He apparently did not believe that the forces built up in Saudi Arabia could destroy him, nor did he have any advisors who could provide him with such unwelcome advice.

The ultimatum ran out at midnight, eastern standard time, on 15 January. The following night was moonless, and the air attack against Iraq began at about 2 A.M. (local time). By 2:30 Baghdad was under heavy attack. It was already clear that the Iraqi national air-defense system had failed: bombs were exploding in quantity, but no sirens were sounding. Film of the attack shows, moreover, Iraqi air-defense guns hosing the sky to no avail. Whatever radars existed were having no useful effect. The first of several preconditions for victory, the elimination of Iraqi air defenses, was in train. It was also the first of several happy surprises. Prewar estimates of allied aircraft losses had been quite daunting. Iraq was one of several countries credited, in 1990, with advanced integrated air defenses that could be breached (at reasonable cost) only by stealthy aircraft. In fact the loss rate throughout the air war was extremely, even surprisingly, low.

The Iraqi air-defense system was originally built by Soviet advisors and, despite considerable infusions of Western technology, it retained its Soviet-style centralization. The Iraqi system gained some protection against countermeasures because it employed a wide variety of radars. However, that also made it difficult to maintain, and probably also problematic to reconstitute after severe damage. Before the war, the Iraqi system had also been described as difficult to analyze, precisely because of its hybrid character. By a happy coincidence, before the crisis erupted, U.S. Naval Intelligence was in the process of analyzing major Third World integrated air-defense systems, many of which might have to be penetrated by naval strike aircraft. As it happened, the analysis of the Iraqi system was completed just before the crisis began in August 1990. Fortunately, too, the coalition had more than five months (between the invasion of Kuwait and the opening of hostilities) to observe the Iraqi national air-defense system in detail. Although prewar Iraqi spokesmen claimed that they were hiding and moving their sets, the main early-warning unit, Tall King, is hardly mobile.[1]

Iraq's was described as an integrated air-defense system (IADS), meaning that its fighters, various missiles, and antiaircraft guns were all centrally controlled so that they could operate in complementary fashion. An approaching attacker can choose either to fly at low level, risking destruction by short-range missiles and guns, or at medium or high altitude, subject to attack by longer-range missiles and by fighters. Integration is necessary because otherwise the fighters cannot operate in areas protected by missiles (missiles may accidentally kill the fighters). The fighters, in turn, should make it impossible for an attacker to evade defense merely by skirting areas covered by the missiles. Long-range missiles, which may be ineffective against low-altitude attackers, are protected by shorter-range missiles with better low-altitude performance. Similarly, the long-range search radars used for early warning of attack (and thus for vectoring fighters) are covered by shorter-range, lower-altitude sets.

Most countries use combinations of fighters and various missiles. What was new (at least in theory) in the IADS was the central control that made it possible for all elements to work together in depth, with mutual support. Without that control, each defensive site was on its own. For example, many countries have air defenses concentrated along their borders. A section of border radars could be jammed and then destroyed by antiradar missiles. Such an attack is complex and requires a substantial force devoted merely to neutralizing the radars, but it suffices if the enemy is limited to a border defense. Once a break had been made in the border, follow-up attackers would be free to attack any targets they liked, subject only to the requirement to deal with surface-to-air missiles concentrated around a few particularly important targets. That seems to have happened in Libya in 1986.

The U.S. Navy and the U.S. Air Force were well equipped to deal with this sort of unintegrated defense. In a naval attack, for example, EA-6B Prowlers would jam radars and might also launch antiradar missiles (HARMs) at them. If the radars shut down, accompanying attack aircraft could cluster-bomb them. Otherwise the HARM missiles, homing on the radars, could destroy them. Special antiradar decoys (TALDs—tactical air-launched decoys) would further confuse the defenders. The attacking force would generally be accompanied by aircraft assigned specifically to kill surface-to-air missile sites. The naval version of such a SEAD (suppression of enemy air defense) attack employed an EA-6B jammer supported by three or four A-7E or F/A-18 (or sometimes A-6E SWIP) attack aircraft armed with HARMs.

Air force SEAD tactics differ somewhat from the navy's. They emphasize attacks by "Wild Weasel" aircraft whose presence induces the enemy to turn on his missile fire control radars (in a naval attack the TALD might be used for this purpose). The Wild Weasel hunter may itself also attack the missile-directing radar with antiradar missiles, or it may direct a "killer" airplane carrying missiles and cluster bombs. The Wild Weasel force sent to Saudi

Arabia consisted entirely of F-4G hunter-killers equipped with both radar warning devices and missiles.[2]

The air force's equivalent to the EA-6B is the EF-111A Raven, which uses much the same electronics (but which cannot launch any missiles). However, the EA-6B has been updated and extended to a much greater degree. In this war it covered more frequency bands and was the only coalition jammer capable of countering weapons from friendly and neutral as well as Soviet-bloc countries (after all, the navy has already found itself dealing with Western-supplied weapons in places like Iran).

Usually an EF-111A is not part of the SEAD strike itself, although it may support one or more strike packages. It was unusual that one of the earliest attack packages consisted of a full tactical fighter wing (about fifty F-111Fs) supported directly by about a dozen EF-111As. The other two EF-111A jamming profiles are "close in" (about 30 miles out, covering an area) and "stand-off" (over 50 miles from the target).

Air force SEAD tactics also employ specialized communications jamming airplanes (EC-130H Compass Call), which are intended to attack the links between early warning radars and fighters and the similar links between the early warning radars and the major surface-to-air missile sites. There is no similar navy special-purpose airplane, but the EA-6B carries communications jammers.

The two forces also differ somewhat in organization. Because carrier capacity is limited, the navy tends to avoid specialist squadrons. It therefore uses its standard F/A-18s, rather than special Wild Weasels, in what amounts to the Wild Weasel hunter-killer role. As a consequence, the carriers off Saudi Arabia had a much larger number of potential SEAD hunter-killers than the air force could provide in the form of single-purpose Wild Weasels.[3]

Such tactics are effective, but they are also quite expensive in terms of airplanes devoted to suppressing the enemy's air defense rather than destroying important targets. The greater the effective depth of the air defense, the higher the cost of suppression in terms of offensive firepower foregone. This effect is called virtual attrition because it reduces damage to the enemy quite as much as does real attrition (destruction) of the attacking airplanes.

It was widely claimed, before the Kuwait war, that breaching tactics could not efficiently defeat an IADS, because the system could work around any single breach in its outer defenses. If breaching would not work, then the solution seemed to be an airplane that could somehow evade the defenses altogether: a stealthy airplane. The breaching argument was made, for example, in support of the navy's program for a next-generation stealthy attack airplane, the A-12. The economics of breaching were, after all, particularly costly for an attack force limited in total size by the capacity of an aircraft carrier.

Integration opened the system to a different strategic approach. Iraqi fighters all operated under tight ground control (the system is called GCI, ground-controlled intercept). Once the control centers had been destroyed, the fighters were largely useless. The centers themselves should have been relatively safe because they were deep inside Iraq, but breaching tactics opened corridors leading to them. Aircraft flying down the corridors at low level would still have been vulnerable to concentrations of short-range missiles and antiaircraft guns. However, the target acquisition and fire-control radars controlling these weapons could be jammed. Many of them had been provided with optical backups to deal with exactly that threat. Hence the importance of the moonless night, which made the optics ineffective. The darkness also helped in that the Iraqi Air Force had little experience of, or enthusiasm for, night flying.[4] Thus the planners knew that a night attack (particularly one launched on a very dark, moonless night) would have a good chance of avoiding fighters altogether.

The destruction of the control centers opened Iraq to large-scale air attack. Contrary to expectations, the Iraqis never repaired them, so that after the first night they never enjoyed the advantages to be expected of a fully integrated system. Without the control centers, moreover, they could not use their long-range early warning radars, whether or not the radars could be repaired.[5] Had the Iraqis managed to repair the control centers, it would presumably have been necessary to repeat the elaborate coordinated attacks made the first night every few days.

It turned out to be very difficult to be sure that the control centers had indeed been destroyed. Most had been hit only by one or two bombs. Strike videos clearly showed that the bombs had hit as expected, but that is very different from knowing just what damage those hits had done. The coalition strategy was to use whatever time the initial strike had bought to attack the Iraqi fighter airfields, on the theory that for a time at least the loss of the centers would disable the fighters. Airfields also had to be struck because Iraqi aircraft presented the greatest threat of chemical attack against both the main coalition bases and against Israel (it was always essential to protect Israel to the extent needed to keep it out of the war). The airfield strikes turned out to be far more costly than the main attack against the Iraqi national air-defense system.

The surface-based missile defenses remained, but they covered only small isolated areas of the sky over Iraq. They were destroyed by classical SEAD attacks.

It was never really clear why the Iraqi defensive system never recovered after the first night's damage. Several explanations can be advanced. One would be that, as in every other sphere, Saddam Hussein had failed to buy sufficient spare parts. Without spares, the radars could not be revived, and the air-defense centers, with their computers, could never be repaired. The lack of spares may be attributable to the embargo, or it may reflect Saddam's reliance on Soviet equipment. Historically, the Soviets have tended to produce complete units in great numbers without manufacturing spare parts on anything like the same scale. Such practices are almost inescapable consequences of the nature of the Soviet planning and production system.[6] The Iraqis' problems may have been exacerbated by extensive operations (to deal with coalition aircraft feinting toward or over their territory) in the days immediately before the attack.

It is also worth keeping in mind that the prewar Iraqi air-defense system was heavily dependent on foreign, particularly Soviet, technicians for its maintenance. Soviet support of the coalition included not only the withdrawal of those technicians but also the provision of considerable information on the Iraqi system, or at least on the parts of the system for which the Soviets had been responsible, to the United States and Britain.

It seems less likely that, as some have suggested, the first night was the initial indication of the catastrophic loss of morale that became evident in other ways during the war. The Iraqis may have lost their faith in active defense, but they were certainly willing to go to considerable lengths to camouflage prospective targets. They became quite adept at simulating bomb damage so as to convince coalition analysts that targets, in fact undamaged, had already been hit. The notorious bunker in Baghdad, with bomb craters painted on its roof, is a case in point.

Iraqi air defense was split into three components. One was a Soviet-style national air-defense organization controlling both the fighters and fixed SA-2 and SA-3 air-defense missiles mainly protecting airfields. This was the organization struck and largely demolished on the first night. A second missile air-defense system, operated by the Republican Guard, protected key sites. It was probably not operated from the main control centers. Finally, the deployed Iraqi Army had a considerable air-defense system of its own. The national system covered the short-range Republican Guard system. It did not effectively cover the Iraqi Army in southern Iraq and in Kuwait.

The coalition could therefore attack in stages. First it had to neutralize the national system, or at least that system's area coverage. Once that had been done, particular strategic targets could be attacked, though such attacks would generally have to include SEAD to neutralize local defensive missiles. Because the army system was decentralized, it could not be destroyed quickly, and it succumbed only to repeated SEAD strikes on particular missile batteries. The effect of the first night's attacks, then, was to make it safe for coalition bombers to fly almost anywhere in Iraq at medium to high altitude, where the bombers could easily see and attack ground targets using both guided and unguided bombs.

The main air-defense center of the national system was located in Baghdad, with subcenters at Kirkuk, Nasiriya, and Routba, to control four defensive sectors. The principal early-warning radars were Soviet-supplied Tall Kings, with low-altitude cover by Soviet-supplied Squat Eyes. Fighters were controlled by Soviet-type Bar Lock radars.[7] Iraq also had a variety of Western radars, either supplied by France or captured in Iran and Kuwait. It is not clear how many captured radars actually functioned, given the paucity of spare parts and technicians.[8]

The network of fixed radars was supplemented by several Adnans, Soviet-supplied Il-76 transports fitted with license-built French Tiger G radars (the local designation was SDA-G). Adnan-1, displayed at the Baghdad show in 1989, had its radar in a ventral hump under its after fuselage. Although advertised as an early-warning airplane, it was probably intended mainly for ground surveillance. Adnan-2 had a rotodome. Although both aircraft were likened to the U.S. AWACS, the comparison was ludicrous. Tiger could handle only a few targets, and each Adnan could directly control only a few fighters, probably as few as four. Control was verbal, based on manual calculations; Adnan lacked both the computers and the data links of modern early-warning aircraft. Nor, apparently, did it have any data link to integrate its radar data with the national system. From a command and control point of view, then, Adnan was broadly comparable to U.S. aircraft deployed about 1958 (such as the Grumman E-1B Tracer) and replaced from the mid-1960s on: Reportedly one of the three Adnan-2 surrendered in the air during the first night attack on Iraq. Another fled to Iran, and a third was destroyed on the ground.[9]

The two major national air-defense missiles were both well known to the West, SA-2 (Guideline) and SA-3 (Goa, which also serves as the Soviet naval SA-N-1).[10] Both had been encountered in Vietnam. It seems unlikely that reported Iraqi improvements made much of a difference.[11] Both missiles are command-guided, using track-while-scan radars, and countermeasures to both were well known before the war. Neither is particularly effective at low altitude, so important missile sites were covered by radar-controlled light antiaircraft guns (mainly towed, radar-controlled, 57-mm S-60s). Both missiles are limited in range; they are intended for point defense of vital targets. The national system could control these weapons (to integrate them with the fighters), but the missiles were still usable after the control centers had been destroyed. It was therefore necessary to continue to fly suppression missions against the missile sites, that is, against the missile control radars.[12]

There were also national air-defense towed guns (as distinguished from the lighter and more mobile guns operating with field army formations): Soviet-supplied KS-12 85-mm guns (M 1939/1944), KS-19 100-mm guns, and KS-30 130-mm guns, a total of 200 in all.[13]

It appears that there was a separate national air-defense layer, consisting mainly of Roland short-range missile systems supplied by France, protecting particularly important sites: Baghdad itself, Samarra, Tikrit, the chemical/biological weapons sites, and probably the nuclear sites. It seems likely that the Republican Guard, rather than either the air-defense system or the Iraqi Army, controlled these weapons. Rolands protected at least some airfields.[14]

The field army controlled most of the smaller mobile air-defense missiles, all of them Soviet-supplied. The longest-range missile was the Soviet SA-6, broadly comparable in concept to the U.S. Hawk operated by the marines and by Kuwait before the war. It was backed by SA-8 (comparable to the French-supplied Roland, a command-guided, radar-directed weapon) and by vehicle-mounted, infrared-guided SA-9s and SA-13s. Troops also had large numbers (reportedly up to 20,000) of shoulder-fired SA-7s, SA-14s, and SA-16s, as well as a few French Mistrals. Mistral and SA-16 were probably unique among Iraqi weapons in this class in being suitable to engage targets head-on.[15]

Finally, there were light antiaircraft guns such as Soviet-supplied ZSU 57-2, ZSU 23-4, and 14.5-mm weapons. Iraq also used Swiss-made Skyguard—twin 35-mm, radar-controlled guns—presumably captured from Iran. Except when the guns were under radar control, they could not be decoyed, nor could they be counterattacked efficiently.[16]

The Iraqis themselves apparently had little faith in either the ground-based GCI system or in Adnan; shortly after the allied buildup in the Gulf began, they withdrew their fighters to northern bases out of easy range of coalition strike aircraft. Once the allies began to bomb Baghdad, a few Iraqi fighters did enter combat, but entirely without success. Perhaps more important, few if any actually tried to intercept attacking coalition aircraft. The initial air-to-air successes were Iraqi aircraft fleeing north once the attack was in progress.

The coalition spent the few days before the beginning of the war in last-minute jamming and electronic reconnaissance, finding all of the Iraqi early-warning radars. Feints into Iraqi airspace were particularly important because the Iraqi radars were turned on in their war reserve modes (WARMs) rather than in their peacetime modes.

The attack the first night was conducted in several phases. Tall King itself cannot reliably detect low-altitude targets, so it must be protected against low-fliers by separate higher-frequency radars. The initial break into the system was by helicopters firing laser-guided missiles at these radars (special forces designated the targets from the ground): Army AH-64s in the west, Marine Corps AH-1Ws on the coast near Basra. The helicopters were preferable to low-flying airplanes or missiles because they could stay close to the ground, and because the radars used moving target indicators (MTI) to distinguish airborne targets from the considerable ground clutter and helicopters were too slow to register on the MTIs.

The destruction of the low-altitude radars opened the long-range radars, the eyes of the system, to attack. Most of the radars were knocked out by manned bombers carrying HARMs. Some of the Tall Kings and the other big radars were destroyed by Tomahawk cruise missiles (armed with bomblet warheads) launched from the Persian Gulf and the Red Sea. The logic of using Tomahawks rather than relying exclusively on HARMs against the early-warning radars was simple. HARM can be fired only against an operating radar. The coalition air force could not afford to miss any long-range radar that had been deliberately shut down to await its approach. Moreover, the radars were fixed, and thus vulnerable to a missile that self-navigated to a fixed target point.

By way of contrast, local air-defense systems such as Roland were highly mobile and could not be located, let alone engaged, until they were turned on.

Lacking long-range radars (apart from the useless Adnan), the Iraqi system could not detect the strike aircraft following the Tomahawks. The ziggurat-like air-defense control centers were destroyed by laser-guided, concrete-penetrating bombs, dropped mostly by F-117s. One of the first shots of the war was a laser-guided bomb dropped by an F-117 on the Iraqi national air-defense center in Baghdad.[17] Fortunately the air-defense centers were not in deep bunkers similar to those built for Saddam and for the senior Ba'ath party leaders; they were in hardened aboveground buildings. The existing laser-guided bombs could penetrate and damage the buildings, but they could not have dealt with deeply buried structures.[18]

The fixed air-defense missile sites were attacked by fighters armed with antiradar missiles, mainly U.S. Navy and Marine Corps F/A-18s carrying HARMs. These missiles home only on active radar emissions. To trigger the radar sites, the attacking navy and marine fighters generally used glider decoys (TALDs). The air force lacked any real equivalent to TALD, but used a limited number of converted targets (BQM-74s) for the same purpose.

Also on the first night, British Tornadoes made their own attacks using ALARM missiles to help them penetrate (at least some of these attacks were coordinated with the U.S. strikes, a tactic developed at the Red Flag Training site). ALARM, which had not yet been fully tested at the time of the war, incorporates a parachute. It loiters over an enemy radar site, waiting for the radar to become active. Presumably the ALARMs loitering aloft destroyed radars which lit off as the Tornadoes came upon them.[19]

The Iraqi long-range surface-to-air missile systems never recovered; they claimed few or no allied aircraft. It was not that their crews gave up: they sometimes salvoed missiles. But the missiles were unguided. It may be that, although in theory they had a fall-back mode of operation separate from the overall national system, they were in reality heavily dependent on the GCI centers. When the centers went, they, too, lost effectiveness. Such integration was probably a necessary condition for the Iraqi system to use its fighters and missiles in any sort of combination. The Soviets, in this case the Iraqis' mentors, have always tended toward centralization as a means of solving IFF problems inherent in combined arms operations, and mixed fighter-defensive missile warfare would be a major case in point. Certainly very few coalition aircraft were shot down by any high- or medium-altitude surface-to-air missiles.

The Iraqis' integrated air-defense system apparently functioned initially, though unsuccessfully (strike aircraft could generally jam their way through where they had to), but it collapsed within the first two hours. It claimed only one coalition aircraft, an F/A-18, on the first night.

The Iraqis were never entirely cowed, and their army air-defense system (which was not lost when the national system collapsed) was reasonably effective at low altitude. There was even some tactical ingenuity. For example, some army units set up their guns to force airplanes into turns that should have opened them up to attacks by IR-guided missiles. However, such tactics were futile against an enemy who, having defeated the national medium- and high-altitude system, had little reason to face the low-level weapons.

Surely there are some lessons here. One might be that a Soviet-designed integrated air-defense system can be quite satisfactorily broken by conventional aircraft cleverly handled. In that case stealthy airplanes, which are very costly, may not be as essential as has been assumed. However, it might also be argued that Saddam's system was more vulnerable than it had to be. His control centers were not deeply buried and, consequently, were vulnerable to the weapons used the first night. Had he gone to the trouble to bury them like his own command center, only the very heavy penetrator used at the end of the war (which could be carried only by an F-111 or, probably, by a B-52) could have destroyed them. It is entirely possible, then, that ultimately Saddam lost his integrated air defense because he did not want air-control centers to be invulnerable to his own counter-coup forces. Future Saddams may think differently. It seems likely that future air attacks on Third World countries will often have to be mounted by carrier bombers. No current or planned airplane of this type can carry the 4,500-lb earth-penetrator that destroyed a deep bunker. Carrier bomb elevators probably also cannot accommodate so long a weapon. One lesson, then, is probably that the navy will have to be able to accommodate this type of weapon in the future (and also, for that matter, that it will have to be able to carry and deliver the current 2,000-lb hard-target killer, which is not currently carried aboard ship).[20]

Perhaps the best alternative, given the brilliant success of Tomahawk, would be to deploy a stealthy cruise missile capable of killing hard targets as a precursor to future attacks on integrated air-defense systems. Most such attacks will surely be mounted from the sea, if only because they must be conducted in urgent fashion, before ground-based forces can assemble. Ideally, the missiles would be fired, not by the carrier or her consorts, but by ships well away from the main group, to preserve the element of surprise. The main candidate for such a launch platform is an attack submarine, simply because it is so covert and because it can survive well out of the protective umbrella of the battle group. The submarines that launched Tomahawks from the Red Sea and from the Mediterranean presage this type of attack.[21]

It may also be possible to disguise some or all of the GCI centers as civilian buildings. One clear lesson of the war was that the United States was extremely reluctant to attack truly civilian targets. In the case of Iraq, there was sufficient preparation time to accumulate a mass of information from the foreign contractors who had actually built most of Iraq's command and control facilities. Thus, on the night after the one potentially embarrassing bombing of the dual-use bunker/air-raid shelter, the Defense Department briefers could actually display a contractor's drawing of the building, and they could speak with considerable confidence. It seems unlikely that we will again have so long a period of preparation against a specific Third World target; crises just do not normally take so long to peak.

The lesson would seem to be that the naval intelligence practice of studying Third World air-defense systems in turn is essential for the future. It is nice to be informed enough to know which targets to hit, but the prerequisite for hitting them at all is surely a full series of regularly updated air-defense-system analyses.

The attempt to destroy the Iraqi Air Force on the ground, and thus permanently to eliminate the air defense, was less successful. This part of the initial offensive was not merely a means of opening up Iraq to further air attack; it was also intended to eliminate the most effective Iraqi threat to the staging area in Saudi Arabia. For example, the only means of attacking Saudi Arabia and Israel with gas was air attack (the Scud missiles did not have chemical warheads).

Most Iraqi aircraft were sheltered in concrete hangarettes similar in concept to those built by the Soviets in Eastern Europe (a few of the very large aircraft, such as the Badger [Tu-16] medium bombers, were too large to shelter except by revetments, and they were quickly demolished by bombing). Such shelters could be destroyed only by very precise attacks, either by guided bombs penetrating their doors or by special concrete-piercing bombs passing through their roofs. The shelters were relatively easy to build, and Iraq had more shelters than aircraft. The coalition had only a relatively limited number of laser-guided bombs capable of penetrating hard structures (I-2000s), and they could be delivered only by F-117s and F-111Fs. Initially they had to be used against more vital targets. That led to attacking the runways themselves with conventional bombs, Gator mines, and the British JP233.[22]

These attacks proved both expensive and inconclusive. The only effective coalition antirunway weapon was the JP233, a bomblet dispenser that a Tornado bomber must carry right over the enemy airfield at very low level. That type of attack was developed because, in the European context for which the Tornado was designed, the British considered it safer to face antiaircraft fire than to fly at higher altitudes where missiles might be effective. In theory, an airplane roaring over locally controlled antiaircraft guns and hand-held missiles at really low level and at very high speed may survive simply because gunners cannot react quickly enough. In Iraq, the medium- and high-altitude missiles were almost completely neutralized on the first night. It was impossible, however, to wipe out small antiaircraft weapons, so they became major killers. Tornado low-altitude attacks were very dangerous for two reasons. First, the Tornado had to fly directly over a possible mass of ground fire, including small missiles. Second, because it flew so low at high speed, the Tornado could easily fly into the ground in the event of either a system failure or light damage to its fly-by-wire controls.[23]

Many runway attacks were made at higher altitude, using more conventional munitions. They had little effect, but they were not as costly as the British strikes.[24] As was expected, the Iraqis proved proficient in repairing runways, and in simulating bomb damage to deter the coalition air force from striking some of their airfields. That was acceptable, since the runway attacks were intended to keep the Iraqis on the ground until airplanes capable of destroying hard targets could be concentrated on the shelters containing the airplanes themselves.

Within a few weeks Central Command abandoned attacks on runways and concentrated instead on the shelters. Those attacks were apparently quite successful, since the Iraqis began to shelter airplanes in ones and twos in sanctuaries such as residential neighborhoods and even in important archaeological sites, such as the ziggurat at Ur.[25] Once the aircraft had been moved out into the open, they could be repositioned relatively easily. The coalition lacked organic reconnaissance; it could not easily target these aircraft on a timely basis. National assets (reconnaissance satellites) could indeed spot them, but their information, relayed through CENTAF in Riyadh, was generally too late to be useful.[26] It is possible that the mass flights of Iraqi aircraft to Iran were prompted by the shelter attacks.

The coalition was never certain that either the Iraqi national air-defense system or the Iraqi Air Force had been put permanently out of action; apparently there could be no unambiguous intelligence indication. As a consequence, many strike missions had to be supported by what proved to be unnecessary defense suppression escorts. In that sense the Iraqis did achieve some virtual attrition of the weight of the air attack that could have been brought against them. Similarly, the husbanding of Iraqi attack aircraft suggested that Saddam planned some last-minute counterstroke. For example, there was real concern, at least by the British Ministry of Defence, that aircraft were being prepared to drop gas on the coalition forces as the battle stabilized north of Kuwait. This latter concern seems to have been prompted in part by the sudden appearance of about ten Iraqi aircraft in the open (where they were promptly destroyed, on the ground).

The dismal performance of the Iraqi national air-defense system soon led Saddam to retire its chief by killing him. Not too long afterward, Iraqi aircraft began to fly to Iran; ultimately about 150 were interned there. The reason for these flights was never entirely clear. It seems most likely that individual pilots, and then entire groups, had decided that their chances of survival were minimal: their choices seemed to be suicide by air-to-air combat or execution by Saddam Hussein or by his security forces. There were instances of transport aircraft passing back and forth between Iran and Iraq, but it is possible that, given the confused circumstances (brought about by the allied bombing) pilots were trying to ferry their families out of Iraq. Certainly the Iranians consistently claimed that the Iraqis who landed in their country were defectors (and, moreover, that they would not release either pilots or aircraft until the war was over).

Iran was probably the only realistic place to seek asylum. An Iraqi pilot landing in Jordan would soon be handed back to Iraqi security forces. To land in Saudi Arabia would be to court destruction by coalition air-defense aircraft, that is, by precisely the aircraft the pilot was fleeing. A flight to Iran carried the risk of being shot down, and the Iranians might well remember the air attacks of the recent war, but they would also be unlikely to hand a deserter back to Saddam Hussein.

The counterargument is that, with his air force melting visibly, Saddam Hussein made a positive decision either to save it for postwar use or even for a surprise attack to be mounted from Iran. He might well have reasoned that any aircraft flown to Jordan would quite possibly have been destroyed by Israel. When the aircraft began leaving Iraq, Saddam Hussein was still saying that the coalition would be broken by the great land battle to come. Given his assumptions, he might well have been most concerned with preserving aircraft for use after the war. Advocates of this interpretation thought that the Iraqi transport aircraft were making round-trips to provide the spares and technicians needed to preserve the combat aircraft intact for further use.[27]

Any such intention surely required a prior deal struck with the Iranians. Logic would suggest that the Iranians would not have been very willing to help the man who had started the Iran-Iraq War, and who was the main obstacle to their desired status as the single dominant regional power. It was certainly in Iran's long-term interest that the United States and its Western partners thoroughly damage the Iraqi military machine. To willingly preserve some of that machine's most aggressive elements (such as the Su-24s) surely was very much against Iranian interests. Saddam had lost his leverage over the Teheran government when he returned their land and their prisoners of war. It may be that Saddam convinced himself that the Iranians would favor him over the Great Satan. It is even possible that the Iranians led him on, and that he could not imagine that they would be so devious as to deceive him.

It now seems unlikely that the Iranians permitted the Iraqis much access to the airplanes once they had landed. Initially they said that the airplanes would be interned for the course of the war; ultimately the Iranians said that none would be returned. If indeed any secret deal had been struck, the Iranians did not honor it. It seems more indicative of their views that they supported the anti-Saddam demonstrators (with weapons as well as rhetoric) in Basra during the week following the temporary cease-fire.

The composition of the group in Iran suggested something other than operational logic. It included not only the best of Saddam's combat aircraft, such as his Su-24 Fencer bombers, but also a mixed bag of transports and even trainers. The fact that many aircraft crashed on landing suggested that their pilots were inexperienced, that they had stolen aircraft in order to defect. Early in the mass flights, some aircraft peeled off as they ap-

proached the border. That was initially interpreted as the departure of escorts that had accompanied officially sanctioned flights,
but later it was theorized that these airplanes had turned back
when they were painted by Iranian air-defense radars, that is,
when they became subject to interception. That certainly pointed
the way toward something other than Iranian connivance in an
Iraqi plan.

Moreover, Saddam eventually made a quite different attempt
to save his air force, as mentioned earlier, placing airplanes in
residential areas and near archaeological sites in the knowledge
that they would not be attacked. These aircraft thus became unusable (their supporting equipment, fuel, and ammunition could
not be moved), but they remained in Iraq. Aircraft flown to Iran
were even less usable.

There is little question but that the offensive against the Iraqi
national air-defense system was stunningly successful. Very few
coalition aircraft were lost to the weapons it controlled, the Iraqi
fighters and the long-range surface-to-air missiles. To the extent
that Iraqi air-defense concepts mirrored Soviet thinking, the initial strike was a test of NATO concepts for attacks on the Soviet
system in Europe. The results tended to vindicate the prewar
U.S. (as opposed to British and German) view of the course of a
likely European air war.

The U.S. Air Force invested heavily in SEAD aircraft, technology, and tactics in hopes that it could control the missile threat
to airplanes flying at medium and high altitudes. A higher-altitude
attacker can see much more of the area he is attacking. Because
navigation is almost never perfect, the pilot will want to acquire
a planned target before dropping bombs or missiles. The greater
the visible area, the better the chance that the target can be located. Similarly, a target seen from a greater distance is easier to
attack, whether with a precision-guided bomb or with unguided
bombs dropped by fire-control computer. Moreover, an airplane
that could fly unhindered at medium or high altitude could freely
use navigational or targeting radars to detect distant targets. Medium-altitude approaches were particularly well adapted to the de-

livery of guided bombs, since they gave a pilot time to acquire the target before marking it for the missile to hit.

By way of contrast, the pilot of an airplane flying at very low altitude hardly has time to acquire his target before it flashes past beneath him. He must rely heavily on information provided before he takes off and often he cannot bomb accurately. Most important, an airplane flying at medium altitude need not fear the numerous, independently targeted, light antiaircraft guns and SAMs. Each has only a short range, but together such weapons carpet the area over which the airplane flies. They were the main killers in Vietnam, and many expected the same situation to apply to Iraq.

The European view was that the SEAD effort was prohibitively expensive in terms of the number of airplanes used to support rather than to execute a strike. The number of aircraft in excess of actual attackers is sometimes described in terms of virtual attrition, that is, the extent to which the enemy has reduced the attacking force. Airplanes flying at medium altitude against unsuppressed long-range missiles would not survive long, because each missile battery would get many shots at each airplane. The Europeans therefore preferred to fly at low altitude and to take their chances against the sort of random fire that light antiaircraft guns and missiles could put up. It followed that attackers could survive only by flying at extremely low level, attacking prebriefed targets. The Tornado bomber, with its JP233 antirunway weapon, was the main expression of that belief. It did not even have provision for a laser designator, which would have been used for precision medium-altitude strikes.

The U.S. Air Force conceded that, at least in Europe, initial attacks would have to be made at low altitudes, to evade the medium-range SAM cover. However, if those attacks were concentrated on the enemy air-defense system, then deep follow-up strikes could be made at medium or high altitude. U.S. Navy tactics tended more toward the initial penetration strike with early follow-up, but they were similar in overall concept. The most important difference was in the sheer number of airplanes involved. The air force always thought in terms of large numbers, so it evolved separate Wild Weasel and other special strike-support aircraft. Because carrier-borne resources were more limited in terms of numbers of aircraft, the U.S. Navy had to rely more on multimission aircraft. Many of the same airplanes would conduct the SEAD attack and then the follow-up bombing strike. For this reason U.S. Navy SEAD-capable aircraft far outnumbered the small number of special-purpose air force Wild Weasels. The navy therefore was responsible for a large proportion of SEAD strikes.[28]

In Iraq, the U.S.–style SEAD effort was practicable because the medium- and high-altitude SAM batteries were not very numerous and because their coverage did not interlock. Sites could therefore be attacked one by one, often from beyond effective SAM range. The Iraqis had relied on their fighters to fill in the areas between the SAMs, but the fighters had been neutralized by the destruction of their control centers. In theory, the Adnan airborne early warning airplanes could have controlled fighters bereft of the ground centers, but they were not nearly sophisticated enough, and they never functioned that way.[29]

After initial losses in low-altitude attacks, both U.S. Air Force and U.S. Navy aircraft were generally directed to attack from above about 10,000 ft. The B-52s, which made their first attacks at 500 ft, switched to 20,000 to 30,000 ft or more. These relatively safe attack altitudes were not always practical. Airplanes could generally fly toward their targets at high enough altitudes to avoid any sort of damage en route, but in many cases (particularly when guided bombs or missiles were not available) accurate weapon delivery was impossible except at low altitude. Similarly, a Navy A-6 was lost delivering mines, which had to be laid precisely, that is, at low altitude. No initial air offensive could have solved the low-altitude problem.

Probably the best measure of success against Iraqi air defenses is the scale of coalition air losses. Intense air operations in Vietnam (such as Linebacker III in 1972 or Route Package 6 in 1967) generally cost 2.6 to 3 aircraft per thousand sorties. Before the war began, this sort of figure suggested that an intense air war in Iraq and Kuwait would cost about 150 aircraft. However, in the end, well over 50,000 fixed-wing sorties into enemy-held territory cost only about forty coalition airplanes, a rate below 0.9 per thousand sorties. Initial navy losses in low-level attacks did reach Vietnam proportions (2.7 per thousand sorties), because the Iraqis were in fact able to put up low-altitude fire not too different from that encountered in Vietnam. The difference was that, with the high- and medium-altitude threats all but eliminated, pilots did not have to face that threat.

Overall, the campaign against the Iraqi air defenses could not have been accomplished without extensive electronic reconnaissance. The United States had no fixed listening posts in the area, so a listening capability had to be built up. Much of it came from the U.S. Navy, which maintains land-based aircraft to monitor Soviet and other naval activity on a constant basis. Ultimately three to five EP-3Es (of squadrons VQ-1 and VQ-2) and one to three P-3s (of VPU-1 and -2) were deployed to the Persian Gulf. Another two to three EA-3Bs (VQ-2) were deployed to western Saudi Arabia (Jeddah). Finally, two EP-3Es and two EA-3Bs (all from VQ-2) were deployed to Souda Bay, Crete. Of these aircraft, the P-3s and EP-3Es were relatively slow and could not survive without considerable protection. The EA-3s were fast enough to survive (they were converted attack bombers), although they were elderly (they had been retired from carrier service).

VQ-1 came on station in the Gulf early in the buildup; VQ-2 arrived in December. Their aircraft were intended for battle group indications and warning (I&W), pre- and post-strike reconnaissance, threat warning to strike packages entering Iraqi airspace, and HARM targeting. They also provided information directly to the air force's AWACS (E-3A), EC-130H Compass Call, and RC-135 aircraft. The VPUs (photo aircraft) were used for strike reconnaissance and real-time bomb damage assessment for coastal and island strikes.

The EA-3Bs were provided for pre-, during-, and post-strike reconnaissance for the Red Sea carriers. They were tied directly to E-2, EA-6B, and S-3B aircraft to identify and triangulate electronic targets (one airplane gets only a line of bearing, so two are needed for a positive location), both for general reconnaissance and for HARM targeting. Typical sorties lasted 6.5 to 8.5 hours. EA-3Bs were on station for each Red Sea carrier strike into Iraq.[30]

The Mediterranean EP-3Es were the only signals intelligence aircraft in the area. They performed strike reconnaissance for the U.S. Air Force strikes against northern Iraq, working with air force E-3, EC-130H, and EF-111A aircraft and also passing threat warnings directly to air force strike aircraft. In addition, the EP-3Es and EA-3Bs made daily eastern and central Mediterranean flights to maintain a current Mediterranean intelligence picture, that is, to monitor possible threats to the vital supply shipping heading for the Suez Canal and for the Red Sea and the Gulf beyond.

The air force brought three RC-135s (including two Rivet Joint aircraft), roughly its equivalent to the EP-3E, into Saudi Arabia to act as its ferrets in that area. They flew prewar intelligence-gathering missions along the Iraqi border and were presumably part of the intense effort to locate and identify Iraqi radars (and to discover their WARM modes) just before the air war began. The Rivet Joint aircraft have side-looking radars used, reportedly, to track Soviet missile re-entry vehicles during tests. At least two of these communications intelligence aircraft were kept in Saudi Arabia throughout the war, apparently primarily to detect Scud-related signals.

9

The Air Campaign

THE STUNNING success against Iraqi national air defenses opened Iraqi territory to an offensive air campaign that lasted five weeks. But work on the air offensive actually began in August. The air force decided that its most valuable contribution to war planning would be a strategic bombing campaign. Soon after Iraq invaded Kuwait, the air force Checkmate unit began to list potential targets. Air force doctrine required elaborate prestrike planning. Relatively few bombs would be available, so it was crucial to decide just where a target was most vulnerable. The airplanes approaching the target needed offset aim points that they could detect and track. Checkmate, augmented by a few naval officers (who joined seven to ten days after work began) compiled a bombing encyclopedia, describing each target in detail and selecting a weapon and a desired mean point of impact (DMPI). Checkmate's bombing plan (at this point really a target list) was presented to the president late in August. Ultimately the plan was code-named Instant Thunder.

Like the strategic air plan against the Soviet Union on which it was modeled, Checkmate's Instant Thunder plan was based on data collected by national intelligence assets such as satellites. As will probably be typical of future Third World situations, there was very little data with which to start. The Iraqi problem was so

169

urgent that the national assets were redirected to support it, for example to find the offset aim points that bombers would need to attack their targets. It seems likely that a parallel effort was made to map Iraq more precisely so that Tomahawk missiles could be used effectively (the missiles need digital maps for their guidance). That work, too, would have been executed by satellite. Once the war began, satellites were extremely important because reconnaissance assets in the theater were so limited. Much of the data actually used for tactical targeting in the KTO, therefore, came out of satellites that reported to Washington rather than to Cent-Com. In a notable example of self-discipline (presumably enforced by the administration) Washington limited itself during the war to an advisory role, for example, recommending restrikes when its own analysts doubted that a target had been thoroughly enough damaged. With perhaps a few exceptions, Washington avoided any attempt to decide which targets should be hit.

Although not the final strategic air plan selected for the war, it was a basis for planning. In September air planning responsibility moved to CentCom in Riyadh. The Checkmate target list was greatly expanded. Although CentCom was a joint staff, air planning remained primarily an air force role, albeit with strong navy representation (given the large percentage of CentCom air resources in the aircraft carriers). Altogether, the targeting group consisted of twenty to thirty air force officers and seven naval officers.

The two services had very different concepts of the nature of the air campaign. The navy's operational experience, in places like Libya in 1986, was concentrated in the penetration of an enemy's national air-defense system. What happened afterward tended to be quite limited, intended to demonstrate that worse could follow. Targets were chosen for their political impact. The navy's main experience of more strategic targeting was its extensive analysis of attacks against Soviet bases. Naval officers assigned to CentCom probably thought mainly in terms of close air support of the soldiers and marines they expected would eject the Iraqis from Kuwait. The air force, which dominated U.S. strategic targeting, saw a potential war against Iraq as a miniature version of the big strategic attack against the Soviet Union. It hoped that a sufficiently intense strategic air campaign would win the war.

As presented to General Schwarzkopf, Instant Thunder was a phased air plan. Phase 1 (seven to ten days) was the simultaneous attack on the Iraqi national air-defense system and on the strategic targets it protected. Phase 2 was a day-long attack on Iraqi air defenses in the Kuwait Theater of Operations (KTO) as a prelude to battlefield attacks. Phase 3 was a lengthy series of attacks on those ground forces preparatory to a ground attack beginning between day 30 and day 39. General Schwarzkopf did not like the separation between strategic attacks and those attacks needed to prepare for the ground campaign, so the latter began at the outset of the war. There was no distinct Phase 2, and Phase 1 strategic attacks continued through the war. Very bad weather greatly reduced the value of the optically guided precision weapons used by the coalition. It was blamed for adding about a week to the length of the air campaign. The great Scud chase also consumed valuable air resources, equivalent to perhaps another week.

Numerous studies as well as numerous exercises at the Red Flag strike school convinced the air force that success in attacks against well-defended targets depended on saturation. The defense (particularly its longer-range elements) can handle only so many distinct targets at a time. Airplanes bunched together present only a single large target, so the air force had to try to mount attacks from many different directions at once. All of those airplanes had to arrive in the shortest possible total time. There would indeed be a concentration over the target, but it would be transient. Attacks with nonnuclear bombs were particularly difficult because each bomb would cause relatively little damage. Therefore the largest possible number of bombs—carried by the largest number of airplanes—had to be dropped against an important or extensive target. The problem of coordination was further complicated by the need to suppress close-in defenses. At one time, this sort of attack might have been mounted by a massed force breaking up at a prearranged point short of the target itself. However, a modern, integrated air-defense system can defeat that sort of coordination by detecting and attacking the strike force before it can approach the dispersal point.

The air force's solution was to coordinate air activity throughout the enemy's airspace, so that airplanes for attacks against one target could be drawn from several different bases. They would no longer have to fly together anywhere in the defended area. That demanded what the air force came to call full four-dimensional (space and time) control over virtually all airplanes in the enemy's airspace. Airplanes attacking several targets simultaneously would seem to be rushing randomly in all directions. They had to be kept out of each other's way, and even their radio frequencies had to be carefully coordinated.

Coordination became more important as the number of airplanes involved increased. Aircraft in Iraqi airspace included not only the strikers, but also the fighters shielding them from enemy fighters, the electronic warfare aircraft trying to neutralize enemy air defenses, and also the reconnaissance aircraft examining targets and following up the strikes. The air force argued that only by weaving all air activity over Iraq and Kuwait into a single integrated air plan under one commander could all of these airplanes be used to greatest effect. Moreover, not to weave their activities together would be to invite self-inflicted damage when different groups of airplanes came into unexpected contact.

Such coordination was extremely difficult. Each day's air activity had to be specified in a rigid plan, the ATO (air tasking order) created by a computer-assisted flight management system (CAFMS). The computer could optimize total attacks against known enemy air defenses. For example, attacks could be designed to use terrain to mask airplanes against enemy air defenses without fear that those approaching from different directions would collide. Fragments (frags) of the ATO go to the squadrons that are to execute the plan. The squadrons do their own planning, but much of their operation is determined in advance by the ATO. Moreover, the success of the concentration tactic requires that the ATO control virtually all air effort in the enemy's airspace. Any strike packages that do not conform with the ATO run a real risk of colliding with aircraft flying to make planned strikes. The strike airplanes are expected to defend themselves against enemy airplanes, and their ability to quickly identify airplanes they encounter is quite limited. Thus any exceptions to the ATO invite accidental destruction of friendly airplanes by other friendlies.

The computer is powerful enough to concentrate air resources simultaneously against several targets. However, its degree of coordination carries a heavy burden of inflexibility. The plan as a whole cannot be rewritten very quickly. Its typical turn-around cycle, between the acquisition of intelligence and the launch of strike aircraft, is probably at least 48 hours (squadrons receive their frags the day before they fly). A targeter planning an attack on any particular target must predict just how much ordnance is needed to destroy it. That is reasonable if the target is a typical strategic or deep-strike structure, such as an oil refinery.

This is not to say that all airplanes in the ATO must necessarily flit rapidly through the enemy's airspace. The ATO will generally make some allowance for loitering airplanes, such as fighters on combat air patrol. It can allow them considerable freedom of action by restricting other air activity near them, or by laying out lanes (for strike aircraft) that they must avoid. However, any such restrictions on free use of the enemy's airspace concentrate the attackers to some extent, and thus present the enemy's air force with opportunities to ambush them. The wise ATO planner, then, will minimize devices such as combat air patrols and barrier patrols.

ATO-ordained strikes in Iraqi and Kuwaiti airspace were controlled by an airborne command post, ABCCC III (airborne battlefield command and control center III), a capsule carried on board an EC-130E. Presumably its computers corresponded to those that produced the ATO in the first place; it was linked directly to AWACS and JSTARS aircraft. ABCCC was conceived as a way of coordinating close air support, but seems to have had a larger overall ATO management role in the Gulf.[1] In effect, the ABCCC is an attempt to protect the fairly rigid ATO against the consequences of inevitable surprises, including accidents and failures. An ABCCC could redirect a strike (within fairly narrow limits set by the overall concept of the ATO). In at least one case, it directed search and rescue forces to a pilot sending a distress signal from a crashing airplane.

The ATO was conceived as an alternative to the Vietnam War system of "route packages," in which each available air unit was assigned its own corridors into (and out of) the target area and its own targets there. The route package system was unavoidable in Vietnam because no existing fieldable computer could possibly have produced a plan coordinating hundreds of airplanes appearing from several different bases. On the other hand, because it was less highly integrated, the route package system was probably much better at handling disparate air-support requirements. The ATO system became practicable only with the advent of large fieldable computers.

The navy had never subscribed to the ATO system; war at sea, or even against a coast, is just too unpredictable to brook so rigid a planning technique. Carriers did not have computers compatible with the air force's ATO-generating equipment (they had their own mission planning systems). Nor did they have the necessary secure communications compatible with the air force's. Carrier participation in the ATO therefore required that the orders planned for execution a few days hence be physically carried to the ships, a job performed by S-3s. For example, each of the carriers in the Red Sea flew an S-3 to Riyadh each day, getting her frags the day before she was to attack. Each carrier generally launched two large strike packages each day.

The degree of air coordination enforced by the ATO was sometimes presented as an interservice issue. The navy and the marines saw matters very differently from the air force: they were much more willing to accept inefficiency as the cost of operational flexibility. However, coordination also had international implications. The Israelis repeatedly argued that they should be permitted to attack the Scud areas in western Iraq. Many in the United States thought that the only real military (as opposed to political) barrier to such operations was that the Israelis were denied the U.S. IFF (identification, friend or foe) codes. However, the highly integrated air operating plan was a much greater obstacle. To fit within it, the Israelis would have had to accept, in effect, U.S. operational control once their airplanes crossed into Iraq. Otherwise their operations would quite possibly have inadvertently interfered with those of the coalition.

The planners had other political problems. Ultimately each coalition air force was controlled by its own government, not by CentCom. In particular, the French government demanded the right to review all targets assigned to its aircraft. It is not clear how many targets, if any, the French government rejected. Presumably the French approval process stretched out the time cycle represented by the ATO process.

Overall, the ATO system is ill-suited to targets that are fundamentally unpredictable, such as moving enemy ground forces or areas in which Scud launchers may or may not be found. The basic method of the ATO cannot be adjusted so that coordinated strikes occur in one area and tactically responsive ones occur somewhere else; such variation merely invites catastrophe. The ATO concept was originally formulated to fight a war in Europe, where the main weight of the air force effort would have been concentrated on fixed targets in the enemy's rear and on the defeat of enemy air attackers. The rise of the ATO probably coincided with the decision that attacks on moving enemy formations well beyond the front line would be conducted, not mainly by airplanes, but rather by the army's new generation of tactical missiles (directed by JSTARS radar aircraft). The ATO would not apply to operations near the battle line or its equivalent, because they were inherently so unpredictable. The only impact of the ATO on such operations would be careful planning of corridors down which the strike aircraft could fly and return without being shot down.[2]

In the case of Iraq and Kuwait, the problem was that tactical and deep-strike areas could not be separated neatly. The relatively inflexible ATO had to cover most of the enemy's airspace, yet it had to deal with unpredictable mobile targets like enemy tanks and Scud launchers. The solution seems to have been twofold.

One was to use the ATO method and to accept inefficiency. "Kill boxes" in areas of expected enemy vehicle concentrations were defined. Aircraft were timed to appear over the boxes, and given a limited time in which to find and destroy as many vehicles as they could. Attacks of this sort could be kept up as long as successive groups of airplanes were despatched to the "kill boxes." None of the fast tactical airplanes (which carried most of the bombs) could be allowed to stay in a box for very long; the set time above the "box" had to be estimated well in advance by a targeter. The entire philosophy of the ATO and of transient concentration would prohibit any attempt to hand over a kill box from one group of airplanes to the next. All strike groups had to operate independently. Only rarely would the same aircraft or the same squadron visit the same box on a regular basis. Moreover, because there was always a severe shortage of tactical reconnaissance airplanes, it was not easy to monitor any given box on a continuous basis.[3] One consequence was that the Iraqis were more successful than they should have been in decoying, for example by fixing wrecked tanks just well enough to make them look operable (hence worth hitting). Similarly, wrecked or unserviceable aircraft were sometimes mocked up to appear viable. Throughout the air campaign against the Iraqi Army, there were considerable disagreements between CentCom and the U.S.–based analysts (who used satellite data) as to just how well the attack was proceeding.

Moreover, inevitably those attacking vehicles in the "boxes" often found themselves forced to leave before they had expended all of their weapons. After all, the targeters could never say in advance exactly where those movable tanks would be when the airplanes turned up.

Some continuity (and efficiency) could be assured by flying a spotter (forward air control) airplane over the kill box, but it was soon discovered that classical slow spotters (in airplanes such as OV-10s) could too easily be shot down. The air force solution was to switch to fast (hence survivable) forward air control (FAC) airplanes, the "fast FACs." Each loitered near a kill box (presumably a single loitering airplane could be accommodated within the ATO). The spotter F-16 carried no ordnance except marking rockets; its pilot designated targets. This practice had been tried, unsuccessfully, in Vietnam (the fast FAC pilot whizzed past too fast to see much), but probably worked better in Iraq, where the desert floor presented a much less confusing picture.[4]

The alternative was to abandon the ATO altogether in selected areas so far from the main targets that what happened there would not interfere with the strategic attacks. The Marine Corps AV-8Bs, for example, operated outside the formal ATO. Much of the carrier air contribution did as well. One effect of excluding the early carrier air effort from the ATO was that carrier aircraft could quickly be called up to assist the ATO-assigned forces (they could, presumably, piggyback with groups that had already been assigned their routes into and through Iraqi airspace). That was particularly important in suppression of enemy air defense (SEAD). The carriers could and did provide "walk-away SEAD packages" on short notice to the U.S. Air Force, the Royal Air Force, and the other coalition air forces. The navy estimated that it performed 60 percent or more of total SEAD.

Similar considerations certainly applied to helicopters, such as the army's Apaches, and probably to A-10s assigned to tank-killing near the Kuwaiti-Saudi border (A-10s assigned to Scud-hunting were probably more rigidly assigned, as they had to fly deep into Iraq). The absence of helicopter statistics in the published accounts of the air war suggests strongly that helicopters were never part of the ATO (from which the statistics were generated). In Europe the air force and army developed combined (JAAT, joint air attack team) tactics in which A-10s and AH-64 attack helicopters supported each other. The helicopters flew very low, popping up to attack the short-range, antiaircraft weapons that otherwise would have threatened the A-10s. They cleared the way for the A-10s to kill tanks from a higher altitude. A JAAT is controlled by an air force forward air controller (in a helicopter, an OV-10, or a ground vehicle) and by an army "battle captain" in a scout helicopter. When the war began, the air force was in the process of converting some A-10s to forward air-control aircraft (OA-10s) on the theory that the slow OV-10s could no longer survive. The attacking A-10s were to be replaced by fast F-16s, which could survive but could not be expected to acquire ground targets effectively. In one case in Kuwait, an A-10 and an AH-64 were shot down; presumably they had been a JAAT team.

The Scud campaign exemplified the alternative solutions to the inflexibility of the ATO. The "kill box" concept was used against areas thought to contain Scud launchers. F-15Es were assigned to fly combat air patrols over two stations (western and southeastern Iraq). They could respond when Scuds were fired (they generally tried to follow launch vehicles back to their storage areas, then bomb the storage areas). The CAP airplanes were cued by JSTARS and also by national-asset information (such as detections of the hot plume of the rising missile) passed through AWACS. Finally, airplanes such as A-10s and navy S-3s and A-6Es were assigned to road reconnaissance, in hopes of finding Scud launchers driving out to their launch sites.

The degree of coordination demanded by the ATO system was greatly reduced as Iraqi air defenses crumbled. For example, the air force used pairs of F-15E strike fighters both for deep attacks against enemy vehicles and to search for Scuds. Missions early in the war took 5 to 6 hours to plan, whereas later planning was pared to one hour per mission.

The ATO system is effective only as long as the U.S. forces hold the initiative, because in that case preplanning can be realistic. If the enemy moves quickly enough, the minimum 24- or 48-hour turn-around time inherent in the system makes it worse than inefficient; the system breaks down. It invites a classic application of the sort of blitzkrieg tactics described by retired air force Col. John Boyd (see the command and control discussion in the final chapter of this book). That actually happened at least once at the air force's tactical school, Red Flag. In Iraq and Kuwait the ATO worked well because the Iraqis were generally fairly passive, so that the United States determined the tempo and nature of the war.

ATO planners try to introduce flexibility in several ways. One is to break the overall operation into packages, with a commander for each. In this case typical packages might have been the KTO, Scuds, Baghdad, and industrial sites. This is a considerable advance on earlier techniques, which probably were too stiff to run as many as five or six packages at once (and which probably could not have controlled as many airplanes as the coalition launched simultaneously). Even so, any preplanned targeting scheme cannot readily allow for an enemy's unpredictable tactical movements on land or at sea.

One by-product of the ATO system is automatically produced detailed mission statistics. The raw number of sorties is deceptive in two ways. First, it is not broken down into the number of targets actually hit. Thus it does not distinguish between an efficient strike that, say, uses three airplanes to hit a target and an inefficient one that uses, say, thirty (one amounts to three sorties, the other to thirty). Second, it is terribly easy to forget that those statistics exclude numerous important missions outside the ATO's primarily strategic framework, yet nonetheless rather important to the ultimate success of the war. Indeed, the issue of ATO statistics is not too different from the fundamental question raised by the air effort in World War II: How important is the strategic air offensive as compared to tactical air attacks and close air support of ground troops?[5]

The ATO system also lent itself to misuse. The war was fought in the context of an ongoing political (interservice) war at home. Before August 1990, it seemed likely that the navy, the service best adapted to projecting U.S. power into the Third World, was the great winner. The decline of the Soviet threat made strategic airplanes, such as the air force's new B-2, seem less and less important. The air force apparently saw the ATO as an opportunity to redress the balance, in particular to prove that the navy's carriers were inefficient means of attacking a Third World enemy. Naval officers have suggested that the ATO was especially well suited to emphasize land-based air attack. Moreover, the ATO permitted the air force to use those assets it most wanted to showcase. Before the war, the air force as an institution badly wanted the stealthy B-2 strategic bomber. The only operational example of stealth technology was the F-117 light bomber, used for the first time in Panama the previous year. It was no great surprise that F-117s were extensively used during Instant Thunder.[6] The larger question is whether the F-117's stealthiness made much of a difference once the Iraqi medium- and high-altitude air defenses had been knocked out. It was probably much more significant that only it and the F-111 could deliver the laser-guided, I-2000, hard-target bomb.[7]

At heart, Instant Thunder was a strategic bombing campaign against fixed targets. It had two quite distinct objectives. One was to destroy the threat Iraq presented to other countries. That was an unstated coalition objective, and it was never endorsed by the United Nations. Because of these considerations, it was unlikely that the coalition would ever overrun much of Iraq. Any attempt to eliminate Iraqi superweapons (such as chemical and biological plants), then, would have to be made by air. This campaign would have little impact on, or direct relevance to, the ground war. The only real question was whether it succeeded. Unfortunately, bomb damage assessment is uncertain at best. Unless and until the sites are visited on the ground, we cannot know.

The second objective was tactical. Iraq's army had to be cut off from its commanders and its supplies and badly damaged before the ground war could begin. The ATO's fixed targets included various Iraqi headquarters and also the Iraqi bridge, road, and rail systems. There is some evidence that early concentration on the more strategic targets rather reduced the efforts on these more tactical ones. Moreover, given the constraints implied in the ATO system, it is not clear that tactical targets could always be efficiently attacked.

The coalition had five strategic objectives:

1. To prepare for a later ground campaign by exacting the maximum damage to Iraqi troops in and around Kuwait. It was never really possible to measure the effects of these attacks. However, an air intelligence officer pointed out that the declining cohesion of the Iraqi ground forces showed as they became less and less enthusiastic about defending themselves. Initially the Iraqi troops tried to shoot back in organized fashion, but later they acted as little more than frightened individuals, trying to dig in to survive assaults rather than responding to broader orders from Baghdad. This of-

fensive involved the destruction of the bridge and road network between Baghdad and the future area of military operations to the south. The Iraqi rail system, including its marshaling yards, was attacked and destroyed.

2. To eliminate Iraqi long-range offensive capability against both Saudi Arabia and Israel. The latter requirement had to be met if Israel were to be kept out of the war; that, in turn, was generally seen as virtually essential if the coalition was to be maintained. The Iraqis began the war with two long-range weapons: aircraft (Su-24, Tu-16, and Tu-22 bombers) and missiles (Scuds and modified Scuds). Some of the long-range aircraft could have been used for reconnaissance. To the extent that the coalition war plan depended on successful deception, it was particularly important that the Iraqi air force be eliminated.

3. To eliminate the current and future Iraqi threat of nuclear, chemical, and biological warfare. Iraq had a small uranium mine near the Turkish border, a uranium separation plant, and four other nuclear-related sites (including a reactor under construction). All were thoroughly bombed. At least one chemical warfare installation in downtown Baghdad, camouflaged as a "baby milk plant," was destroyed.[8]

4. To destroy Saddam Hussein's ability to control his forces or, at the least, his ability to do so in a secure manner.[9] From the opening night of the war, allied aircraft attacked Saddam Hussein's command centers and his communication relays. Saddam's main secure means of communicating with his southern group of forces in and around Basra was a multiple fiber optic link that crossed the Euphrates on the bridges over that river. By the eve of the ground offensive, all but two of the bridges had been dropped into the river, and consequently only two optical fibers were still usable. These fibers were destroyed by special forces as the ground offensive began. With the fibers gone, Saddam had no remaining fully secure communication. He was reduced to radio, which could be intercepted and jammed.

5. To destabilize Saddam Hussein's regime by a combination

of direct threats to the Iraqi leadership group and demonstrations of capability against important Iraqi resources. Under this head come direct attacks on the main ministries and command centers in Baghdad and also attacks on or near Tikrit, Saddam's hometown and the place from which his important associates were drawn. The destruction of the Iraqi steel industry (a matter of national pride) was probably intended to dramatize the extent of Iraqi punishment.

The requirements translated to a broad series of industrial targets:

- the electrical power grid—Iraq ended the war with only 15 percent of its electrical power system intact. By way of comparison, in 1945, after heavy bombing, Germany had *lost* only 15 percent of its electrical grid. Many Iraqi military installations had their own electrical generators, but Iraqi industry could not function without the national grid. The Iraqi sewage system was disabled as a by-product, since its pumps could not work without electrical power.
- oil, the basis of Iraqi military operations—The oil gathering, preprocessing, and transmission systems were destroyed, as were the dozen Iraqi refineries. The destruction of the Iraqi power grid made repairs futile, since oil cannot be moved without electric power (both for pumping and for heating the oil sufficiently to make it flow through pipes).
- water, which is required for many industrial processes including oil treatment.
- petrochemical plants, which use naphtha refined from oil to manufacture vital chemicals—Petrochemical products included missile fuel, ethylene oxide for the fuel-air bombs Saddam claimed, and basic chemical weapons such as mustard and cyanide gases.
- agrochemical plants—Insecticides produced at these plants are closely related to nerve gases (the earliest nerve gases, sarin and tabun, are actually insecticides). In at least one case, a pharmaceutical facility was attached to an agrochemical plant; it presumably made biological weapons.

- fertilizer plants, because they produce explosives (or at the least the precursor chemicals required for such production).
- the small Iraqi military industry devoted to missile production.
- the civilian telephone system—Knocking this out overloaded the parallel secure military system, since without civilian phones the government had to rely entirely on the military system even for the most trivial messages. As the military land-line system began to suffer, the Iraqis were forced to put more and more of their traffic into radio messages, which the allies could intercept and disrupt.[10]

There was also some hope that attacks that demonstrated Saddam's impotence would lead to his overthrow. Three targets were proposed: the 40-ft statue of Saddam himself in Baghdad, the triumphal arch (consisting of two crossed swords arching over a main street), and Saddam's private amusement area (described by one analyst as his "Disneyland") near Baghdad. Accounts vary, but it appears that at least "Disneyland" was hit. This was an unusual example of purely political targeting, a concept that had gained prominence in U.S. strategic thinking in the 1970s.[11] The headquarters of the Ba'ath party was also hit, but that was more likely an attempt to destroy key files that made it possible for the party to maintain control (the attack is analogous to 1970s proposals to make the KGB headquarters a major target in any strategic attack on the Soviet Union).

Some of the timing of the strikes was probably dictated by the need to eliminate Saddam Hussein's strategic attack capability (for example, chemical and nuclear weapons) before the air campaign could be aborted by a sudden Iraqi decision to withdraw from Kuwait. In the event, Saddam never did decide to surrender to air attack, but the coalition always had to be aware that he had the option of stopping the attack before its real objective (the elimination of Iraq as a regional threat) had been met. This problem was an inescapable consequence of the coalition/U.N. character of the war.

The coalition character of the war imposed some other important limitations. From the beginning, the coalition partners had proclaimed that Saddam, not the Iraqi people, was the enemy. All were well aware that scenes of vast destruction imposed on an Arab country by a coalition headed by the United States would make for public outrage within the Arab world. Some considerable damage was inescapable, but strenuous efforts were made to minimize civilian deaths. For his part, Saddam seems to have been well aware of the coalition's fears. Through the war, he used the Arab and Western press to publicize the damage the allies were doing in hopes of generating counterpressure.[12]

Although a large number of tactical aircraft were available to the coalition, the total number of sorties flown daily against Iraq and Kuwait was generally limited to about 1,200. That figure includes all fighter cover, both for strikes and for the protection of Saudi Arabia, all jammers, and all of the nonstrike elements of each strike package. The percentage of actual strikes presumably rose as Iraqi antiaircraft defenses were eliminated. However, because the allies never did eliminate the Iraqi air force, fighters always had to accompany strikes, and fighter patrols always had to be mounted on the Saudi border and on the seaward flanks (Persian Gulf and Red Sea).

Resources, both of aircraft and of precision weapons themselves, were always limited.[13] The main precision weapons were laser-guided bombs. Only certain airplanes could designate targets while delivering them: F-111s, F-117As, F-15Es (but only when equipped with LANTIRN targeting pods), and navy A-6Es. Because the LANTIRN targeting pods did not become available until quite late in the war, many missions that might otherwise have been flown by F-15Es were instead flown by F-111s. Eventually some RAF Tornadoes were equipped with laser designation pods. In some cases an airplane with a laser designator could control bombs dropped by one without (as in the cases of RAF Tornadoes buddy-bombing with Buccaneers, and of U.S. Navy F/A-18s buddy-bombing with A-6Es). In at least one case a group of A-6Es attacked even though two had inoperable designators (the working designators guided the bombs dropped by the others). Given the great success of laser-guided bombs in the war, one lesson was that strike fighters such as the F/A-18 needed laser designators of their own, to be fitted internally so that they did not detract from bomb-carrying capacity (a pod may occupy a bomb rack position). Even among the laser-designator aircraft, not all were equal. Only the F-117A and the pod-equipped F-15E had auto-tracking lasers that could faithfully follow airplane maneuvers. Otherwise a second crewman is needed to keep the laser on target as the bomb falls.

Quite aside from any political factors, the limitation on precision-bombing resources made it essential that strikes be planned on a surgical basis, and that weapons be brought back if targets could not be identified. That generally meant visual identification, since the most precise weapons attacked targets that had to be designated visually. Bad weather could therefore virtually shut down the strategic attacks. Weather that was worse than usual cost the air campaign about a week (low clouds, predicted 18 percent of the time, were actually encountered 39 percent of the time; they prevented the force from striking 40 percent of its primary targets in the first ten days). Tomahawks, the principal all-weather precise weapons, were used extensively to keep up the pressure when weather precluded aircraft strikes. In all, 284 Tomahawks were fired, with an average success rate of 80 percent.

Through about the first ten days, it was claimed that 80 percent of all strike missions had reached their targets. That was incorrectly interpreted to mean that 80 percent of Iraqi targets had been destroyed. The figure really meant that 80 percent of planned attacks had been conducted. If about 90 percent of all laser-guided weapons hit their targets, about 72 percent of the highest-priority targets were hit in these strikes (some were re-strikes, so the overall percentage hit was higher).[14] What no one could know with any certainty was whether individual hits had destroyed their targets. That was particularly true of bombs dropped into hardened buildings, whose structures would remain standing even if their contents were quite thoroughly destroyed.

Because they were in limited supply bombs had to be used efficiently.[15] That often meant relying on secondary damage (for example, fires lit by bombs) for most of the desired effect. That would not have been possible with the more numerous but infinitely less accurate weapons of previous air wars. For example, hits on the computer control station and electrical plant of a petrochemical complex touched off extensive fires, which the Iraqis could not extinguish. The result was that by the end of hostilities the Iraqi oil industry had largely been destroyed.

The limited supply of precision weapons was assigned on a target-priority basis. Before they could be assigned, some difficult targets absorbed surprisingly large numbers of sorties and bombs. For example, the attack on Iraqi bridges began early in the campaign, prosecuted mainly by F/A-18s dropping unguided bombs. Photos of the bridges suggest that, as in Vietnam, hits were frequently insufficient to drop spans. One report suggested that nothing short of a hard-target guided bomb could do the job properly. Considerable improvements in bombing accuracy (in delivering unguided bombs) did not suffice to solve this problem.

Overall, the coalition air force always found itself badly limited in its ability to assess the effect of its strikes. The precision weapons often used televisionlike cameras to display their targets for designation, and the videos produced that way were often the only way of doing bomb damage assessment (BDA). Unfortunately, most such videos merely confirmed that a weapon had hit, and that it had caused some damage (indicated, for example, by blast emerging from a building's wall). It was also important to be able to revisit such a target within a few hours in hopes that more could be learned, for example, from apparent repair efforts. The air force found itself with far too few RF-4s for strike reconnaissance or BDA. Much of this work was done by seventeen navy F-14 fighters carrying TARPS pods. They covered all of Kuwait as well as Iraqi targets as assigned (the F-14s could range over most of Iraq). These TARPS aircraft were so important that eventually the S-3 flights to Riyadh were valued at least as much for the TARPS images they brought as for the ATO frags they carried away. This issue is separate from the lack of real-time reconnaissance that limited the effects of the great Scud hunt described below.

Satellites were also used for BDA, but they were limited because they only passed over the target areas at set times. If that was too many hours after the strike, the Iraqis had time to simulate bomb damage in hopes of avoiding a later attack. One trick, adopted after the first week of the air war, was to time Tomahawk missile strikes for an hour before an expected satellite pass, so that the satellite could do effective and timely BDA. Air strikes were far too numerous for such timing to apply to any of them. One peculiarity of the situation was that the satellite images passed through Washington en route to CentCom, whereas products of local air reconnaissance did not. As a result, during the week or so before the ground offensive there was a considerable dispute between CentCom and some of the Washington intelligence analysts as to the extent of damage to Iraqi tanks.

There was some electronic BDA, mainly by navy EP-3Es flying out of Bahrain and by EA-3s flying from Jeddah. S-3Bs were sometimes able to use their new ESM equipment to detect whether missile sites were or were not operating. They also used their new ISAR radar for the first time in combat.[16] The new ESM on board the S-3Bs was very effective in verifying that air-defense sites had been knocked out. The EP-3Es and EA-3s were the main electronic surveillance aircraft available to CentCom.

One other electronic measure is worth mentioning here. Before the war, the air force had developed a radar-equipped airplane, JSTARS (joint services tactical airborne radar system), capable of detecting and tracking individual vehicles on roads. Both JSTARS (E-8As) under test in August 1990 were deployed to the Gulf. They orbited under fighter cover near the Kuwaiti and Iraqi borders. For example, it was JSTARS data that showed that the flow of Iraqi trucks toward Kuwait and the forces there had been cut from 20,000 tons per day to about 2,000 tons per day. JSTARS detected the Iraqi buildup leading to the border battle at Khafji (see Chapter 10). JSTARS was developed specifically to coordinate the deep (second echelon) attacks required to prosecute the U.S. Army's new AirLand Battle doctrine of the 1980s. The two aircraft in Saudi Arabia were prototypes operated in part by civilian contractor personnel. They were assigned to Saudi Arabia after very successful tests in Europe during the fall of 1990. Each

JSTARS airplane combined a side-looking precision radar (to detect vehicles on the ground) with airborne radar operators and analysts. Earlier airborne vehicle-surveillance radars, such as those carried by TR-1s, sent all their data down to ground stations for evaluation. JSTARS was superior in that it could support a ground force that did not include a ground analysis station.

The air force also deployed TR-1s (modified versions of the U-2) to Akrotiri in Cyprus; presumably they overflew western Iraq, from whence the Scud missiles were launched toward Israel. The TR-1 carries a long-range imaging radar, and presumably it operated somewhat like an E-8, albeit without the onboard analysis capability.

One great surprise of the air campaign was the complete absence of self-inflicted aircraft losses (blue-on-blue). It is tempting to ascribe the latter to vastly better command and control, capable of disentangling a complex air picture. It seems more realistic to assume that, fighting a relatively immobile opponent, aircraft could be assigned relatively rigid lists of targets, centrally controlled, so that interlopers were relatively easy to detect. The ATO, AWACS, and a rigid rule of engagement interlopers (ROE) were all very important.

It was probably even more vital that antiaircraft responsibility was limited to fighters, which were subject to fairly tight control. Antiaircraft guns and missiles, much more difficult to control, were all but prohibited from firing. For example, the two Iraqi Mirages that were shot down by the Saudi F-15 had been tracked for some time by a Hawk missile battery, which was denied permission to fire due to the proximity of the pursuing Saudi F-15. The mass of light antiaircraft weapons on board ships in the Gulf carried a particularly dangerous possibility of shooting down friendly aircraft. Those installed hurriedly to improve ship self-protection were not coordinated with any overall system that might have precluded firing on misidentified friendly aircraft.

CENTAF imposed rigid rules of engagement to avoid accidental fighter-on-fighter combat; it was always afraid that a U.S. airplane would shoot down a coalition fighter of a type also used by Iraq. Control was exerted in two ways. Each fighter had to obtain two independent forms of electronic identification before obtaining a positive approval from an E-3 AWACS control airplane. Navy E-2s fed the AWACS with radar data, but they did not have the authority to approve engagements. The F-15 has two forms of electronic identification besides IFF (NCTR, noncooperative recognition based on jet engine turbine or compressor blade rate and another, classified, system); the F-14 is limited to a long-range TV and IFF; the F/A-18 has NCTR. The air force therefore assigned only F-15s to the main overland combat air patrol (CAP) stations. The navy initially had the overwater CAP stations. Since the Iraqi air force chose only once to fly seaward, the air force F-15s had the opportunities to make most of the kills. Many navy pilots believed that the F-14s had no air-to-air opportunities because the Iraqis fled whenever they detected the radiation of their distinctive AWG-9 radar (which had also been used on board Iranian F-14s during the Iran-Iraq War). Late in the war the navy was given responsibility for CAP stations in the northern Persian Gulf.[17]

This system of ROE was relatively cumbersome, but it functioned well enough in a sky filled with friendly fighters, against a fairly unaggressive enemy air force. The appropriate lesson is probably that we still have not solved the blue-on-blue problem for the more likely future situation in which the enemy will be substantially more active.

Problems would have arisen, for example, had the Iraqis chosen (or had they been able) to attack during the later phase of the war, when aircraft had to be assigned to fluid, transient ground targets, so that it was much more difficult to know where they would be. By that time, however, the Iraqi Air Force was essentially gone, either dead or seeking asylum in Iran, so that air forces could generally assume that any aircraft they saw were friendly.

One surprise was that the weapons were less lethal than many had expected. The reliable electronics made them remarkably accurate, but accuracy did not always assure that a given target had been destroyed completely. This is not entirely unexpected: a modern 2,000-lb bomb is not inherently much more lethal than a 2,000-lb bomb dropped in 1943.[18] One reason for limited lethality is that U.S. and NATO forces (and, by extension, allied forces equipped with our weapons) are largely designed to fight a particular sort of war, against a Soviet or Warsaw Pact army pushing across Europe. In such a war, the main targets are vehicles and temporary fortifications. The main dug-in targets are concrete aircraft hangarettes. To the extent that there are strategic targets at all, they are secondary and may well be attacked in a later nuclear phase.

In Iraq, however, the situation was very different. The United States and its allies would be the attackers. The air offensive had to soften Iraqi forces for the ground war, and it therefore had to be directed against numerous bunkers, many of them built up during the lengthy Iran-Iraq War. Merely finding bunkers had to be a major problem. Evaluating damage to them must have been nearly impossible. Matters were certainly not improved by the absence of recently retired reconnaissance systems, particularly the SR-71. Thus the lesson of the importance of bomb damage assessment, which is taught by every air war, has been reinforced in this one.[19]

Perhaps the most significant bunkers of all, the deeply buried command bunkers built to house Saddam Hussein himself, were most symbolic of the problem. Whatever the rationale for attacking or not attacking Saddam Hussein himself, it is certainly arguable that a direct and credible physical threat to him was the only realistic deterrent. It might be argued further that only by denying Saddam his deeply buried command bunker could he be exposed to the likely fury of Iraqis unwilling to share defeat with him. Thus the ability to destroy such bunkers would have offered important advantages. It was most unlikely that any single 2,000-lb weapon would penetrate to their depth, let alone destroy them. Ironically, the deep-bunker problem had been solved as early as 1944, in the form of heavy thick-cased bombs capable of accelerating to supersonic speed as they fell and then of surviving a trip through up to 80 ft of earth, then detonating beneath their targets. These bombs could be carried by contemporary heavy bombers and by their early nuclear successors. In the West, the only survivor of this generation is the B-52.[20]

The problem seems to have been understood early in the campaign; an urgent request went out for a bunker-busting, laser-guided bomb. A 5,000-pounder, GBU-28, capable of penetrating 30 ft of dirt and concrete was developed. Two were rushed to the theater in time to be dropped by F-111s on a major Iraqi command bunker on the last morning of the war. At present such weapons can be delivered only by the F-111.

The brief naval war provided another example of limited lethality. Several Iraqi craft, including ex-Kuwaiti fast attack boats, were engaged and hit by British helicopters carrying Sea Skua missiles. There was no question that they had been put out of action, but it also appears that they were not sunk. That is a general problem of modern antiship missiles: they hit and often they disable, but they do not sink. That is enough at present, since the ships generally have centralized command/control systems and cannot really function after taking superstructure (particularly bridge) hits. However, the next generation of patrol boats and ships will probably have more distributed and more survivable systems, and any hit that does not sink them may well also fail to disable.

There was also an issue of lethality against land targets. The air force developed a hard-target killing bomb (I-2000 or BLU-109) specifically to attack hard aircraft shelters in Eastern Europe. It turned out to be quite effective against the same sort of target in Iraq. The navy had no such requirement; it generally expected to hit softer targets. In the Kuwait war it found its Mk 80 series bombs and Walleye guided weapons ineffective against the Iraqi bunkers (typically two Mk 84 laser-guided bombs on the roof and a Walleye on the armored door produced no great effect). On the other hand, an I-2000 would not be effective against many softer targets. The lesson for the future is that a broader mix of weapons will be needed almost everywhere.

Saddam Hussein failed to conduct any effective offensive air campaign of his own. A single night attempt to raid Saudi Arabia was turned back after the strike escorts were shot down. The Iraqis were not, however, entirely passive. They fired Scud ballistic missiles at Israel, Saudi Arabia, and Bahrain. The missiles were grossly inaccurate, and they accomplished little. Their only real menace was chemical or nuclear attack, and apparently the United States was assured by the Soviets that Iraqi Scuds could not carry either type of warhead. As a consequence, the Scuds were considered a minor sort of threat, and it appears that little of the first-night ATO was devoted to destroying them. That proved an expensive mistake.

Scuds mattered because they had immense political impact. That translated to very real military impact, in a way that the targeters seem not to have anticipated. Every Scud that fell on a Saudi Arabian city was visible evidence that the coalition forces had failed to shield the kingdom, and therefore that the decision to fight Saddam Hussein had been wrong. Every Scud that fell in Israel raised the cry for retaliation. It was quite obvious from the beginning that most forms of retaliation would entail military actions that the populations of the Arab members of the coalition would find hard to accept. At the least, it would be difficult for governments that had been so active in their anti-Israeli rhetoric to assist Israelis in killing Arabs.

In both cases, a Scud attack was so visible that it could not be explained away. Worse, the attacks were broadcast on television worldwide at a time when virtually all details of military operations in the Gulf area were necessarily being kept secret. Thus these events could not be submerged in news of larger events. Reporters confined to Riyadh, for example, could describe only the daily briefings and the nightly Scud attacks. The Scud attacks gained personal significance every time a reporter was urged to put on a gas mask because a missile was incoming. Hints that the Scuds could not possibly carry chemical warheads were automatically discounted, particularly after the Israelis said just the opposite.

Thus it became crucial to neutralize the Scuds. As in any other sort of strategic missile warfare, there were two complementary approaches: counterforce and direct defense. Counterforce in this case meant destroying the missiles before they could be used. It failed miserably, as indeed it had to, given the small number of Scud launchers and the extent to which they could be concealed and dispersed. Direct defense meant providing a useful antimissile weapon to protect the major targets. Fortunately the Patriot antiaircraft missile was adaptable to this task. Ironically, Patriot had been designed, many years before, soon after the Soviets had first fielded the Scud. Initially it had a limited antimissile capability. That potential was only developed into a useful capability during the 1980s.[21]

Patriot could not reach an incoming Scud far enough out to deflect it altogether. Nor could it generally destroy a Scud altogether by fusing its warhead (one reason was that too many Scuds turned out to have dud warheads). Thus even an intercepted Scud produced damaging debris. Remarkably few people, however, were killed. The sole, very sad exception, was the last Scud to fall on Saudi Arabia, which killed twenty-eight soldiers. It was the only such Scud not to have been intercepted. Ironically, the missiles of the battery that would have been involved were being upgraded for improved antimissile performance. Patriot's success was a powerful pointer toward a need for future longer-range antimissile systems, particularly for use when an enemy could not fire many missiles in quick succession.

The Iraqis had two quite different types of launcher: an elaborate fixed site, and a truck carrying an erector-launcher. The fixed sites were well known, and at the outbreak of war it was thought that they accounted for most of the Scuds. They were promptly attacked and were counted as largely destroyed.

Unfortunately, these attacks did not eliminate most of the Scuds. The Iraqis had numerous mobile launchers, and these vehicles did not look too different from other semi-trailers on Iraqi roads. They could indeed be seen when missiles were being launched, but that happened only when an airplane chanced to be nearby.

Before the war it was assumed that a Scud launching was a relatively cumbersome affair. The weapon had to be erected and fueled just before launching. The launch site had to be surveyed and weather balloons launched to measure winds aloft, which would affect the missile as it rose through the lower atmosphere. Given a few hours, a good crew could hope to hit a target reasonably well. This sort of procedure, however, made the Scud crew quite vulnerable to air attack. An erect missile made a quite visible target. Iraqi crews well understood the problem, and they seem to have learned to erect and fire their missiles very quickly. The missiles fell quite erratically, but then again a hit anywhere in the target urban area was considered acceptable.

The campaign was not too different from the campaign against the German V-2s in 1944–45; Scud itself is a direct descendant of the German missile.[22] The Germans initially wanted to store and launch V-2s from massive concrete emplacements. The emplacements were visible, and they were hit hard from the air. The Germans soon discovered that a V-2 could be fired from a simple steel table, erected into position by a truck-mounted crane. The mobile launchers were virtually impossible to find, and the V-2 threat was eliminated only when the storage and manufacturing facilities were overrun.

The great Scud hunt failed because the Scuds were really vulnerable only at the outset of the war, when they were concentrated and ready to move out. Presumably their bunkers were unknown or, at the least, considered relatively unimportant. Once the Scuds had dispersed, they were almost impossible to find. However, the political impact of Scud hits was such that the coalition had to make every attempt to find and kill them. Scud attacks absorbed at least 100 to 150 strike sorties per day, about 10 percent of the total available. On some days as many as 200 additional Scud attack sorties were mounted. Scud spotting absorbed more. The air force later stated that the resources spent on the Scud hunt were equivalent to about a week of air effort.

The great problem was the lack of sustained real-time reconnaissance over Iraq. The JSTARS radars could detect every moving vehicle, but they could not readily distinguish a Scud carrier from, say, an oil tanker. The air force was largely reduced to reacting to observed Scud launches (which could be detected by satellite or AWACS). By the time the orbiting F-15s, F-16s, or A-6Es arrived, the launchers were already well away. Sometimes they could be tracked down, and then the bombers tried to follow them to the storage areas where several mobile launchers huddled together. In this way they did considerable damage, but they could not shut down the Scud attacks.

Similarly, some bombers dropped scatterable land mines over road areas frequented by mobile Scud launchers. The hope was that the Scud vehicles would have to stay on the roads, from which the mines could be cleared relatively easily, and out of the surrounding countryside. They might therefore become easier to find. However, they were not found easily enough.

Moreover, the Iraqis seem to have been successful in decoying coalition pilots by constructing fake launchers. They did not find it terribly difficult, either, to repair the fixed launchers, which were not very elaborate. Nor did they find it hard to manufacture new mobile launchers. A Scud just did not make great demands on the device setting it up for firing, just as its ancestor, the V-2, had not in 1944.

The great and largely failed Scud hunt carried a particularly important implication for future U.S. defense policy. The stealthy B-2 bomber has been sold mainly as the only way of finding and killing "strategic relocatable targets," that is, Soviet mobile land-based ballistic missiles. The argument is that only a stealthy airplane can survive long enough at sufficiently high altitude to make a sustained search for such weapons. A cruise missile must be sent toward a predetermined target. A conventional bomber, which depends for its survival on flying below most enemy radars, cannot fly high enough to search.

The great Scud hunt was a miniature version of exactly this mission. After the Iraqi air-defense system had been thoroughly wrecked, all coalition airplanes were, for all practical purposes, stealthy. The Iraqis did not know that they were present. They could look as long as they liked, without any great difficulty. In fact, while searching they could use such distinctly nonstealthy sensors as imaging radars; they could do better than a B-2. And yet they very largely failed.

One other surprise, this one largely logistical, deserves mention here. The war required most airplanes to fly very long distances, so large numbers of tankers had to be used. Many of the air force's tankers had been bought primarily to support a small number of strategic bombers, each of which required a great deal of fuel. Naturally these tankers had only a single boom, so they could handle only one bomber at a time. Tactical air strikes, however, involve large numbers of airplanes, each of which has limited capacity. A formation trying to fuel together from a single-boom tanker finds airplanes running low while others are still awaiting their turn. The navy, at least, found the situation very distressing; it often had to use KA-6D "buddy" tankers alongside the air force's tankers. It also found the RAF's three-hose tankers preferable to the air force's. To further complicate matters, naval aircraft were not fully compatible with the standard air force boom system, so some of the air force tankers were modified to suit. The air force, therefore, ended the war with two largely incompatible tanker forces.[23]

10

The Test: Khafji

SADDAM HUSSEIN could not passively accept the destruction of his country by air attack. He always believed that, whatever the firepower the coalition could deploy, its members lacked the stomach for ground warfare on the scale his army had survived during the war with Iran. His first hope, then, was to achieve an early and telling success on the ground, perhaps analogous to the Tet Offensive during the Vietnam War. As in Tet, it would not matter whether, in the end, his troops triumphed in any conventional sense. It would matter much more that they caused severe casualties. He attacked a small abandoned northern Saudi town called Khafji. The battle that followed did not seem very intense (mainly because the Iraqi attack was so incompetently mounted), but it was extremely significant. It pointed clearly to just how the ground war would go.

When the air war began, the U.S. Marines and allied Arab forces were dug in near the Saudi coast and the border with Kuwait. Saddam personally planned an attack that he hoped would draw in a substantial marine force, perhaps a battalion, and either destroy or capture it. His objective, Khafji, was the only junction on the coastal road leading to Kuwait City. The coastal road there runs through marshland, and the rise at Khafji is relatively easy to defend. It is not clear whether the Iraqis knew that the town had been abandoned.

Because the coastal road was so important, the Kuwaiti side of the border was strongly held, in this case by one of the better and larger Iraqi divisions, the 5th Mechanized.[1] The corps of which this division was part planned a simultaneous assault by three divisions. A small frontal attack would draw marines into the town and pin them down. Then they would be hit by a strong tank force coming from the west. They would be cut off by troops landed by an Iraqi convoy headed by a T43-class minesweeper (and including some of the ex-Kuwaiti missile attack boats). Any attempt to relieve them would be harried by commandos landed from small boats.

The attack began on 29 January. The three attacking columns (three brigades of the 5th Mechanized Division) were spaced out between the coast to the "elbow" in the Kuwaiti-Saudi border, 60 miles to the west. The plan called for the columns to the west to penetrate the border and turn east toward the coast, to meet the third column that would run down the coastal road directly into Khafji. Further brigades assigned to the attack started 12 to 24 hours late and never really entered the battle.

Overall, the attack plan was fairly complicated; it required a high degree of coordination, which the Iraqis could not supply. The attackers were first detected (and recognized as attackers, rather than as logistical convoys) while they were forming up on the Iraqi side of the border. JSTARS radar aircraft operating inside Saudi Arabia recognized the dispositions (and thus, in effect, could detect enemy intentions). They could also count the approaching vehicles in each of the three separate attacks. This was quite a new capability for the U.S. forces.

Iraqi POWs captured in this battle were surprised to encounter U.S. forces so close to the border. They apparently expected to meet only Saudis. The Tet Offensive aspect of the plan seems to have been to trap U.S. forces drawn north to rescue the Saudis in Khafji. The Iraqis' ignorance of troop dispositions quite close to the border, in a sector of considerable importance to them, must have suggested to U.S. planners that deception (which was very important in the ground campaign to come) would not be too difficult to enforce.

One Iraqi tank brigade ran down along the border and behind the berm on the Saudi side of the border. It collided with the light armored infantry battalion of the 1st Marine Division, about 50 to 60 miles from the coast. There was a running gun battle at the border, marine and air force aircraft hitting the tanks. The marine vehicles on the Saudi side of the border were LAVs, very lightly armored vehicles never intended to engage battle tanks. However, the marines found that their night sights made it possible for them to outrange and destroy the Iraqi tanks that survived the air attacks. This was the battle during which an A-10 destroyed an LAV with a Maverick missile. A second LAV was killed by an Iraqi tank.

A second Iraqi brigade tried to approach the border about halfway between the first battle and the coast, near the Wafra oil field. It engaged the 2d Light Armored Infantry (LAV) battalion of the 2d Marine Division. Hit hard, it stalled and then retreated. During this battle, a marine corporal managed to destroy two Iraqi tanks with TOW missiles carried by his LAV.[2]

The third brigade (mechanized infantry) attacked Khafji itself, which was held by Saudis and Qataris with U.S. Marines in support. The town was struck from the west by tanks of the Iraqi 15th Mechanized Regiment. They ran directly into a Qatari tank unit equipped with AMX 30s, and the unit was wiped out.[3] Meanwhile the accompanying mechanized infantry entered Khafji itself. That first night the allies chose to hit the tanks, which were still outside the town, rather than begin house-to-house fighting inside Khafji.

Air and vehicle attacks destroyed about eighty of the Iraqi tanks on the border and outside Khafji.

The attack on Khafji itself included an element of deception, apparently planned by the attacking brigade. For some time Iraqi troops had been heavily leafletted from the air. They were called upon to surrender. In the case of tanks, the intention to surrender would be signaled by approaching with turret reversed. In this case the Iraqi tanks approached the Saudi and Qatari special forces troops on the border with their turrets pointed backwards. The accompanying Iraqi infantry had their hands up. As soon as the Saudis emerged from their foxholes to accept the defectors, the tanks turned their turrets around and opened fire. The Iraqi infantry drew weapons from their boots and they also began to fire.[4]

It was never entirely clear whether this deception was intended as more than an attempt to gain a temporary advantage. There was some speculation that its real purpose was to convince coalition troops to fire upon future Iraqi defectors. The Iraqi leadership may have reasoned that word of such incidents, passed within the Iraqi lines, would convince troops that defection was pointless. Certainly there was later abundant evidence that, almost from the first, the Iraqi leadership feared that its troops would bolt.[5]

The survivors of the original attacking force held Khafji, but they were not alone. A U.S. Marine reconnaissance team remained inside the town, directing fire against the invaders. The corporal leading the team cleverly called in artillery fire only when coalition aircraft were overhead, so that the Iraqis would think that the airplanes, not troops on the ground, were involved.

The allied troops were in no hurry to retake the town at a high cost, particularly after they had cut off any hope of an Iraqi withdrawal. It was significant, however, that the Iraqis never managed to defend themselves in anything approaching house-to-house combat. They were generally happy to surrender to Saudi troops driving through the town and spraying houses with machine gun fire. The Iraqis did manage to destroy three Saudi armored cars with RPG-7 antitank rockets. After two days and at least sixty-five deaths (mainly resulting from the destruction of armored personnel carriers), the surviving 400 Iraqi troops in Khafji surrendered. Some of the prisoners claimed that they had advanced only at the point of their officers' guns.

There was also physical evidence of Iraqi incompetence. Many of their armored vehicles were found abandoned. Although troops in towns generally will dismount from their vehicles, they will always leave a driver and a machine gunner to provide a base of fire. In this case, no one stayed; destroyed vehicles were often empty. By way of contrast, the destroyed Saudi vehicles still had many of their crewmen inside: they had fought and died at their places, as they should have.

The two seaborne forces were both destroyed well offshore. Because they were so much slower than larger ships, the commandos in their little boats (comparable to, but larger than, Boston Whalers) set out first. These boats were detected by the radar on board a British frigate in the Gulf, and Lynx helicopters were sent out to search. They began to pick boats off using their Sea Skua missiles, and the battle was then joined by other helicopters (further Lynxes, Sea King Commandos, and U.S. LAMPS IIIs), by A-6 Intruder attack bombers from the U.S. carriers, and by British Jaguars. Many of the helicopters of the second group used their door machine guns and even hand grenades. Of seventeen small boats, fourteen were sunk and three were driven ashore.

The convoy carrying a heavily reinforced Iraqi regimental combat team appeared the next day. As in the previous case, it was detected and engaged by the British frigates in the northern Gulf area. The convoy consisted of the Iraqi T43-class minesweeper, three ex-Kuwaiti TNC 45–class fast-attack boats, and three Polnocny-class landing ships. As in the previous engagement, the attack began when Lynxes firing Sea Skua missiles stopped the convoy by hitting the bridges and superstructures of the ships. The Polnocnys were hit by British Jaguar fighter-bombers, and the TNC 45s by Rockeye cluster bombs dropped by U.S. A-6s from the carriers. Not all of these ships were sunk (the T43 survived quite far into the war), but the attack was broken up. Secondary explosions seemed to show that all of the ships were carrying troops and explosives.

The marines lost eleven men. It later turned out that seven of them had been killed when a U.S. Maverick missile hit their light armored vehicle during the night armored battle. Another Maverick destroyed a Saudi armored car.

Saddam Hussein proclaimed a great victory.

Small as it actually was, the battle proved most enlightening. Before Khafji, the U.S. Army believed that it alone could expect to fight at night, and that the Iraqis lacked any real night vision capability. Khafji demonstrated that, in fact, the Iraqi Army had bought some useful equipment, though probably not on a large scale.[6]

On the other hand, Khafji demonstrated clearly that the Iraqis lacked the ability for the sort of coordination necessary to make efficient use of their equipment. The battle plan for Khafji, like the plans drawn up late in the Iran-Iraq War, was reasonably sophisticated. However, no allowance was made for any sort of deviation. There was no feedback channel by means of which the command could tell how well the attack was going. A more flexible command structure might have been able to modify the attack plan to take account of early surprises and of poorly understood enemy (that is, coalition) dispositions. Instead, Iraqi forces continued toward their attack positions even after the logic of the plan had been overthrown. The plan was not modified when some of the attacking units failed to reach their attack positions. Failure was, moreover, caused not only by the superiority of the defenders but also by the ineptitude of the Iraqis themselves. Most of the forces that should have taken part in the action never appeared at all.

Saddam seems not to have imagined that the attack could fail. He proclaimed success, not so much because he needed a victory to boost public morale, but because without any evidence he really assumed that his plan had won. It followed that he would be unable, or at least unlikely, to detect major weaknesses in his other military plans. After Khafji, General Schwarzkopf could rest easier because he could expect to exploit the gross Iraqi vulnerability in the west without too much fear of being led into a trap. In a larger sense, Saddam had demonstrated a credulity that made operational deception a particularly attractive option.

The battle showed that even a good Iraqi Army unit lacked much will to fight. The infantry that took Khafji and then retreated surrendered after only a few casualties. The tank units did not know how to fight, and they were massacred by tanks and then by Marine Corps helicopters and Harriers. Many of them did manage to get off a few rounds of antiaircraft fire, but totally without effect.[7]

Khafji was Saddam's only attempt at a ground offensive. No other probes were mounted, although there was some random artillery and rocket fire along the border. Saddam learned that his forces lacked the ability to take the offensive, but he still presumably thought that they could inflict severe losses on an invader, as in the Iran-Iraq War. Thus his failure in the initial border battle would not have convinced him to abandon the war. On the other hand, by deterring him from further border probes, the Iraqi disaster did make it most unlikely that the coalition's movement and buildup toward the ultimate ground offensive would be detected in advance.

Perhaps most important of all, the battle demonstrated that the Arab allies, in this case the Saudis and Qataris, who had never really had much of a military reputation, definitely had the will to fight, to risk losses in taking back a town. Moreover, their own success would surely encourage them to achieve even better performance in the coming major battle.

Then there was the loss to friendly fire. The air campaign had managed to avoid any such problems, but only because the aircraft were so rigidly controlled and because so few Iraqis were in the air at any one time. Ground combat was necessarily more confusing. Vehicles were far too numerous to be protected by the sort of rigid control applied to airplanes. Moreover, situations developed far too rapidly. At night, the problems inherent in close air support were exacerbated by a lack of FLIRs (forward-looking infrared devices) on board close-support aircraft, particularly A-10s. A-10 pilots made up for this deficiency by using the IR seekers of their Maverick missiles as FLIRs. Unfortunately the seekers presented pilots with considerably less detailed images than more conventional FLIRs. Vehicles were difficult to distinguish. The only remedy available at the time was a night-visible recognition marking made of strips of fluorescent tape. The other possibility was to try always to engage the enemy at maximum range, so that air support would be attacking far from friendlies. Further allied losses to friendly fire could not be avoided, but they were minimized.

11

The Seaward Flank

SEA POWER tends to act invisibly but powerfully. By the time hostilities began, the coalition had already benefited enormously from U.S. domination of the world ocean, which had made it possible for the United States and its allies to transport huge forces over vast distances. That same sea power had cut off most of Saddam Hussein's supplies of military spare parts and other basic materiel, and thus may well have been crucial in precluding him from repairing his damaged national air-defense system.

Moreover, unlike the coalition's fixed air bases and other facilities in Saudi Arabia and the Gulf states, the carriers and other ships in the Gulf and in the Red Sea were relatively difficult for Saddam's forces to attack. The coalition had no way of knowing, before war broke out, that Saddam would be unable to use his relatively large offensive forces to hit those fixed facilities. A single gas warhead on board a Scud, for example, might well have put an air base out of action. In the event of such attacks, the only land-based coalition offensive units likely to survive would have been B-52s at distant air bases (beyond Scud range). However, the carriers and the Tomahawk ships and submarines, all of them mobile, might well have been immune simply because Saddam lacked the means to locate them and to track them well enough to attack them.[1]

The U.S. ships in the Gulf differed from forces ashore in another important way. They were U.S. sovereign territory. Bases ashore, no matter who operated from them, were ultimately under the control of the host government. The U.S. ships could therefore stow weapons that could not possibly have been allowed ashore. The coalition repeatedly threatened Saddam with "terrible escalation" should he resort to chemical or biological weapons. In other contexts such language generally implies the possibility of nuclear retaliation.

The threats could only be realistic if the United States had usable nuclear weapons in the theater of operations. Nuclear weapons are special; governments do not lightly allow them to escape national control. Certainly the Saudis would not have welcomed U.S. nuclear weapons to their country. The fleet offshore solved the problem. For example, the cruiser *San Jacinto* was designated a "special weapons platform." That was interpreted by the press to mean that she was armed primarily with Tomahawk missiles rather than with antiaircraft weapons (the two can be fired from the same launcher), but "special weapons" more usually means nuclear. Thus the availability of powerful offensive naval forces in the theater made it possible for the United States credibly to threaten a degree of escalation that proved quite important to the coalition.[2]

The carriers also derived some advantages from their locations. Aircraft based on ships in the Red Sea (the *Saratoga* and *J.F. Kennedy*) could reach targets, such as the crucial H-2 and H-3 airfields, without flying over major concentrations of medium- and high-altitude Iraqi missiles; they faced only early warning radars and shoulder-fired weapons. This was a unique opening, and it was heavily used. It required a 5 1/2-hour flight, the navy bombers being tanked by the air force. Typically a carrier would launch twenty to thirty aircraft per strike package, twice a day, operating 18 hours on and 9 hours off (the two carriers overlapped their operations).

Carriers in the Persian Gulf enjoyed a different advantage: at a range of less than 200 nautical miles, they were closer to southern Iraq than any airfield ashore. Once the carriers were in position well up the Gulf, then, they could deliver very high sortie rates against targets such as Basra. The USS *Theodore Roosevelt*, in particular, achieved a very high sortie rate attacking the Republican Guard. Typical strike-package strengths for these operations were sixteen aircraft, and the bombers (A-6Es and F/A-18s) achieved very good accuracy using their bomb computers to direct unguided weapons against Iraqi troops. Initially it was not clear whether Iran would interfere with carrier operations, and considerable effort had to be expended to protect against possible flanking attacks from that country. In addition, there was what amounted to a naval roll-back campaign to clear the northern Gulf (for example, of Iraqi gunboats).

Carriers typically replenished every three to four days. They did not lose much operating time because their support ships could operate quite close by. That, in turn, was possible only because the Iraqi threats to coalition naval forces were so thoroughly demolished.

The system of command and control was set up during the U.N.–sponsored embargo. The U.S. Navy had operational control of all warships in the northern Persian Gulf, and also of warships in the Red Sea. The southern Persian Gulf was a Western European Union (WEU) responsibility, in theory under the admiral of the country that held the WEU chair. [3]

The sea, both the Persian Gulf and the Red Sea, flanked the land battle area. The northern Persian Gulf was the point of contact closest to such critical areas of Iraq as Basra, the center of control for Kuwait and southern Iraq. The most impressive naval contribution was clearly the massive air attack effort, described above, which could be mounted from places in the Gulf much closer to Iraq than the ground air bases in Saudi Arabia. Although the head of the Red Sea is fairly far from western Iraq, in fact there are few air bases in western Saudi Arabia, so carriers in the Red Sea were ideally placed to attack extreme western targets such as H-2 and H-3 as well as Baghdad itself.

Tomahawk missile firings from the ships and from some of

the submarines were really an essential part of the air campaign, particularly the initial break into the Iraqi air-defense system. Like the carrier air attacks, these weapons exploited the mobility of sea power to get into launch positions around the ends of much of the Iraqi air-defense system. Several Tomahawks, launched from the Mediterranean, flew through the weakly defended western border region. No Mediterranean country would have provided the base needed to make just that sort of attack. Although the submarines fired few Tomahawks, their launchings were an initial demonstration of an important capability in support of future air attacks on heavily defended targets.

To exploit the positions of the carriers, the aircraft had to fly over a chain of offshore islands and oil drilling platforms. All were occupied by Iraqi troops, and all were valuable observation points. They did not matter too much as long as Iraq possessed a large and active national radar system. However, as soon as the radars had been destroyed, the islands became quite important. Airplanes flying overhead could be seen well before they approached such targets as Basra and even Baghdad. Experience in Vietnam showed quite clearly that such visual sighting could be used to direct an effective national air-defense system. The observers had to be put out of action. That was done in a series of commando and frigate actions, in many cases involving troops landed by helicopter. As in the case of Khafji, quick Iraqi surrenders in these actions were valuable indicators of the likely future performance of the Iraqi Army.

This campaign began when the frigate *Nicholas* (carrying army special forces AHIP helicopters) and a Kuwaiti patrol boat cleared Iraqis from eleven oil platforms (from which small surface-to-air missiles had been launched) on 18 January: twenty-three Iraqis surrendered after five had been killed and three wounded. This action caused the Iraqis to begin to evacuate all of the offshore islands and the remaining platforms. Helicopter-borne naval special forces teams secured other islands; in one case the Iraqis spelled out "we surrender" in stones before they were even attacked. The frigate *Curts* took fifty-one prisoners when she captured Jazirat Qurah Island. None of these engagements was terribly significant in itself, but the net effect was to clear the Iraqis from their observation posts in the northern Gulf—a worthwhile endeavor.

A more subtle naval contribution was the classic one of tying down large ground forces. As in so many other cases, it takes many more or less fixed units to deal with the possible attacks a seaborne force can mount. As discussed earlier, the afloat marines certainly held down many Iraqi divisions, which otherwise might have been able to mount an effective defense against the ground thrust up along the coastal road into Kuwait City. Moreover, the marines presented a viable alternative to the long left hook that the army ultimately executed. Allied control of the Gulf made it quite practical for them to move up the Shatt-al-Arab and land in the Iraqi rear. The navy and marine commanders pressed hard for this option. That General Schwarzkopf chose not take it up does not invalidate it.

The amphibious operation depended on naval gunfire support. On 3 February the battleship USS *Missouri* began a bombardment of prefabricated concrete structures (bunkers) on the Kuwaiti coast. She was relieved by the USS *Wisconsin* on 6 February. On 8 February the *Wisconsin* supported a Marine Corps probe into southern Kuwait defenses.[4]

Throughout the war, the amphibious option had to be maintained—either as the feint it ultimately was, or as a live possibility. General Schwarzkopf seems to have vacillated on this several times. In January some marines apparently told the local reporter for National Public Radio that there would be no amphibious landing (he very wisely kept this information secret). However, the final decision against a landing was reportedly taken only a week before the ground offensive began.

The Iraqis had only a few ways to preclude such an operation. They began the war with a small fleet, including a few ex-Kuwaiti fast attack boats and a training frigate. The Iraqis had an unknown but probably large number of Exocet antiship missiles, which could be carried by their airplanes and their heavier helicopters. They also had a variety of other potential airborne ship-killing missiles. Ashore, they had Chinese-built Silkworm antiship missiles on mobile launchers. Finally, they had invested fairly heavily in mines.

Each of these threats had received what now seems ludicrously impressive prewar press coverage. There was a general belief that fast attack craft, properly handled, could endanger any large warship. From the beginning of the war, coalition destroyers and frigates, precisely the ships generally advertised as natural victims of inshore attack boats, operated in the northern Gulf, not least in hopes of ejecting the Iraqis from the offshore islands.

The British ships in the northern Gulf were all equipped with Lynx helicopters, which carried Sea Skua antiship missiles. Sea Skua is a small missile, and the helicopter that fires it has to remain within radar range of the target, illuminating it so that the missile can strike home. That is not too difficult if the target is unarmed, but before the war it was generally assumed that a high-speed boat equipped with a modern fire-control system could drive such a helicopter off before any damage could be done. Surely the Iraqi boats, both ex-Kuwaiti (which had good modern gun antiaircraft fire-control systems) and ex-Soviet, should have been able to dart out, fire their missiles, and throw the allied surface navy out of the northern Gulf.

In fact, the small fast boats proved useless. The better boats among them could lock their fire-control radars onto the British helicopters. However, as the boats accelerated they vibrated. Small movements by the helicopters threw off the boats' radars. The same movements did not throw off the helicopters' illuminating radars, and the missiles struck home. They were not very large missiles—the helicopters could carry only so much—but they were large enough to stop the boats in the water. Airplanes finished them off with unguided bombs, which they could drop easily because the damaged boats were defenseless.

The destruction of Iraqi ships is chronicled in Appendix G. By the end of the war, the allies claimed the destruction of thirteen Iraqi combatants, three auxiliaries, and three amphibious ships; they had damaged one combatant, four auxiliaries, and one amphibious ship.

In retrospect, the Iraqi Navy seems a joke, put out of business by massive coalition sea power. In fact, however, before being eliminated it had posed the same threat that many other Third World navies seem to present. The significance of the successful helicopter attack was that frigates could expect to deal with missile-armed fast attack boats before the latter could bring their weapons to bear. It is not clear to what extent these engagements prove that a light vibrating hull cannot support the sort of antiaircraft weapons system needed to protect that hull. Note, however, that the light missiles did not sink their targets: they made disabling hits. It would seem to follow that larger craft could have remained in action, since a single missile hit would not have damaged enough of the ship (that is, enough of her control positions) to disable. The craft sank because, once disabled, they were easy prey to airplanes carrying heavier weapons.

Then there was the airborne missile threat. At no time could it be discounted altogether because the Iraqi Air Force never really vanished, it merely became inactive. There was no concrete assurance that the Iraqis would not try a final push. After all, they had used air-launched Exocets through much of the Iran-Iraq War, including the nearly fatal attack on the USS *Stark*. The consequence was that the carriers in the Gulf had to maintain a constant combat air patrol, over and above the air patrols protecting Saudi Arabia. To this extent, Saddam's decision not to risk most of his air force in air-to-air combat had the side effect of reducing the air effort that could be mounted against him; aircraft on combat air patrol might otherwise have attacked Iraq.

The shore-based missile threat was more serious. Throughout the war, naval aircraft did their best to destroy the Silkworm launchers. However, as in the air campaign, one clear lesson was that small mobile launchers could never be fully accounted for. The Iraqis still had Silkworms at the end of the war. That was not to say that the missiles bought very much. Only two were fired, on 24 February at the USS *Wisconsin* while she shelled their coast. One fell into the water. The other was shot down by a Sea Dart fired by HMS *Gloucester*, a British missile destroyer escorting the battleship. Attack aircraft from the carriers destroyed the battery thus revealed.[5]

Saddam's most effective threat was the sea mine. Although he displayed a number of supposed locally developed mines at the Baghdad show in 1989, he actually seems to have had only four major types: the Italian Manta ground mine (locally modified to incorporate a magnetic sensor in a separate body floating above the basic acoustic mine body), a Soviet-designed but locally made moored contact mine, a Soviet-designed anti-invasion ground mine, and a Soviet-designed ground mine using a locally made case and Soviet electronics.[6] In addition to these the Iraqis placed land mines atop piles off the Kuwaiti coast in hopes of catching landing craft at high tide.

The planned Iraqi mining density along the Kuwaiti coast was 60 mines/nm for depths between 10 and 40 ft, 800 to 1,600 mines/ nm between the 10-ft line and the beach, and 3,200 to 6,400 mines (of much simpler type)/nm on the beach itself. Further mines were laid offshore. In fact, no mines were found on the beach, but the anti-invasion mines were laid in the intended density between the 10- and 40-ft depth marks.

Mine countermeasures were largely a U.S. and British responsibility. The flagship was the USS *Tripoli*, which carried six MH-53E sweeper helicopters. Responsibility for surface mine countermeasures rested with the Royal Navy. (The ships involved are listed in Appendix C.) In addition, several other navies, including the Royal Australian and Saudi, contributed mine disposal divers. The U.S. and British navies had already conducted mine countermeasures, mainly against Iranian contact mines, during the Iran-Iraq War. This time sweeping could not suffice, because it might well fail to pick up ground mines (that is, mines on the bottom triggered by a ship's magnetic, acoustic, or pressure field).[7] The slow, but unavoidable, choice was to hunt down the mines one by one, gradually clearing channels.

The main mine countermeasures technique seems to have been for U.S. minesweeping helicopters to conduct a precursor sweep for influence (magnetic and acoustic) mines. Often they were led by British Sea King helicopters (probably mainly to deal with any Iraqi small surface craft that might have interfered). The precursor or coarse sweep was intended to protect the sweepers/

hunters following from mines set to destroy them, rather than to attack larger ships. The hunters, most of them British, followed.

The sweepers/hunters and the helicopters were all quite vulnerable to Iraqi air or surface attack.[8] Their survival thus depended on the cover that the carriers and the surface combatants could provide from farther down the Gulf, outside the mined area. As the cleared area spread north, this cover was extended.

Five months of continuous prewar observation provided a good picture of where Saddam had been able to lay mines. Once the war began, attacks on Iraqi minelayers were a major mine countermeasure. The combination of a large prewar coalition naval presence in the Gulf and wartime attacks confined Iraqi mining to the northern Gulf.

These measures could not be completely successful. For example, the Iraqi *Spasilac*-class salvage tug *Aka* laid several mine fields during the war, and then hid inshore or up the Shatt-al-Arab. This minelayer was detected, largely by satellite sensors reporting to analysts in Washington. Their conclusions were relayed to the targeters in Riyadh, whose naval officers were responsible for attacking targets of particular naval interest. Unfortunately, the ATO drawn up in Riyadh was not well suited to attack targets that relocated within its 48-hour minimum cycle (between target detection, planning, and attack). In some cases, actual cycle time could be as long as five to six days. The salvage tug was repeatedly targeted, but it was not caught.

That might seem a minor quibble, but mines did inhibit coalition operations in the Gulf. To the extent that coalition movements tied down large Iraqi ground forces, mine countermeasures (beginning with the destruction of minelayers) were quite important to the success of the later ground offensive. The quicker and more complete the mine-clearance operation (that is, the less the Iraqi mining), the wider the area the marines' feint could have covered, and the larger the Iraqi ground force that could have been tied down. The ATO, which was well suited to a relatively static phase of the air war, was not well suited to the naval war, which was always much more dynamic.

Some ships and helicopters were equipped with mine-detection devices, such as high-resolution sonars. They were intended for mine evasion, not mine hunting. This technique was first tried in the Iran-Iraq War. Ships so fitted could avoid mines, and they could also guide other ships. On 3 February the USS *Nicholas* guided the battleship *Missouri* into firing position off the Kuwaiti coast in this way.[9]

Of course there were problems: on 18 February the USS *Tripoli* and the USS *Princeton* were both mined. The *Tripoli* struck a moored contact mine, which blew a 16 × 20-ft hole in her starboard bow. That damage, however, did not put her out of action. Helicopter sweeping continued unabated. The USS *Princeton*, an Aegis missile cruiser, was providing local air cover for the sweepers. She triggered a bottom (influence) mine while proceeding at high speed. She was badly damaged aft, losing half of her power plant. However, her missile system and battery were not put out of action. Had a significant air threat developed at the time, she could still have done her job. Since the air threat was not very intense at the time, she was towed out of the area for major repairs.[10]

These two incidents were widely reported as demonstrations of U.S. failures in mine countermeasures. However, it was not noticed that the U.S. Navy had been able to operate close inshore without any other losses from the beginning of the war. The mine-avoidance sonars, which were very much an emergency measure, worked quite well. Given the extent of Iraqi mining, a coalition fleet that had been grossly unsuccessful in mine clearance would have suffered much worse losses. There is little question, then, that the proposed amphibious operation could have been conducted.

After all, Saddam Hussein thought so, and he had every reason to seek evidence to the contrary. From his point of view, the mine threat failed. The amphibious threat was quite real.

12

The Mother of All Battles

SADDAM HUSSEIN repeatedly told his public that the ground contest for Kuwait would be the "Mother of All Battles," that his troops would inflict such heavy casualties that the coalition forces would withdraw in dismay. The reality was, of course, rather different. Saddam's generals were presumably unenthusiastic critics, but Saddam did get some warning from his former patrons, the Soviets. Uncomfortably aware that the ground war would probably be a humiliating disaster, the Soviets tried to broker a cease-fire. They failed because, unwilling to believe what was coming, Saddam Hussein refused to accept the unconditional terms the coalition (led by the United States) demanded. Saddam apparently hoped that he could end the war simply by withdrawing his forces from Kuwait, without either renouncing its annexation or paying for the damage they had done. That was unacceptable to the coalition because it left Saddam's forces intact.

In Saddam's political system, any humiliation might well be fatal. If defeat was inevitable, better to stand and fight and inflict some casualties on the enemy. If Iraq's army put up a good enough resistance, then Saddam might even emerge a sort of hero, having stood against so much of the world. The 100-hour coalition victory was so thorough that Saddam presumably lost even this consolation prize.

The outcome was quite surprising. No one had been able to estimate the degree to which Saddam's army had been broken by air attack. Nor had anyone guessed just how effective the U.S. assaults would be, even when they met serious resistance. Some Iraqi units did stand and fight, but they lost, and lost badly. Readers will recall that throughout the war, the president and senior military officers had constantly cautioned that, although progress up to that point had been very quick, some serious reverses probably lay ahead. These counsels reflected real intelligence data and real skepticism. For example, analysts in Washington, who had their own satellite and other data to hand, were quite doubtful of CentCom's claims of damage inflicted on Iraqi armor and artillery. It is not possible to check now, since so much of the area attacked never fell into allied hands.

Central Command began planning a military campaign to force Saddam out of Kuwait as early as September 1990. As in the case of the air campaign, it was an option, a possibility to be selected if Saddam refused to leave Kuwait. The great issue was always the same. Saddam's troops were digging in. The great equalizer that the United States would wield would be tactical air power, and that air power would be nearly useless against well dug-in troops. The question, then, was always how to force the Iraqis out into the open.

General Schwarzkopf's initial plan, in September, was to rush into western Kuwait, coming around the corner at which Kuwait meets Saudi Arabia and Iraq. He had limited forces, but they were reasonably mobile, and he was already building up a large air arm. The wadi forming the western border of Kuwait was a traditional invasion route. The general's hope was that the Iraqis would have to emerge from their bunkers to meet his incoming force, and that their movement would expose them to bombing. In retrospect it is not clear that the Iraqis would have had to come out, since the thrust toward Kuwait City would not necessarily have threatened any vital target. The Iraqis might well have been content to pull the attacking Americans into costly street fighting in Kuwait City itself. Certainly it would have been Saddam Hussein's view that the U.S. forces would have halted rather than risk so gruesome a contest.

Events soon overtook this plan. During the fall, as the force in Saudi Arabia was built up, the Iraqis fortified Kuwait, including the western border. There was no longer an easy way into Kuwait. Planners in XVIII Airborne Corps, the force in place in Saudi Arabia, now argued that it would take at least four divisions just to make the left hook. However, there was an attractive way *around* the Iraqi Army, and that way had the additional advantage of being one the Iraqis could not ignore. They would have to come out and fight or risk having their supply lines cut off. That was the deep left hook General Schwarzkopf chose in October 1990.[1]

The left hook was not, however, the only such option he had. The navy and marines argued forcefully for an amphibious thrust, not (as many imagined) onto the fortified Kuwaiti coast, but up the Shatt-al-Arab toward or beyond Basra. Such an operation would have been altogether feasible, and it would have placed a powerful force deep in the Iraqis' rear. Just like the deep left hook, it would have crushed Iraqi forces between allied armies. Unlike the deep hook, it would not have required as much logistical preparation in the Saudi desert, and so would not have risked betrayal by whatever air reconnaissance Saddam Hussein might have mounted. On the other hand, some form of left hook would still have been needed to cut off the escape of the Iraqis toward Baghdad. General Schwarzkopf vetoed the idea. Before the end of January the marines knew that quite probably they would be fighting mainly as ground troops, and that the amphibious fleet would perform a feint. The debate actually continued up to about a week before the ground war began.

For a time it seemed that the air campaign itself might be decisive. Certainly the daily briefings suggested to many in Washington that Iraq was being damaged so badly that it could not continue to fight. Only those in the field were aware that bomb tonnage was quite limited and that bomb damage assessment was almost impossible in the most crucial cases. As a long-time ground combat veteran, moreover, General Schwarzkopf was well aware

The ultimate enemy and the ultimate loser: Saddam Hussein. *(CNN)*

The ultimate winner: President George Bush visits marines in the Saudi desert, November 1990. President Bush won the diplomatic war. He also made the key decision to leave the war itself to Central Command. *(The White House—Susan Biddle)*

Remarkably, the defense establishment in Washington had the self-control not to involve itself in day-to-day military decisions. Here, Secretary of Defense Dick Cheney and the senior U.S. military officer, Gen. Colin Powell, Chairman of the Joint Chiefs of Staff, meet troops in Saudi Arabia, 21 December 1990. *(Department of Defense)*

Gen. H. Norman Schwarzkopf, the Central Command chief, visits troops in the Saudi desert. *(Department of Defense)*

The Central Command air component commander was Lt. Gen. Charles Horner. *(U.S. Air Force—K. Yearyean)*

The Central Command ground component commander was Lt. Gen. John Yeosock. *(U.S. Army—P. Ybanez)*

The two Central Command naval commanders, Vice Adm. Stanley R. Arthur (right) and his predecessor, Vice Adm. Henry H. Mauz, Jr., at the latter's change of command ceremony, 1 October 1990. *(U.S. Navy—Russo)*

Soldiers boarding transport for deployment overseas. Troops could be flown rapidly to Saudi Arabia but not so the ammunition and heavy equipment needed for combat. (*U.S. Army*—M. Hixson)

The problem of transporting materiel overseas was well understood prewar. The air force maintained ammunition on board Afloat Prepositioning Ships at Diego Garcia in the Indian Ocean. This is the lighter-aboard-ship (LASH) ship *American Veteran*. (*U.S. Navy*)

Carriers were the first U.S. forces to arrive in the Saudi area to defend against further Iraqi attack. The USS *Dwight D. Eisenhower* transits the Suez Canal, September 1990. (*U.S. Navy—F. Marquart*)

USS *Tarawa* tied up in Saudi Arabia alongside munitions being staged for U.S. and British forces during Operation Desert Storm. (*Les Farrell*)

These army vehicles are on a dock in Savannah, Georgia, awaiting their ship. The tracked vehicles are M2 Bradleys, armed with
25-mm guns. *(U.S. Navy—S. Allen)*

Even many helicopters had to go by sea. Cocooned CH-53s are
visible on board the M/V Maersk *Constellation*. *(John Bouvia)*

The merchant ships were vulnerable not only at sea but also in the ports at which they unloaded. Special U.S. Coast Guard port security units protected the ports against unconventional attackers, such as swimmers. The ship in the background is the flagship used by the navy during Desert Shield/Desert Storm, the USS *Blue Ridge*. *(U.S. Navy—E. Bailey)*

The U.S. Navy transported its mine countermeasures ships on board the float-on float-off ship *Super Servant 3*. Here she submerges for unloading. *(U.S. Navy—J. Roach)*

Through the fall of 1990, the United Nations sought to pressure Iraq to withdraw from Kuwait, mainly through an embargo. It had to be enforced by allied navies. Here a U.S. F-14 Tomcat from the USS *Independence* makes a pass over the Iraqi merchant ship *Zanubia*. *(John Bouvia)*

Surveillance was the key to a successful embargo. This is a P-3C Orion used for maritime patrol over the area. Other versions of the P-3 provided essential electronic surveillance. *(John Bouvia)*

The embargo was very much an international effort. Here both the USS *Ranger* and the French destroyer *Latouche-Treville* are refueled by the USNS *Passumpsic*. (*U.S. Navy—R. Bos*)

Kuwaiti forces fought the Iraqi invaders and then retreated to fight another day. This is the Free Kuwaiti Navy, consisting of two missile boats and their tender. The boats dueled invading Iraqi tanks, and they later carried Kuwaiti marines who retook the first Kuwaiti territory, some small islands in the Persian Gulf. (*Greg Mathieson/MAI*)

Saddam Hussein was not entirely bereft of friends. Coalition forces captured large amounts of Jordanian ammunition after they liberated Kuwait. (*U.S. Navy—E. Bailey*)

Much of the Kuwaiti air force also escaped to attack Iraqi targets in Kuwait after mid-January 1991. Lieutenant Colonel Mubarak is shown in front of his A-4KU attack bomber. (*U.S. Air Force—J. Wright*)

The United Nations operation was the first occasion since 1945 for several countries to show independence in their foreign policy. Poland and Czechoslovakia were both very proud to send their own forces to the Gulf to serve alongside their World War II Western allies. Here the Polish hospital ship *Wodnik* leaves the Baltic harbor of Gdynia. (*Associated Press*)

If the tone of U.S. self-imposed restraint in Vietnam was set by the decision not to "go downtown," the tone in Desert Storm was set by spectacular attacks on downtown Baghdad on the first night. Here the Iraqi Ministry of Defense burns the morning after the first raids. *(Reuters/Bettmann—Patrick de Noirmont)*

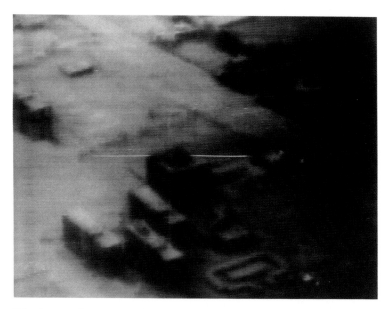

The key to destroying the Iraqi national air-defense system was to attack the ziggurat-shaped control centers. This is a pilot's view, through the infrared camera of his laser designator. *(Department of Defense)*

Some of the Iraqi radars and other air-defense systems were destroyed by Tomahawk missiles. This one is being launched by the USS *Princeton. (U.S. Navy—Benjamin)*

The attack against the Iraqi air-defense system included extensive jamming of radars. The crew of this EF-111A had flown thirty jamming missions (as indicated by the attack symbols) by the time this photo was taken. *(Greg Mathieson/MAI)*

Submarines also launched Tomahawks. Because the subs were not visible, they could achieve a greater degree of tactical surprise even against an alert enemy. This is a periscope photograph taken during Desert Storm. (*U.S. Navy*)

Hard and soft kill: an air force F-111 bomber taxies for takeoff with an EF-111A jammer in the background. The F-111 was one of only two air force aircraft types capable of dropping laser-guided bombs when the war began. *(U.S. Air Force)*

Air force F-117A stealth attack planes dropped the laser-guided bombs on Baghdad. *(U.S. Air Force—S. Stewart)*

All missions had to be supported by aircraft attacking enemy radar-directed antiaircraft weapons. The carrier aircraft and the Marine Corps F/A-18s performed the great bulk of these attacks. Here an A-7E Corsair II aboard the carrier USS *John F. Kennedy* armed with a HARM antiradar missile prepares for a night launch. (*U.S. Navy—C. Madden*)

Navy SEAD (suppression of enemy air defense) missions always included the EA-6B Prowler, this one moving to the catapult on deck of the carrier USS *Independence*. (*John Bouvia*)

The air force SEAD strike force consisted of F-4G fighters in Wild
Weasel units. *(U.S. Air Force)*

Once the missile radars and the fighter direction centers were gone, the Iraqis were reduced to a variety of light antiaircraft guns, precisely the weapons that had been so devastating in Vietnam. This time, however, there were no higher-altitude weapons to drive coalition aircraft into their teeth. This gun was captured west of Kuwait International Airport. (*U.S. Navy—E. Bailey*)

Some of the coalition's air weapons had been designed specifically for low-altitude delivery, to avoid exactly the medium- and high-altitude weapons that the coalition air strategy neutralized early on. This British Tornado drops JP 233 antirunway munitions. *(British Aerospace)*

Most of the precision bombs dropped by the coalition aircraft were laser-guided Paveways. This one is carried by an F-111. *(Greg Mathieson/MAI)*

Most of the coalition aircraft could not direct laser-guided bombs, so they had to be armed mainly with unguided ("dumb") weapons. This F-16 is armed with a combination of Sidewinder air-to-air missiles and CBU-87 unguided cluster bombs. (*U.S. Air Force—M. Lynchard*)

The Iraqis sheltered their airplanes, but some of the coalition bombs, such as the BLU-109 (I-2000), were designed specifically to penetrate those shelters, leaving the planes within unprotected. (*U.S. Air Force—K. Yearyean*)

This shows the damage to an aircraft shelter after an attack. (*U.S. Air Force—P. Heimer*)

This Qatari Mirage, which flew missions against Iraq, is virtually indistinguishable from an Iraqi Mirage, exemplifying the problem of identification of friendly forces. (*U.S. Air Force—F. Corkran*)

Perhaps the greatest surprise of the air campaign was that coalition aircraft avoided shooting each other down or even colliding in night raids. Coordination was assured partly by positive control, using E-3A AWACS (airborne warning and control system) like this one. (*U.S. Air Force—D. McMichael*)

Long-range air operations involve extensive tanking. Here an air force KC-135 refuels a navy A-6E while A-7Es await their turn. They are carrying iron bombs (Mk 83s) and HARMs for SEAD strikes. Desert Storm would be the navy A-7's last combat use. (*U.S. Navy—J. Leenhouts*)

A Royal Saudi Air Force F-15 approaches a U.S. Air Force KC-135 Stratotanker for refueling. (*U.S. Air Force—H. Deffner*)

An A-6E and an F/A-18 are prepared for a strike mission on board the carrier *Midway*. The SH-3 helicopter overhead is generally used both for antisubmarine protection and to rescue downed pilots. In the Gulf, however, SH-3s were used for many other purposes, such as landing commandos and even attacking small enemy surface craft. The F/A-18 in the foreground carries a Rockeye cluster bomb underwing and has Sidewinder missiles at its wingtips. During the war, two MiG-21s jumped a pair of F/A-18s on a strike mission. The F/A-18s turned, shot them down with their missiles, and then proceeded on their strike mission and dropped their bombs. Earlier fighter-bombers would have had to drop their bombs before fighting other aircraft. (*U.S. Navy—E. Bailey*)

A Marine Corps F/A-18D of VMFA(AW)-121 flies over the Al Burgan oil field in southeastern Kuwait. (*Maj. Harmon Stockwell, USMC*)

Aircraft designed for very different missions were used successfully for strikes during the war. These S-3s were designed to hunt submarines, but they successfully detected and even attacked enemy radars, and they were also used to hunt Scuds. (*John Bouvia*)

The B-52 was the heaviest of the coalition bombers. These aircraft dropped about a quarter of all Desert Storm bombs. *(U.S. Air Force)*

The F-15 was the standard U.S. and Saudi interceptor. This F-15C is from the 27th Tactical Fighter Squadron, 1st Tactical Fighter Wing. *(Greg Mathieson/MAI)*

The F-14A is the standard U.S. Navy interceptor. It can also carry the navy's standard TARPS (tactical air reconnaissance pod system) pod, a very important capability given the paucity of reconnaissance aircraft in the theater of operations. *(U.S. Navy—D. Parsons)*

The Iraqis were very adept at camouflage. This U.S. Navy TARPS photo shows an Iraqi Tu-16 Badger bomber, already unserviceable at the outbreak of war, placed at an airfield to attract coalition fire—which it did. *(U.S. Navy)*

AL BASRAH MOSQUE

18 FEB 91

IRAQI DEMOLITION

Saddam Hussein soon lost the ability to shoot down coalition aircraft, but he never abandoned other attempts to blunt the air attack. One tack was to simulate damage to unacceptable targets in hopes that Western public opinion would stop the air offensive. This is the Al Basrah Mosque, its dome neatly sheared off. The nearest bomb crater, made on 30 January, is visible at the top of the photograph, just under the caption. This photograph was shown by the Department of Defense on 19 February 1991. *(Department of Defense—H. Stikkel)*

Saddam's main offensive weapon was the Scud missile. Derided prewar as militarily useless, it nonetheless diverted considerable air effort into the attempt to kill mobile missiles. These are Iraqi-modified Scuds. *(Soviet Military Power)*

The United States deployed Patriot missiles to counter the Scuds; this battery is in Saudi Arabia. *(Greg Mathieson/MAI)*

Patriot missiles proved remarkably successful in intercepting the Scuds: this Patriot launches to protect Riyadh. *(Gary Kieffer/Foto Consortium)*

The aftermath: remains of a Scud near Riyadh, early February 1991. *(Department of Defense—P. Williams)*

Saddam also tried a ground offensive, into the small Saudi town of Khafji. His invading force was largely demolished by coalition ground forces including these Qatari AMX 30 tanks. *(AP/Department of Defense Pool—P. DeJong)*

Marines of the 1st Division fire their 155-mm howitzer into Iraqi positions near Khafji. *(Reuters/Bettmann—C. Platiau)*

Iraqi naval operations in the Gulf appear to have been intended to support the Khafji attack; they were broken up by coalition naval aircraft. Lynx helicopters like this one from HMS *Cardiff*, shown here on board the USS *Curts*, fired Sea Skua antiship missiles. The symbols under her nose cowling appear to show one patrol boat and one missile killed, the latter presumably a shore-based Silkworm. (*Greg Mathieson/MAI*)

The most serious naval threat Saddam Hussein could offer was the mine. This is a recovered contact mine. (*U.S. Navy—E. Bailey*)

U.S. warships in the northern Gulf captured a series of oil platforms and small islands. These Iraqi weapons were displayed on
board the USS *Curts*. The shield of her 76-mm gun shows one
patrol boat symbol. (*Greg Mathieson/MAI*)

Coalition mine countermeasures included sleds like this one, towed by helicopters from the carrier USS *Tripoli*, visible in the background. *(Reuters/Bettmann—J. Mahoney)*

Once the northern Gulf had been sufficiently secured, the navy could directly attack Saddam's coastal fortifications. Here the USS *Wisconsin* fires her 16-inch guns. *(U.S. Navy—B. Morris)*

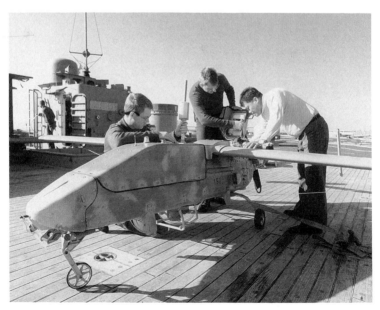

Much of the battleship fire was supported by small, remotely piloted vehicles like this one. They were also used extensively by the marines. *(U.S. Navy—E. Bailey)*

Iraq had very powerful tank forces. The M1A1 was the coalition's most effective tank. *(U.S. Army—S. Henry)*

Most of the Marine Corps tanks were older M60s, fitted with applique armor to defeat antitank missiles, as shown here in Kuwait City after its liberation. *(Greg Mathieson/MAI)*

The AH-64 Apache was the army's most effective tank-killing helicopter. This one is armed with Hellfire antitank missiles. Unlike most of the air force aircraft assigned to army support, it has an effective FLIR (forward-looking infrared device). (*U.S. Air Force*)

The A-10's main antitank weapon is its 30-mm gun, being loaded here. During the war, two A-10s used their guns to shoot down Iraqi helicopters. (*U.S. Air Force—T. Prentes*)

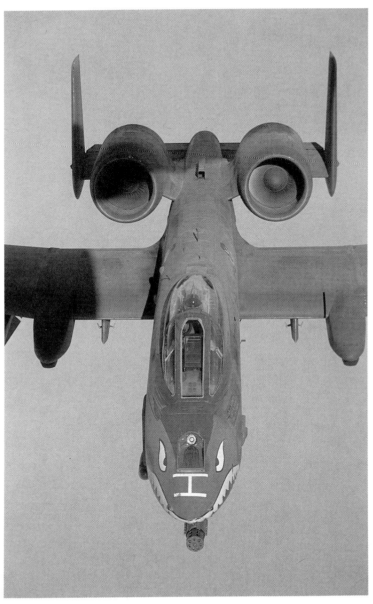

The A-10 was the primary air force tank-killer. Unfortunately it had no FLIR; at night, pilots often used the seekers of their Maverick missiles as a substitute. *(Greg Mathieson/MAI)*

Maverick was the standard heavy antitank missile fired by airplanes. Here one is loaded onto an A-10. The glass dome at the
nose of the missile covers its IR (infrared) seeker. (*U.S. Air
Force—T. Prentes*)

TOW was the most effective coalition vehicle-borne antitank missile. This one is aboard an HMMWV of the 101st Airborne. *(U.S. Air Force—Ford)*

The standard marine attack helicopter is the AH-1W Super Cobra, two of which are shown. Super Cobras and army Apaches made the first breaks in the Iraqi national air-defense system. *(Gary Keiffer/Foto Consortium)*

The marines were unique in having an airplane, the AV-8B Harrier, that could operate equally well from the desert and from a small carrier. Here AV-8Bs fly from the assault carrier USS *Nassau*. (U.S. Navy—S. Allen)

Antitank victory: a burned-out Iraqi T-55 tank. (*U.S. Navy—Holmes*)

The U.S. Army has a greater investment in helicopters than any other army in the world. It bought the mobility used so effectively by the XVIII Corps. Here army UH-60 Blackhawk and Apache helicopters fly out from a Saudi base. (*U.S. Air Force*)

This sand battle map, created by the Iraqis in the basement of a residence in Kuwait City, shows the attacks the Iraqis expected: from the sea and from the south. There was no inkling of the deep swing out into the desert. *(Greg Mathieson/MAI)*

Mobility is bought by cutting weight drastically. This is the standard M102 105-mm howitzer used by the 101st Airborne Division *(U.S. Army)*

The marines must buy tracked vehicles that function both off the beach and deep in the desert. These are amphibious assault vehicles (AAV-7s). *(U.S. Marine Corps)*

A marine LAV-25 is shown in the Saudi desert. (*U.S. Marine Corps—M. Hughes*)

The break into Kuwait had to be preceded by mine-clearing tanks, many of them fitted with rakes like this one. (*U.S. Army—S. Henry*)

Oil was another means of counterattack. By dumping enough of it into the Persian Gulf, Saddam hoped to clog the inlets of the Saudi desalination plants, thus imposing unacceptable damage on Saudi Arabia. This is one result. (*U.S. Coast Guard*—C. *Kalnbach*)

The weapon that wasn't: one of the great surprises of the war was that Saddam did not use gas. Soldiers of the 82d Airborne Division wear protective masks and clothing during training in Saudi Arabia. The weather was then very hot, and these men could not have functioned for long as they were dressed. By the time they fought, the weather was far less troublesome. (*Department of Defense*)

Saddam tried one last act of revenge: he set the Kuwaiti oil fields afire. Like others, the oil fields shown here may well take several years to extinguish. *(U.S. Army—B. Mol)*

Victory: Gen. H. Norman Schwarzkopf and the senior Arab ground commander, Saudi Lt. Gen. Prince Khalid, meet with the Iraqi commanders, Lt. Gen. Mohammed Abdez Rahman al-Dagitistani and Lt. Gen. Sabin Abdel-Aziz al-Douri to dictate terms for a temporary cease-fire, 3 March 1991. *(U.S. Army—J. Trejo)*

that troops almost never surrendered to air attack. They might be badly demoralized, but they would surrender only when armed troops arrived to take over the ground on which they were standing. The air campaign could prepare the battlefield, but it could not end the war.

Through early February, then, Central Command spokesmen stated that the prerequisite for a ground offensive was that half of all Iraqi tanks and artillery pieces be destroyed by air attack. The same spokesmen repeatedly tried to downplay the manifestly pressing time factors. It now seems likely that both efforts were disinformation intended to convince the Iraqis that the battle was not yet imminent.

The enemy force was huge, and it seemed most doubtful that it could be defeated without substantial casualties. Iraqi losses were unknown; it was estimated that up to 545,000 men, in twelve armored and thirty other divisions, were in the Kuwaiti theater of operations. Based on these estimates the 24th Division commander predicted 500 to 2,000 killed and wounded. The XVIII Corps commander thought the marines would suffer 10 to 20 percent losses.

Given the enormous projected human cost of a ground campaign, the actual decision to engage in one had to be made by President Bush. He sent Secretary of Defense Cheney and Chairman of the Joint Chiefs of Staff Gen. Colin Powell to Saudi Arabia to evaluate the situation there. At a meeting on 9 February, General Schwarzkopf recommended an attack between 21 and 25 February. The president approved, and on 14 February General Schwarzkopf set last-minute measures into motion for an attack to be made on 21 February. The offensive was delayed until 24 February so as not to embarrass the Soviets, who were then making a last-minute attempt to broker a cease-fire.

The main problem the coalition commander, General Schwarzkopf, had to solve was the numerical superiority of the Iraqi Army. Classical combat theory requires advantages of 3:1 to advance, and 5:1 to advance into heavy fortifications. Overall, Central Command had to cope with a numerical inferiority of about 4:3 in tanks and worse than 5:3 in artillery.[2] Total numbers of troops were not very different, but the U.S. forces had a much higher ratio of "tail" to "teeth"—that is, support troops to fighting forces (which, incidentally, was why they were so mobile). The only coalition numerical edge, and a heavy one at that, was in aircraft.

These figures were deceptive in a critical way. They were over-all totals, not the numbers that would count in any particular engagement. It was the task of Central Command to pin the enemy down in such a way that our forces could be concentrated to achieve the necessary local superiority. Central Command planned conservatively, assuming no particular superiority for the allied troops or their equipment. The combination of strategy (to achieve the sort of numerical edge that would have beaten good troops, albeit at a high cost) and superior equipment and people proved devastating to the Iraqis.

Whatever his private estimate of the quality of Iraqi troops, General Schwarzkopf could not afford to act on an assumption of innate allied superiority. He planned to wear down Iraqi resistance by air attack, and then to win by a deep flanking armored attack. The Iraqi flank was open along the Saudi-Iraqi border to the west of Kuwait, presumably largely because there just were not enough troops to man both the Kuwait land border and the new defenses along the Kuwaiti coast. This type of flanking attack looked so attractive that General Schwarzkopf had to take special measures, such as deep reconnaissance by special forces, to make sure that he was not being lured into a trap.

Achieving local superiority required deception. The main pre-condition was to deny the Iraqis accurate information as to coalition dispositions. They had lost much of their reconnaissance capacity when their air force was driven from the sky. Other intelligence sources, such as radio direction-finders, were presumably destroyed during the air campaign. That left the Iraqis only whatever they could glean from the news media, and the strict censorship imposed in Saudi Arabia (particularly as to the location of allied units) was crucial. Here the cooperation of the Soviets was extremely valuable. They alone could have supplied the Iraqis with extensive reconnaissance data from their satellites (since the war began it had been obvious that they were observing it with intense interest).[3]

Central Command's own descriptions of the air offensive were an important means of disinformation. The daily briefings suggested that the main weight of the attacks was falling on the Republican Guard divisions, whose importance had been so inflated prewar. Since it is probably nearly impossible for dug-in troops to determine just how badly they have been bombed, the Iraqi command could never really judge the relative weight of air attacks on the Kuwaiti border and farther inland. That denied it an important potential source of intelligence.

In this sense air bombardment offered an important advantage over classical artillery fire. An army planning a breakthrough must concentrate artillery pieces around the point of attack. If that point has been heavily fortified, it generally follows that substantial bombardment is needed, and the target army soon knows where the attack is likely to be made. An enemy particularly strong in artillery might make a dummy bombardment, but resources generally preclude that. Certainly the Iraqis' experience in the war with Iran would have taught the usual lesson.

Aircraft are different. They could attack any part of the Iraqi Army, and once the Iraqi air defenses were gone such attacks carried essentially no cost. They could, then, be used not only for tactically necessary bombardment but also for purposes of suggestion or disinformation. Central Command seems to have been particularly inventive, combining disinformation by action (bombing) with disinformation through its briefings (reinforced by censorship).

Central Command had to destroy large Iraqi units, which it had to assume were still intact (it could never be sure that the bombing had been entirely effective). Both the units in central Kuwait and the Republican Guard were heavily dug in, and direct assaults on their positions could well be costly. Moreover, Central Command could have little enthusiasm for house-to-house fighting in Kuwait City, yet it could not reasonably solve the problem by flattening the place it was fighting to liberate.

The solution was to concentrate on destroying the Iraqi Army rather than seizing Kuwait itself. Once the Iraqis had given up, Kuwait would inevitably fall into allied hands. To accomplish this, the dug-in Iraqi forces had to be forced into the open, where superior coalition tanks and aircraft could destroy them quickly and cheaply. There was, after all, one place the Iraqis absolutely had to move out to defend: Baghdad. Any major offensive into southern Iraq, then, would concentrate Iraqi attention and pull the Republican Guard out of its bunkers. Even if his force did not go all the way to Baghdad, Schwarzkopf would place a powerful allied armored force operating in the Iraqi rear, and capable of encircling (and thus ultimately destroying) them.

For their part, the Iraqis could not cross the destroyed bridges over the Euphrates River, but they could try to cut off the armored thrust by pushing toward the Saudi border behind its spearhead. Thus it was essential that they be forced to deal with simultaneous attacks up from Saudi Arabia. The slower-moving marine and Arab forces near the coast applied the necessary pressure. Depending on the extent to which the border defenses had been wiped out, they could either pin down large Iraqi forces at the border, or they could push inland toward Kuwait City in hopes of forcing the Iraqi defenders out of the city. In the event the Iraqis decided to stay and fight, Kuwait City could be cut off and bypassed, the units moving up from the south closing a trap around the Iraqi regular and Republican Guard divisions.

From the first, the Iraqis had been impressed with the possibility of a Marine Corps amphibious landing.[4] Their countermove had been not only to fortify the Kuwaiti coast but also to mass troops along it. As long as the amphibious threat could be maintained, these divisions would concentrate on the threat from the sea, and they would be unable to move inland to support the other divisions. Moreover, forces concentrating their firepower pointing out to sea might be rolled up by a strong flank and rear attack mounted along the coastal highway.

It was essential that the Iraqi command not sense the preparations for attack. The Iraqis had, unbelievably, left their western flank entirely unprotected. That presented Central Command with an irresistible opportunity, to thrust its large mobile armored force deep into southern Iraq to encircle and destroy the Iraqi forces both inside Kuwait and just north of the Kuwaiti border. Making the thrust, however, required that enormous supply dumps, sufficient for sixty days of combat, be prepared well to the west of the Saudi-Kuwaiti border. Moreover, the armored units had to be moved from positions blocking the Iraqi border forces to their jump-off positions to the west. That took time, and the armored units were vulnerable to flank attacks while they moved west. Moreover, once they had moved, much of the border was no longer protected.

At least three large logistics bases were built in the western Saudi desert, including an ammunition dump covering 40 square miles. General Schwarzkopf deferred construction of the two westernmost bases until after the air war had eliminated most Iraqi air reconnaissance. Once bombing had begun, XVIII Corps moved 500 miles west in twelve days. It left a 100-man deception cell in eastern Saudi Arabia, using inflatable decoys and radio deception measures. The big armored VII Corps began its shorter move only on 16 February. It, too, left behind a deception cell, mainly using electronic measures (a published account cites false Hawk missile radar signals as well as the usual false radio messages).

When the ground offensive began, the French 6th Light Armored Division occupied the extreme western position. To its right, and separated from it, was XVIII Airborne Corps. These units were intended to cover the left flank of the main strike force, VII Corps. To the Corps' right, on the western border of Kuwait, was the U.S. 1st Armored Cavalry Division. On the central part of the Kuwaiti-Saudi border was Joint Forces Command North, the Egyptian-Syrian force. Then came 1st Marine Division. On its right, between the main coastal road and the coast itself, was Joint Forces Command East (five Saudi, Kuwaiti, Omani, and UAE mechanized infantry brigades). The 2d Marine Division began the ground war just to the rear of the 1st Marine Division, and moved up to its left flank.

As in several other cases of coalition success during the war, it was difficult to believe that the Iraqis had not opened their west-

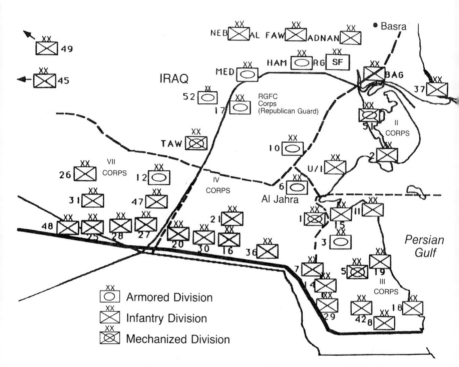

Iraqi Forces in the Kuwait Theater of Operations, 21 February
1991, 0245. (*U.S. Department of Defense*)

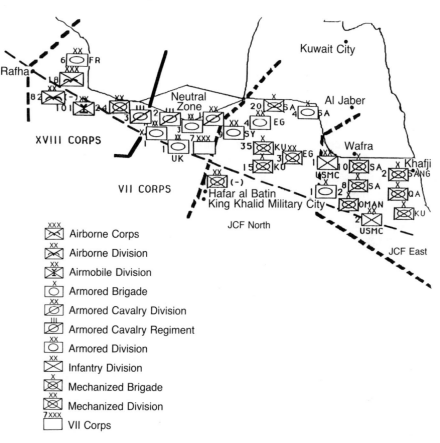

Allied Ground Order of Battle, 22 February 1991, 0120. (*U.S. Department of Defense*)

Definitions of Abbreviations: EG = Egypt; FR = France; JCF = Joint Coalition Forces; KU = Kuwait; QA = Qatar; SA = Saudi Arabia; SANG = Saudi National Guard; SY = Syria; UK = United Kingdom; USMC = U.S. Marine Corps.

ern flank as a deliberate attraction to some sort of allied disaster. General Schwarzkopf cannot have been sure that his own intelligence had detected all of the Iraqi units. He therefore took special precautions. The planned route of the main armored advance was reconnoitered by Special Forces, which ended the war at the Euphrates River.[5] Both XVIII and VII Corps had their own deep-penetration scouts.

Put another way, General Schwarzkopf could not believe that the Iraqis had not seen the same opportunity he had.[6] After the war it was reported that he thought the Iraqis had seen it but had rejected the possibility on the ground that no one could drive that far quickly without losing his tanks. After all, a major reason the Iraqis had not gone into Saudi Arabia after taking Kuwait was that so many of their tanks had broken down. That was, moreover, under relatively benign conditions.

The Iraqis may also have doubted that the massive coalition forces could find their way through the trackless desert to the west. That made the two main tracks especially important, even though the desert itself could easily be crossed for many miles around the inland track to Kuwait City. After all, navigation had presented enormous problems to previous desert campaigners, to the point that the U.S. Army had to do special research on the subject after the formation of the Rapid Deployment Force in 1979. This time new technology, in the form of the GPS (global positioning satellite) system, solved the problem. Using a simple GPS receiver, a vehicle or even an individual soldier can find position within a few tens of feet, anywhere in the world. The Kuwait war was the first combat use of the system, and it was hugely successful. It made possible all the big night maneuvers that in the past would have required numerous scouts and guides along the routes of advance. GPS can be switched to coded transmissions that can be used only by special receivers. In the event, not enough special receivers were available, so the GPS network could not be switched to the coded mode. That meant anyone, including the Iraqis, who had a standard GPS receiver (which is widely available commercially) could use GPS to find his own position. Considerable publicity was given to this apparent lapse in U.S. equipment, but it made little difference, since the GPS itself does not give away the positions of attackers.

GPS made it possible for the attackers to shift their attack plans back and forth virtually up to the moment of attack, since forces using it had no need for fixed markers on the ground. The marines reported that they kept adjusting their breaching point as they received fresh intelligence of Iraqi positions, and as the Iraqis moved their forces.

The Iraqis had placed a large reserve force astride the western Kuwaiti border. The presence of these troops had forced General Schwarzkopf to drop his original attack plan, and in February it appeared that these soldiers could strike at the flank of the advancing VII Corps. The force had to be neutralized. The 1st Armored Cavalry Division was assigned to attack along the Wadi al-Batin, the western border of Kuwait, to pin down the Iraqi force (which VII Corps would eventually overrun from its own flank and rear). Resistance proved lighter than expected, and the division was turned in through the western border of Kuwait, toward Kuwait City.

The attack began at 4 A.M. (local time) on 24 February. Before dawn, the advance elements of the 101st Airborne Division flew into Iraq to set up an advanced base (Objective Cobra), which they needed to leapfrog forward. The assault troops moved out by helicopter, then seized and defended an airhead. The division's 700 trucks linked up with it to provide the fuel and other supplies needed for the next jump forward.

The two key early objectives were Highway 8, the road leading up the Euphrates from Kuwait, and a choke point (between a lake and sand dunes) that any Iraqi reinforcements (or escapees) had to pass, the Iraqi logistics base near Nasiriyah (Orange). General Schwarzkopf could get to Highway 8 before any Iraqis because he had a fast helicopter assault force, the 101st Airborne. Although the helicopter-borne troops could not take much with them, their TOW missiles sufficed to hold their position against any early opposition. The follow-up on the ground would seal off any Iraqi attempt to escape from the trap General Schwarzkopf was springing in the Iraqi rear and up out of Kuwait. The first

Phase I

⊠⊠ (xxx)	Airborne Corps
⊠⊠ (xx)	Airborne Division
⊠⊠ (xx)	Airmobile Division
⊘ (III)	Armored Cavalry Regiment
▢ (xxx)	Armored Corps
▢ (xx)	Armored Division
⊠⊠ (xx)	Mechanized Division

Phase II

Advance into Iraq and Kuwait. (*U.S. Marine Corps*)

Definitions of Abbreviations: CAV = cavalry; EG = Egypt; FR = France; JFCE = Joint Forces Command East; JFCN = Joint Forces Command North; LT = light; MARCENT = Marine Forces Central Command; SA = Saudi Arabia; UK = United Kingdom; USARCENT = U.S. Army Forces Central Command; USMC = U.S. Marine Corps.

sixty-six troop-carrying Blackhawk helicopters reached Highway 8 on the afternoon of 25 February.

More generally, XVIII Corps was assigned to cut off the Iraqi Army. The early successes of the 101st Airborne and also of the marines advancing into Kuwait were so encouraging that the XVIII Corps' Heavy Division, the 24th Mechanized Infantry, jumped off 15 hours early, at 3 P.M. on the 24th. It reached the Euphrates Valley near Nasiriya on 25 February, turned east toward Basra, and destroyed Iraqi airfields at Talil and Jabilah. Between them it destroyed a large Iraqi logistics center (Objective Gold).[7] As in the other offensives, many of the Iraqis the division found were only too glad to surrender. They had had enough of bombing and short rations due to the air offensive. But others did fight. An Iraqi commando regiment near Talil airfield fought for 4 hours despite the heavy bombing it had withstood. Ultimately the 24th Division encountered the Hammurabi Division near Basra. It stood and fought—and lost. Heavily bombarded by divisional artillery, it broke and fled on the morning of 28 February. The remnants survived only because of the unilateral 28 February cessation of offensive operations.

Further west, the light French division, supplemented by a brigade of the 82d Airborne Division, pressed deep into Iraq toward the Euphrates. It was a vital flank guard against any Iraqi attempt to attack the developing envelopment. This protection was quite necessary. The French destroyed an Iraqi division en route to the Euphrates.

XVIII Corps cut off the Iraqi Army. The heavy armored VII Corps was assigned to destroy it while the marines and the Arab forces in northern Saudi Arabia pushed up to preclude any escape south. The corps was joined by the British 1st Armoured Division. This powerful combination exemplified the size and weight of large ground units. In motion, it covered an area 60 miles wide and 120 miles long, consuming 3 million gallons of fuel each day. The U.S. units alone included 59,000 vehicles and 1,600 aircraft. These figures explain why the buildup in Saudi Arabia had to be accomplished by sea, and why it took so long.

The heavy armored force was the most powerful single unit the

U.S. Army had assembled since 1945. The 1st Infantry Division was assigned to make the initial breach through the Iraqi border defense. It conducted a full-scale rehearsal on a replica built in the Saudi desert, the entire British 1st Armoured Division passing through the breach it made. The heavy attack was enormously successful; the initial day's objectives were all met within the first 12 hours. VII Corps crossed the Iraqi border early Sunday morning, and by Monday morning its scouts (2d Armored Cavalry Regiment) were 80 miles into Iraq. By that time this force had already accounted for 270 tanks, including 35 T-72s. The Republican Guard counterattack, led by a column of 80 tanks, failed completely.

The U.S. 1st Infantry Division made the breach on the right flank of VII Corps, and 1st British Division passed through it to deal with the three-division Iraqi operational reserve (12th, 52d, and 17th Armored Divisions) in the Wadi al-Batin. That insured against any flanking attack on the deep strike force (2d Armored Cavalry Regiment leading 2d and 3d Armored Divisions) heading for the Republican Guard.

While VII Corps pushed in behind the Iraqis, the two marine divisions and the Arab units attacked from the south. 1st Marine Division and Saudis and Kuwaitis jumped off at 4:00 A.M., attacking up the coastal road. Next to them the 2d Marine Division and the Saudis approached Kuwait City from the southeast, jumping off at 5:30 A.M. 1st Marine Division took Al Jaber airfield and the Al Burqan oil field the first day; 2d Marine Division destroyed an Iraqi armored column that advanced toward it from Kuwait City. Given these successes, and the weakness of Iraqi resistance, General Schwarzkopf advanced his timetable by 24 hours, and ordered Joint Forces Command North (Egyptians and Syrians) to attack toward the northeast. Initial resistance was surprisingly light. The Egyptians did have to penetrate a burning Iraqi anti-tank ditch that had not been disabled (elsewhere these ditches had been burned out), but Iraqi troops on the border did not fight very well.

Most of the Iraqi defenses were somewhat less elaborate than advertised. At least where the marines penetrated, they consisted only of mine fields, trenches, and gun emplacements (the marines saw no antitank trenches and no high berms). The Iraqis did form the multiple defensive lines with which they had been credited.

Considerable effort went into breaching the Iraqi border mine fields. The two marine divisions attacked side by side, with the 1st Marine Division on the right and the 2d on the left. They differed in technique. The 2d Marine Division deployed a light armored infantry battalion (LAVs) the day before the attack to screen it and to ensure a clear passage from the border berm (on the Saudi side) to the first line of Iraqi obstacles. It captured 400 to 500 Iraqis the first night. The division advanced at night with the reinforced 6th Marines in the lead (three battalions on line). The regiment advanced in a straight line until it hit the breach in the first obstacle, then turned and came out at the breach in the third line of obstacles. This sort of navigation, particularly at night, was a considerable feat. It was achieved by using a combination of GPS satellites and PLRS.[8]

Typically the first vehicles through the mine field were M60s with antimine bulldozer blades, followed by amphibious assault vehicles (AAVs) towing trailers carrying line-charge rockets (MCLCs). The rockets fired about 150 meters ahead of the lead tanks, and their explosions cleared a path about 10 meters wide. The follow-up plow tanks passed through to test the clearance of the lane.[9] The most effective Iraqi mines turned out to be British-supplied bar mines.[10]

The 1st Marine Division found a gap in the Iraqi mine field and penetrated up to the second Iraqi defensive line on its own right flank. On its left flank, it located the mine field exactly. Thirty hours before the attack was to begin, it infiltrated major elements of two of its regiments. One passed through on the right to seal off the approach lane against possible Iraqi antitank missile operators concealed on the ground. The regiment on the left captured an Iraqi who revealed a gap in the mine field. The regiment then passed through, sealed off the gap, and hid itself in preparation for the attack.

Both units expected the Iraqis to use chemicals and antitank missiles in the breaches, as well as counterattacks by the Iraqi immediate mobile reserves. In fact there were no counterattacks until the 2d Marine Division had penetrated about halfway up the coastal road (abreast Al Jaber). Even then, Iraqi attacks were often abandoned after the leading vehicles had been hit. Many of the Iraqi vehicles were no longer threats when they were hit (the advancing marines could not know whether or not they were still manned).

The 2d Marine Division found the going rougher as it advanced because it had to clear Al Jaber. That was an infantry operation, and the advancing force had to stay clear of large numbers of unexploded bombs left over from the air campaign. By the second day, the division was on the escarpment to the west of Kuwait City, on the city's outskirts.

The 1st Marine Division entered Kuwait at an angle to the border and came up alongside the Burgan oil field. The Iraqis counterattacked out of the oil field, and the division had to pass through the smoke from the many fires the Iraqis had set there. The division could not actually penetrate the field, which was filled with above-ground piping and other ground cover behind which enemy troops could hide. Firing into the oil field could easily cause further explosions. The division went up the west side of the oil field, using small infantry units to clear the ground ahead of itself. On its left, it cleared Al Jaber. It was the 1st Marine Division that attacked Kuwait International Airport on 26 February.

By the time the battle was over the division had destroyed 250 T-55/T-62 and more than 70 T-72 tanks. The airport was cleared on the 27th, the division opening its lines to allow Joint Forces Command East, including the Kuwaitis, the honor of entering Kuwait City. The 2d Marine Division stayed near Al Jahra to form the bottom of the box that caught the retreating Iraqi main force. In all, the marines claimed 1,040 enemy tanks, 608 armored personnel carriers, and 432 artillery pieces destroyed or captured, about a quarter of the enemy total.

Several marine amphibious operations were considered. It is not entirely clear at what point they were dropped in favor of the feint. The marines considered a landing on Faylakah Island (eventually such a landing was faked). The landing was dropped only quite late, when the 5th MEB flew its troops ashore to form the operational reserve for the 1st Marine Division. The second major option was a helicopter assault south of Kuwait City to link up with the marines advancing from the south. It was presumably abandoned only when it was discovered that there was no serious Iraqi resistance south of the airport. Even then there was still a possibility that a light force might be inserted by helicopter in the rear of the Iraqi positions. Probably no final decision was made until the last two days of the war. It was to keep these air-assault options alive that the 4th MEB (which had by far the greater helicopter capability) was retained at sea through the ground campaign. Some of its Harrier jets attacked Iraqi positions from their assault carriers (this was the first time Marine Corps Harriers had flown bombing missions from ships).

Disinformation continued as the attack began. Central Command told reporters that the big offshore Kuwaiti islands, Faylakah and Bubiyan, either were under attack or had been taken. In fact no troops had landed, but the amphibious carriers offshore launched Harriers (AV-8Bs) to make ground attacks in support of the spurious reports. There was also radio disinformation, in the form of at least one counterfeit order from a false Radio Baghdad.

As in many other cases of coalition warfare, coordination among the diverse forces presented real problems. The U.S. solution was to attach bilingual Special Forces and tactical air-control personnel to the two Joint Forces Command (Arab) units.[11] Even so, the Arab corps assigned to the left of the marines moved more slowly than expected. For example, even unopposed, it took 4½ hours to breach the main Iraqi defensive line, although that was partly because air preparation had not been as complete as expected.[12] The Egyptians failed to reach their first-day objective, an army barracks about 20 miles inside Kuwait, and the Saudis were also considered slow. Their own armies had never worked together very much, so they were poorly coordinated. At one point the Saudis and the Egyptians exchanged fire (U.S. air liaison officers soon stopped the inadvertent duel).

Iraqi border resistance had largely been crushed by the air bombardment. On the eve of battle, Central Command estimated that the Iraqi divisions on the border were less than 50 percent effective (formations on the coast and farther inland had not been hit nearly as badly). It later turned out that desertion rates throughout the theater ranged from 30 to 60 percent.[13] The passage through the border fortifications was made partly by combat engineers who cleared mines and partly by following the observed paths of enemy patrols. Saddam's oil-filled ditch was burned out, some of its key valves destroyed by laser-guided bombs delivered by F-117s. In one area, however, the Egyptians did have to bridge a burning tank trap.

The Iraqis had indeed laid enormous numbers of land mines, but fortunately they were not as sophisticated as had been feared. For example, there were no reports of casualties to the reported gas mines (although gas mines certainly were found). Allied intelligence was able to plot many of the fields by watching lanes habitually used by enemy soldiers. In one lucky break, the allies captured an Iraqi soldier who had been the driver for a senior officer. Thus he knew just which areas were too dangerous to cross, at least in his sector of the front.

Moreover, many of the mines had been laid either on the surface or buried shallowly. Wind often shifted the sand away from them. Some fields were detonated by light-case 15,000-lb bombs ("daisy cutters" dropped by C-130s), others by fuel-air explosives.[14] Lanes were also cleared using explosive rope trailed by rockets and by mineclearing bulldozers.

The great fear was that troops stalled on the border would be bombarded by Iraqi guns firing chemical shells. In the weeks before the ground war began, there seemed to be considerable evidence of large shipments of 130-mm chemical shells to the border.[15] Great emphasis was therefore placed on physically destroying the dug-in Iraqi guns. Through the period before the ground assault, coalition artillery made nightly attacks on the Iraqi border positions. Iraqi return fire revealed the positions of the long-range Iraqi howitzers. Massed British and U.S. artillery began to shell the Iraqi artillery on 22 February, the day before the planned offensive.

There was also some evidence that Iraqi artillery completely lacked any form of fire control. Reportedly guns were zeroed on particular fixed points, and the Iraqis made no attempt to move the point of aim to hit targets that might reasonably have been expected to move after the first shots. Such tactics recalled World War I experience, when targets were relatively immobile. They did make sense if Saddam expected allied units to become stalled in his border fortifications (on which the guns were presumably zeroed).

Once the dimensions of the disaster were clear, Saddam made one last attempt to extricate his army intact. He announced that his forces were pulling out of Kuwait, a move which fortunately precluded either a house-to-house battle or a siege. However, it was clear that the pull-out would have preserved the Iraqi Army intact. The coalition reply was that Iraqi units moving in military formation would be attacked. Only deserters on foot would be safe.

For example, an Iraqi motorized column was spotted leaving Kuwait City in panic. Attacked by air at either end, it formed a 3-mile traffic jam. Aircraft completely destroyed it. Afterwards it turned out that, even in their final panic, the Iraqis had not been able to resist looting Kuwait. The remains of the column stank of looted perfume.

It is not clear to what extent Saddam's order further demoralized an already unhappy Iraqi Army. There were claims postwar that units who knew that their government was giving up would hardly be willing to fight. Yet the Iraqi tank units did stand and try to fight their way out of the trap. Some surrounded units even tried to fight well after the unilateral cessation of offensive action which effectively ended the war. None succeeded.[16]

Much of this last battle was conducted in weather much too overcast for effective air support. It was a classical tank battle, with a very nonclassical outcome. Thanks to their superior vision equipment (mainly FLIRs), the U.S. tanks spotted their targets well before they were even seen, at ranges beyond 3,800 yds.[17] Their superior ballistic computers insured that they could make killing hits at these ranges. Even when they could engage, the Iraqi tanks were unable to penetrate the M1A1's armor. That was true even of T-72s, which were armed with the best Soviet-made gun, the 125-mm, and which, before the war, had been considered quite impressive.

The sheer speed of the offensive was shocking. Limited Iraqi resistance showed in the small U.S. ammunition expenditure; VII Corps used only 10 to 15 percent of the 70,000 tons it had built up, although some of its units did run short due to the pace of the advance. Perhaps the greatest surprise was that the Iraqis never used gas. There was no question that they had it, and many U.S. officers expected it. On the other hand, they had been heavily leafletted with threats of dire consequences if gas were used. It may also be that, despite Saddam Hussein's public statement that his corps commanders could use gas whenever they wanted to, they still had to wait for specific orders from Baghdad. The word could not come over jammed and destroyed channels.[18] It is also possible that individual Iraqi unit commanders were leery of using gas for fear that their own troops would die if the gas clouds drifted the wrong way or if gas shells burst as they were being loaded (both quite common risks). It turned out that the Iraqis' gas masks were largely worn out (as was first suspected from the condition of masks carried by deserters encountered early in the war).

The ground attack was stunningly successful. Total casualties were ludicrously low: eighty-eight Americans killed in action, plus forty-one Egyptians, Saudis, and Kuwaitis, sixteen British, and two French. Of those killed, twenty-eight of the Americans were victims of one of the few Scuds not intercepted (they died in Dhahran, Saudi Arabia). Many of the others fell victim to friendly fire, and at least seven were killed by mines they were defusing as part of the French division. Overall, the enormous Iraqi Army achieved remarkably little.

It would be easy to attribute the result to the crushing air offensive. However, along with many Iraqis only too glad to surrender, the advancing coalition ground force did encounter many quite willing to fight, even after the coalition suspended its own attack. They stood, fought, and died. The coalition could thank both its superior weapons and the sheer inventiveness of the attack plan (which worked only because the force was so flexible and so mobile).

13

Lessons Learned
and Mis-learned

THE WAR FOR Kuwait was a spectacular, virtually unprecedented victory for U.S. and allied arms. It followed a series of less-
well-publicized but very significant successes, such as the Libyan
raids of 1986, Operation Praying Mantis against Iranian forces in
1987, and the attack on Panama in 1989. Each showed just how
well the new generation of U.S. weapons worked, but none really
sufficed to overcome pervasive criticism of expensive and supposedly oversophisticated equipment. The victory in Kuwait and
southern Iraq confirmed what the U.S. military had been saying
all along: sophistication helped. A point came at which more sophisticated weapons were also inherently more reliable and even
easier to use. What was never said, but much more significant,
was that, once the sophistication had been combined with great
reliability and ease of use, attention could turn to tactics, to how
to use them to win. The earlier generation of high-technology
weapons could achieve much the same peak performance, but
only at the cost of almost total concentration on making them
work at all.

The great lesson, then, is not new but is easily forgotten. People, well-trained and well-led, win wars. Weapons help, but they
do not decide the issue. The best troops cannot win if they are
badly equipped, but good equipment in the hands of poor troops

or badly led troops also cannot win. The outcome cannot be predicted merely by comparing weapons on both sides. Even when weapons are compared, what counts is often how easily they can be maintained and used, not necessarily their maximum performance. In the past, maximum performance has been so difficult to attain that many, even within the military, have tended to concentrate on it rather than on the many other factors, most of them difficult to quantify, that decide the outcome of a war like this one. Saddam Hussein and his inevitable successors will surely have access to very modern weapons, particularly if the decline of the Cold War makes arms producers even more export-conscious. On paper, Saddam's large and modern army and air force should have bought him a reasonable degree of military success. They did not, because his troops were poorly led and because they themselves were not particularly competent.

Human factors like these are difficult to measure. To the extent that intelligence failed during the Persian Gulf war, that failure can probably be laid to the decision, implicit and explicit, that intelligence should be focused on measurable objective issues, not on subjective ones, on how many tanks Iraq had rather than on the quality and motivation of their crews and their maintenance. During the war, an air force officer, looking through endless high-quality, satellite photographs, is said to have offered to exchange the lot of them for a single good spy on the ground. That is the great lesson of wartime intelligence: people, ours and theirs, do not merely make a small difference in a situation determined by hard data about the machines, they usually dominate the situation. We forget that to our cost.

A second point well worth keeping in mind is that the Gulf has some very special characteristics. The flat and largely empty terrain is practically made for air attack; an army literally cannot hide. It can reduce its vulnerability, but the war showed that precision-guided weapons largely negate classical measures like digging in. The war also showed, however, that even a primitive army can be quite inventive in camouflaging itself. Decoys may sometimes be even more effective than the terrain masking to be expected in Europe, since they actually absorb many of the relatively scarce precision-guided weapons (a pilot who cannot find targets takes his weapons home). Extensive reconnaissance, both pre- and post-strike, is probably the only counter to that sort of protection.

The desert was also ideal for the very mobile U.S. Army. Units had been designed to achieve high speeds in much rougher European terrain; they really raced through the flat desert. The main impediment to mobility there, the lack of landmarks, disappeared with the advent of the GPS navigational satellite.

Moreover, it was Saddam Hussein's particular ill fortune that a great deal of U.S. training and weapons development is done in desert environments (the Mojave and White Sands). Critics have long charged that these areas have little relationship to likely battle zones such as Central Europe; this time they were totally wrong. They argued, for example, that targets were just too easy to acquire in the flat desert; that was also true in Kuwait and in much of Iraq.

The United States fought Iraq at a time of transition for its armed forces. It seems likely that, at least for the next decade, the Soviet threat of the past will give way to a series of Third World problems not too different from the one just surmounted. Saddam Hussein was in many ways particularly threatening, but he is not too different in kind from his counterparts in other Third World countries. It is not unreasonable to think that any Western intervention in the Third World is staged not merely for the current antagonist but also for the benefit of other Third World troublemakers. The more effective the intervention, the less stomach those potential enemies have for action against us or our friends. Conversely, a botched intervention has far-ranging consequences. Saddam Hussein was encouraged by what he considered the lessons of the last big U.S. war, Vietnam. On the other hand, several Third World powers probably were impressed by the successful U.S. attack on Libya in 1986, which prefigured Desert Storm in its neutralization of a Soviet-style national air-defense system.

Any lessons to be drawn from the war against Iraq will be read against a background of inevitably declining U.S. defense spending. The real question will be how to distribute spending cuts, not whether to make them in the first place. Each of the services involved in the war has its own views on appropriate priorities. To some extent the tactics adopted in the war, and the lessons that the war appears to teach, have to be evaluated in terms of those expectations, both within each service and in interservice terms. It is easy to believe that what worked well in this case will work as well the next time, but circumstances never quite repeat, and it seems wiser to try to extract those factors that were special to the war for Kuwait.

The Gulf was a most unusual theater of operations. Almost alone among potential areas of conflict in the Third World it is lavishly equipped with air bases, many of them designed specifically to accept U.S. aircraft. Saudi Arabia itself is unusual in its dependence on imports, and therefore in its very well-developed port structure. The prehostilities buildup depended heavily on both the airfields and the ports, and Saddam Hussein failed to use the considerable forces at his disposal to deny either to the coalition. Any future Saddam is unlikely to be so reticent.

Two great lessons of the war are the contributions of the two least visible elements, sea power and overseas bases. Sea power, in the form of carriers and marines, was the block that prevented Saddam Hussein from immediately pressing on into Saudi Arabia, and these forces were also the main defense of Saudi Arabia for some months after the crisis began. Moreover, the other forces that fought the war could not have been brought to Saudi Arabia without massive amounts of sealift. Fortunately, Iraq could not challenge that deployment. However, it is unusual among potential major Third World enemies in lacking submarines and other long-range, antiship forces, and also in lacking friends willing to help more or less anonymously. Just as in the NATO war that no longer seems likely, U.S. forces operating in the Third World live or die depending on whether the United States can guarantee the security of their seaborne lifeline.

The U.S. deployment also depended heavily on foreign acquiescence, not only in Saudi Arabia itself, but also in dozens of bases abroad. Air force fighters could indeed fly directly to Saudi

Arabia, but only because they were able to refuel several times in flight. The tankers used in the refueling process had to fly from friendly bases, bases over which the United States has no sovereignty. With the fading of the Soviet threat, we can no longer take for granted that our current allies will provide us with such facilities, at least on a no-questions-asked basis. Indeed, there is no particular reason to think that the United States will continue to head a cohesive Western alliance. It is telling, for example, that several of the European allies have suggested that command of their warships remaining in the Gulf after the war be transferred to the Western European Union, as was indeed the case with the antimine effort during the Iran-Iraq War.

Despite much wishful talk about a new world order built around the United Nations, it is difficult to imagine that U.S. military policy should be made dependent on the agreement of particular key allies. It is too easy to imagine circumstances (for instance, in a new Arab-Israeli war), in which something like Desert Shield/ Desert Storm would have to be mounted without the assistance of our current European allies. After all, it was difficult enough to secure base rights in 1973, when in theory our allies badly wanted our help owing to the very real Soviet threat. Similarly, none of them was terribly enthusiastic about assisting the United States in Vietnam, even though enmity on their part risked our turning away from the defense of Europe itself, and thus could have been considered extremely irrational.

Quite aside from direct assistance to the coalition, the Europeans denied Saddam Hussein important intelligence. Had he had access to SPOT images through the war, U.S. strategic deception, which turned out to be such an important force multiplier, would have been far less effective (though not entirely impracticable). It seems likely that commercial satellite imagery will be available on a much larger scale within a few years, and that neither the United States nor its coalition partners will find it easy to block access (at least without physically destroying the satellites in question). Thus, in future, the destruction of an enemy's air force may well not suffice to deny him vital tactical intelligence, albeit intelligence usually delivered a few days late. Recent U.S. government interest in limiting commercial satellite photography is unlikely to be too effective.

The *only* U.S. forces that can be deployed without the consent of current allies are naval or sea-based forces. Really long-range air operations are technically possible, but only if the airplanes are tanked, and only if foreign governments agree to overflights. For example, some years ago a squadron of F-15s deployed to Saudi Arabia as a show of strength. It took several months for the necessary agreements to be given, and even then the airplanes had to fly with their guns taped over and without ammunition (that is, without the missiles they would have needed for self-defense).

Beside naval forces, space assets are the only ones the United States can deploy without foreign assistance or acquiescence. The Kuwait war was the first war in which space systems had a decisive role. Given the lack of reconnaissance assets in the theater, much of the tactical work normally done by airplanes had to be done by satellites that were redirected specifically for that purpose. That was the outgrowth of a program, TENCAP (tactical exploitation of national capabilities), begun in the 1970s, to use national sensor systems (the outputs of which are normally closely held in Washington) for tactical support. Without the satellite systems, the war could not have been fought. However, the war also demonstrated the inherent limitations of these systems; tactical reconnaissance aircraft are still extremely important. The retirement of the SR-71 had not been a terribly fortunate decision.

One national sensor, the DSP (defense support program) satellite, was used to detect and locate Scud launches, to provide likely targets with a few minutes of warning. The DSP satellites were originally intended to detect the launching of Soviet ballistic missiles. During the Persian Gulf war, two of them could generally locate a Scud launch plume within 120 seconds of firing. Location was not nearly precise enough to engage the missile directly, but it was enough to alert the targets and the Patriot missiles protecting them. The entire system (DSP, communications, ground-based missiles) was a crude version of the projected U.S. strategic-defensive system. It was put together remarkably quickly.

The space program also provided GPS, the navigational satellites, without which the coalition land forces probably could not have made their decisive deep attack (GPS was probably also essential for the sort of stealthy navigation used by the F-117A). If anything, GPS is likely to become much more important in future as tactical missiles use it for their own navigation. That capability was demonstrated in the Kuwait war (by the navy's SLAM missile), and it will be incorporated in the next version of Tomahawk. One consequence of this development should be much-relaxed requirements for mapping potential areas of conflict, since a GPS Tomahawk will not need elaborate terrain maps by which to navigate.

As might be imagined, most Tomahawk mapping is done from space. The Defense Mapping Agency had to work around the clock to map Iraq so that Tomahawks could be used against it. That was acceptable in a war with a five-month preparation, but not in the sort of pick-up battle the navy (whose airplanes Tomahawk would support) will presumably fight in the future Third World. That makes GPS-Tomahawk quite important.[1]

Neither GPS nor TENCAP figured in any earlier war. The one well-tried space asset, communications, was also, of course, vital, but ironically it was probably most important as a channel via which TENCAP data could be relayed from Washington to Cent-Com. As in past wars, the most important communications lesson was that there was never enough capacity. One solution would be more use of small satellites which would not last very long but which could be launched quickly in a crisis. Naval Space Command and the Marine Air Wing in Saudi Arabia used a small experimental satellite to relay logistics data back to the United States. The main communications satellites dedicated to the operation were two DSCS-2, one DSCS-3, and the FleetSatCom net.

The greatest single question is, Why did the coalition do so well? One answer would be that Iraq was in a hopeless situation from the beginning, that Saddam Hussein was all bluff and no teeth. That is difficult to reconcile with respectable military performance during a lengthy war against another regional power,

Iran. Moreover, even at the end, after Iraq had, in effect, surrendered, some Iraqi armored units were quite willing to stand and fight. It is more interesting to note that they achieved nothing, not even much in the way of coalition casualties. For example, the British army lost more troops to friendly than to Iraqi fire, which is extraordinary.

The next answer would be that coalition weapons so completely outclassed those of the enemy that Iraq had no chance. That is certainly true in some respects (for example, in tank fire-control systems), and the coalition did enjoy a crushing air advantage. However, if it is the main or the sole explanation, then the outcome of the war is not particularly cheering. Much of the coalition's technology was new only in the sense that it had not seen combat before. Virtually all the weapons had been in the inventory for years, and many of them were built around electronics substantially more primitive than that available at consumer computer shops. It seems likely that a future Saddam Hussein will be able to invest in a better line of weaponry, particularly since the technology itself is becoming much more widely available.

The technology explanation is particularly tempting because it is so easy to compare military forces on the basis of the weapons they use, and because so much of current military discourse is really about the weapons themselves. It might be added that the bloated prewar estimates of Iraqi effectiveness were very much based on numbers of weapons (and men) and on the technical characteristics of the weapons themselves, the only data easily on hand.

The coalition won for much less visible reasons: superior training, superior command and control, and superior logistics. None of these factors is easy to evaluate in objective or numerical form. To the extent that they are much more important than some of the numbers, however, it is essential that Western observers, be they military intelligence analysts or the many civilians who advise the government, find some way of taking that reality into account. Otherwise we will always find ourselves deterred by what ought not to frighten us, or too willing to jump into circumstances that really should be deterring.

The modern revolution in training dates back to the Vietnam War, when the U.S. Navy decided that its pilots were not performing nearly well enough against the North Vietnamese. Its solution was full-scale training against special aggressor squadrons on fully instrumented ranges that could show a pilot how and why he had won or lost. The basic idea of full-scale training was not, of course, new; war games have always been a feature of military instruction. What was new was the ability to reconstruct realistic operations, including simulated hits, in exquisite detail thanks to modern radars and lasers. The navy's Top Gun fighter school was copied by the air force. Both services have strike warfare schools at which the tactics used in the air campaign were developed (Red Flag [now Desert Flag] for the air force, "Strike U." for the navy).

The larger the force, the more difficult it is either to simulate operations or to achieve the sort of tactical coordination that wins battles. To a great extent, the massive tank and air-to-surface battles of the desert war were won at the army's National Training Center in the Mojave Desert. After the Korean War the army developed an "aggressor force" against which to train, but it lapsed during the Vietnam War and was not revived until the 1970s, when it acquired much the sort of technology used in Top Gun. The battles around Kuwait were won by extremely smooth coordination of different arms (artillery, tanks, and attack aircraft and helicopters) to a degree unknown in the past. Fortuitously, the Mojave Desert is more like the terrain in which U.S. troops actually fought than it is like the European battlefield for which the U.S. Army was designed.

The marines have a similar full-scale training facility, the Marine Corps Air-Ground Combat Center (MCAGCC), at 29 Palms, California. It runs combined arms exercises (CAX), originally called Palm Tree. They were initially fire-support coordination exercises, but now they are much more elaborate. A CAX differs from an NTC exercise in that the marines use a great deal of live-fire training, although now they place more emphasis on troop involvement and maneuver. They went so far as to build an expeditionary airfield at 29 Palms to support the CAX exercises. The marines also have their own version of Top Gun, Marine Air

Weapons and Tactics Squadron One (MAWTS-1) at Yuma. "Strike U." was partly patterned on MAWTS-1.

All of this training is done at the tactical level. It creates units capable of fighting their own battles, but victory in a war depends on how well those engagements can be tied together in a coherent strategy. Even more than excellence in weaponry, excellence in command and control provided General Schwarzkopf with the ability to design a winning strategy.

Prewar Western assessments of Iraqi military prowess were particularly lacking in any discussion of their command and control capability. For example, a credulous Western defense press was glad to equate Adnan-2, a Soviet-supplied transport carrying a French air-defense radar, with the U.S. AWACS. The reality was very different, and the difference was characteristic of the contrast between Iraqi and U.S. forces. The AWACS radar is far more effective than that of the Adnan. However, the most striking difference is in the extent to which the two airplanes can process and use the information provided by their radars in order to control fighters in an air battle. Adnan-2 looks vaguely like an AWACS, but its command and control facilities, which are its ability to use its radar, are so much more primitive that the two airplanes are not even remotely in the same class.

Saddam managed to buy a great deal of the outward appearance of military power—the guns and tanks and missiles. He was unable to buy, or to maintain, a modern command-and-control system to back up that outward power. It is possible that Saddam's failure to appreciate the importance of command and control was the key to his defeat in the war that followed.

Command and control is, after all, an abstract and colorless business, apparently far removed from the reality of combat. The one man who dominated Iraqi policy, a military amateur, was unlikely to appreciate the extent to which only effective command and control permits a commander to realize the full potential of his battlefield weapons, coordinating their effects in a fluid and timely way. A weapon like a long-range gun is typically described by its maximum possible performance, for example, its maximum range. Saddam made tremendous efforts to buy weapons with the highest possible maximum performance, such as the G5 series long-range howitzers. However, maximum range in itself is irrelevant. What matters is the range at which the gun normally engages targets, and that in turn depends upon command/control, most immediately on the extent to which distant targets can be identified to the gunner. Command/control also affects the gunner's ability to engage multiple targets, because it is the means by which he is informed of their existence and position. The better the command/control system, the more quickly forces in the field can react to changing circumstances, and the wider the area over which deployed forces can cooperate.

It is difficult to quantify the character or the effects of command and control, but the results are clear. In an important sense, the victory in Kuwait was a triumph of effective and robust command and control over brute force and paper (maximum, but not actual performance) capability. The outcome is much like that of the blitzkrieg in France in 1940. The attacker moves in steps, and at each step the defender tries to react. The pace of the steps, and the pace of the reaction, are both determined by the quality of command/control systems. Some years ago Col. John Boyd, USAF (Ret.) observed that an attacker might be able to move from step to step so fast that the defender might find himself reacting to step one while the attacker was executing, say, step four. The result would be the equivalent of a nervous breakdown on the part of the defender. Boyd believed that this sort of process explained the success of the blitzkrieg. In that case, the key was that the leader of the German armored thrust could make his own decisions, whereas French decisions had to be made at a central headquarters served poorly by communications and therefore unable even to perceive the shape of the battle in time. This point was demonstrated by the great Scud hunt and by the attempts to attack other mobile Iraqi targets: our own command and control system, as exemplified by the ATO, sometimes had too slow a decision cycle. A more aggressive and determined enemy might have done much better by exploiting its inherent lags.

The best modern command and control systems provide a central commander with a very current picture of the battle, and with the ability to maneuver all of the forces nearly continuously to match the shape of that battle. This requires enormous computer power as well as dense and robust communications. Large numbers of educated operators are needed to run the system. It is quite possible that, for all of its mobilization, Iraq lacked sufficient numbers of educated men outside its officer class. The next best method is to decentralize, relying heavily on officers in forward positions, whose knowledge of the current situation can make up for the lack of information at headquarters. Saddam rejected this sort of plan for fear of political instability.

The worst system is the one Saddam chose—all decisions were concentrated in his own hands. Given the technology he had, Saddam could not hope for the sort of detailed current knowledge such a doctrine required. He could not, for example, change his plans to accommodate a shifting tactical situation. The fight at Khafji was a telling demonstration. Saddam designed a fairly elaborate battle plan, converging on what he hoped would be a mass of marines drawn into a trap. The marines refused his bait, and some of the converging forces never made it to Khafji. That did not change their orders. Moreover, because he apparently could not imagine the failure of the plan, Saddam announced that he had won a great victory at the time the plan should have succeeded. It is by no means clear that he imagined the consequences of so obvious and public a failure.

The third absolutely vital factor in the coalition victory was logistics, on two levels. One was the ability to move large forces from the United States and Europe to Saudi Arabia in what was, in military terms, a stunningly short time. The United States succeeded in the buildup because it had a spectrum of units, with different levels of mobility, available. The laws of physics impose, in effect, a trade-off between strategic mobility (the ability to bring a unit thousands of miles) and unit combat power (generally its firepower and tactical mobility); this trade-off is explored further in Appendix A. Local armies do not suffer from similar limitations, and thus a considerable buildup will generally be necessary if they are to be defeated.

Some have already drawn the lesson that the army ought to be more like the rapidly deployable marine units with their Maritime Prepositioning Ships. They miss the fact that, to be so deployable, the marines must make some sacrifices. A heavy army division *could* be provided with preloaded ships, but only at an unbearably high cost, and even then it would be only a single division. The U.S. choice, therefore, has been to limit the number of fully mobile units and back them with units requiring conventional sealift. The war experience strongly suggests that the policy of maintaining a largely inactive shipping reserve against the need for such deployment is insufficient. The ships themselves cannot be manned without a pool of trained seamen. An active merchant fleet provides just such a pool, but over the past decade the U.S.–flag merchant fleet has virtually disappeared. Its seamen remain, but they are aging.

Thus one conclusion from the Kuwait experience is that, unless the United States finds some way to revive its merchant fleet, all of its heavy ground forces and ground-based air forces may be unusable in a future conflict. There is no guarantee whatever that foreign merchant ship owners will be willing or able to steam their ships into a combat zone. Moreover, in a future intervention the enemy may well deploy its own antishipping forces, and such deployment will further discourage foreign shipowners. This is not an issue for the naval budget; it is a Defense Department–wide problem, and it cannot be solved merely by buying and laying up more fast sealift ships, or even by forming a merchant marine reserve.

Aircraft are the other leg of strategic airlift. They probably can never move more than about 5 percent of all materiel (again, thanks to the laws of physics), but they are essential for quick movements of badly needed equipment, such as Patriot missiles. Aircraft are also the only way the United States currently moves troops, on the theory that long ocean voyages are debilitating and inefficient.[2]

To a much greater extent than the navy, the air force maintains a large active transport operation. The justification is that, because air transport is used for unexpected emergency shipments, this capacity always must be available. To depend on commercial carriers is to accept their scheduling to at least some extent. As it happened, the commercial carriers had considerable trooping capacity during the fall of 1990 because air travel had virtually collapsed, owing to Saddam Hussein's terrorist threats.

The other aspect of logistics, which is applicable to all military forces, is shorter-range supply within a theater or within a battle area. Logistics imposes a kind of overhead cost on a unit, taking away resources (troops and vehicles) that might otherwise contribute directly to combat power. This overhead includes personnel to amass, move, guard, maintain, and distribute supplies, as well as those who maintain and repair equipment in the field. The overhead pays off by allowing a unit to keep fighting longer, but on paper it often seems to impose too high a "tail to tooth" ratio. Third World and Soviet-style armies generally have not paid this price (which is why their divisions often seem to dwarf ours in firepower). This war strongly vindicated the U.S. position.

This logistical support enabled the U.S. striking force to keep going at high intensity, all the way from the Saudi border to Basra. In contrast, the minimally supplied Iraqi divisions could not remain viable when air attack drastically cut the capacity of their supply lines. Even fixed in place, a division eats 50 to 70 tons of food per day. That amounts to 2,000 to 2,800 tons of supplies per day for the forty divisions in the Kuwaiti theater of operations, *not* counting ammunition and water. The air strikes that cut the supply lines were particularly effective because these divisions had brought so little with them when they deployed from Iraq.

Logistics includes maintenance, which sops up skilled personnel. In a society with few such people it competes unsuccessfully with the need to maintain combat firepower. Like supply, it determines whether a force can actually achieve what its paper organization suggests it can. One of the shocks of the war was the poor state of much of the Iraqi equipment, beginning with the armored vehicles sent into combat at Khafji.[3]

Logistics, training, and command and control are essentially invisible attributes. They contribute enormously to real, but not to paper, military power. For that reason, they are generally the province of established military forces. Inexperienced armies, or, more likely, inexperienced dictators, will choose the maximum apparent military power per dollar. Most of the time, after all, they expect to win more by bluffing than by actually fighting. It is tempting for the United States to follow much the same path as the military budget declines. The war demonstrates clearly just how bad a mistake that would be.

What, then, is the place of all that advanced and remarkably reliable high-tech weaponry? Once the weapons are known to work, and to work reliably, an army or navy or air force can spend most of its time learning how to use them in combat, in combinations that will defeat an enemy. There is a vast difference between building a single defensive missile capable of shooting down an enemy ballistic missile and using those defensive missiles in some coherent fashion. It may be remarkable that a single laser-guided bomb can destroy a bridge, but to design an air campaign around the use of such weapons is a very different proposition.

Through the period after 1945, new technology has been both military god and demon. It has promised extraordinary performance, but at a high cost, for example, in terms of operator and maintainer training. The revolution of the 1970s provided electronics that was, for the first time, both inexpensive and reliable. By the early 1980s the new electronics was in widespread production, and the height of performance could finally be reached on an everyday basis.

This tale is not confined to the military. From about 1945 to the 1970s, computers showed rapid increases in capability, from the point at which they were limited to a few mathematical problems to the point at which they could control vast amounts of data such as credit-card charges. All of these machines, however capable, were delicate. They had to live in air-conditioned rooms, attended by expert operators, with very highly trained repairmen instantly available. A failure, for example of an air conditioner, stopped any large computer dead.

There are still large computers, but the surprise of the 1980s was the creation of small yet highly capable ones so reliable that they could be brought home to operate. They could live in average conditions, and they rarely, if ever, needed repairs. Their immense power, moreover, was applied in large part to make them quite easy to use. The remarkably reliable and usable weapons of the Kuwait war are products of exactly the same electronic revolution.

In the computer world, the effect of the revolution was ultimately to turn attention away from making the computer function electronically (hardware) to making it function in a useful way (software). Tactics and strategy might be considered the military equivalent of software. Full attention can be focused on them only after the hardware issues have been resolved, since otherwise enormous attention must be paid to avoiding disaster caused by hardware (weapon) failure.

To some extent, it may be argued that Saddam Hussein's tactical, training, and logistical failures were a result of the limited cadre of educated men in Iraq; that is, they were a consequence of Iraq's Third World character. The same might be said of Saddam's lack of modern social organization. To the extent that such generalizations are correct, the war carries a fascinating lesson: Third World countries are unlikely to defeat reasonably competently handled First World forces unless they modernize their societies—that is, unless they emerge out of the Third World. Mere purchases of sophisticated weaponry will not do. They may have an impact, but only a temporary one.

That is much the lesson of the colonial wars of the nineteenth century. At least until midcentury, both the Europeans and their victims had access to much the same technology. Yet small European armies almost invariably demolished quite large armies in Asia and Africa (which is why the Europeans were able to establish empires). It is difficult to escape the conclusion that military superiority was a function of social organization, and that this is still the case.[4]

The great lesson is probably that any society wishing to stand up to modern Western forces will have to modernize. It cannot merely buy equipment; the society itself has to change. The change need not mimic the West (probably it will not), but it must produce a larger leadership and technically adept class. Such a class must almost inevitably collide with established centers of authority, so modernization cannot be an entirely peaceful process. The modern Soviet Union is probably a case in point. The hope must be that, once a society has become more pluralistic, it will also become less aggressive.

The training, logistics, command and control, and high-powered weaponry were prerequisites for victory. They did not ensure it, and they cannot do so in future. The coalition won because its leadership in the field, headed by General Schwarzkopf, used its resources intelligently. Fighting 8,000 miles from home, the United States can assemble large, but not overwhelming, military forces. A local power will generally be able to gather more troops and more tanks. Ours may be better, but that will count only to the extent that we plan and fight skillfully. Throughout the war, the public impression was of overwhelming allied firepower achieving withering results. The reality was that the allied forces, though quite impressive, had very finite resources. Because the enemy never quite realized just how finite they were (the sortie-counts are the most obvious case of disinformation intended for that purpose), he was demoralized and probably deterred from ever taking the initiative.

In that sense, the psychological or morale aspects of the war were extremely important. Saddam saw the United States in two quite different ways: as a technological giant capable of miracles, and as a morally weak country unwilling to sustain casualties. The giant aspect seems to have deterred him from striking at Saudi Arabia soon after taking Kuwait, and ultimately it probably discouraged him from offensive action. The exception, Khafji, was likely conceived as a sort of Iraqi Tet Offensive, designed to cause the sort of casualties that would make the superpower cringe. Overall, however, the passivity of the Iraqi forces must be a remarkable aspect of the war. That passivity was bought, not by what was done on the ground, but by the reputation of U.S. technology and of the U.S. forces. Similarly, it seems likely that the marines were able to tie down large Iraqi forces along the coast not because of some sober analysis of the effect of a landing, but because of the aura of power they have built up.

Large Iraqi ground units surrendered quite early in the ground war. It is probably not too far-fetched to say that the U.S. military reputation made it possible for them to consider surrender honorable. Psychology may not be objectively measurable, but it can be extremely important.[5]

The outcome of the war cannot have hurt any of this.

Weighed against the good news, there were some major failures. The great Scud hunt was a miserable, and telling, disaster. Allowed to roam quite freely over a flat Iraqi landscape, the air force could not find a handful of mobile missile launchers, even though the launchers were not masked in any way. It killed those it could, but the evidence is clear that it often attacked decoys, and that it could never really be sure what it had hit. The result casts serious doubt on the value of the new B-2 bomber. The B-2 has been justified for its ability to hunt mobile targets within the Soviet Union (unmanned missiles can hunt down and kill any fixed target). It can hunt, its advocates say, because it is stealthy; it can spend its time looking for elusive targets. But, once the Iraqi air-defense system had been destroyed, *every* coalition airplane was, in effect, stealthy. All of them could search at will. They even had the advantage that special reconnaissance systems could spot Scuds as they were launched (the Soviet problem would have to be solved rather more urgently).

It is difficult to avoid the conclusion that the only viable solution to the Scud hunting problem would have been to land highly mobile troops in the Scud basing areas and allow them to hunt night and day, supplying them by air.

Bomb damage assessment was often virtually impossible. We will probably never know just how many Iraqi airplanes were killed in their shelters. It is just physically impossible to tell, from the air, what has happened inside a closed building. Much of the assessment made in wartime amounted to little more than careful viewing of strike videos. We were well aware that bombs had struck their designated targets, then, but not of whether those targets had been destroyed, and not even whether they had been real, as opposed to decoy, targets.

More generally, it is very difficult to be sure that particular targets have been destroyed unless they are visited on the ground. For example, the Iraqi chemical weapons stockpile was a major coalition air target, and during the war there were repeated claims that all or most storage sites had been destroyed. However, the Iraqis claimed that much of their chemical arsenal had survived the war. If their figures are accurate, the air campaign accounted for only about a third of the storage sites, and even then many weapons can probably be salvaged. That is not to be considered a failure of the air campaign as such, but, rather, yet another in a long line of demonstrations that what looks quite badly damaged may, in fact, be intact.

During World War II, vast tonnages of bombs were dropped on a variety of industrial targets. Aerial photographs, the contemporary equivalent of the videos used in this war, seemed to show total devastation. However, inspection on the ground later on showed that destruction had been less than total and that repairs were often far from impossible. The force attacking Iraq probably did better because it had very precise weapons that could be aimed at points of particular vulnerability, but its bombs were not much more lethal than those of World War II.

It seems likely that the United States entered the war with a somewhat exaggerated sense of the destructiveness of its aerial weapons. For many years, after all, U.S. strategic air planners had worked with nuclear warheads. In most cases they had been more concerned with guaranteeing that a warhead fell on a particular target than with its detailed effects (which were generally underestimated in any case). Iraq was a very different affair. The effects of nonnuclear bombs are very limited.

Those who wish to fight us in future will also learn some military lessons. If they cannot reform their societies, then they probably will get very little out of large investments in conventional weapons and the more or less incompetent troops serving them. They may well become even more enamored of nuclear and chemical weapons. After all, we might have been far less enthusiastic about fighting Iraq if Saddam had had a bomb and the means to deliver it to Washington. That argues strongly that we should intensify efforts to prevent the proliferation of such weapons (for example, through sabotage) and at the same time move toward building defenses against limited strategic attacks.

Then there is the lesson of time. Saddam may have been naive about how long it would take us to get into place to attack him, but the secret is now clearly out. His successors will probably be intelligent enough to move much faster. Those advantages we gained by virtue of time may well be denied us in future. The same applies to the Saudi port and air-base system. It would not take a genius to realize that we would have been badly handicapped by their destruction.

The other lesson is timing. The invasion of Kuwait was like the invasion of the Falklands. In each case the invader was careful to attack just *before* some devastating military cut had been made. In the case of the Falklands, a few more months would have seen the British dispose of the carriers that made their counter-invasion practical. In the case of the United States, unless the current schedule for cuts is changed, it will be very difficult to mount anything like the Kuwait operation in 1995. Similarly, the operation depended heavily for its success on the defense systems bought in the 1980s. It could not have been mounted the same way in 1984, when everything was on order but not yet delivered.

Costs apply to munitions as much as to airplanes and tanks and ships and radars. Again and again, recent conventional but limited wars have involved rates of expenditure far in excess of the estimates made for the big war against most of the Soviet military. It is too easy for military organizations to absorb cuts by reducing munitions (and, incidentally, spare parts) purchases rather than higher-visibility items such as airplanes.

All of these military points having been made, the most important points are surely the political ones. After nearly two decades, the United States showed that it could indeed fight and win a war. The apparent lesson of Vietnam, that the public would not tolerate the cost of combat, seemed to have been disproven. Even though critics of the war predicted casualty rates in excess of

Vietnam experience, the public was generally willing to support President Bush (Congress was far more cautious, having caught the Vietnam bug in a more intense form). The great political question, then, is why a public already supposedly war-shy due to the unpleasantness of Vietnam was so supportive this time.

One conclusion would seem to be that the supposed lesson of Vietnam, that the U.S. public will not tolerate conventional war, has probably been grossly overstated. The public did accept a very long period of costly warfare before its support collapsed. One might venture that the Vietnam War ultimately failed in the United States because the government itself fought with only limited conviction. It never defined an objective against which alternative strategies might be weighed: preserving South Vietnamese freedom was far too vague a goal to be translated into concrete military terms. Ultimately the message to the public was that the war might go on indefinitely, and the American public would not accept that. It is willing to pay heavily, but for finite durations and well-defined goals. Finite need not be limited to 100 hours or 100 days, but it cannot be 100 years, either.

The public eventually grasped that the statistics being churned out (in this case, largely body counts) had little or nothing to do with the only important question: Were we winning and, if so, how long would the war take?[6] Nor, it seems likely, could the public accept fighting under limitations so severe that it seemed unlikely that Washington was really interested in winning in the first place. Without any measure of progress, it was very difficult to understand just what we were doing in Vietnam. Once the public had decided that progress could not be made, any attempt to claim progress seemed like little more than a cynical attempt to improve the war's image.

In war, then, the U.S. public much prefers a sharp, high-intensity conflict to an ill-defined and lengthy, low-intensity war. High-intensity war capitalizes on our technology and presents us with a well-defined enemy and, usually, with inherently well-defined military goals. A low-intensity guerrilla war has no such goals. Success is always incremental—we secure one region after another, we kill off or lock up one guerrilla cadre after another—but it is never totally clear what stroke (if any) will be decisive. Such a war seems dirty precisely because the enemy is so ill-defined. Success requires enormous amounts of intelligence merely to identify the enemy, and often the enemy must be hunted down one by one. This sort of intelligence (not too different from police intelligence) is difficult and unpleasant to acquire, and many of the victims of the hunt are likely to be innocent. Moreover, the enemy may employ many apparent noncombatants. Results may well include massacres like My Lai.

An alternative formulation would seem to be that the United States should try very hard to convert any war in which it finds itself into the sort that the public can support or at least tolerate: a finite, sharp affair rather than the sort of gradual escalation experienced in Vietnam. There, the overriding perceived risk (as understood in Washington) was Chinese intervention. That precluded adopting the one clearly decisive strategy, the invasion and occupation of North Vietnam. Washington was unaware that there was another and, in fact, greater risk, that an apparently indecisive strategy, requiring a sustained commitment, would prove intolerable at home.

U.S. public opinion is much affected by an unstated national ethic, in effect an ideology, violation of whose tacit tenets carries real costs. The ideology is our form of democracy, the idea that every individual is equal, deserves a say in his or her fate, and should be protected from the weight of government. It is taken so much for granted in the United States that few would call it an ideology, yet it is quite distinctive in the larger world. It is taken for granted in only a very few countries. To the governments of most of the others it is the rankest sort of subversion. We are so used to it that we hardly notice, to the point where we saw the Soviets as the ones on the ideological offensive. However, any country that allies itself with us also finds itself accepting some infusion of our way of thinking. That may not be particularly popular with the local rulers alongside whom we fight, but it is inescapable.

A strong undercurrent in U.S. public opinion is the idea that the world would be at peace (or at least much happier) if all countries were democracies more or less like us. There is a tacit assumption that democracies all think more or less alike, so that a more democratic world would also be friendlier to us. We like to think, then, that our foreign policy really is (or really should be) a world moral policy, not U.S. self-interest. Although these words may seem naive, the careful reader will observe that they still apply, long after most observers of President Wilson blamed his adherence to this kind of policy, applied just after World War I, for the disasters of the 1930s. For example, in the 1950s the United States once tried to force Iraq to hold free elections in hopes that the result would stabilize the area because the elected government would be friendlier to Israel. Local observers knew that any such hopes would be frustrated: an elected government prefers its own national sentiments and interests to our own.

The U.S. public quite naturally badly wants to think that the wars it supports are moral ones (in our own terms). It does respond to the national interest, but only grudgingly: it is not popular to fight for such crass purposes as making sure that we retain access to our economic lifeblood, oil. Moreover, particularly in the case of a war, the public is quick to perceive any apparent contradiction between U.S. foreign policy goals and the national ideology. During the 1950s and 1960s, Communists tried hard, and sometimes very successfully, to exploit this possibility by advertising themselves as fundamentally populist and democratic. Sentiment favoring "Uncle Ho" over an apparently corrupt Saigon government was a case in point.

President Bush was well aware of these considerations. He understood that the public would support a war it considered moral and one that seemed directed at a well-defined goal. In this case Saddam Hussein provided the moral purpose. The goal was simple: the liberation of Kuwait. For all his cleverness in trying to deter the United States from fighting, Saddam Hussein could not avoid making himself easy to hate. Even those opposing the war generally avoided any direct support for Saddam. However, as in Vietnam, the moral justification for the war did run afoul of perceptions that some of our allies did not even remotely conform to our ideology or morality. Moreover, many supporters of the war could not accept limitation to the finite goal of liberating Kuwait: if Saddam was all that bad, surely the United States must eliminate him and impose a more moral government in Iraq.

Many in the United States preferred maximum political goals (such as the overthrow of Saddam Hussein and the reform of the Iraqi political system) to minimum ones (such as the ejection of the Iraqis from Kuwait). Some of those who opposed the war from the right even argued that the war would inevitably escalate into exactly that sort of crusade, at unwarranted cost.

For many of the coalition partners, however, these maximum goals were anathema. Accepting a war to bring democracy to Iraq would be almost as terrifying as accepting Saddam's seizure of one of his neighbors. Local rulers had to balance their self-interest in beating off an aggressor against fear that the United States would export its ideology or its political culture effectively enough to destabilize them. The war was rife with examples, some of them described as cultural. The Saudis, for example, found it difficult to accept U.S. female troops, probably particularly female officers who issued orders to enlisted men. U.S. pressure on Kuwait to reinstate the earlier elected assembly exemplifies overt application of U.S. ideology.

The Kurdish situation is probably the most interesting case in point. As noted earlier, the Arab coalition partners could not cheerfully accept a nationalist triumph that broke up Iraq, particularly if that triumph brought power to the Shi'ites in southern Iraq. On the other hand, it is grossly inimical to the West to stand by while the Kurds are massacred, particularly if the massacre is carried out by the man Westerners have just died to defeat. The interplay between realpolitik (Kurdish autonomy would cause serious problems in Turkey and Syria, both coalition partners) and U.S. national ideology (which strongly favors self-determination) has been visible ever since the end of U.S. offensive operations. Initially there was a sort of unofficial support for the Kurdish rising. Then the U.S. position cooled, while the Kurds themselves were driven north. Then the U.S. ideology, as reflected in popular sentiment here, asserted itself; the Kurds were being sold out, and that was intolerable. As these words are written, the United

States is withdrawing from southern Iraq but building and maintaining Kurdish refugee camps in the north of the country. There is even some evidence that these camps will be defended by European (British, Dutch, and French) troops and that the United Nations will be called upon to sanction that protection.

The Iraqi government presumably cannot tolerate any such enclave, because its existence will encourage thoughts of independence among other groups opposed to the central government, such as the Sunnis of the south. The situation differs from that in January and February 1991 in that the Kurdish enclave in the north is being defended by troops from countries which, broadly, share the American preference for self-determination, whereas the coalition that fought the war included countries whose rulers would not long survive any move to real democracy. It is impossible to predict the direction current events will take. One scenario is that the Kurds are finally achieving a sort of homeland and that what is left of the Iraqi forces (mainly surviving Republican Guards) will soon find itself in combat with the United Nations forces shielding the Kurds. A likely outcome would be the destruction of the Guard and then of Saddam Hussein himself.

The great lessons, then, are about people, not machines: good troops, well led; the human dimension of intelligence evaluation as compared to counting machines; the effect of U.S. public opinion (and of foreign rulers) on an administration's war plans. The machines are all spectacular, but in the end the sailors and soldiers and airmen decide what happens on both sides.

A

Ground Units and Their Equipment

THE GROUND UNITS that fought in Iraq and Kuwait were shaped largely by the requirements of other wars. The Western armies had designed their units and their equipment for the most part to fight a major NATO ground war in central Europe. The Iraqi organization was mostly patterned on what the Soviets had designed for much the same purpose, but modified to take account of some local limitations. Thus, for example, although there was little possibility that the Iraqis would have tactical nuclear weapons, all the Western armies show traces of efforts to deal with just that threat. Similarly, the tactics and overall strategy that defeated Iraq on the ground were largely developed to defeat a Soviet ground thrust into Western Europe.

Although the titles of ground units on both sides and in the several coalition armies were similar or identical, organizations and scales of equipment varied radically. So did tactical doctrine, which was reflected in part in organization and equipment. Each army has a largest natural tactical unit, which has a fixed table of organization and can be combined in flexible fashion into the next larger formation. In the U.S. Army, for example, the largest such unit is the division. Divisions and variable numbers of supporting units form a corps. In the British army the largest fixed

unit is the brigade, and the division is the mix-and-match formation adjusted to the task at hand.

Overall divisional size is limited by several considerations. First,
beyond a maximum number of soldiers it is difficult to exert any
sort of coordinated tactical control. That is why all armies limit
their divisions to between 10,000 and about 18,000 troops. Second, tactical coherence requires a unit to travel together (at the
least, close together) over ground. That usually means using roads
(the hard desert can actually support much larger movements
than can normal country), and a road can pass only so many
vehicles or troops per hour. Any attempt to exceed its capacity
merely produces a traffic jam without adding anything in the way
of firepower at the divisional frontage. Similarly, the division's
supplies must come up a road or a series of more or less parallel
roads, and their capacity limits total divisional size. Within the
maximum size, there is always a trade-off between firepower and
support ("tooth" and "tail"). Support may include the vehicles
that make the division mobile. In some armies, smaller total numbers of men may be formed into a division that is largely "tooth"
and has little staying power or long-range mobility. That is one
reason the standard Soviet division is smaller than the standard
U.S. division.

At least in conventional war, a division's firepower depends
upon how many weapons it can concentrate in a given area,
which in turn ultimately depends upon how many men can be
concentrated to fire and serve those weapons. Automation clearly
makes a difference (one machine gun is far more destructive than,
say, ten rifles), but choices must still be made at any given level
of technology. Since 1945 armies have had to choose between
conventional concentrated firepower and dispersion about the
battlefield. The more concentrated the force, the more vulnerable it is to destruction by a single nuclear hit or by a single chemical attack (by aircraft or missile; chemical artillery shells present
a somewhat less concentrated problem). There has always been
a degree of dispersion, but in recent times it generally has meant
breaking a division down into independent brigades or regiments.
Such dispersion guarantees that no single hit can destroy the

entire division. However, it becomes increasingly difficult for the subunits to be mutually supporting. On a nuclear or chemical battlefield, really destructive single weapons can be handled by the subunits. However, as soon as the mass destruction weapons disappear, the subunits prove too small to deal with more conventional formations. They just cannot develop sufficient firepower.

Independent formations below division size are also useful when an army has to be spread out over a country, as during an occupation or counterinsurgency. Thus, in the 1950s the Soviets developed independent regiments that could, in theory, fight effectively on a nuclear battlefield. They were also well adapted to the occupation of Germany. However, they could not survive in conventional warfare, which in the 1970s seemed more and more likely to be the norm. The Soviet solution was the small firepower-heavy division.

Similarly, in the 1950s the U.S. Army developed a "pentomic" infantry division in which the old structure of three infantry regiments (each of three battalions) supported by divisional artillery (three battalions) was replaced by five battle groups (essentially large battalions), a tank battalion (five companies), five 105-mm field-artillery batteries (one per battle group), and divisional artillery for general support (four 8-in howitzers, twelve 155-mm howitzers, and two Honest John missile launchers). The Honest Johns were unguided missiles for nuclear or chemical warheads. The one post-1945 armored division retained much its original structure.

This type of division could not easily concentrate firepower on a conventional battlefield because its battle groups were too weak. A new structure (ROAD, the Reorganization Objectives Army Division) was adopted in the mid-1960s to match the new flexible-response doctrine, in which the army might have to fight either a conventional or a nuclear war. The emphasis shifted to permanent maneuver battalions as building blocks (not independent battle groups) added in variable numbers to a nearly standard division base (including cavalry and air-defense battalions, a divisional HQ, and three maneuver-brigade HQs). An aviation company or battalion was added as needed.

During the late 1970s the emphasis shifted largely to non-nuclear warfare. NATO, for which the U.S. and other Western army organizations were developed, had little defensive depth within which to absorb and stop a Soviet thrust, particularly after France withdrew from the military structure of the alliance. Moreover, political cohesion demanded that NATO not concede that it would have to surrender much territory at the outset of a war. As Soviet forces became more powerful and gained mobility through the 1970s, these goals became less and less practicable. It would take time to absorb and stop a Soviet blow, and that time automatically translated into territory at least temporarily ceded. At the same time, the one crushing asset available to NATO, tactical nuclear weaponry, was largely neutralized as the Soviets, too, armed their troops with short-range nuclear weapons.

NATO sought a political solution in the doctrine of flexible response. Initial resistance to a Soviet attack would be by conventional arms (which implied that special nuclear-only formations were not needed), but any massive Soviet incursion would be met first by a demonstration nuclear response and then (in the event that the Soviets were insufficiently impressed) by a large-scale, NATO, tactical nuclear attack.[1]

This sort of doctrine implied that NATO troops would try to hold a line, absorbing a Soviet blow and only then counterattacking to regain lost territory. The main issue in such a defense is how to concentrate resources at the point of attack, a point that cannot easily be predicted in advance. As far as possible, then, the defense must rely on long-range weapons that can be held to the rear and used almost anywhere along the frontline. Since the frontline will almost inevitably have to withdraw, there is little point in positioning these valuable weapons very far forward. Much of the overall NATO firepower resided in a large air force that could be applied to the area of the line under attack.

The United States was never really comfortable with this sort of doctrine, and beginning in the late 1970s it became interested in beginning the counterthrust at the outset of the war. The army and air force reasoned that an attacking force could not maintain a firm defensive stance in its rear, and that it could best be defeated by being cut off there. This type of strategy was called nonlinear, because it gave up any attempt to maintain a firm defensive line. It depended on mobility and on individual initiative. The weight of resources had to be transferred from the corps to the divisional level.

The new doctrine required early attacks on the enemy's rear, both on his fixed installations and on the logistical tail feeding his advancing spearhead. In part, these attacks were needed to prepare the battlefield for the advance of the heavy ground units. The U.S. Air Force thus became much more interested in deep attacks on fixed targets in Eastern Europe, including the concrete hangarettes sheltering Warsaw Pact tactical aircraft. It and the army collaborated in projects to attack the moving logistical tail. Products of this effort included the JSTARS radar airplane used so successfully in the Gulf. Conversely, the air force lost interest in close air support at the point of contact, leaving that area largely to army attack helicopters.

The new AirLand Battle doctrine (described in chapter 7) thus could be considered an attempt to gain defensive depth to the east of the inter-German border, where battles would not damage NATO territory. This U.S. offensive doctrine was not entirely popular within NATO; it was often described as provocative. However, it was fully adopted by the U.S. Army, and it was the technique used so successfully in Desert Storm.

AirLand Battle grew up together with the new generation of highly mobile equipment needed to accomplish it, particularly the M1 Abrams tank, the M2/M3 Bradley infantry fighting vehicle, the Apache (AH-64) attack helicopter, the Blackhawk (UH-60) transport helicopter, and the MLRS rocket launcher. The combination of doctrine and equipment shaped a new Army 86 structure. Heavy divisions built up according to this new structure (Division 86 within Corps 86, which are described below) fought in Iraq and Kuwait.

These are not merely theoretical points. Sometimes armies fight in units smaller than divisions because they lack the organizational ability to operate on a large scale. For example, the Iraqis generally fought in brigades. Like the small units that other armies preferred for nuclear or chemical warfare reasons, the brigades were wiped out when they faced the much larger U.S. and other coalition divisions.

In ground warfare a distinction is often drawn between tactical, operational, and strategic levels of war. The differences are most easily seen in the context of a battle with a well-defined front line or zone (also called a FEBA, forward edge of the battle area, or a FLOT, front line of troops). Tactics describe what happens when troops and their vehicles collide in and near the FEBA. The operational art describes maneuvers to be carried out by units that can break through the FEBA to operate well beyond it. For example, General Schwarzkopf's left hook deep into southern Iraq can be characterized as war at the operational level. Such attacks still have as their objective the destruction of particular enemy units (e.g. by encirclement). However, really deep penetrations of the FEBA can also bring decisive results (e.g., the capture of an enemy's capital). For example, had General Schwarzkopf headed not for Basra but for Baghdad, his advance would have been more clearly strategic than operational, although the distinction is somewhat fuzzy.

Strategic is also used in terms of depth beyond the front, as in the concept of strategic, as opposed to tactical, air attack. Here the point is that the destruction of strategic targets may affect the overall course of the war, whereas tactical targets are struck to achieve immediate military objectives. However, strategic movement also means movement of ground units over long distances to put them into place to fight. In this war the movement of units from the United States to Saudi Arabia was strategic. Once in place, they moved tactically and then operationally.

These distinctions are useful because they explain different armies' choices of equipment for various degrees of mobility. One way to characterize a ground unit is by the sheer weight of its weapons and vehicles. Another is by the weight of ammunition and other supplies it expends on a daily basis. The less the unit weighs, the easier it is to move on a strategic basis, either by ship, airplane, or road. Once the unit arrives, however, its mobility on the ground (tactical or operational) depends on how mechanized it is. A lightly equipped unit can be moved great distances into a combat zone, but once there it has limited capability. That is most true of the army light divisions (which were not used at all in this war) and of the two airborne divisions; it applies to a lesser extent to the marines.

Mobility on the battlefield generally means armored mobility, and that can be purchased only by accepting great weight and, thus, limited strategic mobility.

Mobility is how quickly a unit can move. A distinction must be drawn between movement up to a combat zone and mobility within that zone (i.e., in the face of enemy fire). For example, tanks are generally moved large distances outside a battle zone aboard wheeled transporters to avoid wearing out their tracks and engines. Precombat movement, then, will be dominated by factors such as the availability of tank transporters.[2] Similarly, protracted movement in and after combat requires large numbers of fuel trucks and recovery vehicles at the division level. These mobility resources must fit within the overall size of the division, so there is always a trade-off between the number of combat units, vehicles, or weapons and overall divisional mobility.

Mobility in a combat zone will depend not only on whether a tank or wheeled vehicle can make some particular speed, but also on how well it can move in the face of enemy fire. That is why mobility generally entails weight, in the form of armor. There is, of course, a limit to acceptable weight, in that tracked vehicles must be transportable over long distances (e.g., by ship and then by rail or road transporter). At least in Europe, tank weight is also limited by the capacity of some critical bridges (the alternative, to design tanks to cross rivers either by swimming or by traveling underwater, has been tried but is not generally practical). Thus the appearance of better pontoon bridges was critical for NATO tank developers.

There is also a direct trade-off between firepower (as carried over the ground) and mobility, since firepower entails weight (of weapons and of ammunition). The coalition forces avoided this trade-off to some extent by putting much of their ground-attack firepower in airplanes and attack helicopters, which could range over the moving battle zone from more or less fixed bases. It was therefore crucial that the Iraqis failed almost completely to provide effective antiaircraft cover for their troops.

This air adjunct to the ground forces had its limitations. Aircraft range over so large an area that they cannot be tied to specific ground units. Pilots often find it difficult to distinguish friendly from enemy vehicles, and distinction becomes almost impossible at night and when weather or fog closes down so that vehicles can no longer clearly be seen.[3] Weather limited the U.S. forces very largely to reliance on ground vehicles, particularly tanks, during the final battles.

Mobility must be linked with endurance. Even when it is not moving, a unit consumes a considerable weight of supplies (at the least, the troops must eat). Once the unit begins to move, its consumption rises rapidly, because its vehicles need fuel and water. If it is to fight, it must be supplied with many tons of ammunition per day. The more mobile and powerful a fighting unit, the greater its daily consumption of fuel, ammunition, and essential spare parts. True overland operational mobility, then, requires a combination of heavy vehicles, large dumps of materiel, and large numbers of support vehicles moving between the dumps and the fighting unit. Without these vehicles, the fighting unit cannot move very far or for very long. The U.S. Army has been particularly concerned to achieve great tactical mobility combined with great endurance. In particular, experience at the National Training Center showed dramatically that fast heavy attacks could shatter enemy units. This doctrine, in turn, explains why the U.S. Army invested in the M1 Abrams series tanks, which are almost unique in the world (they are matched only by the German Leopard II) in their ability to hit distant targets while moving over rough ground at 35 mph.

The U.S. Army pays a considerable price in limited strategic mobility: it took numerous ships, and thus considerable time, to move each division to Saudi Arabia. Once the division had landed, it also took much time to move it into an attacking position, and vast dumps of materiel had to be assembled in the Saudi desert to support the offensive.

Experience over the past two decades has shown that many Third World armies have been willing enough to buy the fighting vehicles that should guarantee some operational mobility, but that they have failed to buy the sort of logistical tail needed to make that potential a reality. Often they cannot sustain intense combat for more that three to five days before stopping to resupply. For example, in 1973 the need to refuel halted a Syrian tank offensive that might otherwise have broken through in the Golan Heights. Much the same might be said of the Iraqi Army; it may have been just such a logistical shortfall that made it impossible for Saddam Hussein to continue moving south immediately after securing Kuwait in August 1990.[4]

The Soviets have a high tooth-to-tail ratio, but for a rather different reason. They do not anticipate that individual formations, such as divisions, will survive for long in combat. They are expected to do maximum damage, then to be replaced, unit for unit, when they are beyond the point of viability. There is little reason, in the Soviet view, in providing each formation with more in the way of reserve ammunition or operating lifetime than enemy firepower will allow it to use. This is much the same philosophy that, on a much smaller scale, provides Soviet tanks with limited stores of ammunition corresponding to limited expected combat lifetime. A Third World army mimicking Soviet organizational practice, but without the large number of units the Soviets have, will find that it lacks the ability for sustained combat.

The U.S. Marines achieve great strategic mobility at a cost in tactical and operational mobility, with the important caveat that an amphibious operation will transport them, in combat-ready form, over tactical or operational distances. Once they have landed, however, their tactical mobility is limited by their lack of fast, heavily armored vehicles. In the absence of some technological miracle, this is an inevitable sort of trade-off.

The U.S. airmobile and airborne divisions represent yet another choice. They achieve high operational mobility because they are transported point to point by helicopters. To some extent, troop-carrying helicopters actually replace conventional armored personnel carriers, and, in theory, attack helicopters replace conventional tanks. This spectacular mobility, over a range of perhaps a hundred miles, inevitably carries costs. The helicopters cannot move a great weight, so the unit must restrict itself to lightweight equipment, which limits its firepower and its staying power. For example, its artillery pieces are small, towed 105-mm and 155-mm guns. Endurance is limited, too; units have to be relieved within three to five days by armored or mechanized forces. Even so, the combination of the light unit and its numerous helicopters is fairly heavy, so the unit as a whole is not extremely mobile on a strategic level (it is quite mobile when shorn of its helicopters, however).

These units, then, are designed to seize critical points, such as road junctions, and to hold them until heavier units can link up on the ground. These considerations explain why XVIII Airborne Corps had to stop to build up a forward base when it arrived deep in southern Iraq, and also why the base was largely supplied by trucks arriving in its wake. Once the base was ready, the Corps's airmobile units could jump forward again, seize and hold an airhead, and wait to link up with Corps ground troops. These units, then, might be described as designed for operational rather than tactical mobility, with the option of gaining strategic mobility at the cost of their operational mobility (i.e., moving long distances by airplane, without their helicopters).

The Syrian, and to a lesser extent the Egyptian, divisions followed a Soviet style of organization, much heavier in tooth than in tail, although they did not necessarily embrace Soviet doctrine. The Iraqi Army still reflected the British organizational ideas of its early period, modified by Jordanian and Indian advice (both also reflecting British influence) during the Iran-Iraq War. There was also, of course, input from the Soviets, and the Soviets were responsible for tying together the disparate elements of the Iraqi communications system.

In each army the unit designations are quite similar: from largest to smallest they are corps, divisions, brigades/regiments, companies, platoons, and squads. The significance of the designations, however, varies considerably from army to army. The point of organization is that units under a higher command can be coordinated to support each other (i.e., that they can fight according to some coherent plan). It is a useful rule of thumb that the "span of command" extends over three to five subordinate units. For example, to the extent that a general is to exercise coherent tactical command of his division, it cannot have more than three to five principal tactical subunits, in this case brigades or regiments. Hence the typical U.S. figures given below. A higher command with many more than five subunits either is not a tactically useful command (it is presumably used primarily for logistics) or it exercises command through some intermediate level not immediately obvious. A scheme of units divided into thirds has been popular since the end of World War I. For example, two units can attack while the third is held in reserve to reinforce or to replace one of the two units in combat.

The higher the level of a unit, the more complex its operation, and the greater the degree of staff competence its tactical handling demands. Third World armies, such as that of Iraq, generally have found it difficult to handle organizations above brigade size (up to, say, 5,000 men) tactically in any coherent way. Their tables of organization include divisions and corps, but tactical reality, as for example at Khafji, is likely to be quite different. Similar, a higher-level unit covers more space. In theory, it needs longer-range supporting weapons. They must, after all, be capable of firing to cover subunits at greater and greater distances from their emplacements.

In the U.S. Army's case, which is typical, the smallest subunit is the squad (nine to twelve individuals under a sergeant). Three squads make up a platoon, under a lieutenant. In some armies there is an intermediate unit, the section (fifteen to thirty troops under a senior sergeant; the British use this term for the squad). Three or four platoons are a company, under a captain. A troop is a company-sized unit of cavalry (the British use this term for a platoon-sized armored or mechanized cavalry unit). Three to five companies form a battalion or squadron (cavalry), under a lieutenant colonel. The British use the term squadron for a company-sized tank or armored car unit. The battalion/squadron is the largest nearly homogeneous unit. At the next level up, two to five battalions plus supporting units form a brigade or regiment, under a colonel or brigadier general. Three brigades plus additional supporting units form a division, under a major general. Two to five divisions, again with supporting units, form a corps, under a lieutenant general. During World War II several corps could be grouped together as an army, under a general, and there were even army groups.

Armies differ quite considerably on the makeup of the different units. The current U.S. organization, Army 86, makes the company a lean organization employing only a single major type of weapon. Administration is concentrated at the next level, the battalion. According to the Army 86 final report, "the battalion commander integrates and fights the combined-arms battle; the brigade commander mixes arms and allocates ground; the division commander locates the enemy, interdicts, concentrates, and fights the AirLand Battle."[5]

The U.S. Army force that fought in the Gulf area had been developed as part of a 1982–83 reorganization intended to form Army 86. The objective was a mix of heavy forces largely for NATO missions (Division 86, Corps 86, and higher-echelon units) and lighter forces for CentCom and similar contingencies (Infantry Division 86, Contingency Corps 86, and higher-echelon units). In effect, VII Corps was Corps 86 and XVIII Corps was Contingency Corps 86. Because the army had insufficient manpower, it cut the planned divisional organizations by one-fifth as of June 1983 and planned to rely on reservists to fill out the active units (a plan that generally failed during the Gulf war). Some forces drawn from the divisions were moved to the corps level. The new concept was called the Army of Excellence (AoE). In addition, further attention was focused on low-intensity conflict. The army's solution was to form four infantry divisions (light) to supplement the two airborne and airmobile units and the experimental 9th Motorized Division (the "high-technology testbed," now being cut down to brigade level). These units are still fairly heavy, but they lack the stamina of the more conventional divisions (they are presumably closer to the Soviet divisional concept). At the same time two more divisions were formed, for a total of eighteen: eleven heavy and seven light divisions.

The unit descriptions that follow are taken from standard doctrine (such as Div 86 organization charts). In practice, units are tailored to some extent to fit circumstances.

Corps 86 consisted of an armored cavalry regiment scouting for three divisions (two armored and one mechanized infantry or the reverse), supplemented by a corps combat aviation brigade, corps artillery (four brigades, typically one of Lance missiles [eighteen launchers], one of MLRS [four battalions, twenty-seven launchers each], one of 155-mm howitzers [144 guns], and one of 8-in howitzers [144 guns]), a corps combat electronic warfare intelligence (CEWI) group, an air-defense artillery group (one gun battalion, three light antiaircraft missile battalions armed with Chaparral, and one heavy antiaircraft battalion armed with Patriot).

The U.S. Army is the world's largest user of helicopters. The planned corps combat aviation brigade consisted of ten battalions:

—1 general support aviation battalion (35 OH-58 scouts, 20 UH-1s, 5 fixed-wing reconnaissance aircraft)

—1 medium helicopter battalion (64 CH-47Ds, 4 UH-1s)

—2 combat support helicopter battalions (each 45 UH-60s)

—6 attack helicopter battalions in 2 groups (each group HQ with 3 UH-60s and an OH-58 scout, each battalion with 18 AH-64s or 21 AH-1Ss and 12 OH-58 scouts)

The VII Corps, the army's main striking force in the Gulf, exemplified the Corps 86 structure: a cavalry regiment (2d), two armored divisions (1st and 3d), and a mechanized infantry division (1st).

The contingency corps equated to XVIII Airborne Corps: an armored cavalry regiment (3d) to scout, two light divisions (82d Airborne and 101st Airborne [Air Assault]), and two U.S.–based heavy divisions (1st Cavalry and 24th Mechanized Infantry). The planned structure included the 6th Air Cavalry Combat Brigade as a corps asset, but this unit was not combat-ready in August 1990. Instead, the 12th Aviation Brigade and the aviation brigade of the 3d Armored Division, both in Europe, were deployed to Saudi Arabia.

1st Cavalry deployed with two organic brigades plus 1st ("Tiger") Brigade of the 2d Armored Division (two tank, two mechanized infantry, and one artillery battalions).[6] The "Tiger" brigade was later transferred to reinforce the 1st Marine Division. 24th Mechanized Infantry Division deployed without the Georgia National Guard roundout brigade (48th Mechanized Brigade) normally assigned to it. Instead, it was given the 197th Separate Mechanized Brigade, the school unit from Fort Benning (one tank, two mechanized infantry, and one artillery battalions, and one cavalry troop).

U.S. heavy divisions are built around ten maneuver battalions (six tank and four mechanized infantry in an armored or cavalry division, four tank and six mechanized infantry in a mechanized infantry division, five of each of the 24th Infantry Division) and one divisional cavalry (mechanized reconnaissance) squadron (battalion).[7] The maneuver battalions operate as three brigades, each of which includes supporting artillery (one battalion of twenty-four 155-mm guns per brigade). The division contributes a battalion of twelve 8-inch guns and a battery of nine long-range multiple rocket launchers (MLRS). The division also has its own air-defense artillery (self-propelled Vulcans) and supporting battalions (e.g., engineer and signal).

The standard army tank battalion is built around 58 tanks and 32 lighter armored vehicles.[8] The standard mechanized infantry battalion is built around 107 light armored vehicles, including 54 Bradleys.[9] Because it is expected to operate semi-independently, the cavalry squadron is not a homogeneous unit.[10]

Each division also includes one or two combat aviation battalions, each comprising a headquarters company (with a few observation and utility helicopters) and three attack helicopter companies (each with a scout/observation platoon of four OH-58 Kiowas and a gunship platoon of seven AH-1Ss or AH-64s). Objectives for helicopters within the heavy division have varied considerably over time. Division 86 was to have had twenty-four UH-60 troop carriers, six UH-1s, fifty AH-1S attack helicopters, fifty-four

OH-58 scouts, and three EH-60s for ECM and ESM. By 1988 the army's objective was a divisional strength of twenty-four UH-60s, six UH-1s, thirty AH-64s, forty-two OH-58s, and three EH-60s.

Total personnel: 17,027 in an armored division; 17,330 in a mechanized infantry division.

An independent armored cavalry regiment is built around three armored cavalry squadrons, a combat aviation squadron, a field artillery battalion (twenty-four M109 155-mm howitzers), and an air-defense artillery battery (twelve guns). The main fighting vehicle is the M3 armored cavalry vehicle (111).[11] The combat aviation squadron consists of twenty-four scout helicopters (eighteen OH-58Cs and six OH-58As), twenty-five utility helicopters (UH-60s), and twenty-six attack helicopters in two attack helicopter companies and three air cavalry troops.[12] Each air cavalry troop includes a scouting platoon (six OH-58s) and an attack helicopter platoon (four AH-1Ss or Apaches).

The airborne division includes nine infantry battalions, which can form three brigades. There is a single armored battalion (airborne), currently equipped with 54 old M551 Sheridan light tanks. This division includes an aviation battalion and an air-cavalry squadron, and an air-defense artillery battalion (towed Vulcan guns). The airmobile division is similar but has a six-battalion aviation group. It lacks any armored component.

The nominal airborne division includes a helicopter battalion (forty-four OH-58s, seventeen UH-1s, thirty UH-60s, twenty-one AH-1Ss or eighteen AH-64s) and an air cavalry squadron (thirty OH-58 scouts and twenty-seven AH-1Ss or eighteen AH-64s). The airmobile (air-assault) division includes six helicopter battalions in its air group: a general support battalion (thirty-two OH-58s, fourteen UH-1s), a medium helicopter battalion (forty-eight CH-47Ds to lift heavy equipment plus two UH-60s), two troop-carrier (combat-support) battalions (forty-five UH-60s each), an attack battalion (thirty-six OH-58s, nine UH-60s, sixty-three AH-1s or fifty-four AH-64s), and an air-cavalry squadron (thirty OH-58s, twenty-two UH-60s, and twenty-seven AH-1s or eighteen AH-64s).[13] In combat, the OH-58s designate targets for the AH-64s; the two types operate in teams.

Based on all of these breakdowns, approximate U.S. Army aviation strength in the Gulf should have been:

	Heavy Divisions (5)	Airborne Division (1)	Air-mobile Division (1)	Corps Aviation (2)	Cavalry Regiments (2)	Total
UH-60	120	30	123	192	50	515
UH-1	30	17	14	48	—	109
CH-47	—	—	47	128	—	175
OH-58	210	74	62	218	84	648
AH-64	150	36	72	216	52	526
AH-1S	250	48	88	252	52	690
EH-60	15	—	—	—	—	15
Fixed-wing	—	—	—	10	—	10

Figures for AH-64s and AH-1Ss are alternatives; the force in the Gulf was mixed. Figures for the heavy divisions are for the army objective as specified in 1988. Approximate actual figures were generally somewhat lower: 370 UH-60s, 315 UH-1s (replacement by UH-60s was not yet complete), 150 CH-47s, 425 OH-58s, 250 AH-64s, 140 AH-1Ss, 30 EH-60s, and several reconnaissance aircraft.[14]

The principal U.S. heavy tank used in the Gulf was the M1A1 Abrams, armed with a 120-mm gun. The heavy U.S.–based divisions that arrived in the Gulf during the Fall of 1990 were equipped with the earlier M1 (armed with the earlier NATO-standard 105-mm gun), because the divisions in Europe, which had to face the best Soviet tanks, enjoyed priority for the better-armed M1A1. It is not altogether clear whether all M1s in Saudi Arabia were replaced by M1A1s before war began. The U.S. Army in Saudi Arabia probably had about 1,900 M1A1 tanks.

The Abrams tank combines a new composite armor with high off-road speed (due to its powerful gas turbine) and a ballistic computer and stabilized gun mount that permit them to fire reliably when moving at speed over rough ground, a capability that proved quite valuable in the Gulf. In prewar exercises, the computer and other human-engineering features made it possible for Abrams crews to aim at and hit their targets in remarkably short time.[15] The Abrams tank also has a FLIR, an infrared vision device that proved effective not only at night but also in the dust and smoke of Kuwaiti daytime (note the account in the main text of the major ground battle). On average, an Abrams outranged an Iraqi tank by about 1,000 meters.

In combat, Iraqi tanks armed with the best Soviet guns could not penetrate the new composite armor. Seven M1s were hit by T-72 rounds, the best in Iraqi (or, for that matter, in Soviet) service, and none sustained discernible damage. Only four Abrams were disabled, and four more were damaged but repairable.

The companion to the Abrams is the M2/M3 Bradley. M2 is the standard armored personnel carrier, replacing the earlier M113. M3 is the companion armored cavalry scout variant. The Bradley, which carries a nine-man infantry squad, was approved for full production in 1980, and it entered service in 1983. The main design requirements were mobility comparable to that of the new Abrams tank (the Bradley has the highest power-to-weight ratio of any tracked armored personnel carrier); main armament (25-mm gun) sufficient to handle enemy light armor and support the infantry squad when it fights dismounted; and sufficient armor to withstand fire from enemy infantry fighting vehicles (the Bradley is probably the most heavily armored personnel carrier in the world). The Bradley also carries a dual TOW anti-tank missile launcher (with seven missiles), a controversial feature chosen by the U.S. Army on the theory that these vehicles would sometimes find themselves facing enemy tanks without friendly tanks in company. The Bradley is also armed with a 7.62-mm machine gun alongside its 25-mm cannon, and with modified M16 rifles that its mounted squad can fire while it moves (this option has been less and less important of late, however). Maximum road speed is 42 mph, and range is 300 miles.

The very similar M3 (cavalry fighting vehicle, or CFV, rather than infantry fighting vehicle, IFV) carries a five-man cavalry squad. It lacks the M16s of the M2 and carries twice as many stowed 25-mm rounds (1,200 rather than 600; both have 300 rounds in belts feeding into the 25-mm cannon) and ten TOW missiles.

Of about 2,000 Bradleys in the Gulf, three were disabled or destroyed (probably one by a Hellfire missile and two by Iraqi tank fire).

The marines in the Gulf were the I and II MEFs, each normally consisting of a marine division (1st and 2d, respectively), supported by an air wing. In this case the marines used a single, heavily reinforced air wing. Afloat were the 4th MEB aboard Amphibious Group 2 and the 5th MEB aboard Amphibious Group 3; there were also the smaller 13th and 22d MEUs, with backup in the form of the 26th MEU aboard the Sixth Fleet amphibious ready group.

The Marine Corps is organized primarily for strategic mobility. It generally operates below divisional size, and ground and fixed-wing air units are always organized together in Marine Air-Ground Task Forces (MAGTFs). The amphibious ready group (ARG) in each of the two forward-deployed fleets (Sixth and Seventh) carries the smallest such force, a regiment-sized Marine Assault Unit or Marine Expeditionary Unit (MAU or MEU). The brigade team (Marine Expeditionary Brigade, or MEB) is the unit supported by a Maritime Prepositioning Squadron (the assault equivalent is the Marine Assault Brigade, or MAB). Similarly, the prepositioned equipment in Norway supports an MEB. The largest marine unit is the division-wing team, the Marine Expeditionary or Assault Force (MEF or MAF). The current U.S. goal is to have sufficient amphibious ships to support simultaneous MAF and MAB assaults. This goal corresponds to the current "one and a half" war policy (i.e., one large war requiring an MAF-level assault and one small one for which an MAB-level assault would suffice).

By law, the Marine Corps maintains three full active divisions (the 3d, in Okinawa; the 1st, at Camp Pendleton in California; and the 2d, at Camp Lejeune, North Carolina) plus a reserve division. Thus the deployment to the Gulf of two active marine divisions consumed about two-thirds of the strength of the corps.

The standard Marine Corps division is built around three infantry regiments, an artillery regiment, a reconnaissance battalion, a tank battalion, an assault amphibian battalion, and a light armored battalion.[16] Each infantry regiment is built around three rifle companies (a fourth is added in wartime) and a weapons company (a regiment deploying as an MEU or MAU has four rifle companies).[17]

The tank battalion consists of four tank companies, a company of HMMWVs armed with TOW missiles, and a reconnaissance platoon (HMMWVs), plus recovery and bridging vehicles. At the outset of the buildup, the marines were planning to replace their obsolescent M60 tanks (some with applique armor) with the newer M1A1s already in army service. The first M1A1s were scheduled for delivery in November 1990, and ordinarily they would not have entered full service until late 1991. The army provided some M1A1s on an emergency basis from vehicles held in storage (in lieu of later production), but the deployed marine units still had numerous M60s when the war began.[18]

The assault amphibians (AAV7A1s) are the marines' equivalent to army armored personnel carriers. They are intended to swim ashore during an assault; each carries twenty-five marines. The full assault amphibian battalion has four combat companies and a total of 200 vehicles. An afloat MEU has an attached assault amphibian company (twelve troop carriers, two command vehicles, and one recovery vehicle). Because it is intended to swim in surf, the assault amphibian must be more lightly built than a land-based armored personnel carrier like the M113 or the Bradley. The 1985 redesignation of the vehicle, from LVTP7A1 to AAV7A1, was intended to emphasize its role as an armored personnel carrier rather than as a landing vehicle.

The light armored battalion is a recent creation, built around the fast (65 mph on roads), license-built Piranha (LAV, light armored vehicle) wheeled amphibious armored personnel carrier accommodating six infantrymen and a 25-mm Chain Gun. The battalion comprises three LAV companies (each with two command LAVs and fourteen LAV(25)s armed with 25-mm guns), a weapons company (eight reconnaissance LAVs, eight mortar-armed LAV(M)s, and sixteen LAV(AT)s armed with TOW missiles), and a headquarters company (two command LAVs, three logistics LAVs, and one recovery LAV(R)). The marines in the Gulf found the LAV's mobility and reliability gratifying. Army airborne units equipped with the vehicle also mentioned its low signature, which made it relatively stealthy.

The artillery regiment assigned to each marine division consists of five battalions, the fourth being permanently detached to the associated MEU. Most of the guns are towed, lightweight pieces: 105-mm M101s and 155-mm M114s (old) or M198s (new and lighter weight). Equipment: two battalions (1st and 2d) each with twenty-four 155-mm towed howitzers, one battalion (3d) with thirty-two 105-mm and 155-mm lightweight howitzers, one MEU battalion (4th) with ten M198s and eight M101s, and one mechanized (5th) with twenty-four M109s (155-mm) and twelve M110s (8-inch).[19]

In all, about half the total strength of the Marine Corps was in the Gulf area: 92,500 out of a total of 193,000.

The United States deployed the 5th Special Forces Group to the Gulf area.[20] The operational unit is the twelve- to fourteen-man A-Team. Six A-Teams comprise a company, and three companies comprise a battalion. The 5th SFG has three battalions, or about fifty-four A-Teams, numbered in an A500 series (the second digit is the number of the company, e.g., A592 is the 2d detachment of the 9th company, which is Company C of III Battalion). Reportedly each battalion was assigned to one of the three main resistance movements: the Kuwaiti resistance, the Kurdish resistance, and the non-Kurdish Iraqi resistance. Operations included the deep reconnaissance toward the Euphrates cited by General Schwarzkopf in his end-of-war briefing, the destruction of the remaining Iraqi fiber-optic links at the outset of the ground war, and the destruction of key bridges that might have allowed Iraqi forces to escape the trap at Basra. A Medal of Honor is pending as a result of a mission deep in Iraqi territory beginning with a high-altitude low opening (HALO) parachute insertion by Detachment A544 early in the war. The AC-130 gunship lost to Iraqi fire on 31 January was supporting a 5th SFG operation.

The British Army organization is closer to that of the Marine Corps than to that of the U.S. Army in that divisions are ad hoc units. The permanent tactical unit is the brigade built out of battalions. The peacetime army "family" unit is the regiment, which carries the traditions of the army as a whole and which is often regional in character.[21] A regiment will include one or more battalions.[22] As an exception to the rule of battalion versus regiment, armored cavalry units are called regiments rather than battalions. Compared to the U.S. ground force in the Gulf, the British had much stronger field engineer units (highly specialized combat engineers and pioneers). One lesson of the war may be that the U.S. Army should increase its own field engineer strength.

The brigade is semiorganizational and semitactical, its subunits forming battle groups as needed. The theory was that the army would normally deploy in brigade form, but it would fight in battle groups built out of the brigades. In the Gulf, armored brigades were the tactical units, with attached divisional troops as needed. The brigades can coalesce into higher-level units. British forces in Germany form a four-division corps (1st, 3d, and 4th Armoured Divisions and 2d Infantry Division).[23] Like their U.S. counterparts, these divisions are triangular, each consisting of three armored brigades (three battalions/tank regiments each). The special division formed for the Gulf had only two brigades, one drawn from each of two armored divisions in Germany, owing to limited British resources. However, it also included units that would normally be added only at the corps level.

The standard armored (not tank) brigade consists of two tank regiments and a mechanized battalion; the standard mechanized brigade (also called an armored brigade) is one tank regiment and two mechanized battalions. The tank battalion or regiment nominally operated fifty-seven Challengers (at least one unit was understrength). The infantry battalion operates forty-five Warriors, and thus is slightly smaller than its U.S. counterpart. The standard infantry brigade consists of three or four infantry battalions plus an armored reconnaissance regiment and an artillery regiment (twenty-four M109s). As in the U.S. case, the division adds 8-in howitzers and multiple rocket launchers (MLRS).

The British 1st Armoured Division headquarters organized the British army forces in the Gulf. It combined an armored brigade and a mechanized (armored) brigade for a total of three tank regiments and three mechanized battalions. The brigades were the 7th Brigade from 1st Armoured Division (which recalled the World War II 7th Armoured Division, the "Desert Rats"), comprising two armored regiments (Royal Scots Dragoon Guards and Queen's Royal Irish Hussars) and one mechanized infantry battalion (1st battalion of the Staffordshire Regiment); and the 4th Armoured Brigade from 3d Armoured Division, comprising one tank regiment (14/20th King's Hussars) and two mechanized infantry battalions (1st Battalion Royal Scots and 3d Battalion Royal Regiment of Fusiliers). Each brigade had an attached Royal Artillery regiment: the 7th had 40th Field Artillery Regiment and the 4th had 2d Field Artillery Regiment.

The division had, in addition, a reconnaissance regiment, divisional heavy artillery, and divisional army aviation. The reconnaissance regiment (Scorpions from the Queen's Dragoon Guards and other vehicles from the 16/5th Lancers) operated twenty-four Scorpions, twenty-four Scimitars, and sixteen Strikers (Scorpion chassis carrying antitank missiles). The Scorpions deployed with the 1st Brigade, the other vehicles with the 4th. Divisional artillery comprised sixteen M109 (155-mm) and twelve M110 (8-inch) self-propelled howitzers of the 32d Heavy Artillery Regiment and twelve multiple rocket launchers (MLRS) of the 39th Heavy Artillery Regiment. The helicopter component was the 4th Regiment Army Aviation Corps, with twenty-four Lynx (carrying TOW antitank missiles) and eighteen Gazelle helicopters.

The standard British heavy tank in the Gulf was the Challenger, an improved version of the earlier Chieftain incorporating the same type of composite armor used by the U.S. Abrams. Because it is not a completely new design, Challenger does not have the sort of fully integrated fire-control system used by the U.S. Abrams, and thus cannot hit as quickly. Nor does it share the Abrams's German-developed 120-mm smoothbore gun. Instead, it uses a British-developed 120-mm rifle, which can hit at very long range. One Royal Scots Dragoon Guards gunner decided to test the accuracy of his gun and destroyed an Iraqi tank with his first round at 5,100 meters.

Warrior is the British equivalent to the U.S. Bradley, carrying a 30-mm Rarden cannon. Like the Bradley, it is designed to carry an infantry squad (seven or eight troops), but it has no integral antitank missile launcher (the squad carries a Milan).

Scorpion and Scimitar are the British equivalents to the U.S. M3 cavalry version of the Bradley. Scorpion carries a 76-mm gun which can engage tanks with its HEAT round; Scimitar (30-mm Rarden gun) can engage lighter infantry fighting vehicles. Striker is a Scorpion chassis carrying Swingfire antitank missiles.

French divisions are much smaller than those of the United States and Britain; they have about the manpower strength of U.S. brigades. Thus the five-division rapid deployment force formed in 1985 (FAR: Force d'Action Rapide) is only 47,000 men. These small divisions have little endurance; they correspond to a French national policy that envisages quick nuclear escalation (or at least the threat of such escalation) in a short European war.[24] Characteristically, France designates short-range nuclear weapons as "pre-strategic," to reflect their role in escalation, rather than tactical (as other countries would designate comparable weapons). France also suffers from limited military manpower, even though the French Army is manned largely by draftees, and there is an understandable reluctance to reduce the territorial coverage of the army.

The standard heavy armored division is 10,000 strong. Each of six such divisions consists of two or three armored (tank) regiments (the two divisions in Germany have two regiments each), two mechanized infantry regiments, one motorized infantry regiment, two artillery regiments, and one engineer regiment. There are also two light ("school") armored divisions (about 5,600 to 6,000 men each), consisting of four regiments (two armored regiments, one mechanized and one motorized infantry regiments; or one armored regiment, one light armored regiment, and two motorized infantry regiments). Each of two infantry divisions (7,500 men each) consists of three motorized infantry regiments (four companies each of three platoons), a light armored regiment, and an artillery regiment.

Five special-purpose divisions (two of them formed for the purpose) are combined in the FAR formed 1 July 1985:

— 4th Airmobile Division (formed 1 July 1985): 7,000 troops, 240 helicopters, with 360 HOT and 45 Milan antitank missile launchers. This division consists of 3 combat helicopter regiments, 1 airmobile combat regiment, and 1 HQ/supply regiment (4 transport squadrons, 10 Puma each, and 1 liaison squadron, 10 Gazelles)

— 6th Light Armored Division (formed 1 July 1985; its headquarters was used in the Gulf): 7,400 troops in 2 light armored regiments and 2 infantry regiments; it is equipped for airmobile and amphibious operations. This division includes an artillery regiment.

— 9th Marine Infantry Division: 8,000 troops, 3 motorized marine infantry regiments, 1 armored reconnaissance regiment, 1 field artillery regiment (105-mm guns, to be replaced by 155-mm)

— 11th Airborne Division: 13,500 troops, 6 parachute regiments, 1 airborne reconnaissance regiment, 1 airborne artillery regiment, 1 airborne engineer regiment

— 27th Mountain Division: 9,000 troops, 5 mountain infantry battalions, 1 mountain infantry regiment (battalion size), 1 armored reconnaissance regiment, 1 mountain artillery regiment, and a mountain engineer battalion

Finally, the division-sized Foreign Legion (8,500 men) includes the 2d Parachute Regiment and three infantry regiments (one used for training, one deployed overseas).

The standard regimental building blocks are:

— armored (tank) with 3 (4 for the 2 divisions in Germany) tank

companies (17 AMX 30B2 tanks each, plus 1 or 2 HQ tanks, for a total of 52 or 54 or 70 tanks) plus 10 AMX 10P/PC
—light armored regiment (36 AMX 10RC armed with Milan missiles)
—armored reconnaissance regiment (36 AML and 24 Milan missile launchers)
—artillery regiment (4 batteries, each of 5 155-mm guns)
—mechanized infantry regiment of 1 armored company (3 platoons, each of 4 AMX 30B2, plus 1 AMX 30B2 and 1 AMX 10PC) plus 3 mechanized infantry companies (each with 4 rifle platoons riding 3 AMX 10P each, plus 1 AMX 10PC and 1 AMX 10P with 2 Milan antitank missiles)
—motorized infantry regiment of 1 antitank company (12 VAB/HOT armored cars in 3 platoons) and 3 motorized infantry companies (each with 16 VAB, including one platoon with 2 Milan missiles and 2 81-mm mortars)
—combat helicopter regiment: 1 HQ squadron, 3 antitank squadrons (10 Gazelle/HOT each), 1 combat squadron (10 Gazelle with 20-mm guns), 1 reconnaissance squadron (10 Gazelle), 1 supply squadron (10 Puma): total 60 helicopters
—airmobile combat regiment: 1 light reconnaissance company, 3 scout/antitank companies (15 Milan antitank missiles each), 1 rifle company, 1 engineer company, 1 support company

Most of this substantial force could not be deployed to the Gulf. The French Army consists mainly of draftees, and under French law (motivated by painful experiences such as the Indo-China and Algerian wars) they cannot be made to serve outside the country.[25] The FAR was conceived largely as a means of quickly plugging holes in a NATO defense of central Europe, and therefore had not been designed for emergencies such as the Gulf. The Foreign Legionnaires can serve overseas, but their force was never designed to fight conventional heavily armed ground forces such as the Iraqi Army.

France therefore had to assemble an ad hoc light armored division around the headquarters of the 6th Light Armored Division;

it was sometimes called the Division Daguet, after the name the French gave the operation. In combat it proved far too light, and this experience will probably affect French planning. The 6th Division was actually much heavier than most French divisions, and it did not quite correspond to any of the organizations described above: one understrength armored regiment (4th Dragoons: forty AMX 30B2 tanks), two armored reconnaissance regiments (1st Spahi and 1st Foreign Legion cavalry), one motorized "battle group" (VAB armored cars and AMX 10RCs from 1st Infantry Regiment and 2d Foreign Legion Infantry Regiment), one artillery regiment (11th Marine Artillery), and two helicopter regiments. The French force also included elements of 13th Parachute Dragoon Regiment for deep reconnaissance and stay-behind operations. Some of these men were caught by the Iraqis early in the buildup while placing navigational beacons in the desert.

The standard French main battle tank, the AMX 30, carries much less armor than contemporary U.S. and British tanks deployed to the Gulf. AMX 30 was conceived in the 1960s. Its designers expected it to rely on its relatively high speed; the AMX 30 corresponds more to World War II tank destroyers than to full tanks. The tank's 105-mm gun is not the standard NATO type used by the United States and Britain (and mounted in M60 tanks used by the U.S. Marine Corps and by the Saudis). It fires shaped-charge (HEAT) ammunition that cannot be allowed to spin very rapidly, so the shell has ball bearings to separate it from the spinning driving ring. The gun is not powerful enough to fire the special armor penetrators used in the standard NATO gun. Moreover, newer powerplants provide sufficient power to move much heavier tanks like the Abrams quite as fast as the light AMX 30. The AMX 30B2 version used by the French Army in the Gulf has a laser range finder and some additional armor, but it could not compare with the Abrams, M60, and Challenger.

The French made special efforts to export a desert version of the AMX 30, and it was adopted by the Saudis and Qataris.

AMX 10P is the standard French infantry fighting vehicle, broadly equivalent to the U.S. M2 Bradley. Like the M2, it carries an infantry squad (eight men in this case). AMX 10P carries a 20-mm cannon, but the squad can mount its Milan antitank missile on top. The same chassis is used to carry a HOT antitank missile.

AMX 10RC is a heavy six-wheeled armored car carrying a 105-mm cannon.

VAB is a light reconnaissance armored car, armed only with a 7.62-mm machine gun.

The Western units actually deployed to the Gulf followed standard tables of organization fairly accurately. That is not the case in Third World armies, and for that reason it is difficult to assess Iraqi troop and vehicle strength. Typically a Third World army actually operates at the brigade level. Divisional headquarters will pick up variable numbers of brigades, almost in a task-force type of organization. The notes that follow are, therefore, approximate at best.

The Arab forces were organized outside CentCom control as an Arab-Islamic force under Gen. Khalid bin Sultan, son of the Saudi defense minister. The force at the front consisted of two ad hoc Saudi divisions, an ad hoc Kuwaiti division, the two Egyptian divisions, the Syrian division, and three separate brigades (Egyptian and Syrian commando/special forces brigades and an African brigade). The African brigade consisted of a Senegalese infantry battalion (500 men), a Niger infantry battalion (481 men), and a Moroccan mechanized battalion (reinforced battalion from 6th Regiment: 1,700 men with M113 APCs).

Other foreign contingents included those from Bangladesh (brigade [about 6,000 men] garrisoning Mecca and 1st East Bengal Infantry Battalion) and Pakistan (7th Armored Brigade [probably on the Jordanian border] and infantry battalion as garrison in the UAE). Some Pakistani troops were integrated into Saudi formations. Before the war, an Egyptian brigade and a Syrian commando/special forces battalion were in the UAE.

The Gulf Co-Operation Council (UAE, Qatar, Oman, and Bahrain) formed a rapid deployment force (the Peninsula Shield Force) based at Hafr-al-Batin, about 60 km south of the Kuwaiti border. In peacetime this force consists of a Saudi brigade plus a composite brigade from Bahrain, Oman, Qatar, and the UAE.

The contingents were reinforced and split into task forces with Saudi, Kuwaiti, African, and Asian units, as described below. Total GCC strength was estimated in mid-February as 55,000 ground troops equipped with about 300 AMX30, M60, QF-40, and Chieftain tanks.

The Royal Saudi ground forces are organized as two parallel armies, the regular Royal Saudi Army and the National Guard. Total army strength is two armored brigades (one with M60A3 tanks and M113 armored personnel carriers, one with French AMX 30 tanks and AMX 10 armored personnel carriers), three mechanized infantry brigades, one infantry brigade, one airborne brigade, and three Royal Guard battalions.

Saudi armored brigades each consist of three tank battalions (two HQ tanks and three eleven-tank companies), one mechanized infantry battalion (AMX 10s or M113s), one artillery battalion, and one support battalion.[26] Each of three mechanized brigades (10th, 11th, and 20th) consists of a tank battalion, three mechanized battalions, one artillery battalion, and one support battalion. A brigade equipped with U.S. equipment has thirty-five M60 tanks, eighty-eight M113s, thirty-one M125s (81-mm mortar carriers), twelve M106s (4.2-in mortar carriers), thirty M577s (command vehicles), eighteen M109 howitzers, and eighteen M992 ammunition carriers. Each mechanized battalion consists of a headquarters company (including reconnaissance and engineer platoons), three rifle companies fourteen APCs, three 81-mm mortars, three 4.2-in mortars, three 90-mm vehicles, one Vulcan AAA vehicle, and two TOW vehicles), and an artillery battery (five towed 105-mm howitzers and six towing vehicles, one of them presumable the battery command vehicle). The Saudi 6th infantry brigade is motorized, consisting of three motorized battalions (AML 90 and M3 Panhard armored personnel carriers), an artillery battalion (FH 70 towed howitzers), and a support battalion. The armored brigade with U.S. equipment was originally manned by Pakistanis, who were replaced by Moroccans in 1987.

The National Guard is an outgrowth of the Ikhwan, the military arm of the desert tribes that conquered what is now Saudi Arabia for the Abdul Aziz family, the House of Saud. It consists of two mechanized brigades (using V-150 wheeled armored personnel carriers) and two infantry brigades. There is no permanent higher unit formation.

In this case the Royal Saudi Army on the frontier was organized into two divisions: 1st (4th Armored Brigade, with AMX 30 tanks; 8th Armored Brigade, with M60A3 tanks; and 20th Mechanized Brigade) and 2d (a National Guard brigade and a mechanized brigade). In December 1990 the remainder of the Saudi units were: the Royal Guards Brigade in Riyadh; a tank brigade in Tabuk, a mechanized brigade on the western Iraqi border, a mechanized brigade on the Yemeni border, a parachute brigade (in reserve), and the other National Guard brigades.

The Free Kuwaiti Army fielded a division consisting of 35th Armored Brigade, which was renamed the Martyr brigade (4,000 men, thirty-two Chieftain and seventy M84 tanks), and two mechanized brigades (each 4,000 men, forty M84 tanks). One source, however, gives total Kuwaiti strength early in the operation as sixty Chieftain and M84 tanks. The figures above may indicate later M84 deliveries (M84 is a Yugoslav-built version of the Soviet T-72).

The Egyptian and Syrian special forces were presumably similar in concept to the Iraqi special forces described below. The Egyptian unit was the 1st Ranger Regiment (three battalions plus support troops). The Syrian unit was the 45th Commando Brigade (122d, 183d, 824th Special Forces Battalions, supported by an artillery battalion).

The Egyptian main force was II Corps, comprising two divisions: 7th Mechanized (8th Tank Brigade, 11th and 12th Mechanized Brigades, 39th Artillery Brigade, and 126th AAA Brigade) and 4th Armored (2d and 3d Tank Brigades, 6th Mechanized Brigade, and 4th Artillery Brigade). The standard tank was the U.S.–supplied M60, and the standard armored personnel carrier was the U.S. M113. The standard tank brigade consists of an HQ tank plus three tank battalions (one HQ tank and three ten-tank companies each), an antiaircraft company (equipped with Soviet-type ZSU-23 guns), a motor rifle company, and a reconnaissance company. The mechanized infantry brigade consists of three mechanized battalions, one tank battalion, one mortar company (120-mm mortars), one antiaircraft company, and an antitank company (typically nine Soviet-type BRDMs with Sagger missiles, presumably ultimately replaced by U.S.–supplied improved TOW vehicles). This organization is similar to that used by the Soviets at the time the Egyptians broke relations in 1973. Total nominal tank strength of an armored division, then, is seven tank battalions (217 tanks) plus HQ tanks. The mechanized division has five tank battalions (155 tanks) plus HQ tanks. Total reported strength (presumably including replacement vehicles) is 300 APCs per division, 200 tanks in 7th Division, 250 in 4th Division.

Syria contributed its 9th Armored Division (52d Tank Brigade, 53d Tank Brigade, 43d Mechanized Brigade, 89th Artillery Regiment, and 79th AA Brigade) and one airborne brigade. The standard tank was the T62 or T72, the standard armored personnel carrier/infantry fighting vehicle the Soviet BMP. Syrian unit organization reflected Soviet ideas about a decade more recent than Egyptian. The size of the tank battalion was the same (thirty-one tanks). However, the armored brigade consisted of three tank battalions, a mechanized battalion, an artillery battalion, and a support battalion. No tank strength figure has been published, but it was probably close to the figure, 250, for the Egyptian 4th Armored Division.

At the outbreak of war the Joint Forces Command was divided into two corps (Joint Forces Command North, which was actually in the west, and Joint Forces Command East) plus a covering force (Forward Forces Command). Forward Forces Command consisted of the Royal Saudi Army 5th Airborne Battalion and the Saudi National Guard 41st and 42d Battalions. The Pakistani 7th Armored Brigade, covering the Yemeni border, was under this command.[27]

Joint Forces Command East was divided into a division equivalent directly under the command headquarters, three task forces, and reserve and support units. The direct control units were the Royal Saudi Army 10th Mechanized Brigade (M60 tanks, less its mechanized battalion), a UAE Mechanized Brigade (AMX 30 tanks), and the Northern Omani Brigade (reinforced). The task forces were: Task Force Othman (Royal Saudi Army 8th Mechanized Brigade [M60 tanks], Kuwaiti Liberation Brigade, and Kuwaiti 2/15 Mechanized Battalion), Task Force Baker (Saudi National Guard 2d Mechanized Brigade, and Task Force Tariq (Royal Saudi Marine Battalion, Moroccan 6th Mechanized Battalion, and Senegalese 1st Infantry Battalion). The supporting forces were the Royal Saudi Army 14th Field Artillery Battalion, 18th Missile Battalion, 2d Antitank Company, and 6th Target Acquisition Battery; the Qatari Mechanized Battalion Task Force (AMX 30 tanks), the 1st East Bengal (Bangladesh) Infantry Battalion, and the South Korean medical unit.

Joint Forces Command North comprised the Egyptian and Syrian commandos, the Syrian armored division, the Egyptian II Corps, two task forces, and supporting units. Task Force Muthena consisted of Saudi Army 20th Mechanized Brigade (M60 tanks) and the Kuwaiti 35th (Martyr) Mechanized Brigade (M84 tanks). Task Force Sa'ad consisted of the Royal Saudi Army 4th Armored Brigade (AMX 30 tanks) and the Kuwaiti 15th Infantry Brigade. The support and reserve units were the Saudi Attack Aviation Battalion, the Royal Saudi Army 15th MLRS Battalion, 7th Target Acquisition Company, and 4th Airborne Battalion; the Kuwaiti Haq and Kulud brigades; and the Czech chemical defense company.

For the ground assault on Kuwait, the Arab corps in the west (Joint Forces Command North) was led by the Egyptian commando regiment. The two Egyptian divisions attacked on the left and the ad hoc Khalid Division on the right, with the Syrian division as corps reserve. The Khalid Division consisted of the Saudi 4th Armored Brigade and 20 Mechanized Brigade, with the Kuwaiti 35th Martyr Armored Brigade and the very lightly equipped Kuwaiti Liberation Brigade (trucks armed with 0.50-cal. machine guns).

Several countries contributed medical units:

Czechoslovakia: NBC chemical defense company and field hospital

New Zealand: field hospital

Netherlands: field hospital

Poland: field hospital (hospital ship)

South Korea: medical unit

The Iraqis maintained seven corps (I through VII) plus a special forces corps command and the separate corps-level Republican Guard Forces Command (RGFC). The RGFC actually operated two corps headquarters. Although in theory the RGFC came under the same general headquarters as the army, it seems much more likely that, in view of its internal anticoup role, it had a separate chain of command leading back up to the Ba'ath party and to Saddam Hussein himself. In particular, the prewar Iraqi Army was about 85 percent Shia, and therefore per se not necessarily loyal to the Sunni regime. [28]

There was also a reserve (mobilization) corps structure: one tank and two infantry corps headquarters.

The regular Iraqi Army at the beginning of the war consisted of six regular and one reserve armored divisions (the reserve division was mobilized after the invasion of Kuwait), three mechanized divisions, ten motorized infantry divisions, seventeen regular infantry divisions, fourteen reserve infantry divisions (mobilized after the invasion of Kuwait, some with only two brigades), one naval infantry division, six special forces divisions, one air assault brigade, and twenty-two separate infantry brigades. The special forces divisions were probably administrative formations controlling twenty special forces (sometimes called commando) brigades, one or two per corps. They may sometimes have operated in divisional strength, but the reader should keep in mind that the Iraqis rarely operated any units in divisional form. [29]

When the crisis began, the Republican Guard Forces Command was credited with seven divisions: two armored (1st Hammurabi and 2d Medina), two mechanized infantry (3d Tawakalna and 5th Baghdad), and three motorized infantry (4th al-Faw, 6th Nebuchadnezzar, and 7th Adnan). There is also an 8th (special forces) division. There is some question as to whether all three motorized infantry divisions had operational headquarters at that level (al-Adnan most likely did not function as an organized division). The Guard also included some independent brigades, e.g., around Baghdad and on the Syrian and Turkish borders. Five new Guard divisions were announced in January 1991 and three were named: al-Nidala (the Iraqi name for Kuwait City), al-Abed, and al-Mustafa.

The Baghdad Division was the permanent garrison of the capital. Unlike other Republican Guard divisions, it had four rather than three brigades and was sometimes split into two minidivisions. Presumably it was the Baghdad Division that maintained order within the capital during the February–March rebellions.

Special forces do not correspond to Western special forces (i.e., specially trained commandos). They are selected shock troops among the infantry. During the Iran-Iraq War, the concentration of the best regular army troops in armored and mechanized formations left the line infantry divisions with limited human resources. Similar considerations applied to the five Republican Guard infantry divisions. It was decided, therefore, to concentrate the best remaining troops in special shock units comparable in principle to the German storm troops of World War I. By the end of the Iran-Iraq War, most divisions had a full special forces battalion, and some had a full brigade (two or three battalions). Each corps is supposed to include one or two special forces brigades. As in World War I, this concentration further diluted the already weak infantry. Special forces battalions received extra training and weapons. Any APCs in an infantry division are generally given to the special forces. The special forces divisions were attempts to concentrate these storm troops in formations large enough to be decisive. In defense, the division's special forces battalion is grouped with the divisional tank battalion as a reserve force. In an attack, the special forces (and some tanks) are used as the exploitation force, held back while the initial attackers (regular infantry supported by tanks) finds a weak spot and breaks through. The special forces units are sometimes incorrectly described as commandos.[30]

The standard Iraqi divisional headquarters controls the divisional artillery and air defense. It also includes its own reconnaissance and tank battalions. The corps includes heavier antiaircraft artillery (an artillery brigade) and an electronic warfare battalion, as well as a reconnaissance company and commando brigade(s). Attached corps-level units can include an antitank battalion, a rocket brigade, a tank transporter regiment, and an army aviation wing.

The standard armored brigade was built around three armored battalions (which the Iraqis call regiments) and a mechanized infantry battalion; it includes a chemical platoon and a mortar battery. Nominal strength is forty to forty-five tanks per battalion in three tank companies per armored battalion, forty to forty-five infantry fighting vehicles and armored personnel carriers per battalion in three mechanized companies per mechanized infantry battalion, and six 120-mm mortars in the mortar battery. By way of contrast, the nominal Republican Guard armored brigade had many more tanks (four companies per battalion, a total of fifty-five to sixty tanks per battalion) and it also had two (versus no) artillery battalions (eighteen 155-mm long-range guns per battalion).

The standard mechanized infantry brigade was built around three battalions of mechanized infantry and one battalion of tanks (forty-four tanks in three companies) plus the mortar battery. The equivalent Republican Guard unit had an extra tank company in the armored battalion and also had two artillery batteries (six 155-mm guns per battery).

The standard infantry brigade was built around three rifle battalions, a mortar battery (four to six mortars), and a commando company. Each rifle battalion consisted of three companies (three platoons per company, three squads per platoon, 10 men per squad, a total of 270 men per company). The equivalent Republican Guard unit added two artillery battalions (eighteen 130-mm guns per battalion) and had six 120-mm mortars in its mortar battery.

Nominal manning was 450 for an infantry or mechanized infantry battalion and 170 for a tank battalion. Note that only the Republican Guard brigades had their own artillery (the regular army held its artillery only at divisional level or above). That made it possible for Republican Guard brigades to operate independently (e.g., to destroy fortifications). On the other hand, both kinds of brigades had the same nominal strength in antitank weapons: four antitank guided missile launchers per mechanized infantry battalion (hence twelve per infantry brigade and four per tank brigade). The nominal mechanized infantry battalion also included two SPG-9s or recoilless antitank rifles and thirty RPG-7 light antitank weapons rocket launchers.

In fact, actual strength was always less than nominal, although the Republican Guards were generally better equipped than regular army units.

The regular army units were equipped with T-55 (mainly supplied by Poland), Type 59 (Chinese-built version of the T-54), and a few T-62 tanks (Soviet or North Korean). T-55 was the first of the modern main battle tanks (capable of fighting heavy tanks but with the mobility previously associated with medium tanks); it is armed with a 100-mm gun. The T-62 is essentially an upgunned (115-mm gun) and slightly lengthened version (some have suggested that it is actually inferior to the earlier T-55, because it is more prone to catastrophic internal explosion when hit). Some Iraqi Type 59s were modified with additional Chinese-developed bar or Iraqi-developed applique armor to defeat light antitank rockets (such as RPG-7s). Some (as at Khafji) had Delft night vision sights.

Most Republican Guard tank units were equipped with the T-72, the main current Soviet tank, which is armed with a 125-mm smoothbore gun and has better armor. Most were Polish- or Czech-supplied T-72Gs; a few were T-72M1s license-built in Iraq (most likely assembled from Soviet-supplied components). The T-72M1 turret incorporates the initial (and inferior) Soviet version of the special armor that appears in modern Western tanks. Note that prewar Kuwait was offered the Soviet T-72, but rejected it in favor of the slightly modified Yugoslav-built M84, on the ground that Soviet production quality was unacceptable.

The M60, used by the marines and by the Saudis, could be expected to stand up to the T-55 and T-62, but not to the T-72.

The prewar Iraqi tank force amounted to about 5,500 main battle tanks. This figure apparently included a few elderly British-supplied Centurions, which were brought out after the cease-fire to help crush the Shi'ite rebellion in southern Iraq.

The standard APC in regular army mechanized divisions was the Chinese-supplied Type 354 (formerly known as K 63), which the Iraqis called BTR 63. It is a simple tracked vehicle carrying a heavy machine gun, and broadly comparable to the U.S. M113. The Republican Guard used the superior Soviet-supplied BMP-1 and -2. Both organizations also used the Soviet MT-LB tracked transporter.

Prewar Iraqi doctrine for positional defense, as in the Iran-Iraq War and in Kuwait, was to form triangular zones. Doctrine called for a corps to defend an area 90 to 160 km wide and 80 to 50 km deep. Its front line was divided into divisional areas (45 to 85 km wide, 20 km deep), and each divisional area was divided further into brigade zones (8 to 12 km wide, 7 to 5 km deep) and battalion zones (3 to 4 km wide, 2 to 3 km deep). Companies and platoons were assigned defensive points along the front. Battalions and below were expected to defend their front lines, which were the ditches and berms so publicized before the war. In theory, the centers of the brigade and divisional triangles were kill zones containing antitank and antipersonnel mines, trenches, and wire, with triangular strong points spread along the front.

An Iraqi infantry division was expected to control a security zone along the front about 8 km deep. Most of the force was concentrated in an operational zone about 10 km deep. The divisional administration area was concentrated in the theoretically secure zone 2 km deep, to the rear of the operational zone.

B

Air Units and Their Equipment

FOR THE UNITED STATES, the standard, self-contained, fixed-wing unit is the wing: the air force tactical fighter wing (TFW) composed of tactical fighter squadrons (TFS), the navy carrier air wing (CVW), the Marine Air Wing (MAW) associated with a division within a Marine Assault Force (MAF). In theory, the wing is the smallest unit that includes not only the airplanes but also their maintenance support. It can, therefore, be deployed independently.

The different services' wings are, of course, radically different in composition and in tactical concept. In each case their aircraft are broken down into squadrons that, in theory, can operate independently in combat. Airplanes usually fight in pairs (flights, in the U.S. Air Force), for mutual protection, and the Air Force sometimes uses pairs of flights, for mutual support. The maximum number of aircraft that can operate together is limited by the unwieldiness of the formation. For example, aircraft attacking typically split into pairs. U.S. Navy practice is also to use pairs, but they tend to cooperate more loosely than in the air force.

The air force tactical fighter wing typically consists of three or four squadrons, although an A-10 wing consists of six squadrons

(108 aircraft). Standard squadron strengths in the European theater are: twenty-four RF-4Cs, twelve EF-111As, eighteen A-10s, twenty-four F-15s, twenty-four F-16s, and twenty-four F-111Es.[1] In each case an actual deployed wing may include one or two extra airplanes, but the basic numbers hold. The total size of the wing depends on how complex (i.e., how difficult to support) the airplanes are. Typically an air base will accommodate one TFW of any one type of airplane, so the number of air bases in an area limits total deployable strength. That is one reason why it was so important that Turkey open its NATO bases for F-111 operations against western Iraq.

The wing concept also applies to heavy bombers, but they commonly operate abroad in squadrons. In this case B-52s from different bases were brought together in provisional squadrons.

Special-purpose airplanes typically deploy in squadrons, sharing maintenance and other support facilities with the full wings.

Tactically, the air force expects to operate in large units; elements of different wings and squadrons are coordinated by a central command. The ATO described in chapter 9 is the ultimate expression of this coordination. The larger the number of aircraft sharing the same airspace, the greater the risk of error or collision. In the air force view, coordination is the only way to avoid embarrassment, and such coordination demands discipline on the part of the crews: their flight paths must conform perfectly to the overall plan. A typical remark is that "some idiot always tries to ruin things by being too smart."

Air force units initially deployed to Saudi Arabia by squadrons, since bases were not ready for them. Later entire wings deployed as integral units. The first aircraft flown to Saudi Arabia were F-15Cs for local air defense.

The air force units flown from the United States were:

27th and 71st TFS of 1st TFW (48 F-15Cs) at Dhahran

58th TFS of 33d TFW (F-15C) at Tabuk

335th TFS and 336th TFS of 4th TFW (44 F-15Es) at Thumrayat, Oman

17th and 33d TFS of 363d TFW (44 F-16s) at Al Dhafra

4th TFS of 388th TFW (F-16) at Al Mindhat

69th TFS of 347th TFW (F-16)

353d, 355th, 356th TFS of 345th TFW (A-10A) at Al Jubail

23d TFW (A-10A); also some from 354th TFW at Tabuk

415th TFS of 37th TFW (20 F-117As) at Khamis Mushayt

35th TFW (20 F-4Gs) at Muharraq, Bahrain

some 366th TFW EF-111As and 552d AEWCW EC-130Hs (total 12 EF-111As and 4 EC-130Hs)

117th TRW (18 RF-4Cs)

These units amounted to one TFW of F-15C interceptors, two-thirds of an F-15E wing (the airplane was just entering squadron service), five F-16 squadrons, two wings (six squadrons) of A-10As, and miscellaneous combat aircraft (there were also EF-111As, EC-130Hs, and five E-3A AWACS).

There were also two reconnaissance wings operating from Akrotiri, Cyprus: 9th Strategic Reconnaissance Wing (U-2R and TR-1A) and 17th Reconnaissance Wing (TR-1A). Reportedly the 9th SRW amounted to four aircraft.

European tactical units deployed in August:

48th TFW (initial batches, 32 aircraft, in August; remainder about November; total about 60 F-111Fs) at Taif

614th TFS of 401st TFW (Torrejon, Spain: 24 F-16Cs) (another squadron went to Incirlik to help defend Turkey) at Dayarbakir

Also deployed from the United States was a heavy bomber force (B-52Gs): one Provisional Bomb Wing (about sixteen aircraft) at Diego Garcia and (after war broke out) twenty-four aircraft ultimately based in Saudi Arabia itself. In addition, provisional squadrons were established in England (at Fairford) and in Spain (at Moron), probably amounting to another thirty-two to forty aircraft. The total available B-52 force was thus about eighty aircraft, of which about forty were in the Persian Gulf theater. The aircraft in Europe were operated by the 92d BW; those at Diego Garcia and in Saudi Arabia, by the 42d and 93d BWs.

European units deployed after November:

European-based F-15Cs (24 transferred to Royal Saudi Air Force on an emergency basis) at Tabuk (total remaining in U.S. hands: 24 F-15s)

2d TFS of 50th TFW (Hahn, Germany: 24 F-16Cs each) at Tabuk

20th TFW (Upper Heyford) (60 F-111Es) at Incirlik, Turkey

511th TFS of 10th TFW (Alconbury: 18 A-10As) at Hafar Al Batin

66th ECW (EF-111A)

Further buildup units:

417th Tactical Fighter Training Squadron (F-117A) elements at Khamis Mushayt

1st SOW (4 AC-130s, 8 MC/HC-130E/Ns) at Riyadh

52d TFW (F-4Gs)

There were also Air National Guard units:

106th TFS (Alabama ANG), relieved by 192d TFS (Nevada ANG) (RF-4C) at Riyadh

138th TFS (Syracuse, NY) (F-16A)

157th TFS (South Carolina) (F-16A)

There was also an Air Force Reserve Unit:

706th TFS (Louisiana) (A-10)

The table below gives approximate total strength of U.S. Air Force tactical aircraft after the initial buildup, in January 1991, and at the time of the final deployment, based on standard squadron strengths:

		Initially	January 1991	Final Deployment
F-15C/D	Interceptors	72	96	120
F-15E	Strike bombers/ Interceptors	48	48	48
F-16	Fighter-bombers	120	216	249
F-117A	Light bombers	20	40–45	
F-111E	Medium bombers	—	60	} 84
F-111F	Medium bombers	32	60	
B-52G	Heavy bombers	—	80	
A-10A	Ground-attack	108	132*	144
EF-111A	Jammers	12	18	18
F-4G	Wild Weasel	—	48	48
RF-4C	Reconnaissance	—	18	

* plus about 10 OA-10 for forward air control

All of these numbers are approximate: strengths varied on a day-to-day basis. Many squadrons seem to have had a few extra aircraft on hand. The first two columns reflect standard unit strengths and thus indicate numbers of aircraft available for combat. The third column consists of figures released by the air force as total deployments. It is not clear whether some of the aircraft involved were replacements for those damaged during Desert Shield or in combat itself. These figures may include aircraft at Incirlik not in the other lists. There were also many special-purpose aircraft: two or three EC-135s, two E-8A (JSTARS), 195 KC-135 and KC-10 tankers, and 146 C-130 transports (plus command, jamming, and special operations versions of the C-130). The tanker figures are probably limited to those in and around Saudi Arabia. Total tanker deployments were 256 KC-135s and 46 KC-10s.

It was significant for the conduct of the air war that only the F-117As and F-111Fs had internal laser target designators. The F-15Es were fitted to accommodate an external laser designation pod (LANTIRN targeting pod), but not all aircraft ever received it. The A-10A was fitted to carry a laser pod, but it seems not to have been used in combat.

The navy and marine air wings are mixed because they have to be independent both tactically and in a support sense. Moreover, both operate in environments that are not conducive to rigid planning. The marine aircraft often support ground combat and must react rapidly in a fluid situation. No central commander can necessarily know in advance that one particular company will come under heavy enemy attack while another needs much less support. Elaborate preflight planning will often be counterproductive.

Similarly, the carrier air wing must be able to operate flexibly. Some strike planning is useful, but elaborately planned times on target are difficult to meet. For example, the carrier may have to maneuver to launch and recover her aircraft. She may have to evade enemy attack, too. A rigid schedule will endanger the ship and her air wing.

The standard carrier air wing is about eighty aircraft: a squadron of A-6 Intruders (all-weather attack), two squadrons of A-7s (day attack) or F/A-18s (dual-purpose attack and light fighter), two squadrons of F-14s (long-range interceptors), a squadron of S-3s (ASW aircraft, in this case usable as tankers and also for surface search), a squadron of ASW helicopters (SH-3 Sea Kings), and supporting units of EA-6B Prowlers (jammers, also carrying missiles to attack enemy radars) and E-2C Hawkeyes (airborne early warning). The USS *Midway*, the smallest of the operational carriers, which later joined the force in the Persian Gulf, carried F/A-18s rather than F-14s. The squadrons in the carrier air wings deployed to the Gulf are listed with their ships in Appendix C.

For comparison with the air force figures above, the total nominal wartime air wing strength of the six carriers deployed during the war is shown below (air wing strength of the three carriers initially deployed is given in parentheses):

F-14	100	(60)	Interceptors
F/A-18	100	(60)	Fighter-bombers
A-6E	95	(45)	Medium bombers
A-7E	24	(0)	Day bombers
EA-6B	26	(15)	Jammers
S-3*	50	(30)	ASW

* used for reconnaissance, COD, bombing

Typically one or two carriers were always off-line replenishing so that combat could proceed continuously. The figures for the first three carriers do not match the final totals because one of the carriers ultimately used in wartime, the USS *Midway*, has a smaller air wing without F-14s (but with extra F/A-18s). Squadron strengths vary from ship to ship, and these totals may be somewhat low.

The carrier air wing differs from the air force wing in three important ways. First, its aircraft are necessarily mutually supporting (in the air force, mutual support is on a squadron-to-squadron basis, the squadrons coming from different wings). Second, because the wing is relatively small, many of its aircraft have to be capable of multiple missions. It is therefore difficult to characterize the mission mix represented by an air wing. For example, the navy uses the same aircraft (A-6E SWIP, A-7E, and F/A-18) both for ground attack and for its version of the SEAD strikes on enemy air defenses.

Third, more generally, the division between defensive and offensive action is much less clear at sea than on land. For example, a carrier puts up a combat air patrol, which might seem to be entirely protective. However, because the carrier herself is a major offensive unit, she expects to attract enemy attacks. Much of the rationale for the carrier lies in her ability to attract and then to destroy enemy offensive units (such as aircraft) that would otherwise kill shipping enjoying a lesser degree of self-protection. In this context, then, the carrier's combat air patrol fighters are part of an offensive operation directed against the enemy's anti-shipping air arm. Critics of the carrier tend to forget this duality when they describe the carrier as oriented too heavily toward self defense.

In addition, many of the surface ships operating with a carrier or a battleship carry small multipurpose helicopters (LAMPS I or III, SH-2 or SH-60) with substantial abilities to attack enemy surface targets and to detect and, in some cases, to jam enemy electronics. For example, early in the war an Iraqi-held island in the Gulf surrendered to a LAMPS. The heavier SH-3 Sea Kings, normally carrier-based, were also extremely active. Two SH-3s forward-deployed to a *Spruance*-class destroyer in the northern Gulf. They operated with the SEALs to destroy mines and capture Iraqis. Three of the deployed SH-3 squadrons acquired night vision goggles (NVGs) prewar, and the goggles proved invaluable in identifying surface craft and in conducting search and rescue. On average, each six-helicopter squadron (HS) logged over 600 hours per month.

There was also a squadron of mine countermeasures helicopters (MH-53s) on board the USS *Tripoli*.

The reinforced Marine Air Wing in the Gulf included six F/A-18 squadrons (VMFA-232, -235, -312, -314, -333, and -451), four AV-8B squadrons (VMA-231, -311, -331, and -542), two A-6E squadrons (including VMA(AW)-224), and an EA-6B countermeasures squadron (VMAQ-2). VMO-1 and -2 provided twenty-four OV-10 observation aircraft. There were also two tanker squadrons (VMGR-252 and -352) equipped with KC-130s (twenty-four aircraft total).

Total Marine Air Wing fixed-wing strength (on the basis of standard squadron strength):

F/A-18	72	Fighter-bombers
AV-8B	60	Light bombers (Harrier II)
A-6E	20	Medium bombers
EA-6B	15	Jammers
OV-10	24	Observation
KC-130	24	Tankers

Ultimately at least eighty-four F/A-18s were in marine service in the Gulf. Actual figures for the other types correspond fairly closely to the nominal ones. Overall, 86 percent of the total Marine Corps air arm was deployed to Saudi Arabia, including all the Corps' AH-1W attack helicopters.

Typical marine helicopter strength:

AH-1W	50	Gunships
AH-1J	25	Gunships
UH-1	50	Light troop carriers
CH-46	120	Troop carriers
CH-53	80	Heavy cargo carriers

The Royal Air Force (RAF) is organized in wings and squadrons. Typically one wing, named for its base, consists of three squadrons (nine or twelve aircraft per squadron). Squadrons, which are numbered, are the permanent units. The RAF formed composite squadrons for the Gulf war. Strength at the outbreak of war was:

15(C) Squadron (12 Tornado GR.1s) at Muharraq in Bahrain (elements of 17, 27, and 617 Squadrons)[2]

20(C) Squadron (12 Tornado GR.1s) at Tabuk (elements of 16 and 20 Squadrons)

31(C) Squadron (12 Tornado GR.1s) at Dhahran (elements of 9 and 31 Squadrons)

2 Squadron (6 Tornado GR.1A reconnaissance aircraft) at Dhahran

43C Squadron (18 Tornado F.3 air superiority fighters) at Dhahran[3]

6(C) Squadron (6 Jaguar GR.Mk 1As) at Muharraq[4]

1 flight (4 Nimrod MR.Mk 2s maritime patrol aircraft) at Oman (from 120, 201, and 206 Squadrons of the Kinloss Wing)

The RAF operated three Nimrod R.Mk 1P ESM aircraft of 51 Squadron from Akrotiri, Cyprus, alongside the U.S. U-2Rs and TR-1s based there. Several RAF tankers were also deployed to the Gulf. By late 1990 there were four VC10 K.Mk 2s at Muharraq and two VC K.Mk 3s at Riyadh; the Mk 2s were ultimately replaced by Victor K.Mk 2s (converted bombers).

After the initial Tornado losses, the RAF deployed twelve Buccaneer S.2Bs (carrying Westinghouse AVQ-23E Pave Spike laser designator pods) to Muharraq. In addition, six Tornado GR.1s were deployed to Tabuk with two GEC-Ferranti thermal-imaging airborne laser designation pods (TIALDs).

The French equivalent of the wing is the escadre; it is broken down into two to four escadrons (squadrons). Typically the escadrons of an escadre are numbered within it, e.g., escadron 2/33 "Savoie" is the 2^e escadron of the 33^e escadre (in this case, of reconnaissance). Escadrons can be broken down further into numbered escadrilles. French aircraft deployed to the Gulf were twelve Mirage 2000 RDIs (5^e escadre de chasse), eight Mirage F-1Cs (12^e escadre de chasse), twenty-five Jaguar As (11^e escadre de chasse), four Mirage F-1CRs (33^e escadre de chasse), five C-135Rs (93^e escadre de ravitaillement), one C-160G (1/54 escadron electronique "Dunkerque"), three C-160Fs (61^e escadre de transport), two C-160Hs (61^e escadre de transport), and six C-160HGs (61^e escadre de transport).

The C-160G was equipped with the Gabriel COMINT/standoff communications jamming system. In addition, the French reportedly deployed their only DC-8 Sarigue (strategic ELINT platform) and two modified SA-330 Puma ECM helicopters.

Canada contributed twenty-six CF-18s of the 439th TFS, normally stationed at Baden-Sollingen, Germany. The Canadian ships in the Gulf operated five CH-124A Sea King helicopters. In addition, the Canadians deployed two EC-144A Challenger ECM aircraft and a CP-140 Aurora to Gibraltar to provide electronic warfare training for ships transiting en route to the Gulf area. One of the two EC-144As later flew to Muharraq in Bahrain, supported by a CC-130 transport.

Italy contributed ten Tornadoes and two support aircraft (one C-130 and one G-222). The Tornadoes came from the 6° and 50° stormos (squadrons).

Total reported Royal Saudi Air Force strength at the outbreak of the war was sixty-three F-15Cs, twenty-four Tornado F.3s, thirty-six Tornado GR.1s, 76 F-5E/Bs, twenty-four Hawk trainer/attack aircraft, and five E-3s (AWACS). These figures are totals delivered, not totals operational. Thus, during the war it was reported that a British Aircraft Corp. maintenance team in Saudi Arabia was responsible for an operational force of thirty-three Tornadoes (twelve interceptors, twenty-one attack bombers) and thirty Hawks.

Bahrain and Qatar also contributed combat aircraft. Reported total strengths (as of December 1990) for Bahrain were twelve F-16C/Ds and twelve F-5E/Fs. For Qatar the totals were fourteen Mirage F.1s and six Alpha Jets. All but the Alpha Jet are fighter-interceptor-bombers; the Alpha Jet is a trainer with light-attack capability. These aircraft were available for the defense of Saudi Arabia and the Gulf states, but they were not used for offensive operations in Iraq or Kuwait. This force also included some elderly Hunter fighter-bombers.

Other coalition air contributions were:

—Argentina: 1 Boeing 707-320 and 2 C-130Hs, plus Alouette IIIs on board the two warships in the Red Sea
—Australia: AS 550B Ecureil helicopters on board the frigates *Adelaide* and *Darwin* and several naval S70Bs, all used in the embargo operation
—Belgium: contribution to the NATO force in Turkey, described elsewhere. A proposal to send F-16s to the Gulf failed owing to disagreement within the government and also owing to Belgian air force objections that the aircraft lacked electronic countermeasures.
—New Zealand: 3 C-130 transports
—Egypt: offered Mirage 2000s and F-16s but Saudi Arabia did not accept; similarly, Turkey rejected an offer of 18 Dutch F-16As

A typical unofficial count of the prewar Iraqi air order of battle was: one strike squadron of sixteen Su-24s, eight interceptor squadrons, twenty-two fighter/ground attack squadrons, one reconnaissance squadron, and one bomber squadron.

Aircraft in service were:[5]

MiG-29 Fulcrum	48*	Interceptors
MiG 25 Foxbat	20	Interceptors
MiG 23MS Flogger	50	Fighter-bombers
Mirage F-1	116	Interceptors and fighter-bombers
Mig-21/Xian F-7	150	Interceptors
Su-24MK Fencer	20	Strike
Tu-22 Blinder	5	Medium bombers
Tu-16 Badger	12	Medium bombers
Su-20/22 Fitter	80	Fighter-bombers
F-6 (MiG-19)	40	Fighter-bombers
MiG-27	20	Fighter-bombers
Su-25	30	Ground-attack

* probably including 10 unarmed trainers

There was also a wide variety of helicopters, including ten Super Frelons equipped with Exocet missiles for antiship attack.

To the extent that these figures are accurate, they tally aircraft on hand, not necessarily aircraft in service. For example, it seems to be Soviet practice to provide aircraft as unit spares rather than to provide spare parts for major overhauls. Thus squadrons are considerably smaller than overall figures suggest. Many older Soviet-supplied aircraft, such as the Tu-16s and Tu22s, were no longer effective. Some of them were used as decoys to attract bombs during airfield strikes.

The prewar assessment was that the Mirages were the only really effective Iraqi fighters, and that they could perform either as interceptors or in ground attack. To the extent that Iraqi air defense is a separate organization from the tactical or strike air force, the interceptor force may have been limited to the MiG-25s and -29s, the MiG-21/F-7s, and twenty-four Mirages. The usual assessment was also that the Su-24s were the only Iraqi aircraft capable of penetrating Israeli air defenses. To the extent that missiles could not carry chemical warheads, they were the main Iraqi mass-destruction threat against Israel.

These figures do not include the Adnan airborne radar project. In addition, before the war Iraq was either experimenting with or installing air-to-air refueling equipment on board Il-76 transports and MiG-23 fighters. This capability was not, however, exercised very frequently.

The most striking feature of the Iraqi air order of battle is the great variety of aircraft involved, which must have complicated maintenance and operations.

C

Naval Forces in the Embargo and the War

MOST OF THE SHIPS in the Gulf and the Red Sea were under U.S. operational control. From the beginning of the embargo, there was some question of Western European Union (WEU) command arrangements. At this time the WEU lacks any political-military mechanism comparable to that developed by NATO, so the system had to be informal and consultative. It was based on that developed during the earlier 1987–88 Gulf war. Once war was clearly imminent, WEU ships were placed under U.S. tactical control, but general support was coordinated by the WEU.

There were three tiers of consultation: an ad hoc group of senior politico-military officials (typically chiefs of naval staff) chaired by the French (who held the WEU chair) to set guidelines, define the embargo mission, etc.; a group of points of contact (typically captains) meeting monthly in the naval headquarters in Paris to identify specific areas for coordination and to exchange information; and meetings on the spot for coordination among the WEU commanders in the Gulf and the Red Sea. On board the *Marne* at Djibouti, Admiral Bonneau acted as coordinator, passing WEU decisions and information to the deployed forces.

At a series of meetings between 10 and 14 September 1990 on board the French destroyer *Dupleix*, the British, Dutch, French, and Italians divided up the Gulf/Straits of Hormuz area into five patrol zones, each of which was to be covered continuously by two ships. The French and Belgians were assigned the Bab el Mandeb, and the French and the Spanish the Straits of Tiran. The latter effort was further coordinated with the Greeks and the U.S. Navy.

In wartime, the Spanish, Italians, and French took responsibility for the Straits of Oman. The French and the Belgian frigate patrolled the Bab el Mandeb.

The following list, by country, includes descriptions of special modifications made to improve individual ship antiaircraft protection.

ARGENTINA

Argentina deployed the destroyer *Almirante Brown* and the frigate *Spiro* to the Gulf blockade fleet. It seems unlikely that they had any special antiaircraft modifications.

AUSTRALIA

The initial deployment consisted of the *Perry*-class frigates *Adelaide* and *Darwin* supported by the underway replenishment ship *Success*. The support ship was replaced in January by HMAS *Westralia*, and the two frigates were replaced by the *Adams*-class destroyer *Brisbane* and the Frigate *Sydney*. The destroyer was fitted with Phalanx close-in defensive guns (a modification not made to her U.S. counterparts) abreast her after funnel, atop the extended Ikara deckhouse. As weight compensation, the ship surrendered her 26-foot boat in favor of rigid inflatable boats (RIBs). All of the combatants also received a pair of 0.50-cal machine guns. They had quilted blankets hung on their sides and wrapped around masts where there were permanent rails; these were probably made of radar-absorbing material and were intended to break up their radar cross sections. On board the frigates, the quilts were mounted at the 02 level (projecting out like awnings) and on the sides of the ship (hangar). The support ships were fitted with 0.50-cal machine guns and they carried army RBS-70 handheld, antiaircraft missiles. When the war ended, the Royal Australian Navy was preparing a second destroyer for deployment.

BELGIUM

The Belgian government deployed two Tripartite minesweepers (the *Iris* and *Myosotis*) and the support ship *Zinnia*. Later it sent the frigate *Wielingen* (replaced by the *Wandelaar*) to the Gulf. The minecraft were equipped with Stingers borrowed from the Royal Netherlands Marines. The Belgian government prohibited these units from clearing mines during hostilities, but they went to work after the cease-fire.

CANADA

Canada deployed three ships to the Persian Gulf, the destroyers *Athabaskan* and *Terra Nova* and the AOR *Protecteur*. They were refitted with extemporized, close-in defensive systems before their departure. On board the destroyers, Phalanxes replaced their Limbo ASW mortars. Two single Bofors guns and 0.50-cal machine guns were also added, together with extra chaff launchers. The *Terra Nova* was fitted with two quadruple Harpoon launchers. The AOR received two Phalanxes, two 40-mm Bofors guns, and 0.50-cal machine guns; the twin 3-in/50-mount formerly removed was replaced; and additional chaff launchers and EW equipment were added. On board all three ships, soldiers manned handheld, Javelin, short-range, surface-to-air missiles. The force had five CH-124 Sea King helicopters. Their ASW equipment (including dipping sonars) was removed, and they were fitted with ESM (including the British Kestrel system); some or all also carried 0.50-cal machine guns. All of the Canadian ships were also fitted with C-Tech CTMAS-36 mine-avoidance sonars.

DENMARK

The Danish presence in the Persian Gulf was the frigate *Olfert Fischer*. She had twelve Stingers (borrowed from the Royal Netherlands Army) on board.

FRANCE

As might have been expected of a navy concentrating on power projection, France quickly sent a strong force to the Persian Gulf to respond to the Kuwait crisis: the carrier *Clemenceau* (transporting the troops and helicopters of the 5th Combat Helicopter Regiment), the missile destroyers *Dupleix* and *Montcalm*, the frigates *Cdt. Bory, Cdt. Ducuing, Doudart de Lagree,* and *Protet,* and the replenishment ship *Var.* The carrier withdrew after delivering her troops. Ultimately the French force consisted of the missile destroyer *Du Chayla,* the ASW destroyers *Jeanne de Vienne,* and *La Motte-Picquet,* the frigates *Cdt. Bory, Doudart de Lagree,* and *Protet,* and the corvette *Premier Maître L'Her.* They were supported by the replenishment ships *Durance* and *Marne,* by the maintenance ship *Jules Verne,* and by the coastal tug *Buffle.* The French Indian Ocean force included the support ship *Rhin.* France also contributed the hospital ships *Rance* and *Foudre,* which operated in the Red Sea.

The French also contributed two Tripartite minehunter/sweepers.

The French A69-class corvettes were provided with four 0.50-cal machine guns each, a standard fitting for ships operating in the Indian Ocean (where pirates must sometimes be repelled).

The French electronic intelligence ship *Berry* operated against Iraq.

GERMANY

German forces were not deployed to the Persian Gulf, but they were deployed in support of the coalition. The German constitution limits these forces to operations within the NATO area, which is north of the 25th parallel. However, the German navy did form a minesweeper squadron to operate off the Mediterranean entrance of the Suez Canal, to keep the canal open in the event that Libya, a supporter of Iraq, tried to mine it. The squadron consisted of the depot ship *Werra* (which also functioned as command ship); the ammunition ship *Westerwald*; the minehunters (Type 331B) *Marburg, Koblenz,* and *Wetzlar;* and the minesweepers (Type 343) *Laboe* and *Ueberherrn.* All ships carried Stingers for close-in self-defense (these missiles are standard on board the new Type 343s), and their crews were issued antichemical warfare antidotes. The squadron was specially formed in response to the crisis: in the Baltic and the North Sea, the German navy normally operates its sweepers and hunters separately.

Germany contributed five minehunter/sweepers and six Troika drone boats (with two controllers) to the postwar mine-clearance effort.

GREECE

The Greek contribution to the force in the Gulf was one "Standard" frigate, *Limnos*, later relieved by the *Elli*. These ships were scheduled for Phalanx installation; they were probably so fitted, the gun replacing their after 3-in mount.

ITALY

The initial Italian force in the Persian Gulf consisted of two frigates and two corvettes plus a support ship, with four mine countermeasures ships in the Red Sea. A third frigate was sent in October. As of November, the force in the Persian Gulf consisted of the *Maestrale*-class frigates *Libeccio* and *Zeffiro*, the *Lupo*-class frigate *Orsa*, and the underway replenishment ship *Stromboli*. Later the frigate *Orsa* was replaced by the missile destroyer *Audace*. In January replacements for the original group sailed from Italy: the frigates *Lupo* and *Saggitario* and the support ship *Vesuvio*. The helicopter assault ship *San Marco* also joined the Gulf force in a multiple capacity (hospital ship/spares stores ship for the Italian force, with four Sea Kings on board). The Italian force was responsible for keeping the approach to the Suez Canal clear.

KUWAIT

Two Kuwaiti craft escaped the Iraqi invasion: the *Istiqlal* (an FPB 57) and the *Al Sanbouk* (a TNC-45). Neither had any missiles; the Kuwaiti government in exile had to buy some. The two boats fought an aggressive war in the northern Gulf, supported by the escaped oil field barracks ship *Sawahil* (owned by the Ministry of Ports; the Iraqis had captured a sister ship).

Kuwait also created a Marine Corps, which was carried by her two fast attack boats. It retook the oil platforms and some of the Gulf islands. The Kuwaitis were particularly concerned, given the vagaries of claims to this land, that they, and not their allies, should retake it. They reclaimed the first captured Kuwaiti territory.

THE NETHERLANDS

The Dutch combatant strength in the Gulf consisted of one missile and one ASW frigate. The original pair, the *Witte de With* and *Pieter Florisz*, were replaced in November 1990 by the frigates *Jacob van Heemskerck* and *Philips van Almonde*, supported by the *Zuiderkruis* (which was fitted in two weeks with a containerized Goalkeeper CIWS for the occasion, and which carried Royal Netherlands Marine Stinger missile teams). The frigates were fitted with 20-mm Oerlikon machine cannons, with 0.50-cal machine guns on their bridge wings, and with additional chemical protective gear. The *Pieter Florisz* at least had her Lynx helicopter fitted with 0.50-cal machine guns.

The postwar Dutch contribution to mine clearance was three Tripartite sweeper/hunters.

NORWAY

Norway sent the Coast Guard cutter *Andenes* to the Gulf. This ship was intended to support the Danish frigate.

POLAND

Poland sent the hospital ship *Wodnik* and the salvage ship *Piast*. The salvage ship was armed with four twin 23-mm guns, possibly the new type of mounting that includes a short-range SA-7 series missile. The hospital ship was a converted cadet ship; the salvage ship was intended as her escort. Both are built on the same hull.

PORTUGAL

As of late August, Portugal had planned to send two warships to the Persian Gulf. It actually sent the transport *Sao Miguel*, which supported the German mine countermeasures squadron in the Eastern Mediterranean. Later this ship supported the British force in the Gulf.

SPAIN

The initial Spanish contingent in the Gulf consisted of the *Perry*-class frigate *Santa Maria* and the *Descubierta*-class frigates *Descubierta* and *Cazadora*. They were later relieved by the *Perry*-class frigate *Numancia* and the *Descubierta*-class *Infanta Elena* and *Cazadora*. These ships were supported by an amphibious transport (without troops).

USSR

Soviet ships operating in or near the Gulf were the *Udaloy*-class destroyer *Admiral Tributs*, a missile destroyer, a frigate, and an *Amur*-class repair ship. These ships did not actually participate in either the maritime interdiction or the Gulf war. Early in the Kuwait crisis, there were indications (such as requests for transit rights) that the Soviets planned a much more impressive presence. The contradiction between this early information and the later and much less impressive reality suggests that there may have been some difference of opinion within the Soviet leadership as to the wisdom of actual participation. The Soviets did hint that they would serve under a U.N., but not a U.S., command.

UNITED KINGDOM

Apart from the United States, Britain had the largest naval contingent in the Persian Gulf, built up from the longstanding precrisis Armilla Patrol. By mid-August the British had one destroyer (*York*), two frigates (*Battleaxe* and *Jupiter*), three mine countermeasures ships, and one tanker (*Orangeleaf*) in the Gulf, which were supported by three Nimrod maritime patrol aircraft. They were soon joined by the tanker *Olna*, the replenishment ship *Fort Grange*, the repair ship *Diligence*, and the survey ship *Herald* serving as a mine countermeasures support ship (the specialized ship of that type, *Abdiel*, having been discarded).

As of November 1990, the British contingent included the Type 42 Batch III missile destroyers *York* and *Gloucester* (HMS *Cardiff* left for the Gulf in November), the Type 22 Batch II frigate *London*, the Type 22 Batch I frigates *Brazen* and *Battleaxe*, and the *Leander* Batch 3A frigate *Jupiter*. There were three "Hunt"-class minesweepers (*Atherstone*, *Cattistock*, and *Hurworth*) supported by the survey ship *Herald* (later replaced by the *Hecla*). The force as a whole was supported by the underway replenishment ship *Fort Grange*, the tankers *Olna* and *Orangeleaf*, and the forward repair ship *Diligence*. In addition, the logistics landing ships *Sir*

Galahad and *Sir Percival* remained in the Gulf after the end of hostilities to support the large British army contingent. Before their departure, they were armed with four single Mk 4 Oerlikons (20-mm guns), and *Sir Galahad* was fitted with a terminal for the MARISAT communications satellite.

RFA *Argus*, the merchant ship converted to training carrier, was sent to the Persian Gulf as a hospital ship. Unlike other such ships, she was not painted white or specially marked. Reportedly that was to permit her to help operate combat aircraft, using her large flight deck. The *Argus* was armed with four DS30B automatic cannon.

Later the frigate *Jupiter* was withdrawn. A fourth missile destroyer, HMS *Exeter*, was added, as were two more Type 22 frigates, the *Brazen* and *London* (flagship of SNOME, Senior Naval Officer Middle East). The mine countermeasures group was supplemented by the *Dulverton* and *Ledbury*. Two more LSLs, the *Sir Bedivere* and *Sir Tristram* (for a total of four of the five of this type) went to the Gulf. The replenishment ship *Resource* joined the fleet.

Two British diesel-electric submarines, HMS *Opposum* and *Otus*, operated in the Persian Gulf. Apparently they carried special forces (SAS and SBS). About 27 January it was reported that U.S. aircraft had sunk an Iraqi tanker *under which* a British submarine was hiding, endangering twenty-two special forces men trying to return to her. This was about the time of the great Iraqi oil slick, and the British reportedly complained that the slick had made submarine-borne special operations nearly impossible. At least one of the submarines seems to have entered the Gulf soon after the crisis began in August 1990. Both submarines were camouflaged (in duck-egg blue and black), presumably because they were expected to spend time on the surface launching and recovering special forces men.

In addition to the ships actually in the Gulf, the Royal Navy formed Task Group 323.2 to watch Libya and operate in the Eastern Mediterranean: HMS *Ark Royal*, *Manchester* (replaced by *Charybdis* after 23 January 1991), and *Sheffield*. In the Eastern Mediterranean, they were joined by USS *Virginia* and *Spruance*, both Tomahawk-shooters. These ships were probably the ones that fired their missiles over Turkey into Western Iraq.

UNITED STATES

The U.S. fleet in the Gulf and the Red Sea was the largest such force deployed since World War II, comprising six carrier battle groups, two battleship surface action groups, numerous escorts, and thirteen submarines and four amphibious formations. Ships are listed with the battle groups with which they deployed, but these units were often split up once in the Gulf area. An operational carrier battle group generally consists of a carrier, escorts (CG, DDG, DD, FFG, sometimes FF), and a station (replenishment) ship, usually an AOE or AOR. In each case the carrier is escorted by one or two Aegis cruisers (CG 47 and above). In some cases the battle groups operate with an oiler (AO) and an ammunition ship (AE).

The escorts form a cruiser-destroyer group (CruDesGru, commanded by a rear admiral) consisting of one or more destroyer squadrons (DesRons, commanded by captains). Pacific Fleet DesRons are both administrative and operational organizations. Atlantic Fleet administrative DesRons break up for deployment. DesRon designations given below are operational only.

Combat logistics ships generally deployed with the battle groups (they were convoyed overseas), but they operated as part of a dispersed combat logistics force comprising TF 63 (Mediterranean and Red Sea) and TF 73 (Persian Gulf and Arabian Sea). This force included destroyer tenders (AD), which stayed in port to maintain destroyers and frigates, and aviation store ships (AFS), which normally shuttle between a base and a deployed carrier. In this case, although the replenishment ships were considered part of the individual battle groups, in practice they operated as part of the overall combat logistics force.

Reportedly, Aegis vertical launcher cruisers (CG 52 and above) assigned to the Gulf carried 24 to 48 Tomahawks rather than their usual outfit of 12. The USS *San Jacinto* may have carried mainly Tomahawks (about 100). She fired the first Tomahawks of the war. Tomahawks are also carried by *Virginia*-class nuclear cruisers (CGN 38–41), by some of the *Spruance*-class destroyers (8 each in box launchers on board DD 974, 976, 979, 983, 984, 989; up to 61 each in vertical launchers on board DD 963, 964, 966–971, 975, 981, 990–992), and on board at least some submarines. Ships with Tomahawks aboard are marked by an asterisk in the list below.

Details of submarine deployment in support of Desert Shield/ Desert Storm have not been declassified. However, it has been stated that thirteen submarines were involved, eight of them in prehostilities surveillance and reconnaissance. Five more arrived on station after the war began, operating under CentCom control. Two submarines, the USS *Louisville* (in the Red Sea) and the USS *Pittsburgh* (in the Eastern Mediterranean), fired Tomahawks at Iraqi targets.

Force flagship: *Blue Ridge* (LCC 19)

Carrier battle groups and their air wings (A is the prefix for Atlantic Fleet; N is the prefix for Pacific Fleet):

Midway (CV 41) with CVW-5 (tail code NF)

Squadrons (aircraft in parenthesis): VFA-151 (F/A-18A), VFA-192 (F/A-18), VFA-195 (F/A-18), VA-185 (A-6E and KA-6D tankers), VAW-115 (E-2C), VAQ-136 (EA-6B), HS-12 (SH-3H)

—Surface ships (DesRon 15, augmented by *Hewitt*): *Mobile Bay* (CG 53),* *Bunker Hill* (CG 52),* *Fife* (DD 991),* *Oldendorf* (DD 972), *Hewitt* (DD 966),* and *Curts* (FFG 38)

Saratoga (CV 60) with CVW-17 (AA)

—Battle group consisted of DesRon 24 with the carrier and CruDesGru 8. DesRon 24 established the Red Sea Maritime Interdiction Force (MIF) and developed its initial tactics.

—Squadrons: VF-74 (F-14A+), VF-103 (F-14A+), VFA-81 (F/A-18C), VFA-83 (F/A-18C), VA-35 (A-6E and KA-6D tankers), VAW-125 (E-2C), VAQ-132 (EA-6B), VS-30 (S-3B), HS-3 (SH-3H)

—Surface ships: (DesRon 24): *Philippine Sea* (CG 58, flagship),* *Sampson* (DDG 10), *Spruance* (DD 963),* *Elmer*

Montgomery (FF 1082); (CruDesGru 8): *Wisconsin* (BB 64),*
South Carolina (CGN 37), *Biddle* (CG 34), *Thomas C. Hart*
(FF 1092), and *Detroit* (AOE 4).

Ranger (CV 61) with CVW-2 (NE)

—Squadrons: VF-1 (F-14A), VF-2 (F-14A), VA-145 (A-6E),
VA-155 (A-6E), VAW-116 (E-2C), VAQ-131 (EA-6B), VS-38
(S-3A), HS-14 (SH-3H). This air wing contained two A-6E
squadrons but no F/A-18s as deployed.
—Surface ships (CruDesGru 5): *Valley Forge* (CG 50), *Prince-
ton* (CG 59),* *Horne* (CG 30), *Harry W. Hill* (DD 986), *Paul
F. Foster* (DD 964),* *Jarrett* (FFG 33), *Francis Hammond*
(FF 1067), *Kansas City* (AOR 3), *Shasta* (AE 33)

Independence (CF 62) with CVW-14 (NK)

—Squadrons: VF-21 (F-14A), VF-154 (F-14A), VFA-25 (F/A-
18C), VFA-113 (F/A-18C), VA-196 (A-6E and KA-6D tankers), VAW-113 (E-2C), VAQ-139 (EA-6B), VS-37 (S-3A), HS-
8 (SH-3H)
—Surface ships (CruDesGru 1): *Jouett* (CG 29), *Antietam*
(CG 54),* *Goldsborough* (DDG 20), *Brewton* (FF 1086), *Reasoner* (FF 1063), *Cimarron* (AO 177), *Flint* (AE 21)

America (CV 66) with CVW-1 (AB)

—Squadrons: VF-33 (F-14A), VF-102 (F-14A), VFA-82 (F/A-
18C), VFA-86 (F/A-18C), VA-85 (A-6E and KA-6D tankers),
VAW-123 (E-2C), VAQ-137 (EA-6B), VS-32 (S-3B), HS-11
(SH-3H)
—Surface ships (DesRon 22): *Normandy* (CG 60),* *Virginia*
(CGN 38),* *Preble* (DDG 46), *William V. Pratt* (DDG 44),
Halyburton (FFG 40), *Kalamazoo* (AOR 6), *Nitro* (AE 23)

John F. Kennedy (CV 67) with CVW-3 (AC)

—Squadrons: VF-14 (F-14A), VF-32 (F-14A), VA-46 (A-7E),
VA-72 (A-7E), VA-75 (A-6E and KA-6D tankers), VAW-126
(E-2C), VAQ-130 (EA-6B), VS-22 (S-3B), HS-7 (SH-3H)
[Note: This was the last deployment of the A-7E light attack
bomber.]

—Surface ships (DesRon 36): *Thomas S. Gates* (CG 51),* *San Jacinto* (CG 56),* *Mississippi* (CGN 40),* *Moosebrugger* (DD 980), *Samuel B. Roberts* (FFG 58), and *Seattle* (AOE 3) [Note: *San Jacinto* was designated a *special weapons platform* and carried about 100 Tomahawks, at the expense of Standard defensive missiles.]

Dwight D. Eisenhower (CVN 69) with CVW-7 (AG)

—Squadrons: VF-142 (F-14A+), VF-143 (F-14A+), VFA-131 (F/A-18), VFA-136 (F/A-18), VA-34 (A-6E and KA-6D tankers), VAW-121 (E-2C), VAQ-140 (EA-6B), VS-31 (S-3B), HS-5 (SH-3H)

—Surface ships (CruDesGru 2): *Ticonderoga* (CG 47), *Scott* (DDG 995), *Tattnall* (DDG 19), *John Rodgers* (DD 983), *John L. Hall* (FFG 32), *Paul* (FF 1080), and *Suribachi* (AE 21)

Theodore Roosevelt (CVN 71) with CVW-8 (AJ)

—Squadrons: VF-41 (F-14A), VF-84 (F-14A), VFA-15 (F/A-18A), VFA-87 (F/A-18A), VA-36 (A-6E), VA-65 (A-6E), VAW-124 (E-2C), VAQ-141 (EA-6B), VS-24 (S-3A), HS-9 (SH-3H)

—Surface ships: *Leyte Gulf* (CG 55),* *Richmond K. Turner* (CG 20), *Caron* (DD 970),* *Hawes* (FFG 53), *Vreeland* (FF 1068), *Platte* (AO 186), *Santa Barbara* (AE 28)

Battleship battle groups

Missouri (BB 63)* (CruDesGru 3): *Horne* (CG 30), *Kidd* (DD 993), *Jarrett* (FFG 33), *McInerney* (FFG 8), and *Sacramento* (AOE 1)

Wisconsin (BB 64)* [See above with *Saratoga*, but *Wisconsin* operated independently once on station.]

Amphibious ready groups

Amphibious Ready Group Alfa from Seventh Fleet (13 MEU(SOC) embarked): *Inchon* (LPH 12), *Nashville* (LPD 13), *Whidbey Island* (LSD 41), *Newport* (LST 1179), *Fairfax County* (LST 1193)

Amphibious Ready Group Bravo from Seventh Fleet (ComPhibRon 5 embarked; MAGTF 6-90): *Okinawa* (LPH 3), *Ogden* (LPD 5), *Durham* (LKA 114), *Fort McHenry* (LSD 43), *Cayuga* (LST 1186)

Amphibious Group Two; ComPhibRon 12 (4th MEB embarked): *Nassau* (LHA 4), *Guam* (LPH 9), *Iwo Jima* (LPH 9), *Shreveport* (LPD 12), *Raleigh* (LPD 1), *Trenton* (LPD 14), *Pensacola* (LSD 38), *Portland* (LSD 37), *Gunston Hall* (LSD 44), *Saginaw* (LST 1138), *Spartanburg County* (LST 1192), *Manitowoc* (LST 1180), *La Moure County* (LST 1194)

Amphibious Group Three; ComPhibRon 9 (5th MEB embarked): *Tarawa* (LHA 1), *Tripoli* (LPH 10), *New Orleans* (LPH 11), *Vancouver* (LPD 2), *Denver* (LPD 9), *Juneau* (LPD 10), *Anchorage* (LSD 36), *Germantown* (LSD 42), *Mount Vernon* (LSD 39), *Mobile* (LKA 115), *Barbour County* (LST 1195), *Frederick* (LST 1184), *Peoria* (LST 1183) [Note: One of the three helicopter carriers (*Tripoli*) was used instead as mine countermeasures flagship, so this Amphibious Group had reduced air capabilities as compared to Amphibious Group Two.]

Middle East Force: *La Salle* (AGF 13, flagship), *Worden* (CG 18), *England* (CG 22), *McDonough* (DDG 39), *David R. Ray* (DD 971),* *Leftwich* (DD 984), *Reid* (FFG 30), *Vandegrift* (FFG 48), *Rentz* (FFG 46), *Nicholas* (FFG 47), *Robert G. Bradley* (FFG 49), *Marvin Shields* (FF 1066), *Barbey* (FF 1088) [Note: *Blue Ridge* (LCC 19), naval force flagship, was attached to this force.]

Mine Countermeasures Force: *Avenger* (MCM 1), *Adroit* (MSO 509), *Impervious* (MSO 449), and *Leader* (MSO 490) [Note: USS *Tripoli* acted as mine countermeasures flagship, operating mine countermeasures helicopters.]

Other ships

Other surface combatant ships assigned: *Sterret* (CG 31), *Ford* (FFG 54), *Vandegrift* (FFG 48), and *Taylor* (FFG 50) [Note: These ships were probably in the area and gone before the beginning of hostilities in January 1991.]

Combat Logistics Force (ships not deployed with the battle groups):

Store ships: *Mars* (AFS 1), *Sylvania* (AFS 2), *Niagara Falls* (AFS 3), *White Plains* (AFS 4), *San Diego* (AFS 6), *San Jose* (AFS 7)

Ammunition ships: *Haleakala* (AE 25), *Kiska* (AE 35), *Mount Hood* (AE 29)

Destroyer tenders: *Sierra* (AD 18), *Yellowstone* (AD 41), *Acadia* (AD 42)

Repair ships: *Vulcan* (AR 5), *Jason* (AR 8)

Salvage tug: *Beaufort* (ATS 2)

Hospital ships: *Mercy* (T-AH-20), *Comfort* (T-AH-19)

D

Selected Major Weapons

Smart (LGBs and Electro-Optical Bombs)

A "SMART" BOMB is guided to its target on the basis of some external command. Guidance continues after the bomb has been dropped. By way of contrast, a "dumb" or "iron" bomb receives no guidance at all after it has been dropped; its likelihood of success depends entirely on the accuracy of the bomb-aiming system on board the airplane delivering it. A smart bomb is aimed by a human being. By way of contrast, the next generation of "brilliant" bombs are to be self-aiming, seeking out targets on the basis of onboard sensors. The distinction is somewhat artificial, since many existing guided missiles (e.g., those that attack airplanes and ships) are self-aiming but would hardly be described as brilliant.

Guided bombs first appeared about 1943, and work on them continued for about a decade. They were attractive for two reasons. First, a guided bomb could be dropped from a greater altitude, because it did not suffer from the same inaccuracies as a dumb bomb. Its aimer could correct for aiming errors as it fell. Thus it could be delivered from outside antiaircraft range. Second, guidance made it possible actually to hit small vital targets,

324

such as bridges and maneuvering ships, without dropping impossibly large numbers of bombs, as would be the case if dumb bombs were being used. Early guided bombs had to be manually steered via a radio link, the bomb-aimer following the flight of the weapon by observing either a flare in its tail or, in some very sophisticated versions, the radar or television image as seen by the bomb.

Work on guided bombs eventually stopped because, with the advent of antiaircraft missiles, it seemed unlikely that any guided weapon could be delivered accurately and safely (since the attacking airplane had to remain near the target to guide the bomb in). Nuclear bombs were another matter, since small errors in their delivery did not really matter. During the decade after 1953, what little effort the U.S. government applied to nonnuclear, guided, air-to-ground weapons went into a few powered missiles, mainly Bullpup.

Matters changed radically in Vietnam. Many targets were not defended by long-range missiles, but airplanes trying to bomb them had to survive intense, short-range antiaircraft fire. Greater accuracy would reduce the number of flights (sorties) per target and thus drastically cut losses. A guided bomb that could glide to the target could also be dropped from far enough away (a few miles) to avoid much of the small-arms antiaircraft fire. Such a weapon could be easily and cheaply built, moreover, because the necessary technology, in the form of lasers and televisions, was quite mature. Low cost and simplicity were vital because the weapon had to be available in considerable numbers to deal with the many important targets (bridges, power stations, even particular enemy vehicles).

There was no real question of building entirely self-guided missiles, because the targets too often had insufficiently distinctive signatures onto which a missile could lock itself. Moreover, a missile that could easily hit one class of targets, such as bridges, could not be relied upon to hit other important ones, such as buildings or tanks.

In the case of the Kuwait war, aside from a desire to avoid killing civilians unnecessarily, accuracy was vital for two other reasons. First, bombs and bomber sorties were quite scarce.

There just were not enough to go around to destroy all the key point targets. Second, many key targets, such as hardened buildings, were vulnerable in only a few small areas, such as ventilation shafts. Unless weapons could be aimed a exactly the right points, even large numbers of bombs would have done little good. The deeply buried command post destroyed in the final morning of the war was a good case in point. It was quite small overall, and, therefore, many conventionally aimed bombs would have missed it altogether. There would have been little point in dropping bombs capable of penetrating its roof had the bombs not struck it in the first place. Smart bombs can often be delivered to within a few feet (fewer than 10) of their targets, because they become more accurate as they approach their targets. That is, such bombs guide themselves on the basis of something they see. They see more precisely as they get closer. By way of contrast, a bomb-aimer working at a distance is affected by the limited accuracy with which he can see the target in the first place (he must also compensate for other inherent problems).

Precise guidance turned out to be extremely important in the campaign against dug-in Iraqi armor. A tank turret is a very small target, so conventional iron bombs tended to miss altogether. There were never enough aircraft to saturate the large areas in which the Iraqis had buried their tanks up to the turrets. However, the turrets were quite visible and could easily be designated and hit by precision weapons. One wartime surprise, then, was how valuable 500-lb laser-guided bombs could be (supplies of these weapons almost ran out).

Precision-guided bombs work in two ways: the bomb-aimer either imposes a signature on the target (the laser-guided bomb), or he locks the bomb onto an appropriately distinctive area of the target (as in an electro-optical bomb). In both cases, the bomb-aimer depends on being able to see the target before hitting it. He is, therefore, at the mercy of the weather. That is why cloudy weather in Kuwait and southern Iraq so bedeviled the coalition air attackers.

In the case of a laser-guided bomb, the signature is imposed on the target by pointing a coded laser beam at it. The seeker in the nose of the bomb can easily distinguish the laser spot from the surrounding unilluminated area, and the bomb guides itself to that spot. Laser-guided bombs (LGBs, often code-named Pave-ways in U.S. service) first appeared during the Vietnam War. The main changes since have been in guidance, which now allows the bomb to fly a more elaborate path (e.g., to be released at lower altitude, so that the dropping airplane can evade enemy fire).

Laser-guided weapons can attack targets that the attacking air-plane designates, or they can attack targets designated (lased) by an accompanying airplane or by an individual on or near the ground (as in the initial attacks on the Iraqi radars). In U.S. ser-vice, the Air Force F-111F, F-117A, and F-15E (when equipped with a LANTIRN targeting pod) and the Navy A-6E all carry their own laser designators. F/A-18s, A-10s, and AV-8Bs attacking with laser-guided bombs currently have to rely on designation either by other aircraft, such as A-6Es, or by ground units. The British initially used teams of Buccaneers (lasing) and Tornadoes (bomb-ing), and then provided designator pods for the Tornadoes. They found that the buddy system (designator and separate shooter) required so much attention on the part of the shooter crew that they could miss other important cues, such as missile warnings (a Tornado was lost that way).

Relying on ground designation has an important advantage in close combat. The designator is unlikely to mistake a friendly vehicle for an enemy, so a laser-guided bomb probably will not hit a friend (unless, of course, so much debris is thrown up by an earlier bomb that the later one cannot lock onto the laser spot). That is why the marines, who think of the AV-8B primarily as a close-support weapon, prefer to rely on ground designators.

An airborne laser designator can be held on target by a crew member, or it can automatically track the target. The choice be-tween the two is not obvious. Automatic tracking is done by a video camera that locks onto either the centroid of a dark (or light contrasting) area, or an edge between two well-defined areas of light and darkness. If the target is ill-defined, then no such auto-matic track is possible. If the edge leads away from the target (as in, for example, the dark area between the hull of a ship and the white of its wake), then auto-tracking will merely throw the weapon off. On the other hand, auto-tracking greatly reduces the work load of the crew (it is clearly essential in the case of the one-man F-117A) and allows an airplane to maneuver freely after it drops its bomb.

An auto-tracker generally produces a video of its attack, since it uses just that video signal to aim the weapon. Auto-trackers were the source of most of the strike videos shown on U.S. television during the Kuwait war. They had the additional advantage of providing a degree of instant bomb damage assessment.

Major laser-guided weapons used in Kuwait were the U.S. Paveway series (which included a British variant), the U.S. Hell-fire antitank missile (described separately below), a version of the U.S. Maverick, and the French AS-30L missile (in effect, a pow-ered laser-guided bomb). The U.S. Paveways included GBU-27, the guided version of the I-2000 hard-structure killer (the bomb is also designated BLU-109/B), and GBU-28, the very hard structure killer used at the end of the war.

The main U.S. laser designators used in the Kuwait war were the AVQ-26 Pave Tack, the integrated A-6E laser, and the inte-grated designator on board the F-117A. AVQ-26 has been carried by F-111Fs since 1980. It is a single centerline pod containing a FLIR (see night vision devices, below) and a laser designator/ tracker. The FLIR and laser are stabilized so that the airplane can maneuver violently while attacking. AVQ-26 is about the size of a 1,000-lb bomb, and it can also be carried by the F-4 fighter. The A-6E has a laser ranger/designator, but it does not auto-track. There are also laser spot trackers such as the air force's Pave Penny. They detect and track a laser spot projected either by another airplane or from the ground. Target position and sight angle data are automatically fed into the airplane's bomb com-puter, so that it can attack the target thus identified. Pave Penny is carried by aircraft such as the A-10 and F-16. The navy equiva-lent, on board the F/A-18, is ASQ-173. The AV-8B and the British Jaguar have internal laser spot trackers integral with their bomb-ing computers.

The AH-64 helicopter uses a FLIR/laser combination called

TADS/PNVS (target acquisition and designation sight/pilot night vision system), which includes both a laser and a laser spot tracker. The display is inside the pilot's faceplate. TADS/PNVS is used to aim and guide the helicopter's Hellfire missiles.

British Buccaneers used AVQ-23 laser pods to guide LGBs dropped by accompanying Tornadoes. Later a few of the Tornadoes were provided with their own TIALD pods.

The main disadvantage of the laser-guided bomb is that it cannot see the laser spot through smoke or thick dust. Thus the debris thrown up by the explosion of a single laser-guided bomb will preclude accurate delivery of the next; some time must pass while the dust settles. That makes it difficult for a laser-guided attack to saturate target defenses, and it means that a few such bombs will generally miss, as some did during the 1986 raid on Tripoli in Libya. That was not the fault of the technology; it was inherent in the guidance technique. Future weapons may incorporate inertial guidance that will keep them on course to a designated target without the imposition of any external cue, such as a laser spot.

Electro-optical guidance is the main alternative to laser guidance. Before it is dropped the bomb is locked onto an area on the target. That may be a particularly dark or light area (the bomb aims itself at the centroid), or else an edge. The advantage of electro-optical guidance is that the bomber need not remain anywhere near the target while the bomb is in flight (maneuvering while a laser-guided bomb goes toward a target still entails some risk). On the other hand, not all targets present suitable areas of contrast or edges. Moreover, a bomb that begins fixed on part of a target may wander elsewhere if other nearby areas of contrast attract it. For example, a bomb dropped on a ship can wander into the dark strip between the hull and the white of the wake and strike the water well astern. A bomb dropped on a zebra-striped vehicle will often drift off onto a prominent object nearby.

The main electro-optical weapons dropped during the war were 133 navy Walleyes and a few air force GBU-15s (used against the Sea Island oil terminal, which was spewing oil into the Persian Gulf). Unlike a standard electro-optical bomb, Walleye incorporates a data link by means of which the launching airplane can lock it onto a target after it is launched.

There was also SLAM, an important variation on the electro-optical guidance theme. SLAM carried an electro-optical seeker and a data link. It was fired and flown out to a target area (using a satellite navigation system), and then locked onto a target by an airplane for the final minute or so of flight. In this way a pair of SLAMs were fired into a hardened building, one going into the hole made by the other. In all, seven SLAMs were fired during the war.

Computer Bombing Systems (CCIP)

Quite aside from being equipped with self-guided bombs, many of the tactical aircraft in the Kuwait war had computer bombing systems. The computer measures aircraft motion, and it is connected to a radar or laser that measures the range to the target. It also contains ballistic data on the various weapons the airplane carries. Given precise enough data, iron bombs can (in theory) be delivered almost as accurately as smart weapons; the computer literally flies the airplane while it attacks (the pilot can often choose among different attack paths, or the computer can vary the drop point, maintaining a constant computed point of impact, as he varies the flight path to avoid enemy fire). The basic concept is not new (World War II bomb sights flew bombers just before and after they automatically dropped bombs), but lasers make for precise measurement of target distance (radar often provides a range that averages over the ranges of objects in the fairly wide radar beam).

The current form, CCIP, means continuously computed impact point. That is, the airborne computer always shows the pilot where a bomb launched at that moment would hit. When that matches a target he has designated, the system releases a bomb.

Probably the first such U.S. system to incorporate a digital computer was the attack system in the A-7E Corsair II, two squadrons of which flew from a carrier. Laser bombing systems were introduced in the navy's A-6E Intruder, its standard attack bomber. The F-15E has a much more capacious airborne fire-control computer, and it and the F-16 can both use the LANTIRN attack system, which incorporates a targeting laser (see night vision devices, below). The F/A-18 also incorporates a computer bombing system.

In November 1990 the air force was claiming that F-15Es could regularly drop bombs (using computer fire control) within 10 ft of a target, based on radar ranges. Similar figures were claimed for A-6Es (in both cases, accuracy depended, in part, on just how distinctive the radar target was). The wartime claim was that CCIP was providing an accuracy (CEP, i.e., radius within which half the bombs would fall) of 30–40 ft, compared to 150–200 ft during the Vietnam War. Precision-guided bombs used in the Gulf were credited with a CEP of 1–2 ft, which was probably somewhat too high.

Cluster Bombs

Cluster bombs cover an area with small bomblets. Compared to conventional (unitary) bombs, a cluster bomb can destroy objects over a wider area, with the important caveat that it is effective only if the bomblets have sufficient destructive power on their own. Using a single cluster bomb a pilot may be able to destroy an entire convoy of vehicles in a single aircraft pass, i.e., with a single exposure to antiaircraft fire.

Cluster bombs were first used in World War II, and the earliest modern U.S. type, Rockeye, was extensively used during the Vietnam War. The main current areas of development are the method of dispersion (the goal is that the bomblets be spread evenly over the target area) and the effectiveness of each bomblet. The goal is to develop small yet effective bomblets so that the maximum number can be packed within the size and weight dictated by modern tactical aircraft designs. Typically an antitank bomblet is designed to penetrate the top armor of a tank, which is generally about 60-mm thick. It uses a shaped charge, and for some years such charges have been developed so that smaller and smaller diameters (i.e., smaller and smaller bomblets) suffice to penetrate a given armor thickness.

As a measure of the importance of cluster bombs in close support, they accounted for more than a third of the over 60,000 unguided weapons dropped by U.S. Navy and Marine Corps aircraft.

MISSILES
Antitank (TOW, Maverick, Hellfire, Dragon)

Antitank missiles differ from many others in that they generally cannot distinguish their targets from the background by themselves; the tank does not have a distinctive enough signature. Therefore any long-range antitank missile has to be command-guided in some way (short-range weapons are just aimed; they are unguided). If the operator is on the ground or on board a slow-moving helicopter, there is always a good possibility that he can be distracted during the flight of the missile (the launch point is, after all, revealed by the blast of the missile motor, making the operator vulnerable to enemy fire).

In recent years considerable effort has gone into designing weapons that can distinguish tanks and can therefore guide themselves; they are sometimes called brilliant. Tests under ideal conditions, in which the tank is visible against a desert (e.g., by its infrared image), were fairly successful, but skeptics always wondered whether the seekers would work when the tanks were moving in ground clutter. The desert tests seemed unrealistic. Ironically, they were almost exactly equivalent to the situation in Iraq and Kuwait.

The earlier directed weapons retain an important advantage. Like artillery, they can be fired at other kinds of targets. Accounts of the battle for Khafji, for example, mention antitank missiles used to sweep defenders from buildings. No brilliant munition would be clever enough to do that (the building would have the wrong signature).

Generally, antitank missiles and rockets fall into four categories: large, multipurpose, standoff missiles typically delivered by fighter-bombers or light bombers; missiles fired either from tripods or from vehicles or helicopters; missiles that one individual can carry that are fired from the ground; and unguided rockets. For the United States forces, the standard heavy ground-attack missile is Maverick. At one time the standard medium weapon was TOW, but now helicopters fire the faster Hellfire. The small guided weapon is Dragon. The unguided rocket, the successor to the World War II Bazooka, is exemplified by the AT-4.

Maverick (AGM-65) is the standard U.S. fighter air-to-surface missile and is carried by aircraft such as the F-16, the F/A-18, and the A-10. First used in Vietnam, it has modular (essentially interchangeable) guidance units for laser-guidance, television, infrared (IR), and imaging IR (similar to electro-optical but using a different part of the spectrum). Maverick is quite a large weapon; one hit will blow the turret off a large tank. During the Kuwait war, A-10s used the imaging infrared seekers of their Mavericks as a sort of substitute forward-looking IR (FLIR) night-vision device. Versions of Maverick used in the Kuwait war were both television- and IR-guided, with 125-lb and 300-lb warheads. Maximum range is about 14 miles.

TOW (tube-launched optical wire-guided, designated BGM-71) is the standard U.S. crew-portable or vehicle-mounted antitank weapon. It has been in U.S. service in various forms since about 1972 and it has been widely exported. The gunner keeps the missile heading toward its target by keeping it in his cross hairs. The system keeps track of the moving missile by observing an infrared flare in its tail. A computer in the launcher converts the gunner's movements into flight corrections for the missile, and these corrections are transmitted by means of a wire that the missile unreels behind itself. TOW is launched both from ground vehicles (such as the Bradley and the TOW version of the marines' LAV) and from helicopters (such as the AH-1). It was a great advance on earlier wire-guided antitank missiles, whose operators used joysticks literally to fly them (and which, therefore, required extremely good eye-hand coordination). On the other hand, TOW flies relatively slowly. Its operator must fly it all the way to the target, and the prospective victim may see the cloud of dust and smoke made when it is launched.

The use of an infrared flare for missile tracking opens the system to a countermeasure. If an enemy shines a bright enough infrared source at the operator, the system will mistake it for the flare, tracking will be impossible, and the missile will miss. The Iranians used TOW extensively during the Iran-Iraq War, and the Iraqis bought large numbers of French-made TOW counter-measures.

TOW is fired by U.S. Army and some Marine Corps AH-1 attack helicopters (the Marine Corps AH-1W has been upgraded to fire Hellfire, and AH-1T can fire either TOW or Hellfire). It is also carried on board light vehicles such as Bradleys, some LAVs, and some HMMMVs. In mounting TOW on board its light infantry fighting vehicles, the U.S. Army went against the views of many other armies, which argued that tanks and attack helicopters should be the only mobile tank-killers. The U.S. view was that lightly armored personnel carriers, particularly those used for reconnaissance, might well encounter enemy tanks. In such cases their TOWs would be their only usable weapon.

At Khafji, a marine corporal destroyed two T-72 tanks with two shots from his LAV, a spectacular performance (which, remarkably, did not particularly impress the corporal). During the major land battle, two Bradleys found themselves confronted by a T-72 tank that appeared quite suddenly at a range of about 250 yds. It hit one of them (some of the crew were pulled out to safety before the ammunition inside exploded), but the other destroyed the tank with a TOW.

Hellfire (AGM-114) is the current standard U.S. helicopter missile (the name means helicopter fire). It is laser-guided, either by the firing helicopter or by a ground-based laser whose spot the helicopter detects. Hellfire is substantially faster than TOW, and therefore gives the opposing gunner much less time to react. Moreover, if the weapon is ground-designated, the helicopter can fire and leave. Hellfires destroyed Iraqi radars at the outset of the land campaign; their targets were designated by Special Forces on the ground nearby. Of the three current major U.S. antitank missiles, it is the only one that was not used (in an earlier version) during the Vietnam War. Hellfire is carried by the Army AH-64 Apache and by the Marine Corps AH-1W Super Cobra. Maximum range is 5 miles, compared to 3.5 miles for a TOW, so the attacking helicopter can stay farther from its target.

Dragon (FGM-77) is the smallest of the U.S. antitank guided weapons. It replaces the 90-mm recoilless rifle at the platoon level. Like TOW, the missile is wire-guided, and in this case an automatic tracker mounted atop the missile launcher tracks the missile's tail flare. Dragon can be fired from an individual's shoulder (typically its tube has a muzzle support). Maximum range is 1,000 meters, about 0.6 miles. The warhead weighs 5.5 lbs, compared to 8.6 lbs for TOW. Together, missile and launcher weigh about 25 lbs.

AT-4 is the current individual antitank weapon, replacing the earlier smaller-diameter LAW (84-mm vs 66-mm). The rocket it fires is unguided, and effective range is only a few hundred meters. These weapons differ from the World War II bazooka in that their launch tubes are discarded after firing (they are much lighter than a bazooka).

Hellfire, Dragon, TOW, and AT-4 are relatively small missiles. They rely for their effect on shaped-charge warheads. By way of comparison, the shell from a tank gun penetrates by kinetic energy: it literally forces its way through armor. That kinetic energy in turn can be achieved only at a high cost in the total weight of the weapon, in this case a very long gun barrel and a large propelling charge. A shaped charge does not rely on velocity at all (in fact it is most effective at fairly low velocity), so it can be fired from a lightweight weapon. A conical, metal-lined opening in the face of the warhead focuses the blast forward toward the target. The metal that lines the inside of the cone forms a hot solid slug that is projected forward at high speed to penetrate armor and to damage whatever it hits inside a tank. The advantage of a shaped charge is that it permits a lightweight missile, flying at moderate speed, to penetrate thick armor. However, the shaped charge cannot destroy a tank unless it hits some vital component (e.g., the ammunition, to cause a secondary explosion). Moreover, antidotes have been developed specifically to defeat shaped charges: applique (reactive) armor and compound (e.g., Chobham) armor. Reactive armor contains an explosive charge that drives a metal plate into the path of the developing solid slug and either breaks it up or pushes it out of the way, so that it hits too obliquely to do much damage. All three missiles have therefore been improved with new warheads to defeat reactive armor, for example by using a pair of tandem charges (the first charge is neutralized by—but neutralizes—the reactive armor plate; the second breaks through). Missiles with such improved warheads are designated TOW 2 (later Hellfires with improved warheads do not have new names). Dragon II has a better warhead (85 percent better penetrating power) but it cannot defeat reactive armor. Nor can AT-4.

There is no specific counter to the new tank armor exemplified by the U.S. Abrams and the British Challenger. This type of armor may make it impossible for shaped-charge antitank missiles to deal with modern heavy tanks.

Maverick (or, for that matter, a 500-lb LGB) is a very different proposition: it destroys the tank by brute force.

TOW was used by most of the coalition armies, though sometimes in combination with equivalent European weapons. The main exceptions were France (Milan and HOT only), Qatar (Milan and HOT only), and Syria (Soviet-type AT-3 and AT-4 [not to be confused with the U.S. AT-4] only). Other similar weapons used by the coalition armies were:

—HOT (France, Kuwait, Qatar, Saudi Arabia, UAE) broadly equivalent to TOW, typically fired from a vehicle or a helicopter. Range is about 4 km (2.5 miles) and the warhead weighs about 13.2 lbs. The entire missile weighs 55 lbs at launch. Like TOW, HOT is wire-guided.

—Milan (Egypt, France, Oman, Qatar, UAE, UK) is a manportable antitank missile (weight is limited so that two missiles in their launch tubes can be carried by one person). Range is 2,000 m (about 1.2 miles), the missile weighs 14.8 lbs, and its warhead weighs 6.6 lbs. Milan lies between Dragon and TOW in capability.

—Swingfire (UK) is another missile broadly equivalent to TOW, carried either by a vehicle or by a crew. Range is 4 km (2.5 miles), total weight is 59.5 lbs, and the warhead weighs 15.4 lbs. Unlike TOW, the missile is controlled by joystick (like the Soviet AT-3 Sagger) and thus is relatively difficult to use.

—Soviet AT-4, used by Syria, is equivalent to Milan (the Soviet AT-5 is equivalent to HOT).

Antiradar (HARM)

The High-Speed Anti-Radar Missile (HARM, AGM-88) was the main means of defeating Iraqi radars, particularly those used for antiaircraft fire control. Like other antiradar missiles, HARM detects enemy radar signals and homes on the emitter. It was first used in the 1986 Libyan raids. The missile can be fired in any of three modes: prebriefed, self-protection, or target of opportunity. In the first, the missile seeks out a predetermined radar signature. It can acquire a target after it is launched (e.g., from an altitude below the radar's horizon). Self-protection missiles are fired automatically by an airplane when its radar warning receiver picks up an appropriate radar signal. Finally, the missile itself can function as a radar search receiver; it is fired manually when it receives an appropriate radar signal. The guidance system incorporates a strapdown inertial platform: the missile keeps track of its position (and of the estimated target position), and thus can continue to fly toward its target even if the latter is shut down. Range depends on launch speed and altitude and can be as great as 80 nautical miles.

HARM weighs about 800 lbs and is 163 inches long. It has a 146-lb warhead. Reportedly, about a thousand HARMS were fired during the war, 895 of them by Navy and Marine Corps aircraft.

Air-to-Air (Sidewinder and Sparrow)

Sidewinder (AIM-9) is an air-to-air missile that homes on a hot spot on an airplane. Early models could home only on hot jet exhaust. However, current Sidewinders can often detect the hot forward parts of an airplane. Compared to Sparrow (see below), Sidewinder has shorter range but the launching airplane need not keep the target in sight after it fires. The missile weighs about 188 lbs and is 112 inches long. Maximum range for current versions is about 10,000 to 20,000 yards.

Sparrow (AIM-7) is the longer-range (beyond visual range) complement to Sidewinder. It homes on the launching airplane's radar radiation reflected from a target airplane. Maximum useful range is about 20 nautical miles. In the Kuwait war, Sparrows (AIM-7F and -7M) were carried by air force F-15s and by navy F-14s and F/A-18s.

Sparrow weighs 500 lbs and is about 142 inches long. Maximum range is set by the guidance radar (the missile must be able to detect target reflections at the moment of launch) and is about 24 to 28 nautical miles.

The issue of which missile to use against a given target is decided largely by rules of engagement. In Vietnam, the rules required a fighter pilot to identify a target visually before firing, so the long-range Sparrow was little used. In the Persian Gulf, AWACS control aircraft could give pilots permission to attack beyond their own visual range, so Sparrow was used in the great majority of successful air-to-air attacks.

Naval Land Attack (Tomahawk)

Tomahawk (BGM-109) is a ship- or submarine-launched land-attack missile carrying either a unitary (1,000-lb) or a bomblet warhead. The missile navigates toward its target using a combination of inertial and map-matching (TERCOM); it homes on the target itself by comparing a stored image with the output of its own video camera. The map-matching system compares a series of radar altimeter readings with a series of stored terrain heights. The result is remarkably precise. Observers in downtown Baghdad watched Tomahawks literally flying down streets well below upper-floor height. During the first night of strikes on the city, a Tomahawk neatly clipped a major radio antenna.

Tomahawk was the only all-weather precision weapon available to the coalition force. It was used particularly extensively when clouds precluded laser bomb strikes from medium altitude. Typically Tomahawk strikes were arranged for about an hour before a satellite pass, the latter used for bomb-damage assessment.

The whole flight path of the missile must be worked out in detail and fed into the missile before it can be fired. Typically a large number of alternative Tomahawk missions are designed at a large shore-based Tomahawk Mission Planning Center, then entered into data transfer devices (DTDs—large, detachable, computer hard disks) for stowage aboard ships and submarines. Mission planners at the fleet level select the appropriate missions.

During the war, 297 Tomahawks were fired, of which 282 began their missions successfully (9 failed to leave the tube and 6 fell into the water after leaving the tube). At least 2 (and possibly as many as 6) were shot down, most or all of them in a single quickly arranged stream attack (the missiles had to fly a single mission profile most of the way to their target).

Missiles fired from the Eastern Mediterranean were specially modified with increased fuel capacity.

Ballistic (Scud)

Scud B (SS-1C) is a ballistic missile first deployed by the Soviets in the 1960s, and license-manufactured elsewhere, including North Korea. It is directly descended from the German V-2 of World War II (SS-1 was a copy of the V-2 itself). Scud B weighs about 14,000 lbs and has a nominal range of 110 to 180 miles. Its warhead is permanently attached to the missile body, and thus impacts with great force. Before the war broke out, the Soviets assured the United States that, in this form, Scud could not carry a chemical warhead (the chemicals could not survive impact, and there was no means of distributing them reliably before the missile hit). The Soviets also said that they had not supplied Iraq with any technology suitable for converting Scud to deliver chemicals. Even so, throughout the war there was fear that Scuds were carrying poison gas, and the Israelis maintained that Iraq had converted some missiles for that purpose. None was ever fired, however. Moreover, wartime experience showed that the high impact velocity of a Scud often disabled its fuse and caused it to dud.

The Iraqis modified Scuds for greater range, largely by reducing warhead weight, enlarging their fuel tanks, and burning all of the fuel during the early phase of flight (rather than continuously). Such a Scud therefore came down with a relatively heavy warhead and a heavy motor, separated by the light empty fuel tank.

It was structurally unstable and often broke up in the upper atmosphere. That further reduced its already poor accuracy, but it also made the missile difficult to intercept, since its flight path was unpredictable.

The Iraqis had four versions: Scud itself (180-km range), longer-range Scud (half warhead weight, extra range attained by burning all propellant immediately rather than steadily through the flight of the missile), Al Hussein (650-km, attained by reducing warhead weight to 250 kg and increasing the fuel load by 15 percent), and Al Abbas (800-km, achieved by reducing warhead weight to 125 kg, with 30 percent more fuel). Al Abbas could be fired only from static launchers; all of the others could be fired from mobile or static sites. Only the original Scud and the minimally modified version were particularly successful.

There were two types of mobile launcher: the TEL and MEL. The TEL (transporter-erector-launcher) carried the missile to the launch site and erected it for firing. An MEL (mobile erector-launcher) could only erect the missile; it could not transport it. It was much simpler than a TEL (presumably it did not have to provide so smooth a ride), but had to be accompanied by a special missile transporter.

In theory, a crew firing a Scud must first fuel and erect the missile (erection includes running up the gyros and then actually pointing the missile at its target). The crew must survey the launch site to determine exactly where it is with respect to the target, and launch one or more weather balloons to measure aloft winds, which will affect the rising missile. According to a prewar estimate, a properly fired Scud would be accurate to within about a mile, a figure adequate only if it carried a nuclear warhead.

No accurate figure for total numbers of Iraqi Scud launchers has ever been published. It seems likely that there were three distinct Scud operating areas, western Iraq, central Iraq (Baghdad/Tikrit), and southern Iraq/Kuwait. The Iraqi style of organization would suggest that a brigade was assigned to each area; a brigade consists of two or three mobile missile battalions. There were also fixed launchers, many of which were destroyed at the beginning of the coalition air offensive. Reportedly a Scud support infrastructure was built up from 1985 on, including hardened storage sites and hardened sites in which mobile launchers could hide.

In addition to Scuds, Iraq had shorter-range unguided rockets: Brazilian-made Astros II and Soviet-made FROG-7. During the first night of the war, the Iraqis fired forty-five Astros IIs and three FROG-7s into Saudi Arabia; they fired thirty rockets the next night, and thirteen the following night, and then none for at least several nights (the batteries may have been destroyed by Marine Corps Cobra helicopters). There was considerable speculation before the war that, even though the program for a Scud chemical warhead may have failed, the Iraqis did have chemical warheads for the FROGs.

Air-Defense, Long-Range (Patriot)

Patriot is the current standard NATO long-range air-defense missile. Development began in the early 1960s under the designation SAM-D. The Soviets were deploying Scuds at about the same time, and SAM-D was conceived as both an antiaircraft and an anti-Scud weapon. However, as work proceeded the antimissile requirement was gradually dropped (partly because of political opposition to such weapons). As it was, the antimissile potential was revived in 1984 (it was proposed in the late 1970s), largely owing to increased interest in longer-range antimissile weapons (inspired by, but not included in, the "Star Wars" program). Fortunately, two improvement packages, PAC-1 and PAC-2, were either in service or in early production at just the time that Scud had to be countered. PAC-1 moves the area searched by the ground-based radar up, so that it looks at the zone from dead overhead down to about 45 degrees above the horizon. PAC-1 also includes a means of estimating the missile's point of impact, so that Patriots are not wasted on incoming weapons likely to miss populated or important targets altogether. For example, the missile would not be launched to deal with an incoming missile whose flight path led into the water. One problem in combat was that Scuds generally broke up in midair (see the discussion of Scud), and the pieces then flew much less predictable trajectories.

It was just such an unpredictable missile that killed twenty-eight Americans late in the war.

PAC-2 provides a new warhead (more effective against ballistic missile targets) and a new fuse. Presumably the fuse bursts the warhead against a small target approaching much faster than the airplanes the missile usually engages.

The missile itself uses an unusual form of guidance, TVM (track via missile). Its radar tracks the target and the ascending missile. The rising missile receives radar energy reflected from the target and sends a signal derived from that reception back to the control unit. The unit then orders the missile to fly toward an intercept point on the basis of the combination of radar data and data received from the missile. The result is better than pure command guidance because it benefits from observations made by the missile itself. It is also simpler than other forms of self-guidance because most of the calculation is done on the ground, an important point given the size of the computers available when Patriot was designed. Simplicity of electronics within the missile reduces its cost and weight, and makes space for more (and more energetic) missile fuel.

The PAC modifications were practical because the missile is controlled by software rather than by a hard-wired computer (i.e., one designed to execute only a very specific program). PAC-2 deliveries began in September 1990.

A standard Patriot fire unit consists of eight four-missile launcher-containers. Typically two missiles are fired at a target, but four would have to be fired at a broken-up Scud to insure that at least two attacked the warhead section. The fire unit's radars generally detected Scuds at about 70 miles, and the unit engaged at 10–20 miles. Alerts were often provided by satellites (DSPs) originally launched to detect Soviet missiles, and the time from alert to engagement was typically 6–7 minutes. The time from engagement to the destruction of the missile was typically 15–18 seconds; the Patriots and the Scud closed at 2,000 to 4,000 ft/sec.

Antiship (Sea Skua)

Sea Skua is a British helicopter-borne antiship missile, first used in the Falklands War in 1982. The launching helicopter illuminates the target with its search radar, and Sea Skua homes on the reflected radiation. Sea Skuas used in the Gulf were modified to attack relatively small targets (fast attack boats and similar craft). Sea Skua enjoyed considerable success in hitting its targets, but the small warhead (about 45 lbs), adopted to keep it small enough for helicopter use, limited its lethal effect. It was generally used to stop a target, which was then hit by LGBs or unguided cluster bombs.

NIGHT VISION DEVICES

Although not weapons, night vision devices were so important to the coalition that they deserve special mention. There are two basic types, FLIRs and starlight scopes (ambient light amplifiers). A FLIR (forward-looking infrared) device looks at infrared rather than visible light, i.e., at small temperature differences between the objects in its field of view. Because objects do not cool at anything like the same rate after dusk, they show considerable contrasts in temperature, and these contrasts convert into recognizable images in a FLIR.

Moreover, infrared radiation will often penetrate dust and smoke, which block out visible light. Well before the war it was discovered that tanks equipped with FLIRs specifically for night operation could often see through haze. In Kuwait, FLIR sights on board U.S. tanks and other armored vehicles were able to detect enemy vehicles well beyond their own visual range, with decisive results.

A FLIR generally consists of an array of IR detectors over which an image (formed by a lens) is scanned to create a video signal for display on a television-like receiver. Scanning is necessary because really large arrays are complex and too expensive for current operational low-cost FLIRs. As in most other areas of microelectronics, complexity is becoming cheaper: next-generation tactical FLIRs will probably employ arrays of detectors large enough to see the entire image formed by the lens without scanning (i.e., large enough to stare). Most Western countries use standardized FLIR common modules for many different applications. In each of them, a mirror rotates rapidly to scan over the image formed by the lens.

Because the FLIR has a scanning cycle, it associates each portion of the scene it sees with a particular point in that cycle. The Iraqis had small numbers of FLIR jammers that exploited this feature. They flashed a bright IR light. In theory, if the light is bright enough, the FLIR will see some of it even when it is looking at another portion of the scene. After all, it is looking for a relatively weak radiation, and some leakage cannot be avoided. Since the flashing light is out of phase with the FLIR scanning cycle, the FLIR may well associate the flashes with different portions of its scan. If the jammer flashes at the appropriate rate, it may even cover the FLIR field of view with its light, rendering the FLIR useless.

This type of jamming is quite commonly used against infrared guided missiles, whose detectors usually scan conically (i.e., in a circular pattern) to determine the direction to the target. As in the FLIR case, the flashes confuse the missile's seeker, because it associates each time in its scanning cycle with a particular direction, and because its beam must be wide enough that some considerable leakage from the flasher is inevitable.

Jammers of this type, which were apparently previously unknown, were captured at Khafji. A simple technical fix reportedly solved the problem. Presumably it involved a change in the FLIR scanning rate. This type of jamming will become entirely ineffective as cheaper FLIR arrays, suitable for staring rather than scanning, enter service.

As is implied by the name, a FLIR is generally fixed to look ahead over a limited field of view. It is typically designed for targeting rather than for radar-less (i.e., less detectable) night flying. However, as enemy electronic countermeasures have improved, the overall night-flying capability has become more and more important. The marines' solution, in the AV-8B Harrier, is to combine a FLIR (view ahead) with night vision goggles (so the pilot can look to either side). Marine F/A-18Ds use a FLIR pod plus night vision goggles. Both AV-8B and F/A-18 have color digital maps for navigation in the dark. At least in the AV-8B, the FLIR can highlight objects of a set size and temperature (e.g., tanks) located in areas of concern. That reduces pilot search time.

The A-6E is unusual in having a rotating turret containing a FLIR, a low-light level television camera, and a range-finding laser. The FLIR can be scanned over the area ahead of the airplane, although its more usual function is to keep a target in sight as the A-6E maneuvers.

The air force did not buy night vision goggles (the use of which requires special cockpit lighting). Its main FLIR, the LANTIRN (low-altitude navigation and targeting infrared system for night) pod carried by F-15Es and F-16s, provides a cone of forward vision about 30 degrees wide. Pilots can look periodically to the side by jinking right and left, or they can fly in a special formation to protect each other. Ultimately the solution will probably be a turret-mounted FLIR that swivels with the pilot's head. Its image will presumably be displayed on the inside of the pilot's faceplate. A full LANTIRN installation consists of a navigation pod and a targeting pod. The navigation pod, which was all some aircraft carried, contains a terrain-following radar and a FLIR. The targeting pod carries a dual-field of vision FLIR, a target-tracker, and a laser-designator and range-finder. The combination of FLIR tracking and laser range-finding makes for precision dumb bombing when both are combined with the ballistic computer on board an F-15E or F-16. The F-16 combination can follow terrain automatically. The F-15E, like the navy A-6E, is currently limited to manual terrain-following (the pilot responds to a special cockpit display).

Having failed to buy a night-attack version of the A-10 close air support airplane, the air force used the IR seeker of its Maverick missile as an emergency FLIR. Like the LANTIRN pod, the Maverick looks out over about a 30-degree cone, but it has much worse resolution. This limitation probably explains why A-10s destroyed several friendly vehicles with Maverick missiles (poor resolution would have made vehicle recognition extremely difficult).

A FLIR is a fairly elaborate device. The infrared image has to be formed and scanned before it can be displayed on what amounts to a television screen. FLIR technology therefore is not suited to individual night-vision goggles or small-weapon sights. Existing FLIRs have another limitation. They display a fixed area ahead of the airplane. A pilot trying to fly at low altitude without using his radar wants to be able to turn and look easily in any direction, not to have to stare ahead or maneuver a FLIR turret by joystick. At present, he can choose between night-vision goggles (which are limited in performance and are not integrated into his airplane's weapon-control system) and the limited-view FLIR. Much recent work, particularly for the navy and the marines, has gone into integrating a standard FLIR with the goggles in such a way that the pilot can look out to the side without losing concentration or confusing his focus.

The night-vision goggles are an example of starlight scope technology. Such devices take available light (whence the name) and greatly amplify it to display an image not too different from that provided by daylight. As introduced in Vietnam, starlight scopes were quite massive. They have since been reduced in size to the point where a pair can be mounted on a set of goggles to form night-vision goggles (NVGs), which can be worn by pilots. Although the NVG requires some existing light to work, it is effective under almost all conditions. In the Kuwait war, NVGs were used by both the army (for helicopters) and the navy (for A-6 Intruder attack bombers). Conversion from conventional operation to NVG operation required changes in cockpit lighting (conventional bulbs are replaced by blue-green ones). The result provides up to 7 miles of vision at night. For the A-6, the great advantage is that it can operate at low altitude (about 200 ft) at night without using its usual terrain-avoidance radar, i.e., without providing any warning to an enemy using radar-intercept equipment. One great limitation on such methods is that the pilot is unlikely to see obstacles, such as high-tension wires, which can still bring him to grief. The current solution is a laser radar, which has inherently short range and thus is unlikely to announce the airplane's presence.

ARTILLERY

Artillery is distinguished from other ground weapons in that it fires indirectly: the gunner generally does not see the target. He relies instead on information from an external observer. Thus the effectiveness of artillery fire depends not only on the performance of the individual weapon but also on the quality of the external information. Iraq had some very-long-range guns, but they apparently fired only at preregistered targets. There were no forward observers, and no air spotters. In such circumstances, it is usual for artillery to "search" at maximum range in hopes of finding targets. A modern alternative is to wait for enemy artillery to fire and use a radar to detect and track the shells (and thus to track them back to their point of origin). There is no evidence that the Iraqis tried either solution, although they did have a few artillery-locating radars.

Generally a distinction is drawn between a high-velocity gun with a relatively flat trajectory and a lower-velocity howitzer (with a shorter barrel) that has a higher-angle trajectory and reaches out to a shorter range but attacks targets from above. Greater gun length makes for greater muzzle velocity (hence range) because the powder charge propelling the shell has more time in which to build up that velocity. Thus tank guns have the longest barrels (in proportion to their caliber). The gun-howitzer distinction is being eroded as longer-barrel "howitzers" enter service.

A major traditional artillery role is area attack. Since the 1960s, many armies, such as the U.S. Army, have developed bomblet shells, equivalent to cluster bombs, specifically to attack concentrations of enemy troops and armor. Much the same idea applies to the long-range bombardment rocket (MLRS) adopted by the United States and the NATO armies.

Because artillery pieces fire indirectly, apart from air attack they are subject mainly to indirect return fire. Accuracy is limited, so the classic danger to an emplaced artillery piece is from fragments of shells bursting close by. To the extent that they are protected, then, self-propelled artillery pieces have thin armor sufficient to stop such fragments, but not to stop shells themselves. Thus, despite their vague family resemblance to tanks, self-propelled (SP) artillery is a very different proposition.

There have also been two major attempts to increase gun range without increasing gun length or pressure. One is the rocket-assisted projectile (RAP), which is in current U.S. service. The other is the base-bleed shell, in which chemicals burning at the base of the shell smooth out air flow and thus improve the shell's overall aerodynamics. Base bleed was the technique developed by Dr. Gerald Bull (in combination with longer gun tubes). Both techniques cost some accuracy.

The main U.S. artillery pieces used in the Gulf were the self-propelled M109 howitzer (155-mm), the self-propelled 8-inch howitzer (M110), and the MLRS multiple rocket launcher. Airborne and some Marine Corps units use lighter-weight towed 105-mm and 155-mm (M198) howitzers. M109 range is 18,000 meters (23,500 meters for RAP rounds); it fires 4 rounds/min for 3 minutes. M198 is a new design developed jointly with Britain, West Germany, and Italy; it fires a 96-lb RAP shell to a range of 30,000 meters (maximum range with a conventional shell is 22,000 to 24,000 meters). Similarly, the 8-inch howitzer can reach out to 30,000 meters with a RAP shell (maximum range with a conventional shell is 21,300 meters). It has a heavier shell (200 lbs), so it can fire only one round every 2 minutes on a sustained basis (maximum rate is four rounds in the first 3 minutes).

MLRS was used in combat for the first time in the Gulf. A single launcher can fire twelve rockets (each 9-in in diameter and 13 ft long) in quick succession to a range greater than 30 km. Each rocket carries submunitions. After firing, the MLRS launcher can run to an alternate position before an enemy can fire back (it takes a conventional gun much longer to fire as many as twelve rounds, one by one). About 10,000 MLRS rounds were fired during the Gulf War.

Some MLRS launchers were modified to fire two of a larger semiballistic (inertially guided) rocket, ATACMS (Army tactical missile system). ATACMS was conceived in the late 1970s to attack second-echelon units under an air force–army program called Assault Breaker; ultimately the concept was for it to fire at targets acquired by JSTARS aircraft. Like MLRS, ATACMS spreads submunitions over its target area. ATACMS was tested in 1988–89. In all, 105 missiles were deployed to Saudi Arabia, and more than 30 were fired in combat at high-value targets designated specifically by CentCom: surface-to-air missile sites, logistics sites, howitzer and rocket batteries, and tactical bridges.

The other important coalition artillery pieces were the FH70 towed NATO howitzer, used by Saudi Arabia, whose internal ballistics probably match those of the U.S. M198, and a variety of Soviet pieces in Egyptian and Syrian service (towed 122-mm and 152-mm, self-propelled 122-mm 2S1s and 152-mm 2S3s).

Iraqi artillery was mainly Soviet, with some Western-supplied weapons (most notably Bull-type 155-mm–long howitzers from Austria). The Bull howitzer received particular publicity. It is 45 calibers long, compared to 39 calibers for FH 70 or M198. Maximum range is 39,000 meters, using a base-bleed shell. Iraq also had some North Korean–produced long-range Koksan self-propelled guns (probably 180-mm caliber). The Iraqi guns often outranged U.S. guns on paper, but that range bought little in the absence of effective targeting methods. That did not necessarily imply irrationality. The Iraqis presumably expected coalition attackers to stall in preregistered areas within their fixed defenses, and they would use guns aimed at just those points to pour in fire. The weakness of their system was that the coalition armies did not play by the same rules: they ran over or around most of the fixed defenses and were able to destroy many of the fixed guns beforehand.

CHEMICAL WEAPONS

The Iraqi chemical weapons were mustard and nerve gases. Before the war, stocks were reportedly held at Karbala, Al Fallujah, Baija, and Samarra. Estimates of total stockpile size varied; one estimate was 400 tons in all.

Mustard gas was first used in World War I. It is a blistering agent that damages the skin and, if inhaled, the lungs. The primary defense is a gas mask, since the primary danger is inhalation. However, skin blisters may expose the victim to further attack by other agents.

Nerve gas was invented during World War II; it kills by attacking the victim's central nervous system. It enters the body mainly through the skin (although it can be inhaled directly)—hence the elaborate antigas suits worn by so many allied soldiers during the operation. Nerve gas is generally delivered as a liquid aerosol that evaporates to form a gas cloud. The gas is absorbed more slowly than the liquid, so the victim has a little time to take countermeasures (which generally means rapidly injecting antidotes).

During the war against Iran, the Iraqis learned to deliver a combination of nerve and mustard gases. The mustard gas would have produced skin blisters, through which the nerve gas could be absorbed much more efficiently. That would have been particularly important if the nerve gas itself were impure. There were reports that the Iraqis tried a third synergistic gas, hydrogen cyanide. It is somewhat lethal in itself, but its most useful property is that it deactivates the activated charcoal in gas masks and other chemical filters.

The main defense against gas attack is to keep the chemical away from the potential victims, either by covering them with impenetrable suits (admitting only filtered air) or by maintaining a positive pressure in the vehicles they ride. Suits become particularly uncomfortable (to the point of smothering the wearer) in very hot weather (i.e., in spring, summer, and early fall in the Gulf). However, this type of weather is also unkind to chemical agents, since they decompose fairly quickly. The coalition troops suited up for the advance through southern Iraq and Kuwait, and apparently their suits caused them no great problems.

Chemicals could be delivered by artillery shell or by airplane dispenser. Iraq never demonstrated an ability to deliver chemicals by longer-range missile, and there is reason to believe that it never mastered the technology involved. A ballistic missile warhead reenters the atmosphere at very high speed, becomes quite hot, and then hits the ground with tremendous impact (sufficient, in the case of a Scud, sometimes to make a dud more effective than the intended explosion). Chemical weapons are relatively delicate and are unlikely to come through such stresses undamaged. Ideally, then, they should be released by a warhead properly insulated against the heat of reentry and arranged to burst high above the ground, to form an appropriate cloud. It is not clear whether the Iraqi version of the Soviet short-range unguided artillery rocket (FROG, for free rocket over ground) has a chemical warhead.

By 1990 the Iraqis also had chemical mines. Some were found in Kuwait, but none was encountered by coalition troops.

Given the available means of delivery, the main initial coalition counter to Saddam's gas threat was to destroy or neutralize his air force. Without airplanes, Saddam could not threaten the allied base of operations in Saudi Arabia. The gas threat explains the constant and intense attention paid to the air defense of Saudi Arabia. The relatively small Iraqi bomber force probably could not have done terribly important damage using anything other than chemical weaponry, but chemical attack on those fixed and inviting targets had to be a major concern. That would have been even more the case as the army logistical base was built up in the desert.

One reason the allied ground campaign was driven so fast was the hope that the Iraqi forward formations could not fire their chemical weapons without direct orders from Baghdad. They would therefore be unlikely to engage really speedily moving targets, particularly using short-range weapons (mainly artillery) which would quickly be overrun or bypassed. Saddam seems to have been aware of this consideration, because he publicly stated that permission to fire had been predelegated to corps commanders in the forward area. [1]

Certainly the allies expected chemical attacks as they entered the Iraqi defenses. They found few chemical stocks in those positions (small stocks were found). There are several likely reasons why. One would be that, until quite late in the campaign, Saddam preferred to hold these weapons centrally, rather than let them fall into the hands of individual army officers. [2] Some weapons would have been destroyed in the big arms dump explosion. Surviving ones would have been interdicted by the tactical air campaign. The elimination of most Iraqi chemical-weapons capacity would have helped, since anything lost in the big explosion could not have been replaced.

Another theory is that local commanders had some gas stocks but were inhibited from using them due either to coalition threats (made by radio and leaflet) or to fear that their own protective gear (such as Soviet-supplied gas masks) were useless. Certainly gas masks captured in the Iraqi lines were so badly dried out and cracked that they would have had little effect.

Yet another theory was that Iraqi chemical weapons had a limited shelf life, and therefore that the destruction of the factories precluded timely replacement at the front. This seems unlikely at first blush. Everyone else has found that quite ancient stocks of nerve gas retain rather too much of their lethal character decades after they are made (the problem is that they are both lethal and corrosive, so that the chemical bombs and shells begin to leak). However, it seems likely that Iraqi nerve gas is impure (see above), and that impurity may drastically limit its shelf life.

It is also possible that the Republican Guard stocks, which would have been at the front, were held back for postwar control.[3]

E

Coalition Air Losses

MOST OF the low-altitude losses were either to 57-mm (S-60) antiaircraft fire or to SA-16 hand-held SAMs. Except as noted, Tornadoes are RAF. One of the first few RAF Tornadoes succumbed to bird-ingestion damage (engine failure) after the other engine had been disabled by ground fire. Another was shot down by a Roland. In most cases, dates are those on which losses were announced and may therefore be in error by a day.

Date	Aircraft	Notes
17 January	F/A-18C	From VFA-8 (USS *Saratoga*); by SAM, probably SA-2, near H-3; a fireball, probably this airplane (hit head-on during a HARM attack), was observed between 28,000 and 31,000 ft
	A-4KU	Kuwaiti Air Force; hit by AAA just across the Kuwaiti-Iraqi border
	Jaguar A	French; hit by SA-7s in both engines while attacking Al Jaber. Successfully landed at Jubail despite fire in both engines, but total loss. Three other Jaguars were hit the same night (in one case, the pilot was hit in his head; in another, in the flight control system), but they were repaired.

Date	Aircraft	Notes
18 January	A-6E	From VA-35, attacking H-2/H-3; probably by a Roland missile
	A-6E	Minelaying, near Abadan
	F-15E	AAA fire (4th TFW)
	Tornado	SAM followed by bird ingestion (15C Squadron)
	Tornado	Italian; this airplane, flown by the squadron commander, was the only one to carry out a strike on the first day (the Italian flight-refueling probe proved incompatible with the U.S. KC-135 tanker, and the second airplane's probe broke off in the tanker's refueling boom. This airplane and the others therefore had to abort. The squadron commander pressed on and was shot down
	Tornado	NE Kuwait; probably by AAA during airfield attack near H-2 with JP-233 (617 Squadron)
	Tornado	Royal Saudi AF; probably by AAA while attacking an airfield (W. Talil) with CBUs
19 January	OV-10D	Ras al Mishab (U.S. Marine Corps); probably by a hand-held SAM
	F-4G	Crashed in Saudi Arabia after battle damage (probably attacking AAA)
20 January	F-15E	AAA fire near NW border of Iraq (4th TFW)
	F-16	W. Talil; AAA fire
	F-16	SE Baghdad; SAM
	A-6E	Returned to carrier but total loss due to battle damage
	Tornado	Attacking H-2
	Tornado	Noncombat loss (control column jam) from 31C Squadron
	UH-60	Noncombat loss in medevac mission. This was probably a failed extraction of a special forces team
21 January	F-14A	Shot down over Wadi Amif by medium-altitude SAM (probably SA-2) while on TARPS run; pilot rescued (Iraqis captured RIO). The F-14 was flying at about 30,000 ft and at about 300 kts; the missile was seen at its 2

Date	Aircraft	Notes
		o'clock position. The pilot tried to evade, but its tail was clipped off
	AH-64	Noncombat loss
22 January	Tornado	Attacking H-2 airfield, by AAA (31C Squadron)
	AH-1	Army Cobra; noncombat loss
23 Janauary	F-16	AAA over Kuwait
	AV-8B	Training accident in Persian Gulf
	AH-64	Noncombat loss
24 January	Tornado	Medium-level attack on Al Basrah with iron bombs (617 Squadron)
26 January	F/A-18C	Noncombat loss (mechanical problem)
28 January	AV-8B	Faylakah Island. Made multiple passes over the target; probably by AAA
	AH-1S	U.S. Army; noncombat loss
29 January		U.S.: no details released
31 January	AC-130H	Lost over Kuwait but crashed into the Persian Gulf; probably not immediately critically damaged (by hand-held SAM fire). Reportedly this airplane stayed too long in the target area after day broke. All 14 killed
2 February	A-6E	Near Kuwait City, probably AAA
	A-10	Reported lost to short-range SAM
	AH-1J	Crashed while returning from armed escort mission; crew listed as killed in action. Noncombat loss
3 February	UH-1N	Noncombat loss (U.S. Marine Corps)
	B-52G	Noncombat loss; crashed at sea on final approach to Diego Garcia. Some reports that battle damage was involved
5 February	F/A-18C	Northern Gulf, returning to carrier
7 February	UH-1H	Noncombat loss
10 February	AV-8B	Lost over southern Kuwait to AAA
13 February	F-5E	Royal Saudi Air Force over Southwest Iraq, to AAA
14 February	EF-111A	Crashed in Saudi Arabia after battle damage
	Tornado	Destroyed during a laser-guided bomb attack. This aircraft was flying at the rear of a strike package, with its crew in head-down mode, when hit twice (originally reported as missiles, possibly SA-3s, but more likely by

Date	Aircraft	Notes
		heavy antiaircraft guns; the airplane flew for some minutes before crashing). Loss was blamed in part on distraction due to the need to coordinate with the designating aircraft; the crew was presumably distracted from the FCS radar or missile warning (15C Squadron)
	F-5E	Royal Saudi Air Force, by AAA attacking Iraqi front-line positions
15 February	A-6E	Crashed in Saudi Arabia after battle damage
	2 A-10s	These A-10s were attacking Republican Guards and were reportedly shot down by hand-held SAMs, possibly Mistrals (more likely SA-16s)
16 February	F-16C	Noncombat loss; lost while making instrument landing approach in Saudi Arabia
	UH-1	Noncombat loss
18 February	F-16	40 miles N of Saudi border; pilot rescued
19 February	OA-10	Lost over Kuwait to AAA
21 February	OH-58	Lost in combat (returning from border reconnaissance)
	SH-60	Noncombat loss
	CH-46	Noncombat loss (USMC)
	F-16	Noncombat loss. Engine failure while refueling in midair
	UH-60	Crashed on medevac mission attempting to land in bad weather
23 February	AV-8B	Near Ali Al Salem airfield, Kuwait, by AAA
	CH-46	Noncombat loss, from USS *Seattle*
25 February	AV-8B	Southeast of Kuwait City, by AAA
	OV-10D	AAA fire
	AH-64	
27 February	OV-1D	Combat loss

Some further coalition air losses seem not to have been accounted for: one OA-10 or A-10, one AH-1, one AH-64, one OH-58, and three UH-60s. Some of these may represent errors due to double counting.

F

Iraqi Air Losses

ALL IRAQI aircraft (except the helicopters destroyed by A-10) were shot down by missile fire.

Date	Aircraft	Notes
17 January	2 MiG-29s	One shot down by wingman, who then crashed. It appears that the Iraqi pilots taped down the air-to-air radar button so that it locked onto the first target it acquired. They also held down the trigger so that lock-on caused immediate launch. The second pilot apparently became fixed on the fireball caused by the first MiG.
	1 Mirage F-1	Crashed while pursuing an EF-111A that was standoff jamming over western Iraq; could not follow a hard turn and flew into the ground.
	2 Mirage F-1s	By a 33d TFW F-15C with Sparrows. Part of an attempted raid on Dhahran.
	2 MiG-21s	By F/A-18s of VFA-81 (USS *Saratoga*), on a bombing mission. The F/A-18s turned, shifted to air-

Date	Aircraft	Notes
		to-air mode, and engaged, without dropping their bombs. One fired a Sidewinder, thought he had missed, then fired a Sparrow. The Sidewinder actually destroyed the target, and the Sparrow hit the largest piece of debris. The other destroyed its target with a Sparrow.
	2 MiG-29s	By 4–6 33d TFW F-15Cs (1 probable). Iraqi aircraft were under sporadic GCI control. Sparrow missiles.
	1 MiG-25	By 33d TFW F-15C, with Sparrow
19 January	1 Mirage F-1	By 36th TFW F-15C, with Sparrow
	1 Mirage F-1	By 36th TFW F-15C, with Sparrow
	1 MiG-25	By 33d TFW F-15C, with Sparrow
	1 MiG-29	By 33d TFW F15C, with Sparrow
	1 MiG-29	By 33d TFW F-15C flew head-on at this airplane as it took off; the pilot spun in.
24 January	2 Mirage F-1s	Shot down by a Saudi F-15C over Persian Gulf. Initially thought to have been carrying Exocets, later evaluated as photo flight over Khafji in preparation for the battle there. Sidewinders were used.
26 January	3 MiG-23s	By 33d TFW F-15Cs, with Sparrows
27 January	2 MiG-23s and 2 Mirage F-1s	By 2 F-15Cs about 60–100 mi south of Baghdad (from 53d TFS). Targets were acquired at about 80-mi range head-on; at 40 mi the Iraqis turned away. Targets were flying at about 5,000 ft, F-15s at 27,000–30,000 ft. No. 1 F-15 was tracking 2 MiG-23s in tandem; No. 2, the two F-1s in tight formation. The F-15s descended to lower altitude to attack. No. 1 fired an AIM-7, which exploded but did not kill the lead MiG-23, an AIM-9 did kill it. No. 2 fired

Date	Aircraft	Notes
		an AIM-7 beyound visual range at a MiG-23, but it did not explode. It may have passed between the two tightly paired aircraft. Soon both passed beneath No. 2's nose, and he fired 2 AIM-7s with his airplane inverted, destroying both targets. No. 1 then destroyed the remaining MiG-23 with an AIM-9. The entire battle took 8–10 min.
	1 MiG-23	By 36th TFW F-15C, with Sparrow
29 January	1 MiG-23	By 33d TFW F-15C, with Sparrow
	1 MiG-23	By 33d TFW F-15C, with Sparrow
6 February	2 Su-25s	All four by two 36th TFW F-15Cs,
	2 MiG-21s	while fleeing to Iran at low altitude (about 100 ft). All shot down by Sidewinder missiles.
7 February	3 Su-22s	By two 33d TFW F-15Cs, while trying to fly to Iran (also reported as four aircraft in two incidents); Sparrow missiles
	Mi-8	By a VF-1 F-14A, with Sidewinder
	Bo-105	By a 926th TFG A-10, with 30-mm gun
	Hind	By a 36th TFW F-15C, in northern Iraq, using Sparrow
8 February	Alouette III	By an A-10, possibly the same one that shot down the Bo-105, using a 30-mm gun
11 February	Unid. Helo	By a 36th TFW F-15C, using Sparrow
	Unid. Helo	By a 36th TFW F-15C, using Sparrow
15 February	Unid. Helo	By an F-15 on anti-Scud mission, using a laser-guided bomb (the helicopter was hovering at the time)
20 March	Su-22	By a 36th TFW F-15C, using Sidewinder
22 March	Su-22	By a 36th TFW F-15C, using Sidewinder. A second Su-22 spun in, crashing either as the F-15C approached or as it turned to evade.

In addition, Iraqi AAA shot down an An-12 fleeing to Iran (date unknown).

The official Iraqi list of aircraft flown to Iran during the war is: twenty-four Mirage F-1s, twenty-four Su-24s, forty Su-22s, four Su-20s, seven Su-25s, four MiG-29s, seven MiG-23MLs, four MiG-23BNs, one MiG-23UB, two Boeing 747s, one Boeing 707, one Boeing 727, two Boeing 737s, fourteen Il-76s, one Adnan, two Dassault Falcon 20s, three Dassault Falcon 50s, one Lockheed Jetstar, one Airbus A300, and five Airbus A310s. The Airbuses are officially listed as "stolen from Kuwait Airways." Major Iraqi civil aircraft unaccounted for are one Boeing 727 and two Boeing 767ERs. They may be the aircraft flown out of Iraq to Mauritania just before the war.

G

Iraqi Naval Losses

DATES AND identities are uncertain, since several ships and craft were reported disabled or sunk on multiple occasions. In the notes that follow, PBs are otherwise unidentified patrol boats, which presumably include ex-civilian craft seized in Kuwait harbor. The prewar Iraqi naval order of battle was: one training frigate (*Ibn Khaldum*); six Osa II and four Osa I missile attack boats (of which two Osa Is were retired from service, but presumably still serviceable) each carrying four SSN-2 missiles; three SO-1–class subchasers: five Zhuk-class patrol boats; two Poluchat-class patrol boats: one T-43-class minesweeper/minelayer; three Yevgenya-class inshore minesweepers: four Nestin-class (Yugoslav-built) river minesweepers; three modified Ro-Ro cargo ships; three Polnocny-C–class landing ships; one Spasilac-class salvage ship; and one transport/yacht.

One of the militarized Ro-Ro ships was caught in Libya in August 1990; another was refitting in Germany, her engines having been removed.

The invasion provided Iraq with all but two of the Exocet-armed fast patrol boats (the original total was two FPB 57s and six TNC-45s), but the Kuwaitis managed to sabotage all their missiles. By this time the Iraqi navy was in such bad condition that the captured ships were probably its best.

The Iraqis had substantial special forces (but probably not on the Western model—see Appendix A). Hence the inordinate attention paid to their hovercraft. The Iraqi naval special forces probably took Faylakah Island but made no other great contributions. There was some fear that Iraq had a midget submarine, but that turned out not to be the case.

Very few of the ships survived. Those that did included the Spasilac and one Osa, which apparently escaped to Iran (at Bandar Khomeini). The training frigate was at Umm Qasr at the beginning of the war and never moved (it was probably being refitted). It was hit at least once (there was some fear that it would be loaded with SS-N-2, Silkworm, or Exocet missiles and make a suicide run against the ships in the Gulf). The T-43 was sunk off Bubiyan Island, probably while going back to port to get more mines to lay. All three Polnocnys were sunk. At the end of the war at least one Zhuk survived (it was in Kuwaiti hands late in February), and there were also some river craft, including three Yugoslav-built river monitors.

Iraq had a substantial prewar merchant fleet, but little of it is likely to return home. The main port was being dredged by the Dutch in August 1990, and the Iraqis would not let the Dutch leave until this work had been completed. They then took all their dredging equipment home, and the port is now badly silted. The Shatt-al-Arab is still littered with tankers sunk during the Iran-Iraq War, and it has now been mined. Dredging is, therefore, impossible for the present.

Some ships were sunk. Of four large tankers (the ones emptied to create the big oil slick), one was severely damaged (it is a constructive total loss). The other three are usable. Other Iraqi merchant ships sought haven from the embargo in many ports; they are scattered around Europe, and some are in Mauritania. Six or seven are moored at Aden; others are as far away as Singapore. One is on the ship-breaking beach in Pakistan, but its legal status is unclear.

Much of the Iraqi naval effort was apparently devoted to moving loot out of Kuwait rather than to anything more warlike. This effort included four Japanese-built shallow-draft cargo ships.

Date	Unit(s)	Notes
22 January	T-43	Disabled by 4 A-6E Intruders
	3 PBs	1 disabled, 2 chased off by U.S. ships in the Persian Gulf
23 January	Tanker	Disabled by A-6E Intruders; had been acting as intelligence collector
	Hovercraft (*Winchester* class)	Sunk by A-6Es while refueling from the tanker
	Zhuk	Sunk by A-6Es
24 January	Zhuk	Sunk by A-6Es
	Minelayer (*Spasilac* class)	Sunk by A-6Es
	Minelayer	Sunk by Royal Saudi ship using Harpoon
	Minesweeper	Sunk by Iraqi mine while evading A-6E attack
	4 ships	Hit by A-6Es and F/A-18s in attack on Umm Qasr naval base
25 January	Minelayer	Engaged and hit by U.S. ships while laying mines near Sea Island oil terminal; set part of terminal and surrounding water on fire
26 January	PB	Left burning in Kuwait harbor
	TNC-45	Left buring by A-6Es
27 January[1]	Ship	Sunk by A-6Es
28 January	N.A.	A-6E attacks on Iraqi ships in Bubiyan Channel, at Umm Qasr base, and in Kuwait harbor. No results have yet been made available. Similar attacks on 29 January.
29 January	17 small boats	Detected by SH-60; 12 damaged (4 sunk) by Lynx helicopters from HMS *Brazen* and *Gloucester* using Sea Skuas
	Large patrol boat	Sunk by Sea Skua from HMS *Cardiff* (probably associated with Khafji convoy)
30 January[2]	8 FPBs	Attacked by A-6Es and F/A-18s; 4 sunk, 3 damaged. Included Osa-class missile boats. Another report splits

Date	Unit(s)	Notes
		this into an attack on 2 PBs at Umm Qasr (1 sunk, 1 damaged) and an attack on 4 units near Bubiyan Island (3 PBs sunk, 1 landing craft damaged).
	T-43	Sea Skua hit by HMS *Gloucester* Lynx; left burning
	TNC-45	Sea Skua hit by HMS *Gloucester* Lynx; left burning
	3 LSM	Sunk by Jaguars and A-6Es using CRV 7 rockets, bombs, and cannon. Another report states that 2 were left dead in the water (the third fled). This attack occurred near the Shatt-al-Arab.
1 February	PB	Left burning at Min-al-Bakr oil terminal by an A-6E
2 February[3]	PGM	Exocet-capable patrol boat hit by 2 LGBs; second one straddled by a string of 12, 500-lb bombs; both at Al Kalia naval facility
	4 PBs	Engaged by *Nicholas* helicopters near Maradim Island (1 destroyed, 2 damaged)
	PB	Destroyed by A-6Es in Kuwait harbor with 2 LGBs.
8 February	Training ship and TNC-45	Both neutralized by A-6Es at Cor-al-Zubayr
9 February	Zhuk	Substantially damaged by Rockeye from an A-6E
10 February	2 PB	Sunk by A-6Es in northern Gulf
14 February	Osa	Sunk in Kuwait Bay by A-6Es

H

Scud Attacks

Result	Target		
	Saudi Arabia	Israel	Bahrain
Total fired	48	40	3
Missed target area	11	15	1
Intercepted by Patriot	34	11	0
Hit Target	0	13	0
Debris Hit	7	7	0
Missed country	3	1	2

THE TOTAL number of Scuds fired is the number of harmless hits (missiles that did not reach protected areas) plus the number intercepted plus the number that hit the target without being intercepted plus the number that fell outside the target country altogether. In the case of Israel, the difference between the number of missiles intercepted and the number of debris hits is four Scuds whose warheads were detonated in flight (presumably by Patriots), and which therefore produced no debris.

Published figures vary considerably. The table above was released by the British Ministry of Defence and corrected to some extent by reference to later U.S. publications. An article in the

April 15 issue of the *Wall Street Journal* states that, in all, 158
Patriot missiles were fired at 47 Scuds, intercepting 45 of them.
Generally 2 missiles were fired at each target, but Scuds often
broke into pieces; 2 Patriots were typically fired at each piece. For
example, 5 missiles fired at Saudi Arabia broke into 14 pieces,
attracting 28 Patriots.

Apart from one hit at the very end of the war in Saudi Arabia,
which killed twenty-eight Americans in a barracks, Scud did very
little damage to Saudi Arabia. Of the Scuds that hit Israel, only
two actually killed anyone: one on Ramat Gan on 22 January
killed three, and one on Tel Aviv on 25 January killed one. Others
died of indirect effects of the attacks, such as heart attacks and
suffocation in incorrectly applied gas masks. Scuds wounded 289
in Israel and damaged a total of 11,727 apartments.

Notes

INTRODUCTION

1. The evidence on this point is somewhat contradictory; there were certainly indications that the Bush administration considered war likely as early as September or October 1990. However, many of those in Congress who opposed the war in December (and who quite possibly could have caused a constitutional crisis had the administration chosen to override their votes) were very much impressed by projections of casualties the United States would probably incur in a war to liberate Kuwait. Saddam seems to have been quite aware of the congressional role in ending U.S. support for South Vietnam, and in precluding any U.S. reaction when North Vietnam invaded in 1975. It is difficult to avoid the thought that he actively promoted exaggerated accounts of Iraqi military strength in hopes of deterring the United States.

2. The British had a considerable advantage in this case in their extensive historical links with the Gulf region. It may have been indicative that, at least in public statements, the British were more aggressive earlier than the Americans; it seems that the Foreign and Commonwealth Office called for an immediate and unambiguous military response. Apparently this was at least partly a response to feelers from the Arab world to the effect that an early display of strength was badly needed. The United States soon followed, possibly in response to information from Britain.

3. Iran was probably the most notorious case in point. In 1976, a CIA report predicted that the Pahlavi dynasty would last at least another twenty-five years. The primary source was Savak, the Iranian secret police service, not the man on the street or in the bazaar. The present author well remembers being assured about 1977 by State Department

representatives that the character of the shah's government, particularly its "white revolution," made it far more stable than such shaky regimes as that in Saudi Arabia (the context was a project to draft an arms control impact statement on the proposed scale of F-18Ls to Iran).

CHAPTER 1. BACKGROUND TO WAR

1. The Ottomans first conquered the area that is now Iraq in 1534, but it was later taken over by Persia (Iran) and changed hands several times before the Ottomans finally won in 1638. Enmity between Arab Iraq and Persia dates back much further. In 637 Arab tribes newly converted to Islam defeated the Zoroastrian rulers of Persia at Qadissiyat (Saddam called his 1980 offensive "Qadissiyat Saddam").

2. The Assyrians provided most of the troops recruited by the British after 1920. They were badly battered by the Iraqi Army after the British granted independence in 1932.

3. The *Political Dictionary of the Middle East in the 20th Century*, edited by E. Levine and Y. Shimoni (Jerusalem Publishing House, 1972) describes the Arab Sunnis as the only group for which identity with Iraq exceeds tribal or communal identity, and also as the carriers of Arab nationalism within Iraq. It seems unlikely that Saddam's efforts have really changed matters in the intervening two decades. Certainly the Iranians thought that the Iraqi Shi'ites would rise to support them in 1979–80, and Saddam wiped out the local Shi'ite leadership to preclude that.

4. Iraq includes the two holiest Shi'ite sites, Karbala and Najaf. During the war, the coalition avoided attacks on either, for fear that Iran would enter the war. During the Shi'ite rising immediately after the war, the Republican Guard shelled Karbala for 12 hours. Presumably the Iranians could have taken that attack as a pretext for attacking Iraq. Through the period between independence in 1932 and World War II, Iraq was subject to almost continuous Shi'ite risings, some of them encouraged by political factions in Baghdad.

5. The situation is not really very different from that in Europe up through this century. Nationalism, i.e., identification with an ethnic group, conflicted with loyalty to a king who might unite portions of several different ethnic groups under his own crown. At the same time, many in Europe hoped to achieve some wider unity, perhaps under the emblem of the Catholic church. Nationalism had the wider connotation of being a popular movement, justified by its support from below, and thus was directly opposed to royalty, which, in theory, was justified directly by God. For example, German nationalism directly conflicted with the aims of the Prussian (Hohenzollern) monarchy, to the extent that the kaiser refused to accept a pan-German crown offered by nationalists in 1848. The extent to which modern Islamic kings and princes justify their rule by reference to the Koran would certainly seem to recall the Europeans' divinely justified monarchies. In this sense what is usually

described as Arab nationalism or as a pan-Islamic movement would seem much more like the pre-nationalistic Christian unity of medieval Europe, likely to collapse (as has in fact been the case) as countries develop national identities.

6. This idea, of course, long predates Saddam Hussein and his Ba'ath party friends. Its first modern expression was a plan by Sherif Hussein, who had led the nationalist fight against the Turks in World War I, to form a federation of kingdoms ruled by his sons, Ali, Feisal, and Abdullah, to consist of Iraq, Greater Syria (including what is now Jordan), and Hijaz (what is now Saudi Arabia). However, in the postwar settlement France ruled Syria (Iraq was created, in effect, as a consolation prize for Feisal). Soon after the war, the Hashemite king of Hijaz was ejected by the Saudi family. Later the Hashemite family put forward another Fertile Crescent scheme, uniting Syria, Lebanon, Jordan, and Palestine (this was before 1948). The Syrians later proposed their own Fertile Crescent scheme, without any Hashemite control. The Arab League, formed in 1945 to promote Arab unity, nonetheless rejected all such schemes for merging its members. The next major push toward a pan-Arab state was Gamal Nasser's 1958 creation of the United Arab Republic of Egypt, Syria (which seceded in 1961 after a military coup), and Yemen as the beginning of a larger pan-Arab union; Iraq briefly attempted union with Jordan (their two kings were closely related) as a counterbalance. In 1963 the revolutionary governments of Iraq, Syria, and Egypt briefly planned union; presumably they could have compelled Jordan to join with them. This attempt, too, was unsuccessful. In each case the local rulers were unwilling to submerge themselves in any larger entity. In cases like Saudi Arabia and Iraq, no local ruler was willing to share valuable resources (mainly oil) with the poorer partners. No pretender to pan-Arab unity was able to reach the others' populations to circumvent that unwillingness. Nasser came closest, with his Voice of the Arabs broadcasting from Cairo, but he failed.

7. These were troops occupying the abandoned hotel in Khafji, the day before the allied attack on it. A reporter managed to phone them.

8. The conflict between Iraq and Iran illustrates the difference. Both share the same Muslim (Islamic) orientation. However, Iraq is ethnically Arab; Iran is not. The enmity between Arabs and Persians long antedates the emergence of Islam. The situation is further complicated in that Islam is split into several major sects. Iran is largely Shi'ite. Saddam is a Sunni Muslim, as are the Egyptians and the governing classes of the Gulf states. To make matters more complex, Shi'ism is the faith of more than half of all Iraqis, and Sunnis are in a distinct minority.

9. This was not a new theme for the Saudi government. After 1979 the newly militant Iranians claimed that the Saudis did not deserve their special status as protectors of Mecca, that the Iranians were more pious and should displace them. One interpretation of the extreme reaction to Salman Rushdie's book *Satanic Verses* is that it was an attempt by the

Iranians to bolster their claim to special piety. The Iranians also promoted disturbances in Mecca during the annual pilgrimage specifically to discredit Saudi stewardship.

10. The usual formulation was, "How do you end the war, whether or not Saddam survives it? Surely individual terrorists will still be furious enough to act." That avoids a major lesson of the antiterrorist campaign, which is that terrorist attacks in the West require considerable financing and logistical backup; they are anything *but* the act of a few highly motivated fanatics (although those actually executing the acts may be so described). Presumably the worldwide freeze of Iraqi assets helped dampen any terrorist plans; it is remarkable that so little was done during the war. Most of the attacks (which were largely limited to the Third World) appear to have been the acts of individuals not controlled by the Iraqi government. It is also instructive that, although the gross number of terrorist acts in the world has been rising for some years, the number in the West has been falling. By far the greatest percentage of terrorist attacks in recent years have been intimately related to the ongoing war in Afghanistan, and have been perpetrated in Pakistan; they have nothing to do with the forces operating in the Middle East or in the Gulf.

11. David Pryce-Jones's *Closed Circle: An Interpretation of the Arabs* (London: Harper Collins, 1989) is very much the cynic's view. He argues that ba'athism has no real ideological content whatever, that it was invented to bring its creators into power. In *Republic of Fear* (Berkeley: University of California Press, 1989), Samir al-Khalil seems to take the ideological content more seriously, and discerns a tension between the pan-Arabism of the Ba'ath party and a nascent Iraqi nationalism initially developed under the monarchy (1941–58). The monarchy fell in an army coup in July 1958, and the first Ba'athist coup attempt followed on 7 October 1959. Saddam Hussein, then twenty-two years old, was a member of the hit team. He fled to Egypt. A successful Ba'ath coup followed on 8 February 1963, but the new president, Abd al-Salaam Aref, conducted his own coup against the party, supported by the army and by moderate Ba'athists. Aref's successor, his brother Abd al-Rahman Aref, was overthrown in a further coup on 17 July 1968, and the current Ba'ath regime entered power. All further changes of government have been by the elimination of rivals within the party, beginning with the ejection of all non-Ba'ath allies at the end of July 1968.

12. During and after the Iran-Iraq War Saddam Hussein also tried to promote a sense of pan-Iraqi nationalism, emphasizing the connection between modern Iraq and the great Mesopotamian civilizations. One of his major projects was to rebuild ancient Babylon. These efforts recall the Iranian shah's very public celebration of 2,500 years of Persian/Iranian history.

13. There was a large ethnically Arab minority in southwestern Iran (Khuzistan), around the oil-producing area centered on Abadan. This area contains about 80 percent of Iranian oil production. The Iranians

had long made strenuous efforts to Persianize the area, to the point that by 1979 the Iranians estimated that only 40 percent of the inhabitants had Arab roots. It appears that the remaining radical Arab movement in the area, which was calling for the creation of a separate nation of Arabistan, was largely financed by Iraqi intelligence. It turned out that the Arabs were the least of the Iranians' ethnic problems. (See A. H. Cordesman and A. R. Wagner, *The Lessons of Modern War: Vol. II: The Iran-Iraq War* [Westview Press, 1990]).

The Iraqi reference to what might be called Iraq irridenta recalls pre-1939 German demands that ethnic German areas in countries like Austria and Czechoslovakia be united with the Reich. Saddam Hussein is known to be an admirer of Hitler's, and the parallel is probably not accidental. Cordesman and Wagner suggest that the Iraqis failed to achieve any sort of decision at the outbreak of war because they deceived themselves into thinking that the local population would rise to greet a liberating army. That seems excessive; the Iraqis probably just were not competent enough.

14. The Ba'ath, a very small (1,000-person) party, initially came to power piggybacked on a coup by Nasserite army officers. However, there was a natural enmity between Nasser and the Ba'ath as alternative champions of Arab unity, and the Nasserite officers soon came to oppose the Ba'ath. Well aware of the potential for army opposition, the Ba'ath formed a parallel force, the National Guard, soon after the coup. The National Guard terrorized the cities, and the Iraqi Army must have resented it. The Ba'ath party itself split in October 1963, when a particularly extreme member, Ali Saleh al-Saadi, won. That further infuriated the army. Saadi was arrested and ejected, and there was brief civil war between the army and the National Guard. At one point a pro-Saadi air force officer bombed the presidential palace. The nominal head of state, Col. Abd al-Salam Arif, used his army units to win the subsequent coup. Some Ba'ath members remained in his government. Arif seems to have been less than thorough in the postcoup repression of the Ba'ath, and he died in what was probably a staged helicopter crash in 1966. These events are interesting mainly for the lessons they taught young Ba'ath politicians such as Saddam Hussein. Probably the most important were the need to maintain party unity and to instantly eliminate all potential rivals. The lesson that extreme measures (as were taken by the National Guard) might be counterproductive was never learned: Saddam Hussein generally preferred the stick to the carrot when dealing with potential rivals outside the party. Reportedly Saddam ascribed the 1963 failure to a conspiracy between Ba'ath renegades and aristocratic army elements.

15. Saddam rose swiftly. He worked as a torturer during the brief period of Ba'ath control in 1963. During the unsuccessful attempt to maintain control of the badly split party that November, he supported Michel Aflaq, and was rewarded with a position in the regional command. He was helped by his relationship with his older cousin, Gen. Ahmad Hassan

Al-Bakr, who became secretary general in 1965. This sort of rise was possible because, despite its power in government, the Ba'ath was still so small an organization. Saddam was made deputy secretary general in 1966. He was imprisoned between 1964 and October 1966 (when he escaped).

16. Reportedly the proposed mechanism was a union with Ba'athist Syria, which would have left Saddam as number three in a state nominally run by al-Bakr with the Syrian president, Hafez-al-Assad, as vice president. (See J. Miller and L. Mylroie, *Saddam Hussein and the Crisis in the Gulf* [Times Books/Random House, 1990]). It seems possible that the intense enmity between Assad and Hussein stems in part from the failure of this proposal.

17. For example, after the ultimate failed meeting with Secretary of State James Baker, the Iraqi foreign minister, Tariq Azziz, actually refused to convey the U.S. letter to Saddam Hussein, quite possibly for fear of the consequences of presenting a document Saddam would consider disrespectful.

18. It is tempting to imagine that such measures so destroy morale that troops cannot fight, as General Schwarzkopf later suggested. However, the Soviets took just such measures throughout World War II, and their army did quite well against a much less terrorized German opponent.

19. The Guard predates the Ba'ath seizure of power. They were formed after the 1963 coup as a hand-picked presidential unit, responsible both for personal security and for order in Baghdad. The nominal leader of the 1968 coup, the deputy director of military intelligence, Col. Abd al-Razzaq al-Nayif, convinced their commander, Col. Ibrahim al-Daud, to join by offering a high position. The Guard's tank battalion reportedly refused to resist the coup because of a tribal slight the previous year by the then prime minister. Al-Nayif became prime minister and al-Daud became defense minister, but after 1963 the Ba'ath were very aware that non-Ba'ath allies were dangerous. Thirteen days after the coup, with al-Daud abroad, al-Nayif was invited to lunch and pistol-whipped, apparently by Saddam himself, before being ejected from the country. Eventually he was killed in London. al-Daud was wise enough not to return from abroad. At this time the Ba'ath had only 5,000 members by its own count, and thus could not mount a coup without piggybacking on others' ambitions.

20. Before Saddam's accession to power, Iraqis generally appended the name of their native village to their names, so that Saddam would be called Saddam Hussein al-Tikrit. He personally abolished this practice, reportedly to conceal the fact that all of his high officials came from Tikrit.

21. Cordesman and Wagner in *The Lessons of Modern War* report that, as of 1982, 300 generals had been relieved and 15 shot. Some of the executions at this time may have been intended to prevent a military coup.

22. For example, Saddam Hussein had himself made a general after receiving an honorary degree from the Iraqi military college in 1970. He apparently had no previous military training whatever, a defect that showed to his great disadvantage in both the Iran-Iraq and Kuwait wars.

23. The Popular Army was a militia founded in 1970 and then much expanded in 1975 due to Ba'ath party fears of military disloyalty. It consisted of all male party members between eighteen and forty-five. Despite its considerable nominal strength, it had few active members. The Ba'ath party also maintained a Vanguard Force of 285,000 nine- to sixteen-year-olds, more political than military in character. To the extent that the party modeled itself on the Nazis, the Vanguard Force might be considered its Hitler Youth and the Popular Army its equivalent of the post-1934 SA, with some pretensions toward the pre-1934 role of counterbalancing the German regular army.

24. The Popular Army was similar in principle to the contemporary Iranian Revolutionary Guards (IRGC), which was also a parallel army organization intended in part to substitute political enthusiasm for political competence. In both cases the politically oriented army also could preclude an army coup.

25. Saddam was presumably particularly alive to this possibility because the air force played a key role in the February 1963 coup, bombing the Defense Ministry where the head of state, Colonel Qassim, had taken refuge.

26. Saddam's motive must, of course, be open to speculation. However, it seems suggestive that the bunker construction program continued after the end of hostilities with Iran, at a time when no particularly formidable enemy was in sight. Such a program would be entirely consistent with the needs of internal security, and particularly with a perception that internal instability might follow the end of the Iran-Iraq War. These suggested goals of the bunker-building program would also explain why the Iraqi national air-defense system was *not* hardened to anything like the same extent (the main centers were in hard, above-ground bunkers). It had little relevance to the internal security problem, and was not likely to be severely stressed by the sort of war Saddam expected to fight. Airfields were, of course, hardened, because Saddam could not afford to lose any large fraction of his air arm in a surprise attack similar to that conducted by the Israelis in 1967. It may also be relevant that, according to a prewar report, the Iraqi Navy (which could not have mounted a coup) had more political influence (i.e., presumably was treated better) than the air force (which could have).

27. For example, Saddam's uncle, who had enormous influence over him, wrote a pamphlet entitled "Three Whom God Should Not Have Created: Persians, Jews, and Flies." Saddam had it reprinted and widely distributed in 1981.

28. As ruler of Iraq, Britain fought off a Turkish attempt to regain these provinces in 1925–27. During the Iran-Iraq War, when it appeared

that Iraq was close to collapse, the Turkish government reportedly proposed that in the event of collapse it seize the Mosul area and its oil fields so as to preserve them for Western use. Turkey explicitly avoided any claim against Iraq during the Kuwait war, but its historic claims limited the extent to which Iraq could withdraw troops from the Turkish border.

29. The first major Iraqi offensive began in September 1961, and by the spring of 1962, full-scale guerrilla war was in progress. The war was suspended in March 1970 after the Iraqi government issued a manifesto granting the Kurds important minority rights. The agreement broke down in March 1974. The Kurdish resistance disintegrated after the shah withdrew logistical support about a year later, following his agreement with Iraq. The Kurds live in Iran, Iraq, Syria, Turkey, and the southern Soviet Union, and they have made numerous attempts to form a Kurdish state. During the Iran-Iraq War, Iraq tried to use Iranian Kurds (who were being persecuted by the Iranians) while the Iranians fomented a rising among the Iraqi Kurds (which was put down with, among other things, poison gas). The predictable Kurdish rising followed the Iraqi military disaster in February 1991.

30. U.S. government figures show that, between 1983 and 1987, the Soviet Union supplied 47 percent of Iraqi arms (worth $13.9 billion); France supplied $4.8 billion, China, $3.3 billion, Czechoslovakia, $700 million, West Germany, $700 million, Bulgaria, $625 million, Poland, $460 million, Italy, $370 million, and the United Kingdom, $40 million. Brazil and others (not including the United States) supplied $5 billion worth of arms.

31. It was never clear just how much of the debt could ever be collected. With respect to his Arab creditors, who accounted for about half his postwar debt, Saddam's position was that Iraq had bled to protect the Gulf states from predatory Iranian Shi'ist subversion, and that their wartime loans should therefore be converted into gifts. Reportedly by early 1990 the Saudis had given up hope of collection, but the Kuwaitis felt otherwise. In particular, they brought up the Iraqi debt whenever the Iraqis tried to press them to reduce oil production (which would have helped raise the price of oil).

32. However, note that in November 1990 an unnamed senior Egyptian official claimed that about a year before (i.e., November 1989) Iraq had begun a conspiracy involving Jordan and Yemen to isolate Saudi Arabia and seize Kuwait and the UAE. According to him, Egypt had been approached with a bribe in this connection in February 1990.

33. This account is based on Miller and Mylroie's *Saddam Hussein*. These authors argue that, by presenting himself as an Arab champion opposing Israel, Saddam could deter his victims from calling for U.S. support; by doing so they would only have been identifying themselves with Israel. This accusation, that the conservative states opposing Iraq were backing Zionism indirectly, was an essential element of prewar and wartime Iraqi propaganda. It seems to have had some effect in Egypt,

and more of an effect in the Mahgreb (North Africa: Morocco, Algeria, Tunisia).

34. Miller and Mylroie, in *Saddam Hussein*, report that this offer, which was practically a war warning, was not known to U.S. intelligence for some months, probably not until after Kuwait had been invaded. At about the same time, Iraq placed unusually large orders for U.S. grain, an act which might also be read as preparation for war.

35. On 17 July Saddam Hussein gave a nationally broadcast radio speech in which he threatened force against the excess producers and stated that "policies of some Arab rulers are American." On 21 July the CIA reported that Iraq was moving nearly 30,000 troops to the Kuwaiti border, and the Kuwaitis went on alert. The UAE–U.S. exercise later in July was the first occasion on which the UAE agreed to openly cooperate with a U.S. military exercise.

36. The final Iraqi reinforcement of the force at the border, to 100,000 men and 300 tanks, was prominently reported in the U.S. press on 30 July. The U.S. government asserted publicly that it was a bluff. Miller and Mylroie, in *Saddam Hussein*, report, however, that on 1 August the CIA estimated that invasion was "probable." They also report that on 28 July an American oil expert, a former senior U.S. official, was told by an Iraqi that "by next week, we will be protecting the people of Kuwait" and that the United States would not intervene because it was "a paper tiger." The United States did take some steps. On 28 July the House and Senate voted economic sanctions against Iraq to counter both Saddam's increasing belligerency and his record of gross human rights violations. The Senate voted to cut off $700 million in loan guarantees used to purchase U.S. wheat, rice, lumber, cattle, and commercial goods. The House voted to limit loan guarantees, but with the proviso that sanctions would be waived if the secretary of agriculture determined that they would cause more harm to U.S. farmers than to the Iraqi government. These measures well illustrate the extent to which the United States had built up a trading relationship with Iraq. Earlier, late in April, the administration opposed congressional sanctions on the ground that they would limit President Bush's ability to act as a moderating influence on Iraq.

CHAPTER 2. THE INVASION

1. The first real indication that something was happening was the activation of the Iraqis' long-range Tall King radars. That these border control radars typically were *not* active may indicate that the Iraqis had limited supplies of spare parts (they were husbanded for periods of real crisis), and may help explain why the system could not be rebuilt after it was attacked on 17 January 1991.

2. One peculiarity of contemporary media reporting was the frequently contemptuous description of Kuwaiti performance, apparently calculated to build up the Iraqi success. In December 1990 the Kuwaiti government in exile claimed that 4,200 Kuwaiti soldiers had been killed

and 12,000 captured in the invasion. It is not clear whether the figure for dead includes those killed while resisting after the country had been overrun.

3. One of the more famous recent instances of the boy crying wolf is the surprise attack on Israel in October 1973. The previous April Israeli intelligence received what it believed to be a war warning. Israel mobilized (standing forces do not suffice for a full defensive posture), but nothing happened. Mobilization was, moreover, very expensive (not to mention provocative). When similar warnings were received in October, the Israeli government preferred not to put forces on alert, particularly when the U.S. State Department (in the person of Henry Kissinger) assured them that nothing was imminent. It later turned out that the Egyptians and Syrians had very nearly attacked in April: the war warning had not really been a false alarm. The ultimate cost of the disregarded October alarm was very close to national disaster. Similarly, it is often argued (probably best by Dr. Roberta Wohlstetter) that the U.S. surprise at Pearl Harbor was largely due to the numerous false war warnings previously received. It was just impossible to sift the real signal from the noise.

4. The desire to read military preparations as a message rather than as preparation for action seems to be an unfortunate feature of the modern nuclear age: most political scientists will probably agree that nuclear weapons are, after all, unusable on a large scale. This problem reportedly appeared in its most ludicrous form in 1975, when the North Vietnamese were massing to take Saigon, and the then director of the IISS could only ask what message they were trying to send. The shock of the invasion (not to mention the surprise at having been lied to in Baghdad) apparently disabused the U.S. State Department of this particular illusion, at least with respect to Saddam Hussein. Reportedly after August it entertained little hope for a negotiated settlement, although it tried hard to obtain one.

5. The effect of a pause for looting can be decisive. A comparison with Korea in 1950 is instructive. On their way south, the North Koreans paused to loot Seoul. That delayed (but did not stop) them. It did buy time for the outnumbered Americans and South Koreans to build a series of temporary defensive lines, and ultimately to stop the North Korean advance short of the sea (from which perimeter the allies were able to build up for the counteroffensive, which began at Inchon). The Korean situation differed from that in Saudi Arabia because there was no natural pausing point between Seoul and the rest of South Korea.

CHAPTER 3. FORMING THE COALITION

1. Before the outbreak of war, Iraq had its own uranium mine and was either building or operating the separation plant needed to produce U-235 for a bomb. It also still had the enriched uranium originally imported to run the reactor destroyed by Israel in 1981. This material was

under surveillance by the International Atomic Energy Authority, and it was physically inspected some months before the war. The skeptics argued that the reactor fuel was insufficient for more than a few bombs, and that the separation plant was far from complete. To manufacture the few bombs, Saddam would have had to withdraw from the nuclear nonproliferation treaty, and thus he would have cut himself off from further shipments. This sort of argument is generally used to show that enriched uranium (which can be used in a bomb) is unlikely in itself to be used for military purposes as long as the country owning it submits to international safeguards (i.e., because the penalty for withdrawing from the safeguards is a sufficient deterrent). As of late 1990, inspection showed that Saddam still had not done anything with his stock of U.N.–monitored enriched uranium. He still had no bomb. It would not have been difficult, however, for him to have assembled one or two bombs from that uranium. The nonproliferation argument is that one or two would have been militarily insignificant, and that the embargo resulting from his breakout would have precluded further production. Saddam might have looked at matters quite differently. He had his own uranium mine, and he was buying centrifuges for uranium separation. No one outside Iraq knew for sure just how far that program had gone. Therefore, were he to detonate a bomb, no one could be sure whether that bomb represented most of the legal reactor fuel or some of the uranium enriched by the centrifuges. Thus Saddam would be able to get considerable threat value out of a single bomb explosion, whether in the Iraqi desert (as a demonstration) or in Tel Aviv.

2. Saddam analogized his invasion of Kuwait to the Israelis' seizure of Egyptian, Jordanian, and Syrian territory in 1967, but that had been as part of a war begun by the other nations. There was also some reference to the seizure of part of Cyprus by Turkey in 1974; the Turks have argued that their attack responded to a Greek attempt to oust the Cypriot government and replace it with one entirely beholden to Greece, i.e., that the seizure was defensive in character and was not an unprovoked attack. The fear of disruption over artificial (i.e., colonial) boundaries is such that the charter of the Organization of African Unity specifically binds its members not to use that as a casus belli.

3. The cry for justice for the poor conveniently avoided reference to the oil wealth of Iraq itself, largely squandered on weapons during the Iran-Iraq War. Before the embargo, Iraq produced about 3 million barrels of oil per day, equivalent to an annual gross income of perhaps $21.9 billion. Oil amounted to 98 percent of its export income. Reportedly the prewar Iraqi military machine represented an investment of at least $50 billion, or well over two years of oil income.

4. It is possible that Saudi Arabia first began buying U.S. ground equipment on the theory that the Pakistanis, who were equipped with older U.S. equipment, could use it upon arrival. The Saudis' M60 tanks were quite different from the Pakistanis' M48s, but in the late 1970s the

United States planned to upgrade M48s in the region (in Iran and Pakistan) to M48A5 (i.e., nearly M60) standard at a large new factory in Iran. The factory (and most of the Pakistani M48s) vanished in the Iranian Revolution of 1979, and the Pakistani army had to equip itself with Chinese-built T59s. The Saudis were seen operating their own M60s during the Kuwait crisis.

5. Through the first half of 1990, Pakistan was preoccupied by the possibility of war with India over Kashmir. Any Pakistani interest in substantial assistance to Saudi Arabia after August was quashed by the extent of the Indian threat. The Indians began putting particularly strong pressure on Pakistan in July 1990, about when the Saudis might have asked for Pakistani assistance under their old agreement. The possibility of Pakistani support was significant because it would have been welcome as an Islamic, as opposed to infidel, force. The alternative, open reliance on the West, carried real hazards to a state (Saudi Arabia) whose main claim to importance within the Islamic world was its custody of the holiest city in Islam, Mecca, a place absolutely off-limits to nonbelievers.

6. There were persistent reports that the Korean workers in Saudi Arabia were organized in paramilitary security units; it may follow that the Saudis had some understanding with the Koreans that they would supply assistance in an emergency. It may therefore be significant that the North Koreans began to apply pressure to South Korea at about the time of the invasion. Such pressure would also have made the United States reluctant to withdraw the Seventh Fleet carriers, which provide significant strike support for South Korea.

7. The first U.N. Security Council resolution, demanding an immediate and unconditional Iraqi withdrawal, was passed 14–0 (Yemen abstaining) on 3 August. That same day the United States and the Soviet Union together condemned the invasion in an unprecedented joint declaration. The Security Council voted economic sanctions on 6 August, 13–0 (Cuba and Yemen abstaining); it called for all countries to halt trade, financial dealings, and transportation links with Iraq. Iraq cut off oil shipments through one of the Turkish pipelines on 6 August, apparently due to the cancellation of purchase contracts. The next day Turkey announced that it was cutting off shipments through its other pipeline. Note that the European Community imposed economic sanctions (embargoes on oil and arms) on 4 August, before the Security Council acted.

8. Through the fall of 1990 the French position was somewhat ambiguous. For example, it was widely believed that the carrier *Clemenceau* was sent to the Gulf loaded with helicopters in hopes that a deal could be struck with Saddam by which they would be used to evacuate French civilians from Kuwait. Minister Chevenement publicly questioned French participation in the war even after it had begun, and just after the first air raids he stated that France's 10,000 troops, 54 aircraft, and 12 ships in the Gulf would not participate in hostilities inside Iraq. This decision was reversed by President Mitterand three days later. Chevenement was replaced as defense minister by Pierre Joxe on 29 January 1991.

9. Saddam and other Arabs interested in confrontation with the West were well aware that declining Soviet aggressiveness had lost them a key supporter and arms supplier. Saddam may even have thought that, sufficiently armed with advanced weapons, he could somehow displace the Soviets as the main bulwark against Israel. He seems not to have realized the extent to which the withdrawal of the Soviets freed U.S. hands.

10. The Arab states felt this dilemma; they could not happily be seen as accepting the U.S. lead. On 3 August twelve Arab foreign ministers issued a joint condemnation of the Iraqi invasion. On 8 August President Mubarak of Egypt called a summit meeting and offered to head an all-Arab security force to supervise the withdrawal of Iraqi troops from Kuwait. The Arab leaders met in Cairo the next day, but they postponed their meeting when Saddam Hussein called for a holy war by the Arab and Muslim people against foreign intervention and against the "defilement" of Mecca (i.e., against the Saudis). On 10 August a majority of the Arab League members voted to send an Arab military force to Saudi Arabia and other Gulf states, to protect them against further attack. Twelve countries endorsed a resolution condemning the Iraqi invasion and calling for restoration of the prewar Kuwaiti government. The full twenty-one–member Arab League met on 30 August in Cairo and again condemned the invasion. The net effect was that Arab troops were despatched to the Gulf under Arab League auspices; they did not automatically come under CentCom control. Ultimate command responsibilities had to be delicately negotiated. That is typical of coalition warfare, and the experience of negotiation is an indicator of the character of future possible coalition or U.N.–sponsored operations.

11. The theory was that the black soot from the wells would have drastic environmental effects, at least throughout the Indian Ocean area. There was considerable skepticism that Saddam would actually set these fires, but he did, toward the end of the air campaign and then during the ground war. The low-pressure wells put themselves out, but at this writing it remains to be seen how long it will take to put out the high-pressure wells. In one case a U.S. sergeant managed to turn off the valves feeding the fire, but in most cases the Iraqis destroyed the valves. Saddam also threatened to burn oil-filled tankers off the Kuwaiti beaches, but this seems to have been an empty gesture. Saddam actually did dump oil into the sea, threatening the Saudi desalination plant (not to mention wildlife in the Gulf).

12. This history also connects the Saudi (Abdul Aziz or al-Saud) and Kuwaiti (al-Sabah) royal families. Both first came to power in the eighteenth century. The al-Sauds formed an alliance with the originators of the fundamentalist Wahhabi cult within Islam, and the combination of their military prowess and the attraction of the religious sect gave them control over much of Arabia by the late nineteenth century. However, their kingdom then split up. Abdul Aziz ibn Saud created modern Saudi

Arabia by reconquering the Arabian peninsula, beginning with Riyadh in 1902. In 1915 Abdul Aziz concluded a treaty with Britain, obtaining sufficient arms to eject the rival Rashid dynasty from the Nejd, the area on the Persian Gulf which now contains Saudi oil resources. That left the Hashemite kingdom of the Hejaz (along the Red Sea coast) containing the holy city of Mecca and governed from Medina. Since he governed Mecca, in 1924 the Hashemite king (Hussein's forebear) named himself Caliph of Islam; he would have been the first modern pan-Islamic ruler. Abdul Aziz finally triumphed in 1925. During his wars, Abdul Aziz periodically had to seek refuge in Kuwait. The Saudis remembered their debt when the al-Sabahs had to flee Kuwait.

13. Iran was directly supporting the rebels, many of whom were Shi'ites. That included arming men crossing the border, and providing them with sanctuary and with bases. With terrible massacres being reported, the Iranians asked the United Nations to do something to stop them. It is not clear that the U.N. can do anything of the sort, particularly since most members will be unwilling to allow intervention against their own gross repressions. The United States eventually warned that any Iraqi warplanes trying to fly would be shot down, and in mid-March U.S. F-15s shot down two Su-22s attempting to attack Kurdish rebels. Apparently the destruction of much of the Iraqi Republican Guard Corps deprived Saddam Hussein of sufficient force to deal simultaneously with the Kurds and the Shi'ites.

14. King Fahd of Saudi Arabia first formally approved the deployment of a multinational defense force to his country on 7 August. He had already met Secretary of Defense Cheney in Jiddah the previous day, to discuss U.S. troop deployment to his country. President Bush then ordered U.S. forces moved into the country (Operation Desert Shield). The following day, 8 August, Britain announced that it was sending forces to the Gulf. On 14 September British Prime Minister Thatcher announced that she was sending 5,000 troops and 120 tanks, the largest post-1945 British deployment of heavy armor. Ultimately the British deployed a very heavy division to Saudi Arabia. On 9 August, President François Mitterand of France announced that the French naval force in the Gulf area would be augmented, and that he was sending ground units. However, they would not be part of the U.S.–led multinational command. The first large formal deployment, of 4,000 troops, was announced on 15 September, in response to Iraqi moves against the French and other embassies in Kuwait. The NATO foreign ministers soon formally backed the U.S. action, but did not approve any alliance military action. On 10 September the United States asked the NATO ministers to add ground forces to those already contributed by Britain and France. On 14 September Canadian Prime Minister Brian Mulroney announced that he was sending a squadron of CF-18 fighters to cover the two destroyers and a replenishment ship he had already sent to join the embargo. Chancellor Helmut Kohl of Germany had already announced (16 Au-

gust) that he would send troops to join a U.N. force in Saudi Arabia, but his parliament refused, on the ground that the German constitution did not permit forces to operate outside the NATO area limits. However, the Germans did send naval units to the Mediterranean to replace U.S. units sent to the Gulf. Their other assistance was financial and material. Meanwhile the Arab League offered a joint Arab force to help defend Saudi Arabia, and the first Egyptian troops arrived on 11 August. On 14 August the Syrians announced they would send troops.

15. This is quite aside from the question of whether the U.S. public would cheerfully have accepted the costs of a long-term occupation of Kuwait. President Bush apparently decided that any real intervention in the Iraqi rebellion would have carried just that cost, and he could not see it as justified. The war was fought to protect the coalition partners, not to change the internal government of Iraq, however unpleasant that might be. To have accepted that mandate would have made it difficult not to go on into Syria, another country with a decidedly unpleasant government (which has, incidentally, crushed its own minority citizens quite as brutally as Saddam has crushed Kurds). The difference is that, apart from the ambiguous case of Lebanon, Syria has not invaded its major neighbors.

CHAPTER 4. THE EMBARGO

1. It was well understood that Saddam Hussein's nascent nuclear capability had to be destroyed, but that goal was never made explicit by the United Nations. Nor would the destruction of a potential nuclear force have justified a nuclear attack. Moreover, the sheer destruction to be expected in even the most limited nuclear strike would have had enormous political consequences.

2. The idea of using bombers based in the United States was raised in 1990 in defense of the new B-2 "stealth" bomber. The air force argued that B-2s flying from U.S. territory (albeit using tankers based abroad) could attack any point on the earth. This argument became important as the primary justification for the bomber, attacks against mobile Soviet targets, began to pale with the decline in U.S.–Soviet tension. The idea was that a few B-2s could carry much the same total bomb load as a single carrier air strike. However, the B-2s could not orbit indefinitely above their prospective target areas to provide sustained intimidation.

3. Both kinds of force are designed for quick initial deployment. Airborne and airmobile troops, for example, landed in the Gulf a day or two after they were despatched from the United States. They could not take many of their vehicles with them, however, and they certainly could not have faced Iraqi tanks for very long. If they face serious opposition, the very mobile forces must be reinforced by heavier (hence less mobile) forces. For example, amphibious marines fight as they emerge from their landing craft and their helicopters. By way of contrast, the heavier Marine Expeditionary Brigade (MEB) needs time to marry up its seaborne

heavy equipment, including its tanks, with the marines brought by air. They could get into place very quickly, but not quickly enough to fight a hasty battle against an advancing Iraqi army.

4. By August 1990 Iraq was already short of cash. Many bills remaining from the Iran-Iraq War had not been paid. For example, a new fleet of frigates and corvettes built in Italy had never been released because full payment had never been received. A negotiated release based on partial payment was aborted by the embargo. It seems likely that some of the Third World suppliers on which Iraq had depended, such as Brazilian and Chilean companies, will be bankrupted by the debts accrued through the Iran-Iraq War. To the extent that is true, uncontrolled arms exports to other Third World states may be drastically curtailed by the Iraqi fiasco.

5. There was, however, a report in September 1990 that Iran had agreed to help break the embargo by taking 200,000 barrels of Iraqi crude and refined oil per day. This oil could then be transshipped as Iranian-produced and the proceeds paid back to Iraq.

6. Iraqi aircraft did continue flying, at or above their normal peacetime tempo. Reactions differed. The U.S. forces were surprised at their ability to sustain operations. Presumably that was possible because spares had been bought on a lavish scale (as attested to by a Soviet pilot who had trained Iraqis to fly MiG-29s). However, peacetime tempo had not been terribly impressive. During the two months or so just prior to hostilities, the Iraqis normally flew no more than a total of 200 sorties every 24 hours. In the period immediately preceding 15 January 1991 they hardly flew at all. Pilot readiness inevitably suffered, particularly since the Iraqis were never observed flying anything but the most elementary profiles, never below medium altitude, and virtually never at night.

7. The Defense Department formally proposed a multinational naval interdiction force on 6 August. On 10 August President Bush publicly warned Iraq not to send tankers out to break the embargo. On 12 August he announced that the United States would use force to stop any ships, including those carrying food, attempting to break the embargo. That was the formal beginning of the naval interdiction effort; on 16 August the Defense Department announced the formal beginning of interceptions (President Bush had approved this step the previous day). The secretary of defense signed an order drawing an intercept line at the 27th parallel north. The first two Iraqi cargo vessels were intercepted the next day. Britain and Australia announced they would join the naval effort on the 13th. The Western European Union (WEU) foreign ministers joined in the interdiction effort on the 21st. The U.N. Security Council resolution supporting the naval interdiction was passed 13–0 (Cuba and Yemen abstaining) on 25 August. The first Iraqi ship trying to run through the interdiction, *Zanubia*, was seized on 4 September; she was carrying tea from Sri Lanka to Basra, and was diverted to Muscat.

8. This experience carried two valuable lessons. First, the very rapid

production and distribution of the necessary JOTS terminals was possible because they were standard hardware and because the necessary software can quickly and cheaply be duplicated. This is a radically new experience in naval warfare; typically, large-scale modifications require large-scale efforts. Second, the kind of statistical merging of disparate and intermittent sensor data of the sort that had been developed since the 1970s (since programs called Outlaw Shark and Outlaw Hawk) was finally demonstrated in a realistic environment, with thousands of ships present. The maritime interception operation was, in a sense, the culmination of a revolution in U.S. naval command and control occasioned by the introduction of the Tomahawk long-range antiship missile. Outlaw Hunter is a P-3C with an imaging (ISAR) radar for ship identification, a satellite navigation receiver for precise positioning, and a statistic ship-tracker, which enables it to associate ship identifications with particular tracks. It can communicate with other tracking terminals via the satellite net (OTCIXS), which all the JOTS terminals share. In 1990, Outlaw Hunter was a prototype experimental program that had been applied to only a single P-3; another airplane was modified for the operation. Incidentally, the embargo, like the war, clearly demonstrated just how reliable modern computers had become.

9. *Ibn Khaldoon* was the training ship of the Iraqi merchant marine, and thus had official status. She also had substantial passenger accommodation, hence her suitability as a "peace ship."

10. This is a classic blockade problem. In World War I, the British boarded ships entering the North Sea. They could be headed either for Germany or for the neutral Netherlands or Denmark. At first goods marked for use in the neutral countries were passed. However, many of these goods were actually intended for re-shipment to Germany. The British ultimately resorted to calculations of just how much the neutrals needed, and allowed only that amount to pass. Because Jordan was a neutral, it was inadmissable to cut off all trade to Aqaba, yet the United Nations force could not allow Iraq to continue to import much of what it needed through that port. The through trade to Iraq had been so important that almost all work in Aqaba very nearly ceased when it was interdicted. That and related economic disasters help explain why the Jordanian public was less than enthusiastic about the opposition to Iraq.

11. Cdr. Tom Delery, USN ("Away the Boarding Party!") in the special (May 1991) *Naval Review* issue of the *Proceedings* of the U.S. Naval Institute recounts refusals to muster crews, increasing concealment of contraband, and more instances of nationalistic statements by Iraqi captains. Some used fire hoses to wet down decks so that they became too slippery for helicopter boarding teams to land.

CHAPTER 5. THE BUILDUP

1. Initial options for military response were presented to the president on 3 August. This early work determined the shape of the U.S. buildup

in Saudi Arabia, since the forces concentrated there had to be suitable to execute the military options envisaged. However, this work did not imply that those options would actually be executed, and there is no evidence that as of August 1990 the U.S. government thought that it would have to go through with a war.

2. The CINCs are: CINCCENT (Central Command), CINCEUR (Europe), CINCLANT (Atlantic), CINCNORAD (North American Air Defense), CINCPAC (Pacific), CINCSAC (Strategic Air Command), CINCSOF (Special Operating Forces), CINCSOUTH (Southern, i.e., Central American), CINCSPACE (Space), and CINCTRANS (Transportation). CINCSOF and CINCTRANS were both established in 1987. Sometimes the CINCs are called USCINCs to distinguish them from NATO CINCs.

3. The navy has a particular representation problem in that a large percentage of its officer corps is always deployed at sea, and thus is unavailable for joint staff service. In peacetime, large fractions of the air force and army are not deployed. Moreover, because the air force requires all its pilots to be officers, its ratio of officers to enlisted personnel tends to be high (again, providing a large pool of officers from which to fill joint staff positions). These differences would not be obvious to, say, an air force officer who had spent an entire career in an environment in which many officers were available to serve in Washington. Cynics noted that one of the bill's sponsors, Sen. Barry Goldwater, was a major general in the air force reserve.

It is only fair to add that before the JCS reorganization, many felt that, like any earlier war council, the JCS would never be able to act very decisively or aggressively. Some member would always object to any course of action (as, indeed, many former members actually did during the debate over war against Iraq). Under the old system, then, the JCS would often act as a brake on an aggressive president. Under the new system, an aggressive chairman might well push successfully for action, submerging the objections of other staff members. That is quite apart from the dangers to the services inherent in any potential parochialism on the part of the chairman.

4. The argument echoes prewar disagreements between the battle force and the carrier force; the battleship commanders wanted to know why, in fleet exercises, the carriers always fought a sort of private battle instead of providing such vital support services as scouting and spotting for shellfire. The carrier commanders replied that the "private war," in this case the destruction of the enemy carriers, was a necessary prerequisite: if the U.S. carriers were lost, the battleships would lose any hope of gaining air services.

5. Ironically, the Libyan raid may have been an unusual case in which jointness was *not* a factor. U.S. foreign policy strategists of this period often discussed a concept of "public diplomacy," in which foreign governments and prestigious foreign organizations would be brought into

public support of U.S. policies. The F-111s were based in Britain, so their use forced the British government to acknowledge support of the U.S. policy of attacking a state supporting terrorism. Given the overall political purpose of the raid (to demonstrate U.S. will to punish terrorists), this seems a reasonable explanation.

6. The Strategic Air Command (SAC) was famous for years for its absolute devotion to preplanned and rigid tactics. The rationale was that any individual deviation could ruin the elaborate pattern reflected in the integrated nuclear strike plans. Consequently, its behavior was predictable. That would not hurt in a nuclear strike because it would be executed only once. But similar rigidity caused losses among SAC B-52s attacking in Vietnam, since (at least until the end) the airplanes always followed exactly the same routes and schedules. Tactical air command was always less rigid, but the Air Tasking Order system used in the Kuwait war was typical of air force tactical practice.

7. The aircraft carrier is the most prominent case in point. For many years its critics have pointed to the large investment in apparently defensive fighters; one U.S. Air Force officer (presumably repeating a common jibe) called it a "self-licking ice-cream cone." However, the fighters are also the *offensive* means of destroying one of an enemy's most potent antiship weapons, his own attack aircraft, which, armed with missiles, may be able to fire from outside the range of shipboard defensive weapons. The carrier presents an offensive threat that those enemy airplanes must counter by attacking, and her fighters can then destroy them. In so doing, they eliminate a major enemy force. Which is that, then, defense (of the carrier) or offense (the elimination of the enemy)? The play of defense as offense is not, of course, limited to naval forces. A common ploy in land warfare is to move a force forward into a threatening position, e.g., astride an enemy's lines of communication, then quickly fortify that position so that the enemy expends his own forces trying to destroy it.

8. See the present author's *U.S. Maritime Strategy* (London: Jane's Publishing Group, 1988) for a more extended discussion. The Soviet navy is unusual in that, operating under an army-dominated general staff, it behaves like an army. U.S. maritime strategy has long been designed to use the inherent inefficiency of such operation against the Soviets. One difference between most navies and many armies is that the enemy force (in this case his fleet) is *always* the naval objective, whereas armies often are concerned largely or completely with seizing particular ground areas. When General Schwarzkopf decided to go after the Iraqi Army in southern Iraq in order to liberate Kuwait, young officers in VII Corps reportedly saw his long left hook as an application of naval principles. Some of them rocked the van carrying their commanding officer, Lt. Gen. Fred Franks, while singing "Anchors Aweigh."

9. An example of what happens *without* support can easily be found in the Libyan crisis in 1986. F-111s based in Britain had to fly a much

longer route to attack Libya because France denied overflight. One of the planes suffered an electrical short-circuit and crashed, probably because it had to fly for so long to reach its target.

Moreover, rights are often conditional. In the Kuwait war, France limited B-52 overflights to aircraft attacking military targets it considered legitimate. Limitations are endemic to coalition warfare (U.S. live-fire training in Saudi Arabia was restricted for fear of killing Bedouins in the desert training area) but heavy dependence on fixed bases tends to have particularly constraining effects.

10. A single modern U.S. mechanized division includes over 5,400 vehicles and 125 helicopters. According to standard army figures, such a unit expends 557 tons of supplies per day when in reserve, 2,079 tons/day in pursuit, and 2,743 tons/day when attacking. General Schwarzkopf's sixty-day dump in the Saudi desert, built up to support his long left hook, presumably amounted to about 162,000 short tons per division engaged. These figures do not include water for personnel, amounting to 652 to 800 tons/day, or water for motor vehicles. Such figures explain why heavy divisions are relatively immobile, at least for any great distance.

11. A current projected defense reorganization divides U.S. forces into Atlantic and Pacific commands. As of the early spring of 1991, each was slated to include a single, forward-deployed carrier, with others operating in U.S. waters to provide backup. The Atlantic area includes the current CentCom. Since a permanent U.S. carrier presence would probably involve at least two carriers, it is not clear how the new scheme squares with other requirements, such as carrier operations in the Mediterranean or in the Far East. For the post–Kuwait war situation, the carriers are considered preferable to land-based aircraft because ground-based U.S. forces are likely to cause local governments much more embarrassment. The United States promised that it would withdraw its ground presence at the end of the Kuwait war, but also that it would continue to help stabilize the region.

12. Carrier operations in constricted waters are by no means necessarily a problem. During the 1980s, the U.S. Navy became very interested in operations from within Norwegian fjords, where the geography would have presented special hazards to Soviet submarines and bombers attempting to attack the carriers. There were similar exercises in the Aleutians. Adm. Jerry Unruh, who commanded the *Independence* carrier group, had been air wing commander aboard the USS *Constellation* in just such exercises in the Aleutians, so he was particularly suited to the run up into the Gulf.

13. The marines did deploy containerized, intermediate-level maintenance facilities from two converted merchant ships (T-AVBs). Desert Shield demonstrated that their concept worked well, although a casualty delayed one of the ships.

14. USAFE operates a total of eleven tactical wings in three air forces:

3d Air Force in England (with four TFWs: 10th, with A-10s; 20th, with F-111s and EF-111As; 48th, with F-111Fs; and 81st, with A-10s, F-16C/Ds, and special forces aircraft; plus 513th airborne command and control wing, with AWACS aircraft), 16th Air Force in Spain (with one TFW, 401st, flying F-16C/Ds), and 17th Air Force in Germany (with four TFWs: 36th, with F-15C/Ds; 50th, with F-16C/Ds; 52d, with F-4Gs and F-16C/Ds; and 86th, with F-16C/Ds; plus 56th Electronic Combat Wing and 26th Tactical Reconnaissance Wing; this Air Force also operates a detached F-15 squadron in the Netherlands). PACAF operates a total of five tactical wings in three air forces: 5th Air Force in Japan (18th and 432d TFWs), 7th Air Force in Korea (8th and 51st TFWs), and 13th Air Force in the Philippines (3d TFW). Tactical Air Command operates a total of eighteen tactical wings in two air forces, plus local air-defense forces amounting to another two wings (1st Air Force, organized as two air divisions each equivalent to a wing). 9th Air Force (whose headquarters became the basis for AFCENT) includes eight TFWs (1st, with F-15s; 4th, with F-4Es and F-15Es; 23d, with A-10s; 31st, with F-16s; 33d, with F-15s; 56th, with F-16s; 347th, with F-16s; 354th, with A-10s; and 363d, with F-16s and RF-4Cs) and one tactical air control wing (507th, with OV-10s). 12th Air Force includes six TFWs (27th, with F-111Ds; 37th, with F-4E/Gs; 49th, with F-15A/Bs; 366th, with F-111s and EF-111As; 388th, with F-16A/Bs; and 474th, with F-16s), a composite wing (24th, with OA-37s, in Panama), a tactical reconnaissance wing (67th, with RF-4Cs), and a tactical air control wing (602d, with OV-10s and OA-10s). Of these units, the TFW in the Philippines is scheduled for withdrawal in September 1991.

15. Turkey called on NATO members and particularly on West Germany to provide aircraft to protect it against any possible Iraqi counterstrike under the terms of the NATO treaty (in which an attack on one member is considered an attack on all). West German refusal to send very much must have been an unpleasant surprise. In November, then, Turkey requested deployment of aircraft attached to the Allied Command Europe (ACE) Mobile Force, a kind of rapid-deployment force for use within Europe: eighteen Belgian Mirage 5As (8 Squadron), six Italian RF-104Gs of 3 Stormo (for reconnaissance), eight Italian G-222 transports, and eighteen German Alpha Jets (JBG 43). Turkey declined to grant facilities for eighteen Dutch F-16As of 315 Squadron (augmented by 316 Squadron), which were offered in September. Beside the aircraft, the Germans (and the United States) did send Patriot missile batteries, and the Dutch supplied Hawks.

16. The matchup was tested regularly in REFORGER (reinforcement of Germany) exercises; the stockpiles are called POMCUS. POMCUS was conceived in the 1970s as an alternative to early reinforcement by sea. Its great defect was always that it created an irresistible target for Soviet special forces and deep-penetration troops.

17. Central Command was initially the Rapid Deployment Force, formed in 1979 by President Carter largely in response to the Soviet

invasion of Afghanistan, which seemed to presage a thrust farther south to warm water.

18. Cargo sent by sea amounted to 3.5 million tons of dry cargo and 6 million tons of fuel and lubricants (POL). Cargo transported by air amounted to about 500,000 tons, which was a record amount.

19. The other U.S.–based divisions were the two light infantry divisions (the 6th and 7th), the motorized division (the 9th, to be reduced to motorized brigade status), and the mountain (light infantry) division (the 10th). None of the light units was ever deployed to the Gulf, since none of them could have stood up to the heavy Iraqi forces. The National Guard includes roundout brigades for the 1st Cavalry Division, the 5th Infantry Division, the 9th Motorized Division, the 10th Mountain Division, and the 24th Infantry Division. The Army Reserve includes a roundout brigade for the 6th Infantry Division. To the extent that the roundout units were needed to make divisions fully effective, the war in the Gulf tested the prewar U.S. practice of fully integrating reserve with active units. The National Guard also includes ten separate divisions, but none was called up for service in the Gulf. However, Air National Guard units were called up for combat service.

20. Since 1973 the U.S. military has consisted entirely of volunteers, and the size of the full-time force has been drastically limited. For example, in 1990 the army force targets were 744,000 regulars (more recently increased to about 775,000), 610,000 reservists, and about 472,000 in the National Guard. The marine force targets were 153,400 regulars and 43,600 reservists. Air force figures were 545,000 regulars, 129,000 reservists, and 113,000 in the Air National Guard. The corresponding navy figures were 591,000 plus 359,200 reservists. The distinction between national guard and reserve forces is that the former are controlled by the states in peacetime, whereas the latter are always federally controlled. The full-time personnel were concentrated in front-line jobs that had to be done either in peacetime or by forward-deployed units in emergency. Much of the army and air force logistics work (which was needed to support mobilization) was shifted to reservists. Thus many reservists were needed to load cargo in the United States and then to unload it in Saudi Arabia. Reservists were also mobilized for combat, e.g., in air force squadrons. The navy approach was necessarily somewhat different, but the navy relied heavily on reservists for mine countermeasures in the Gulf.

21. Saddam Hussein is unlikely to have had much understanding of the logistics that dominated the operation. The war he fought involved relatively short supply lines, and they were not vulnerable to attack. The United States is probably alone in possessing even the limited degree of ready mobile force represented by the carriers and the MPSs.

22. In 1981 a congressionally mandated study suggested that the United States needed about 4.6 million deadweight tons of strategic sealift capacity, in addition to the six division sets of POMCUS materiel in

West Germany, a brigade set of Marine Corps equipment prepositioned in Norway, and strategic airlift. Unfortunately the total capacity of the active U.S. merchant fleet was only about 5 million tons of dry cargo (plus a much larger amount of bulk and liquids, such as oil). Hence the Ready Reserve Force. The origin of the active prepositioning ships can be traced back to the creation of the Rapid Deployment Force in 1979. In fact the idea was older; Secretary of Defense Robert S. McNamara proposed construction of Forward Deployment Logistics Ships (FDLS) in the early 1960s, and three preloaded Victory ships were actually deployed to the Far East (their cargoes were used in the initial Vietnam buildup). The first of the Carter administration forward-deployment ships began loading in U.S. ports in May 1980, and what later became the Near-Term Prepositioning Force was on station at Diego Garcia by mid-July of that year. This group of seven ships carried sufficient equipment to support a MAB (equivalent to MEB) and several air force tactical squadrons for two weeks of sustained combat. Later the NTPS became the APS (Afloat Prepositioning Squadron) distributed among several stations. Later the three MPS squadrons were created, by building five ships and converting eight more. One lesson learned in Desert Shield was that the practice of prepositioning and maintaining equipment on board the MPS was considerably more effective than the simple cargo loading of the less sophisticated APSs.

23. One of the FSSs, the USNS *Antares*, broke down at sea and her cargo had to be transferred to another FSS. The ship had been scheduled for boiler repairs before the emergency, but the great need was held to justify the calculated risk of using her. After both her boilers broke down, she was towed into Rota and her cargo was transferred.

24. One weakness in the RRF was that its ships were bought up in the world shipping market. Ro-Ros and LASH ships were too attractive economically to go on sale in any large numbers, and there was never enough money to build such ships in U.S. yards. All seventeen RRF ships of this type were activated. Another problem was that RRF ships were predominantly steam-powered while the world merchant fleet is virtually entirely diesel-powered. Nor had the RRF fleet been fully maintained. In the end, only about half the RRF fleet was activated. Of the first forty-four ships activated, eleven were ready on time, thirteen were one–five days late, ten were six–ten days late, and ten were eleven–twenty days late. Data on the RRF and the sealift organization is taken mainly from Capt. D. M. Norton, USN, "Sealift: Keystone of Support" *Proceedings* of the U.S. Naval Institute (May 1991).

25. This initiative has been criticized on the ground that it does not directly help British shipowners; the incentives apply to any British seaman in deep-sea trade.

26. Such refinement has become important only relatively recently. In the past, most merchant ships (except tankers and bulk carriers) had their own cranes, and thus could unload themselves into lighters off-

shore. From their point of view the only really important port facilities were breakwaters inside that they could anchor and operate. Piers were useful, but they could be improvised. With the advent of cargo containers, most cargo ships could no longer handle their cargo unassisted. Modern ports have elaborate cranes and large open areas in which the cranes can place containers aboard trucks for shipment inland. The result is that a single port can handle cargo at a very high rate using minimum manpower, but also that it is far more vulnerable than in the past to sabotage or attack. Hence the importance of special crane ships that can unload the container ships into lighters offshore. Such ships have little or no normal commercial application, so they had to be converted specifically for the U.S. Ready Reserve Fleet. Hence also the importance of the LASH ships, which carry their cargo preloaded on board lighters they can launch offshore.

27. The coast guard units are unique to the Ninth District; they have been developed over the last five or six years as part of a program in which the coast guard would be responsible for the wartime security of U.S. ports (a role it took during World War II).

CHAPTER 6. THE FORTIFICATION OF KUWAIT

1. In his final briefing, General Schwarzkopf thanked the press for publicizing the buildup, which, in his view, contributed greatly to deterring Saddam from further action.

2. The reality was somewhat more complex. The long-range howitzers achieve much of their performance by using base-bleed shells, which are apparently less accurate than conventional ones. Moreover, there was no evidence that the Iraqis had the ability to acquire targets or to perform effective fire control at the ranges their guns could reach. Quite the opposite proved to be the case.

3. Like the howitzers, these technologies were less impressive than advertised. Fuel-air explosives are notoriously tricky to use, and their only reported employment during the war was by allied forces trying to clear mine fields. It is even more difficult to understand just how cluster bombs could be described as radically new or particularly secret; virtually all bomb manufacturers make them in one version or another. The fuel-air story proved remarkably persistent during the immediate prewar period (such bombs were often rather generously described as miniature equivalents of nuclear weapons).

4. A historical example might have suggested just how bizarre this appellation was. In 1915 the U.S. Navy's General Board, seeking authority to build a larger navy, argued that whoever won World War I would emerge with a combination of large debts and a battle-hardened army. At that point the United States would be the only attractive source of money, and of course the victor would use his battle-hardened army to cancel his debts. Given the bloody disasters of 1915, that idea must soon have seemed ludicrous: no one would volunteer for a new war after

experiencing World War I. It is striking that in August 1990 Saddam Hussein did exactly what the General Board feared in 1915. He was able to do so because, even though Iraq had lived through its own version of World War I, the assault on Kuwait did not involve much further effort. However, the general conclusion, that living through a gruesome war makes one war-weary rather than hard, seems to have been proven by events in January and February 1991.

5. It may be that Western writers describing the Iraqi performance against Iran could not bring themselves to admit that it was pathetic (even in victory) and therefore unworthy of their efforts. This problem, clientitis, would also presumably apply to many intelligence professionals.

6. All potential coup-makers received some material rewards. For example, a Soviet officer training Iraqi pilots to fly the MiG-29 was impressed by their plush accommodations and by the luxury cars provided to their officers. He also felt that some of the best Iraqis had been recruited as potential fighter pilots, men quite as good as those trained in the Finnish and French air forces. However, Saddam did not really want his pilots to become competent enough or aggressive enough to mount a coup against him. He paid them well, but did not let them fly enough to become really skilled. The combat engineers were a different story. They, too, were rewarded, but they were also exercised rigorously. Saddam wanted competent fortifiers. Most contemporary observers believed that he got them.

7. Although Saddam could imagine that Iran would not renew the war against him, he had to reckon with the possibility that Syria, a member of the coalition, would use a war as a pretext to attack. The force facing Turkey was necessary for two reasons. First, Turkey had unresolved claims on Iraqi territory, particularly the oil areas around Mosul and Kirkuk. Second, Saddam had to expect a Kurdish uprising in the event that war actually began (the Kurdish areas are essentially those claimed in the past by Turkey). Therefore Saddam could not simply move all the troops freed up by the Iranian deal to Kuwait.

8. To put these figures in perspective, in the fall of 1990, Iraq was credited with seven army corps; its army included six armored divisions, four mechanized divisions, and forty infantry divisions, plus two special presidential guard armored brigades, two SSM brigades (to control Scud long-range missiles), and three special forces brigades ("Red Berets"). In January 1991, the Iraqi Army was said to amount to 950,000 regulars plus 450,000 reservists. Of this total, about 510,000 men were reported deployed in or around Kuwait as of January 1991. Saddam Hussein apparently considered these forces insufficient, since early in 1991 he ordered conscription of seventeen-year-olds (including all students) as well as men aged thirty to thirty-three. Many of these untrained soldiers seem to have been placed in the forward defenses on the western Kuwaiti border with Saudi Arabia. Figures for overall Iraqi strength are taken

from *The World Defense Almanac* (Monch Publications: special issue of *Military Technology* for January 1991). See also Appendix A.

9. In early October Kurdish spokesmen reported that Iraq had moved twelve Scud B and Al Hussein missile launchers to the border region, within range of Incirlik. The troop strength on the border, five divisions, was reinforced by two infantry divisions and an armored division from the Iranian front.

10. In the Pacific during World War II, unit strength counts were developed to a fine art, using evidence such as the size of unit latrines (which had to be proportional to the strength of the units). The U.S. analysts in the current case may have been able to work from some units' requests for food and other supplies, but much of that information probably went by land-lines which U.S. forces could not regularly tap, or in codes too low-level to bother breaking. The sort of sophistication seen in the South Pacific in, say, 1944 cannot be built up quickly by analysts who have not spent years studying the army in question. Thus it is impossible to blame the analysts for over-estimating Iraqi strength in Kuwait. Moreover, it will never be certain just how many Iraqis deserted during the bombing; strength at the outbreak of war really may have been close to that estimated.

CHAPTER 7. MILITARY CONSIDERATIONS

1. A Soviet merchant ship intercepted by the blockade naval force just before the war began was carrying tank parts. The Soviet authorities refused to believe that this was the case. One interpretation would be that the Soviet army was increasingly willing to defy Soviet official policy supporting the coalition. Certainly there was much public disagreement in Moscow, and much talk of opposition to a U.S. military presence (let alone a victorious presence) so close to the southern Soviet border.

2. The Germans tried to solve this problem in 1917–18 by laying down a quick, sharp barrage, and also by equipping their assault troops with light movable weapons such as mortars. Their storm troops could infiltrate around points offering real resistance, and (in theory) the forward fortifications would not stand up to envelopment from the rear. These tactics worked well on a local scale in the March 1918 offensive, but in a larger (operational) sense they foundered because the Allies could still reinforce more quickly; the Germans never quite made it to their objectives. Presumably the Iranians used hand-carried, antitank weapons in much the same way, but, as in 1918, they could not completely penetrate very deep defenses. The French concluded from the 1918 experience that the defense would always win out; the Germans concluded that something moving a lot faster than a foot soldier was needed to turn a tactical breakthrough into operational or strategic triumph.

3. This sort of attack, which did have the merit of breaking the pattern of trench warfare, is reminiscent of the early armored attacks mounted in 1917–18.

4. In 1973, for example, Israeli tanks advancing toward the Suez Canal found themselves attacked by Egyptians wielding hand-held rocket launchers (RPGs). The Egyptians had hidden in their foxholes until individual tanks passed. A tank cannot engage infantry effectively because its design concentrates on a single very powerful gun capable of engaging other tanks, and also because its crew has limited all-round visibility. Dismounted infantry or infantry in a fighting vehicle (such as a Bradley) can use numerous small weapons to attack infantry near the armor. It does not matter too much that they cannot aim and fire terribly accurately as they advance either on foot or in a moving vehicle; volume of fire may be enough to keep the enemy's head down and then to force him to give up. For example, dismounted infantry preceded the tanks as they penetrated the Iraqi berm. The Bradley (M2) exemplifies the new generation of infantry fighting vehicle *from which the infantry can fight.* The concept has not been altogether popular in the U.S. Army, and in practice troops will generally dismount and advance while the Bradley provides covering fire. The older U.S. M113 exemplifies the earlier concept of the protected "battle taxi" from which infantry must dismount to fight. It is important to distinguish between the machine gun or machine cannon mounted on a Bradley or a similar vehicle, which is intended largely to spray (and thus to neutralize) enemy infantry, and the single, large, aimed weapon on a tank. Generally the infantry fighting vehicle designer will compromise and provide a machine cannon powerful enough to engage other lightly armored vehicles but still capable of firing rapidly enough to deal with infantry. Such a weapon is of course useless against a full-fledged tank. The infantry fighting vehicles are complementary to, not competitive with, the tanks.

This solution has not been adopted by all armies. The Soviet BMP carries infantry and has firing ports, but it is armed with a short large-caliber (i.e., slow firing) cannon and with an antitank guided missile. It can, therefore, engage large vehicles, but it lacks the spraying effect of a large machine gun.

5. The navy did eventually operate strategic bombers and strategic missiles, so it did partly accept the air force's argument. However, through the period of emphasis on strategic nuclear warfare, naval aviation tended to place a much greater emphasis on various forms of close air support largely because the navy must always be ready to support marine landings.

6. The key development was probably an efficient internal combustion engine, which also made it practicable to build fast tanks and airplanes. Thus it was no accident that the United States, the world leader in automotive technology in 1941, was also able to build the largest tank force, the largest air forces, and a huge amphibious assault force. Engines for all three were closely related and competed for much the same industrial resources during World War II. That changed postwar. It is interesting that the same type of engines (gas turbines) now power U.S. aircraft,

U.S. tanks, and U.S. air-cushion landing craft. That is not the case in many other countries.

7. The troops and light equipment are landed by helicopter, while heavier vehicles in the initial wave come ashore on board air-cushion vehicles, which are relatively insensitive to beach conditions such as slope. In World War II, both troops and vehicles were brought ashore by beaching craft whose characteristics severely limited acceptable beach slopes and other factors. A clever defender could guess which beaches would and would not be acceptable. The longer the acceptable beach, the greater the forces required to hold it.

8. It seems likely that the administration's offer at the juncture between air and ground offensives was prompted only by a series of Soviet attempts to broker a way out of the war before Saddam was completely defeated. The administration also benefited by giving Saddam a definite (short) deadline before which the war would escalate. Once hostilities had begun, the administration was careful not to pause for negotiations, a mistake it felt had been made in Korea and Vietnam.

9. The single likely exception was an attack on a key command center, apparently a relay center, on the outskirts of Baghdad. The center was a two-story building, and the Iraqis later claimed that the upper level served as an air-raid shelter. The allies had abundant evidence that at least part of the building was a vital communications relay center, linking a major command post in the basement of the Al Rashid Hotel with forces in Kuwait. An attack on the hotel was ruled out, reportedly because of the casualties it would have caused (including most of the Western journalists in Baghdad), but quite possibly also because existing weapons would not have penetrated into the deep basement area, or would not have done sufficient damage there. The smaller building was hit instead. Persistent thick black smoke strongly suggested a hit in a heavy electrical transformer (the insulating oil burns hot and smoky) of the sort to be expected as part of an electrical installation. It was never altogether clear whether the bodies so publicly recovered from the building were indeed from a shelter, or if they had been brought in from elsewhere. At the end of the war it was reported that, to the extent the building had served as a shelter, it had been restricted to Ba'ath party officials and their families.

CHAPTER 8. SEIZING AIR CONTROL

1. Prewar evaluations of the Iraqi system varied. Secretary of the Air Force Donald Rice claimed that it rated a 6 on a scale of 10, where 10 would be the defense of Vladivostok (a former air force officer thought this a bit high, and preferred 4.5). The Iraqi system was considered far better than that in Libya or Syria due to its sheer mass of equipment, its redundant systems and links, and the raw investment involved. One question is whether such evaluations ever take into account problems of maintenance, presumably far less crippling for the Soviets. The Soviets

provided substantial information on the Iraqi system, verifying much of the existing U.S. intelligence picture. The greatest prewar intelligence problem was identifying updates made by the Iraqis themselves, and there was real fear that Western systems (such as Rolands) in Iraqi hands would confuse Western electronic warfare systems designed to handle Soviet equipment. This problem becomes less and less serious as equipment becomes easier to reprogram, but there is still a problem if the Soviets prefer different frequency bands to those common in the West.

2. Standard air force Wild Weasel doctrine is for the F-4G "hunter" equipped with radar detectors (APR-38 or -47) and HARM missiles to be accompanied by "killers" whose HARM and cluster bombs destroy the radar site neutralized by the HARMs. The two-seat F-4G is used as a hunter because the rear-seat operator (the RIO) can concentrate on finding enemy radars. The current "killers" are two-seat F-4Es and the newer, and higher-performance, single-seat F-16Cs. The F-16Cs can also provide fighter cover for the less agile F-4Gs. Some units lack separate "killers" and use their F-4Gs, armed with HARM (or the older Shrike and Standard ARM) missiles, both to find and to attack enemy radars. Reportedly the separate killers were not deployed to Saudi Arabia because the F-4E was never wired to carry the modern HARM missile, and because the F-16C (which has an interim HARM capability) has no secure means of obtaining target data from the hunter. The Wild Weasel teams either accompany a strike force or hunt down enemy surface-to-air missiles on their own for area defense suppression. The term Wild Weasel has survived from Vietnam; in the wild, a weasel attracts a predator by its presence and then swiftly kills it.

3. In Vietnam, the navy equivalent to Wild Weasel was called Iron Hand. The practitioners were not special units, but instead were regular aircrews with extra training (the current TARPS crews exemplify this practice). Sometimes squadrons within air wings were assigned specific recurring responsibilities. For example, on board the USS *Hancock* in 1972, VA-55 specialized in Iron Hand (using APR-23 radar receivers and Shrike missiles), VA-212 specialized in Walleye glider bomb attacks, and VA-164 specialized in laser-guided bomb attacks.

4. Iraqi night-flying deficiencies were apparently well known. Reportedly the arrival in Saudi Arabia of the first air force F-15 interceptors was timed for dusk specifically to reduce the likelihood that they would be intercepted by the Iraqis.

5. It usually has to be accepted that a radar hit by an antiradar missile can be repaired fairly quickly. The missile has a relatively small warhead (to leave enough volume for a high-speed motor, not to mention its own electronics), and it homes on the radiating antenna, not the rest of the radar. The small warhead limits the radius of the area it blasts. A wise radar operator can often keep the valuable and irreplaceable parts of his system well away from the radiating antenna, just so that antiradar hits will not be totally fatal. Thus, antiradar missiles are generally described

in terms of the number of hours it takes to repair the damage they cause. Thus, attacks on radars themselves buy valuable time for a strike but must usually be repeated as repairs are made. For example, after the Libyan system was successfully breached in 1986, radars were back in operation about two days later.

6. It appears that Soviet clients are expected to operate only a fraction of the total number of tanks or radars or airplanes they receive in any shipment; the others are intended as unit replacements. The Soviets themselves apparently often suffer from low availability rates for much the same reason. The recent Soviet account of the interception of KAL flight 007 mentions that most of the long-range radars (Tall Kings) in the area were out of service because they had not been repaired, i.e., probably owing to a lack of spares for these older sets that were no longer in production. Such poor performance seems remarkable in an area as important to the Soviets as Kamchatka; it suggests that deficiencies are quite widespread, and that they are not temporary lapses. Similar problems presumably affect any Soviet client state.

7. Tall King is a low-frequency (150–180 MHz) radar enjoying long range (reportedly 500–600 km, i.e., 310–370 statute miles) but unlikely to detect low-fliers, particularly small ones such as Tomahawk missiles. However, maximum altitude coverage is 150,000 ft. Tall King scans at 2–4 RPM, which is not sufficient to track fast targets at close range. This radar first appeared about 1955 and was still being used by Soviet air defenses (at least in the Far East) as late as the mid-1980s (when, as the Soviets have stated, the absence of spare parts made several inoperative and thus complicated the interception and destruction of KAL flight 007). Squat Eye is a mast-mounted, C-band radar with a rated range of 210 km (about 130 statute miles). It was also used by the Iraqi Army to support SA-3 missiles. Bar Lock is an S-band (3 GHz), stacked-beam radar (six beams at slightly different frequencies) providing simultaneous height and range readings for fighter control. It operates in track-while-scan mode (scanning at 3–6 RPM), reportedly handling about six targets simultaneously (presumably three attackers and three defending fighters). Effective range is said to be 390 km (about 240 statute miles). The radar has two reflectors, whose elevation angles can be adjusted to move the stacks of beams up or down. This set was introduced in the early 1960s. The national system also used a long-range nodding (at 5–30 cycles/sec) height finder, Side Net (S-band, nominal range 175 km, i.e., 110 statute miles). Like Squat Eye, Side Net would have had a low-altitude surveillance role. Tall King, Side Net, Squat Eye, and Bar Lock are all NATO-assigned, not Soviet, names. These radars should be distinguished from sets associated with surface-to-air missiles.

8. Sources differ on the list. The French-designed Tiger G (TRS-2100) was used for Roland 1 target acquisition. France also supplied TRS-2215 and TRS-2230 radars. These are, respectively, long-range mobile and fixed 3-D planar-array S-band radars, TRS-2230 having a larger antenna.

When overrun, Kuwait had four Plessey AR-3D and six Thomson-CSF TRS-2230D radars. The AR-3Ds were in southern Kuwait and there was sufficient time to destroy them; the TRS-2230Ds were all captured intact and either taken to Iraq or used in Kuwait. Kuwait also had several ITT/Gilfillan TPS-64 long-range, lightweight, transportable, 3-D radars, whose fate is unknown. It is unclear to what extent these captured high-performance Western radars could have been or were integrated into the Iraqi national system. An unclassified U.S. Army summary of Iraqi air defenses also listed the U.S. FPS-8 (early warning and aircraft control, probably taken from Iran) and the elderly Marconi S-266, back-to-back, S-band, early-warning radar (which may have been supplied to Kuwait or to Iran in the 1960s). The Italian RAT-31S (whose antenna is similar in appearance to that of TRS-2230) was listed in the army booklet, but it seems most unlikely to have materialized in Iraq, since the few sets delivered can all be accounted for. Whether the Iraqi civil air-traffic-control system (using French TRS-2054 radars) was, or could have been, integrated into the national air-defense net is not clear.

9. A typical unofficial count of the prewar Iraqi air order of battle was: fighter-interceptors: 48 MiG-29 Fulcrums (probably including 10 unarmed trainers), 20 MiG-25 Foxbats, 50 MiG-23MS Floggers, 116 Mirage F.1s, and 150 MiG-21/Xian F-7 Fishbeds; strike/attack: 20 Su-24MK Fencers, 5 Tu-22 Blinders, 12 Tu-16 Badgers, 80 Su-20/22 Fitters, 40 Shenyang F-6s (MiG-19), and 20 MiG-27s; Iraq also probably had about 30 Su-25 Frogfoots. These particular figures (apart from those for the Su-25s) are taken from *Flight International* (9–15 January 1991). The 1990/91 edition of the *Military Balance* (London: IISS, 1990) gives somewhat different figures amounting to one strike squadron of 16 Su-24s, eight interceptor squadrons, twenty-two fighter/ground attack squadrons, one reconnaissance squadron, and one bomber squadron. The prewar assessment was that the Mirages were the only really effective Iraqi fighters, and that they could perform either as interceptors or in ground attack. To the extent that Iraqi air defense is a separate organization from the tactical or strike air force, the interceptor force may have been limited to the MiG-25s and -29s, the MiG-21/F-7s, and 24 Mirages. The variety of aircraft types apparently made maintenance difficult, so it was standard practice to send aircraft out of the country for that purpose. Similarly, Iraq operated a wide variety of types of helicopters (sixteen types according to *Flight International*).

10. Published figures for numbers of launchers vary from source to source. The Middle East volume of the French encyclopedia of *Military Powers* (Paris: Société I³P, May, 1989), claims a total of 150 SA-2 launchers, delivered in 1971, and 150 SA-3 launchers, delivered in 1972–73. According to the same source, "air defense of the priority zones (cities and industrial sites) is the responsibility of about 60 SA-2 or SA-3 batteries. Their close-in defense is ensured by ZSU-23-4 self-propelled guns." It would appear that this was entirely separate from the Rolands and

the few Crotales, which were special Popular Army/Republican Guard weapons.

11. There was one important exception. For airplanes, missile evasion relies heavily on automatic recognition of a radar, using its distinctive signal pattern. It has long been known that the Soviets habitually reserve particular signal patterns for wartime (they are called war reserve modes, or WARMs). Automatic radar warning receivers must be programmed to recognize specific threats, and they cannot be expected to deal with previously unknown WARMs. It appears that two airplanes, the F/A-18 lost the first night and the F-14A lost somewhat later, succumbed to SA-2 missiles in divergent WARM mode. In at least one of these cases, the airplane may have been optically tracked, the system sending only guidance signals to the missile. In some cases (reportedly including the older ALR-45 on board the F-14A) the airplane's radar warning receiver can intercept and recognize the tracking radar signal but not the missile control signal. One counter to WARM operation is that pilots can often see and evade missiles without electronic warning. The F/A-18 was on a SEAD mission and its pilot may well have been head-down (firing a HARM) when the missile hit him head-on at about 28,000 to 31,000 ft. The F-14A was reportedly on a TARPS reconnaissance mission, flying above overcast in a known SAM area.

12. SA-2 uses the UHF (147–161 MHz) Spoon Rest for target acquisition (scan rate 1–3 or 2–6 RPM, nominal range 200–275 km); Spoon Rest is often supplemented by a Side Net height-finder. The system uses the track-while-scan Fan Song for target tracking and missile guidance. Spoon Rest and Side Net can also acquire targets for an SA-3 battery. SA-3 generally uses Squat Eye or Flat Face (a similar radar with its two, rather than one, antennas mounted much lower) for target acquisition. The fire control radar is Low Blow.

13. Iraq was the last remaining user of the KS-30 gun. The associated fire-control radars are Fire Can for the KS-12 and Whiff (SON-4) for the KS-19. These are old strategic air-defense guns. KS-19 was the first major postwar weapon. KS-30 was conceived as a supplement to the first Soviet strategic air-defense missile, the SA-1. Note, however, that although the Iraqis had heavy national air-defense guns, film of Baghdad clearly shows that defense around key targets was largely by small-caliber weapons (57- and 23-mm). These may have been Popular Army/Republican Guard weapons.

14. The Guard was generally trusted with the more complex weapons. Given the extent of Saddam Hussein's other arrangements to protect himself and his regime against coups, it is reasonable to assume that he would have wanted to provide himself with a specially loyal inner air defense against possible attack by his own air force. Iraq had 100 Roland 1s and 27 Roland 2s at the outbreak of war, plus a small number of Crotales (which are broadly equivalent to these missiles). Roland 1 is mounted on a transportable shelter, and its target acquisition radar is a

separate Tiger (TRS-2100), the same radar that equipped the Adnan airborne early-warning airplane. Roland 2 is mounted on a tank (AMX 30) chassis, which also carries its Siemens MPDR-16 pulse-doppler acquisition radar. Both Roland and Crotale are command-guided. The Soviet-supplied SA-8, which is broadly comparable with Roland, equipped the Iraqi field army.

15. Early IR-guided weapons homed only on the rear hemisphere plume of an airplane's hot exhaust. Mistral, SA-16, and such contemporaries as Singer can detect that same plume from the forward aspect, where the airplane blocks out its hottest part.

16. They were far too mobile for effective counterattack: by the time word had been received of their presence in any particular place, the guns would be long gone. Faced with just this problem during the Vietnam War, the U.S. Air Force proposed a scanning laser that would detect the reflection of the glass lenses of gun sights, then switch over to higher power to destroy the sights or the eyes behind them. No such air weapon was fielded, but the U.S. Army developed much the same sort of device as Stingray.

17. The first shots were Tomahawks attacking the Iraqi national electric generating system as a way of confusing the defenders.

18. Given Saddam's natural fear that the air force might try a coup, it would have been logical for him to house its control in above-ground structures inherently vulnerable to attack by the Republican Guard.

19. ALARM is, in effect, a simpler version of the concept of the U.S. Tacit Rainbow, now canceled. It functions either as a deterrent to radar use or as a way of catching a radar whose crew thinks it is safe because the attacker has already come too close to fire his antiradar weapon.

20. It is not that the bomb is too heavy for carriers, merely that current carrier aircraft (and, incidentally, other U.S. tactical aircraft) are all limited to maximum unit weapon loads of about 2,000 lbs, generally carried externally (an A-6 carries many thousands of pounds, but not in larger packages). There are also important safety limits on weapon length and diameter. Ironically, the earlier generation of carrier attack aircraft, the A-3, had an internal bay sufficient for a 10,000-lb bomb (although it may not have been long enough for a needle-nosed earth penetrator). Against all of this, it may be that the internal space needed for a satisfactory GCI center exceeds that which can economically be buried deep enough to survive. Some such spaces may be altogether impossible to destroy without recourse to nuclear weapons (Cheyenne Mountain is probably the main U.S. example).

21. Full coordination demands sufficient computer software to ensure that the missile, flying a twisting path, arrives at the appropriate time in relation to the air strike. This software (and the Tomahawk mission planning system) is only now appearing on shipboard. Tomahawk's success in Iraq suggests that it is already stealthy enough for the job. It lacks only a warhead capable of killing hard targets.

22. French aircraft attacking runways in Kuwait reportedly used small numbers of Brandt 100 antirunway bombs, the standard French air force type. The U.S. Air Force had bought the French commercial Durandal, but apparently did not use it during the war. Tornadoes accounted for about two-thirds of the runway attacks, with F-16s making up much of the remainder. About a quarter of total airfield strikes during the first three weeks of the war were directed against runways. Most of the strikes were quite large, examples being twelve Tornadoes, four Tornadoes plus twelve F/A-18s (presumably the latter for SEAD), twenty F-111s, and six A-6Es. The Tornado loss rate in these strikes was slightly over five times the U.S. loss rate during intense operations in Vietnam.

23. Postwar there was considerable controversy in Britain as to whether the JP233 weapon required almost suicidal dedication on the part of anyone delivering it. The RAF claimed that only one Tornado had been lost while delivering the weapon, but it seems likely that this was a technicality. Other Tornadoes probably crashed due to damage incurred during low-altitude delivery. It seems to have been accepted that three of the first four combat losses were to light surface-to-air missiles, most likely SA-16s. The cause of the other loss is not known; there was a suggestion that under some circumstances a JP233 bomblet might explode before being ejected from the airplane. Overall, the Tornadoes certainly suffered badly, since six out of forty-two strike aircraft deployed were shot down.

24. Two navy A-6Es of squadron VA-35 were lost in low-level attacks against airfields H-2 and H-3 in extreme northwestern Iraq. That was not required by the weapon they were using, but rather it was due to an unwise tactical choice by their air wing, which decided to go in at low altitude despite evidence and pleas not to do so. H-2 and H-3 were struck early and often because they were the Iraqi airfields closest to Israel. It was considered essential to neutralize them in order to preclude any attack on Israel that might have brought that country into the war, thereby endangering the coalition. These fields also contained fixed Scud launchers. H-2 and H-3 are not code names; these designations date back to the British occupation of Iraq in the 1920s.

25. It is necessary to use words like "apparently" because it was never possible to be certain of just how effective attacks on bunkers such as aircraft shelters had been. It was easy to be sure that a weapon had hit, and often there seemed to be some sort of secondary explosion, but the latter could not always be distinguished from the blast of the bomb itself. There was no way of knowing whether a given shelter had or had not contained one or more airplanes. A figure of sixty-eight shelters destroyed was used repeatedly during the war. However, in his postwar briefing, General McPeak claimed that 375 aircraft shelters (of a total of 594) were damaged or destroyed; he estimated that 141 aircraft had been caught in the shelters (presumably calculated on the basis of aircraft counted in Iran, in the open in Iraq, and known to have been shot down).

26. Aircraft were even moved to airfield fence areas. The carriers in the Red Sea wanted imagery on the basis of which they could plan strikes, but they could get only textual information, which was insufficient. This situation probably also applied to the Persian Gulf carriers. The carriers were important because they were the main long-range strike assets not entirely covered by the ATO, hence available for quick-reaction strikes. One conclusion would be that some means of secure facsimile transmission (of raw intelligence) would be extremely valuable. Another would be that the ATO system itself could not be effective against targets moved on a daily basis. More powerful computers and a compatible USAF/USN satellite communications system would have solved the problem.

27. There was a precedent for planned flights to other countries. Just before opening the war with Iran in September 1980, Saddam dispersed most of his aircraft around the Arabian Peninsula. He apparently feared an Iranian version of the 1967 Israeli surprise attack on the Egyptian Air Force. This action was somewhat bizarre in that the Iraqi strategy at the time was to mount an armored thrust, which could best have been supported by air attacks. In *Republic of Fear*, the Iraqi author, Samir-al-Khalil, suggests that the Ba'ath party was unwilling to accept the losses of Iraqi aircraft to Iraqi guns, a possibility he imputes to poor command and control (but which is actually almost inevitable to some extent).

28. For this reason, the navy dropped a smaller bomb tonnage than might otherwise have been the case: the F/A-18s were frequently conducting SEAD (which contributed heavily to the overall success of the allied attacks) rather than dropping bombs themselves.

29. In theory, an attacker planning to destroy a medium- or high-altitude SAM system can evade its fire by flying so low that he is hidden by the curve of the earth. One virtue of the airborne radar plane is that if it is sufficiently sophisticated its radar can see just such low-altitude attackers. The radar plane also has the great virtue, compared to a surface site, that no preset missile (such as Tomahawk) can destroy it. Adnan should have provided the Iraqis with much of the redundancy needed to frustrate the integrated U.S. attack plan, but it was far too primitive to realize that possibility.

30. The EA-3Bs were requested by the Red Sea carrier battle group commanders, who lacked any comparable airplane on their flight decks. An early navy analysis remarked that the airplanes' mission success proved once again the value of an organic carrier SIGINT (signals intelligence) asset; at least one battle group commander concluded that he would have been far happier with embarked aircraft of this type (an ES-3A program is in train).

CHAPTER 9. THE AIR CAMPAIGN

1. In principle, ABCCC is the ground strike equivalent of AWACS (which is intended to control fighters in air-to-air combat). The ABCCC receives target data both by voice and from electronic sources such as

JSTARS. Each capsule contains twelve battle management work stations. The original manual ABCCC was conceived during the Vietnam War as a means of extending the horizon of the earlier ground-based tactical command and control center. However, the AFCENT commander, General Horner, used it in the Gulf as his survivable command and control platform, from which he could fight the air-to-air and air-to-ground battles. At the end of the war it was reported that ABCCC IIIs had flown more than forty missions, which suggests that one flew each day. Total flight time was 400 hours, an average of about 10 hours daily. ABCCC responsibility grew from 25 percent of mission responsibility to over 50 percent at the end. The first two 46-ft capsules, made by Unisys, were deployed to Saudi Arabia on 5 January 1991.

2. This is not a trivial consideration. Friendly aircraft must be able to fly out and back without revealing corridors to an enemy; therefore the corridors must change quickly and often. This requirement helps motivate concentration on full four-dimensional control of all the strike aircraft. At sea, where circumstances are inherently much less predictable, no such solution is really possible, and the need to avoid blue-on-blue (friendlies killing friendlies) is a major tactical consideration.

3. The clearest evidence of a shortage of damage assessment resources is the extensive use of strike videos for bomb damage assessment.

4. Similarly, though in a different context, the marines adopted the Fast FAC concept (using the two-seat F/A-18D) after losing two OV-10s early in the war. During the ground campaign, the marines flew two fully loaded attack aircraft into the front line area every 7.5 minutes. The FAC provided continuity. If it had no targets to assign, the pair of attack aircraft flew into kill boxes farther beyond the front line, and if there were no targets in the boxes, they were released to attack targets of opportunity. This practice avoided stacking aircraft over the front line area, where they might have been vulnerable to antiaircraft fire. A marine Fast FAC spotted the big Iraqi convoy that tried to escape from Kuwait City at the end of the war. Other marine aircraft cut off the convoy by dropping lines of Gator mines across the road. Three Fast FACs were assigned to control the attack on the convoy, and the marines provided eight attack aircraft every 15 minutes. The attack lasted for several hours, until the weather closed it down.

5. Even at a superficial level the statistics are difficult to interpret. As of 6 March CentCom reported that coalition aircraft had flown 114,000 sorties. However, it is unlikely that this figure includes helicopter flights and other activity entirely outside the ATO. Of the figure given, 58 percent were combat missions, 80 to 83 percent of which were flown by U.S. aircraft. Of 108,000 sorties listed by CentCom through 28 February, the air force was credited with 59 percent, the navy with 16 percent, the marines with 13 percent, and other coalition forces with 16 percent. However, the percentage of total sorties attributed to combat was 65 percent for the navy, 79 percent for the marines, and 53 percent for the

air force. On this basis, the navy and marines flew about 38 percent of all combat sorties. The air force has claimed that the two services' contribution totaled only 10–12 percent of daily sorties, with a high of 16 percent. Even these figures are probably misleading, since they are almost certainly derived from the ATO and thus list essential missions such as combat air patrol (near the carriers) as "support" (i.e., noncombat), probably do not include the "walk-away" SEAD packages, and take no account of helicopters which, for the navy, are often combatants (for the air force they are almost all support aircraft).

6. Gen. Merrill A. McPeak stated that F-117s attacked 31 percent of the day 1 strategic targets, and that they were the only aircraft used against downtown Baghdad the first day. The air force argument was that the F-117 was far more economical than conventional attack airplanes, since it never had to be accompanied by a support package. Nor would it have to evade enemy weapons while attacking. Given the success in breaching the Iraqi air-defense system, it might be suggested that after a point *no* coalition airplane over Iraq needed either a support package or had to evade enemy fire at medium altitude. The question for the future is whether this situation is likely to be repeated elsewhere in the Third World. Compared to other attack airplanes, an F-117 has a limited bomb load (two bombs) because it must carry everything internally to maintain its special antiradar shape.

7. There was some question as to just how stealthy the F-117A had been. The 8 April issue of *Aviation Week and Space Technology* reported that, during one of the early attacks on Baghdad, an F-117A pilot found himself being stalked by a Mirage F-1 equipped with a searchlight. He had the definite feeling that the Mirage was being coached into position, which means that the long-range (probably low-frequency) radar the Iraqis were using for fighter control had been able to detect and track him. However, the much higher-frequency radar on board the Mirage was not nearly so successful (hence the searchlight, which in this case did not help). This experience would not have been too surprising; the F-117A's shape is probably intended mainly to defeat microwave radar of the sort carried by an airplane or used by a ground-based, antiaircraft gun or missile. That happened only once: presumably the radar that tracked the airplane was later jammed. At first F-117s received standard jamming support as they approached their targets, and the jamming alerted Iraqi defenses. There was always a chance that a lucky (but unaimed) shot would hit the airplane, so, during the war, tactics were revised. The F-117 approached unprotected by jammers and then received jammer cover on its way out, when the defenses were alerted by the explosion of the bomb it had dropped. Late in the war the British claimed that at least one F-117A had been detected and tracked by the Type 1022 radar on board HMS *London*, at a range of 40 nautical miles, over the Gulf (the ship also reported that she had locked her Seawolf missile fire control radar, Type 911, onto the target at 10 nautical miles). This, also,

should not have been too surprising. The F-117A reduces its apparent radar cross section largely by reflecting radar reflections up or down, away from the radar transmitter. Over land, signals reflected down would be almost completely absorbed by the earth. However, water reflects radar signals, and a substantial fraction of those signals would probably be reflected back into the beam of a surveillance radar aboard a ship (much the same consideration would apply to the broad fan beam of the radar on board an E-2C). Once the F-117A had been detected by the fan-beam Type 1022, it could be handed over to the Type 911 relatively easily, because the latter's operator would know that the faint returns from the airplane were a real target rather than clutter or noise. The lesson is probably that stealthy airplanes and missiles will be less successful at sea than over land.

8. The "baby milk plant" incident showed Iraqi propaganda at its most blatant and inept. An Iraqi-released movie showed supposed employees of the plant all dressed in uniforms marked "baby milk plant," without any Arabic lettering at all. U.S. briefers made much of the plant's elaborate defenses and guards, hardly the sort of thing required for a thoroughly civilian facility.

9. Most of the major centers in Baghdad were knocked out, beginning with the above-ground portion of the presidential palace. The main exception was a bunker in a secret sub-basement of the Al Rashid Hotel, which was occupied by foreign visitors, particularly reporters. Communications between the Al Rashid Hotel and Kuwait were severed, however, when the bunker in suburban Baghdad whose upper level was being used as an air-raid shelter was destroyed.

10. The Iraqis apparently relied largely on their hard-wired and line-of-sight microwave communications to ensure security without, probably, relying heavily on coding machines (these forms of communications are so difficult to intercept that they generally need not be encoded). They were trained to limit any non-line-of-sight radio broadcasts. However, attacks on the microwave towers and on the bridges carrying fiber-optic communications links to the south forced the Iraqis to rely much more heavily on their radios, whose signals could indeed be intercepted. Little-trained in using the coding equipment for the radios, the Iraqis made numerous errors (which allowed U.S. cryptanalysts to break into their systems) and often operated entirely in the clear. According to an article in the 22 April 1991 issue of *Aviation Week and Space Technology*, the Iraqis were probably using early-generation coding devices that have to be keyed and synchronized with each other. Much of the intercepted operator chatter concerned these steps. Once the United States forces had the Iraqi codes, they could both intercept their signals and substitute deceptive ones of their own; the latter practice was apparently quite important during the final phase of the war. Moreover, the Iraqi military radio net was soon jammed. Troops found themselves listening to Radio Baghdad for their instructions. Early on the second day of the ground

war, a false Radio Baghdad broadcast announced that Kuwait City had already been liberated; Iraqi troops closer to the border thought themselves cut off and began to pull out. The episode is presumably one of many examples of a basic lesson: he who adopts a single technical solution (links difficult to intercept) to a crucial military problem (communications security) exposes himself to an enemy who recognizes just how important that single solution is. His troops, who have never learned the fallback solution, cannot implement it in an emergency.

11. According to *Newsweek*'s account of the air war ("The Secret History of the War," 18 March 1991), Secretary of Defense Dick Cheney personally vetoed the statue and arch attacks. However, one account has the statue toppled and the arch attacked unsuccessfully. The point of hitting the Ba'ath party private complex ("Disneyland") would have been to force the party leadership to recognize the disaster that Saddam was bringing upon them. It echoes the British decision to destroy the Summer Palace at Peking in 1860 as an attempt to do damage that the rulers of the country could not forget. There may also have been some hope that Saddam himself would be caught in one of these attacks (reportedly he was almost caught on two occasions). Political strikes had to be tried because there was no real hope of physically removing Saddam by seizing Baghdad. This is much the same problem as attacking the Soviet Union and trying to achieve a political settlement without facing the high cost of invading and defeating the country's military forces. Political attacks became a major theme in U.S. strategic thinking during the 1970s, as it became clearer that nuclear attacks would not necessarily so devastate the Soviet Union as to end a war in one shot. The decapitation concepts described in Chapter 7 were an example, but there were others.

12. Saddam had two aims. The first was to destabilize Arab regimes within the coalition. One of his arguments was that it was intolerable to allow the infidels to spill Arab blood in Iraq after they had not paid for spilling it in Israel, that the air war was just another manifestation of the root conflict with the West. Riots throughout the Arab world suggest some success in this endeavor, perhaps involving large amounts of Iraqi money. It may have been significant that manifestations of pro-Iraqi sentiment were strongest in Muslim countries, such as those in North Africa, farthest from the war and thus least likely to be involved or damaged. Saddam's other hope was that Western journalists reporting from Baghdad would arouse what he hoped was strong if latent antiwar sentiment, particularly in the United States. In at least some cases, Iraqi photographs of purported bomb damage turned out to be old photographs of prewar earthquake damage. In one celebrated case, an Iraqi woman shouting her anger at the United States (for Western television consumption) turned out to be a senior Iraqi government official. Western government spokesmen pointed out that extensive television coverage of life proceeding almost normally in wartime Baghdad strongly suggested that the citizens were not being terror-bombed. Indeed, movies

of night attacks showed citizens casually wandering the streets, which was hardly likely if they feared random attacks.

13. In his 15 March summary briefing on the war, General McPeak stated that precision-guided bombs had made up only 6,520 tons of the total of 88,500 tons dropped on Iraq (it seems unlikely that this figure included self-propelled missiles such as Maverick). General McPeak claimed a success rate of about 90 percent for guided bombs, but his generally loose tone suggests that the figure should not be taken too seriously (later it was claimed that F-15E squadrons achieved 80 percent success with their laser-guided bombs). The navy did find laser-guided bombs significantly more reliable than the alternative, the electro-optical (fire and forget) Walleye bomb, which it credited with a 60 to 65 percent success rate. Although figures are not available, it seems likely that those few aircraft capable of directing laser-guided bombs were quite thoroughly occupied in delivering them. Presumably a future Third World conflict would involve more airplanes capable of dropping laser-guided bombs, and thus a much higher percentage of such weapons. In particular, it seems unfortunate that the airplane capable of carrying the heaviest load, the B-52, could not deliver guided bombs; over a quarter of the unguided bombs (25,700 tons) were dropped by B-52s flying 1,624 missions. Reportedly at the end of the war the U.S. Air Force was on the point of equipping one or more B-52s so that they could drop laser-guided bombs to be directed by smaller aircraft orbiting a target area at lower altitude.

14. Laser-guided bombs made up the bulk of all the precision-guided bombs dropped. The navy also used 133 Walleyes, an earlier electro-optical missile with a data link back to the launching airplane. It could be used at a greater standoff distance. See Appendix D for details of guided bombs.

15. Much was made of attacking surgically so as to avoid casualties to civilians in nearby buildings, and certainly Iraqi propaganda was quick to point to any instances it could describe as indiscriminate bombing. It seems much more likely that precision was sought mainly because there were numerous targets, and never enough sorties or bombs available to waste on area attacks.

16. Inverse synthetic aperture radar (ISAR) uses the motion of a target to form an image. Different parts of the target move at different speeds toward or away from the radar, depending on how far they are from the axis around which the target turns (for example, on how high they are above a ship's waterline). These different velocities impose different Doppler (frequency) shifts in the signals reflected from the different portions of the target. If the radar beam is sharp enough, it looks at only a limited slice of target, so the Doppler shift from that slice indicates a distance perpendicular to the line of the beam. The combination of slices with shifts amounts to an image of the target. In this case, the motion was probably the scanning motion of a live radar, which would stand out

particularly clearly on an ISAR. The radar would have to rotate even if its transmitter was switched to a dummy load, in order to be able to operate as soon as the transmitter was switched to the live load. Thus the ISAR-equipped S-3 could probably detect radars feigning inaction. The S-3B performed in many other roles (for none of which it had been designed), largely thanks to the excellence of its ISAR radar, which could be used over land (in this case the motion of the airplane provides a target image). The airplane combines ISAR with a very good ESM receiver, ALR-76. This combination was useful in Scud-hunting. S-3Bs also flew armed surface CAP (SUCAP) for the naval force in the Gulf. On one such mission an S-3B sank an Iraqi patrol boat with Mk 82 bombs. S-3s supported naval strikes by launching TALD decoys and by tanking.

17. Late in the war, a handwritten air force point paper surfaced explaining that the electronic identification requirement was a ploy to avoid giving the navy the CAP stations. During the next (fifth) week of the war the navy was given the CAP station north of Basra.

18. Modern bomb fillings are more powerful, but the difference is unlikely to be anything like an order of magnitude. Even if modern explosives have twice the effect of their World War II predecessors, it is well to keep in mind that the largest modern tactical bombs are 2,000 pounders, while 4,000 pounders were common in the past. The difference is largely due to the fact that the modern weapons must all be carried externally, by fighter-bombers or attack bombers, whereas the really heavy World War II bombs were carried internally.

19. For example, just before the beginning of the ground offensive, Central Command claimed that its aircraft had knocked out 1,685 Iraqi tanks, about 40 percent of the total force in the theater. Newspaper reports suggested that this figure had been greatly exaggerated, perhaps by a ratio of as great as 3:1. World War II experience, as reported in the U.S. Strategic Bombing Survey (USSBS), suggests that aerial photos (and, presumably, satellite photos as well) tend to make for a relatively optimistic view of the extent of damage done, and that inspection on the ground can make for considerable pessimism. It is possible that, knowing as much, Central Command was deliberately conservative in its estimates.

20. The bombs used at the time were 12,000-lb Tallboys and 22,000-lb Grand Slams, both conceived by Barnes Wallis. During the 1970s there was considerable interest in an earth-penetrator carrying a nuclear warhead to destroy deeply buried Soviet command centers. There is little question that such a device can be designed to survive after passing through many feet of hardened concrete and earth, and reportedly there is current interest in a nonnuclear version (which would hit the earth at Mach 1.6). The bombs actually dropped on the Iraqi bunker were developed by Lockheed in twenty-two days (from request to use); they were made out of surplus 8-inch gun barrels. They hit at low supersonic speed.

21. There is a considerable irony here. Through the 1980s, advocates of strategic missile defense ("star wars") believed that earlier attempts at such a defense had failed simply because the policymakers would never buy a missile for missile defense because they could not imagine that one bullet could shoot down another (even though just that had been done, at White Sands, as early as 1960). They thought that a demonstration of something radically different, such as a laser missile-killer, was needed to make their case. Then the entire country watched missiles being shot down night after night; Patriot almost always hit its Scud, albeit sometimes at low altitude. The Patriot modification program was not part of the strategic defense ("star wars") project, but interest in tactical ballistic missile defense was certainly encouraged by high-level interest in defending against longer-range weapons. Until the 1980s, there was some nervousness that Patriot missile defense capability would make for difficulty in arms control agreements limiting strategic missile defense.

22. Scud is a NATO code name; the associated numerical designation is SS-1C. SS-1 was a direct copy of the German V-2.

23. This was not an instance of interservice rivalry. The navy generally finds itself using carrier aircraft to fuel other carrier aircraft. They are too small to use the air force's boom system. The booms, however, are preferable if the tankers are large enough to accommodate them.

CHAPTER 10. THE TEST: KHAFJI

1. The 5th Mechanized had nine brigades; the nominal Iraqi division has three.

2. The corporal did not even consider this performance remarkable.

3. The regimental commander, riding a Chinese-built K 63 armored personnel carrier, told his machine gunner to fire on the unit they were approaching. When the gunner saw that he was up against tanks, he refused. The regimental commander promptly shot him, then had his own legs blown off when a Qatari AMX 30 fired at him.

4. The Saudis and Qataris did not stand and die. As intended, they withdrew and reported the attack, remaining in contact with the advancing Iraqis. That indicated a high standard of professionalism, particularly among men raised in a culture that places so high a value on pride and face.

5. Available evidence suggests that the false surrender idea had originated at the brigade level. It was not repeated elsewhere. Later there were abundant reports that many Iraqi units incorporated special political squads intended to kill anyone attempting to desert. When they defected before the opening of the ground war, Iraqi troops that were dug into the border region claimed that they had been told their positions were mined front and rear, so that they would die if they left, and that the Saudi frontier (actually a few thousand yards distant) was three to four days' march away (i.e., that they would not be able to get there on foot). There were also prewar reports that the border fortifications had

been designed with extra works to prevent soldiers from bolting to the rear. The small number who deserted to the coalition during the air campaign would seem to testify to the efficacy of these measures. However, it has also been suggested that at least 30 percent of the Iraqi troops in the theater managed to desert and walk toward home before the ground campaign began. Desertion was so rife, and had so depleted forces, that soon after the end of the war the Iraqi government issued a special proclamation pardoning all deserters.

6. The Iraqis were using Dutch (Delft) equipment. After the war, the U.S. government charged the Dutch firm with illegally exporting night-vision technology that had been transferred for NATO use. The lesson is that advanced technology in itself is virtually impossible to keep out of the hands of at least some Third World troops. The larger lesson of Khafji is that possession of a little advanced technology does not in itself make an advanced army.

7. The conclusion that the Iraqi Army did not know how to fight was not universal. To the outside world, stiff Iraqi resistance at Khafji, rather than coalition distaste for taking unnecessary casualties, seemed to explain why it took two days to retake the town. Also, observers' reactions to events at Khafji reflected very different expectations of Iraqi competence. One young marine, for example, was surprised that their vehicles shot back at all. Clearly he expected that the Iraqis would break and run at the sound of approaching aircraft.

CHAPTER 11. THE SEAWARD FLANK

1. Ships may seem quite visible, hence open to attack. However, about three decades of U.S. and Soviet experience show that considerable reconnaissance support is needed if ships at a distance are to be struck. Scuds just took too much time to target (ships would move too far between the time when targets were found and the time the missile would arrive at the presumed target position). Even Iraqi aircraft would need considerable targeting support, since they could not afford to spend time searching for naval targets (and opening themselves up to counterattack). As it turned out, Scuds were far too inaccurate to hit airfields reliably, and Saddam never fired enough of them at once to overwhelm the Patriot missiles protecting the airfields. No one would have been sure of either fact before the war began. As for the B-52s, their situation would have been far more precarious without shorter-range aircraft (flying from bases within Scud range) to deal with Iraqi air defenses.

2. After the war Saddam claimed that he still possessed large stocks of chemical weapons. If that is true, then it is quite possible that he was deterred from using them.

3. This was the French admiral (France held the WEU chair from June 1990 through June 1991).

4. The battleships' 16-inch shells were probably the only coalition weapons that could have breached Saddam's deep coastal bunkers. The

battleships were the only warships with sufficient firing range to hit the shore without going aground on the offshore shallows. They used small, remotely piloted vehicles (Pioneers) to spot their fire. In a bizarre incident, twenty-eight Iraqis surrendered to the *Wisconsin*'s Pioneer—in effect, to a model airplane.

5. This incident may have occurred as amphibious ships moved toward the coast following mine countermeasures craft in a strong feint. That neither the battleship nor the British destroyer was mined suggests strongly that the Iraqi mine threat could not have prevented the feint assault from turning real.

6. There is some dispute on this point; one writer claims as many as eight contact and eight influence types. It seems unlikely that the Iraqis actually planted many (or perhaps any) of the mines they displayed at the 1989 Baghdad arms show.

7. Contact mines are swept by cutting the cables mooring them to the bottom. In theory, a ground mine might be swept by a device simulating that part of the ship's overall signature to which the mine responds. However, modern ground mines generally incorporate ship counters, so that they will not respond to the first few ships that pass over them. The solution is either to sweep back and forth many times or to examine the bottom in great detail and destroy every minelike object found. Either alternative is quite tedious.

8. For example, a mine countermeasures ship has to be relatively small, to minimize the magnetic, acoustic, and pressure signatures that trigger influence mines. It cannot therefore be particularly well armed, nor can it stand up to air or missile attack. When navies sent their minecraft into the Gulf, they considered the air threat so serious that craft were provided with extemporized weapons (see Appendix C). However, to avoid blue-on-blue air losses, the ships could not be permitted to fire these uncontrolled weapons. It was therefore critical that the fleet provide particularly tight air control over the mine countermeasures areas near the head of the Gulf, i.e., near the Iraqi positions. Similar considerations applied to Iraqi antiship missiles.

9. A high-resolution sonar will surely pick up moored mines. It is less certain that it will detect ground mines, particularly if the latter sink some way into the bottom.

10. The *Princeton* suffered by far the worse damage. That may seem odd but it was to be expected. A contact mine expends its energy in blowing a localized hole in a ship's hull. A bottom mine produces a large gas bubble that expands and contracts as it rises. Often it strikes a ship several times, each time with such energy that it can literally lift the ship out of the water. In the case of the USS *Princeton*, the explosion was out to one side, and the effect was to twist her hull aft of the break in her forecastle (which is a point of relative weakness because it is a structural discontinuity). The weight of explosive was variously estimated at 150, 500, and 1,000 kg (330, 1,100, or 2,200 lbs). At this writing it is not certain

what the triggering mechanism was. Apparently a second mine, triggered by the detonation of the first, exploded about 300 yds off the cruiser's starboard bow. The first mine may have been a magnetic type which explodes only after two looks (to avoid being triggered by a sweep producing a strong magnetic field over a limited length) or an acoustic type triggered by propeller noise (although the ship is very quiet, and she was apparently running at low speed).

CHAPTER 12. THE MOTHER OF ALL BATTLES

1. Much of the army detail in this account is taken from a long article by Rick Atkinson in *The Washington Post* of 18 March 1991. Much has also been taken from General Schwarzkopf's final briefing.

2. In his postwar briefing, General Schwarzkopf showed initial troop strength as 623,000 for Iraq and 443,000 for the coalition. He stated that the ratio of combat troops was closer to 2:1 than to the nominal 3:2 because the Iraqi units contained fewer support troops. Tank strength was given as 4,700 Iraqi versus 3,500 coalition, and artillery strength as 3,200 Iraqi versus 1,745 coalition.

3. The other possible source of satellite information, the French commercial satellite, SPOT, was denied to the Iraqis by government decision. Presumably photographs of the KTO were not provided to any commercial user (Saddam could have used third parties to collect intelligence for him). SPOT has a 24- to 48-hour turn-around time, so it could not have supported Iraqi forces during the attack. However, it could certainly have revealed the coalition attack plan, particularly the left hook. It is possible that the Soviets showed Iraqi Foreign Minister Tariq Aziz satellite data to support their unsuccessful plea that Iraq end the war before a ground campaign could begin. If that is so, the timing of the last Iraqi mission to Moscow suggests that Aziz should have seen evidence of the U.S. preparations for the flanking attack. Presumably Saddam Hussein was not impressed, since the Iraqis did not change their own dispositions to meet the attack. Reportedly the Soviets used a high-resolution photo satellite, Cosmos 2108, to observe the initial stages of the war (it made daily passes over southern Iraq and the Kuwaiti-Saudi border; its film capsule was recovered on 28 January). A second satellite, Cosmos 2124, replaced Cosmos 2108 in orbit on 7 February. Unlike the earlier satellite, Cosmos 2124 reportedly can return data to earth in multiple packages so that it can be used to monitor a developing situation. The Soviet satellite data are taken from an article by John G. Roos in the April 1991 issue of *Armed Forces Journal* (Soviet data supplied by Nicholas Johnson of Teledyne-Brown Engineering).

4. The parallel with Hitler's obsession with the threat of an Allied landing in Norway is difficult to avoid. In several cases in World War II the plausible threat of an amphibious landing far from the actual point of contact was used to pin down substantial German forces. These deceptions could not have been mounted without the presence of considerable

amphibious shipping quite capable of making the notional (false) attacks; the same was true in the Gulf war.

5. The teams, each of six commandos, were sent out by helicopter: four went north to the Euphrates and one went out in advance of the French. Two teams were recalled after being spotted.

6. General Schwarzkopf ultimately decided to take this chance. His subordinates were not unanimous on this point; reportedly some of the army unit commanders feared that the Iraqis would see the deep strike developing and cut it off. Schwarzkopf met this potential threat by deploying substantial forces on the flanks of the striking force.

7. According to the account in the *Post*, the division found 1,700 bunkers full of munitions, weapons, and fuel. At the airfields, the division claimed twenty-five airplanes destroyed by its armored vehicles. It also demolished numerous Iraqi tanks on transporters. That these lucrative targets still existed so late in the air campaign suggests just how limited that campaign was.

8. PLRS (position location reporting system) tells a commander where his troops are. It is a UHF system, in which every station transmits to every other station; station locations are obtained by triangulation. Although some of the lines of sight used by the system are generally blocked, there is always some line of sight to each transmitter. A marine general likened the advance of the units to the movement of ships at sea, navigating rather than running down marked roads.

9. The double system (line charge plus plow) is needed to deal with dual-impulse mines, which will not explode at the first pressure. None of the other hasty antimine measures—fuel-air explosives (FAE), B-52 carpet bombing, and the 15,000-lb bomb—was entirely satisfactory. FAE and B-52s were both extensively tested. It was always feared that the overpressure of an FAE bomb would sensitize any mines it did not explode, so that, if anything, a mined area would become more dangerous. FAE was of interest as a way of clearing an area of antitank guided missile operators. FAE attacks were planned and were almost certainly executed as part of the initial breaching by the two marine divisions. The problem with B-52 attacks was fusing. Bursts above ground could cause mines to explode, but it was important that the bombs not explode too low. In that case they would tend to tear up the ground. Mines in torn-up ground could pass through the prongs of a mine plow. Plows could also be stalled in rough ground. The 15,000-lb bombs had more a psychological than a physical effect.

10. These mines resembled 2 × 4s. The rakes of a mine plow would flip a cannister mine out of the way, but a bar mine would turn between its prongs.

11. Air force tactical controllers were assigned to the Saudi and Kuwaiti brigades (their highest coordinated formations) and to the Egyptian and Syrian divisions. Special Forces A-Teams were assigned down to battalion level.

12. This account is based on a report by David A. Fulghum in *Aviation Week and Space Technology*, 22 April 1991. Fulghum, in turn, seems to have based his article on accounts by forward air controllers traveling with the Arab Joint Forces Command North. His source observed that, had the Iraqis chosen to fight as planned on the border, they had ample ammunition for the long-range guns zeroed on their pre-planned killing zone, and that the guns had by no means been silenced by the pre-attack bombardment. Instead, the Iraqis cracked early, 500 surrendering before the Saudi and Kuwaiti troops reached the breach. The article implies a reluctance to use aircraft close to the Arab force for fear of mistaking their Soviet-type tanks for Iraqi ones. Thus U.S. and British units on either side of the Arab force suffered casualties due to friendly aircraft, but the Arabs did not. Fulghum also states that the U.S. officers with the Arab force were needed "as watchdogs over the Arab advance to ensure that what was being reported in the heat of battle actually was happening."

13. Figures are all approximate. Iraq began the war with an estimated 545,000 troops in the theater. About 100,000 were killed, and perhaps another 150,000 taken prisoner (however, according to some reports the number of prisoners was only about 63,000). That accounts for no more than roughly half the estimated Iraqi force. It may be that the figure for the dead does not include those killed at the border fortifications. Most of the remainder presumably bolted, many of them before the ground war began. It is also quite possible that the original estimates were badly inflated. They were based on orders of battle, on the assumption that the Iraqis conformed to their standard tables of organization. The reason is that it is much easier to identify enemy units as such (for example, from their radio traffic) than to tell how well they are filled out. This fact is the basis for many deception operations, such as the one mounted by the U.S. forces.

14. Only about ten 15,000-lb bombs were used, and they were intended primarily to intimidate Iraqi troops in the frontline bunkers (a particularly crude U.S. leaflet pointed out that these bombs were "our pistol bullets").

15. Small amounts of chemical shells were recovered after the war. It was never altogether clear just how much chemical ordnance Saddam Hussein had been able to move into the theater of operations. One bombing attack on the Republican Guard seems to have hit a major ammunition dump, and a chemical cloud was detected afterwards by a French C-160. There was also some speculation that at least some Iraqi chemicals had limited shelf life, and that the isolation of the Kuwaiti battlefield had precluded the movement of fresh supplies. It may have been more significant that examination of Iraqi chemical protection showed that most of it was obviously defective; troops may have been reluctant to risk firing weapons that might have killed them. Finally, the allies were careful to leaflet the Iraqis with a threat to retaliate severely against any unit

or commander using gas. Before the war, Gen. Stanislav V. Petrov, commander of the Soviet chemical troops, said that Iraq had 2,000 to 4,000 tons of toxic chemical weapons, mainly mustard and nerve gases. In what may have been an attempt to deter the allies from attacking the Iraqi factories, he warned that hits on Iraqi biological weapons factories or stockpiles might have severe consequences. General Petrov mentioned reports that Iraq had strains of Siberian plague and cholera and that it might possess unknown or exotic African diseases, and possibly also botulin toxin. On 18 April 1991, in accordance with the United Nations terms for a permanent cease-fire, Iraq reported its surviving stocks of chemical weapons: nearly 10,000 nerve-gas warheads (presumably mainly gun projectiles), more than 1,000 tons of nerve and mustard gas, nearly 1,500 chemical weapons (bombs and shells), and 30 chemical warheads for Scuds (there were also 23 conventional Scud warheads). Nearly a third of the weapons were inaccessible, in bombed-out storage sites. The United States charged that the Iraqi report was quite incomplete, both as to the weapons described (it omitted cyanide gas) and to its exclusion of biological weapons. The Iraqi statement was the first definite confirmation that Scuds could have had chemical warheads, a claim made by Israeli intelligence but denied by the Soviets and also by an Iraqi emigré involved in missile development. It may also be read as Iraqi boasting (the warheads may not have been usable). Similarly, the Iraqis have claimed binary weapon technology. These data are from the account of the Iraqi report in the *New York Times* for 20 April 1991.

16. At 1:30 A.M. on 1 March, a large Iraqi convoy (300 tracked and 700 wheeled vehicles) was spotted moving north through the Rumaila oil field. Its leading element tried to fight its way through to a causeway over the Euphrates, and 24th Infantry Division destroyed it. A Cobra helicopter gunship blocked the causeway by knocking out the lead vehicle with a TOW missile, and then two battalions of armored fighting vehicles ran down the line of vehicles, destroying them with automatic cannon fire.

17. One company of the 3d Armored Division, commanded by Capt. Tom Nash, claimed 98 percent first-round kills at 2,300 to 3,500 yds, according to an article by P. J. Sloyan in *Newsday*, 10 March 1991. The Iraqis apparently first knew they were under attack when their tanks began to explode. That was largely because their vision devices were grossly inferior. However, it was also because the speed and weight of the coalition attack caught them by surprise. Many Iraqi tanks were overtaken while still dug in, with only their turrets showing. Brig. Gen. Richard Neal (USMC), who was operations officer for Desert Storm, said that most of the tank kills were rear shots; the tanks just were not even pointing toward the oncoming U.S. units.

18. It was also suggested that Iraqi chemical agents had a limited shelf life, and that the destruction of the chemical plants early in the war precluded replacement of stale stocks, or that chemicals were never is-

sued to frontline units because lines of supply had become so tenuous (due to sustained air attack) by the time Saddam wanted to use them. The second explanation seems more likely. Reportedly some, but very few, chemical shells were found in bunkers overrun in the KTO.

CHAPTER 13. LESSONS LEARNED AND MIS-LEARNED

1. According to *Aviation Week and Space Technology* (22 April 1991), coverage of Kuwait and Saudi Arabia was thin as of 2 August 1990. The article states that the United States currently relies on national reconnaissance satellites for mapping; the Defense Mapping Agency would prefer a better-adapted satellite, Landsat 7. The magazine also claims that mapping limitations made it necessary for Tomahawks to be fired at some targets from the Mediterranean rather than from the Red Sea, so that the missiles could use about 500 miles of rough and hence easily identifiable terrain over Turkey to locate themselves before turning south toward Iraq.

2. That still leaves the question of how to move troops into an area lacking airports, as in the British experience in the Falklands. It may be that civilian cruise liners are sufficiently numerous to offer a real ocean-going alternative, but it may also be that the United States should maintain the ability to convert containerships into emergency troop transports by installing containers of the appropriate design. This is an example of a lesson (troops can easily move by air) that may be more limited than it seems. Can the United States always expect or seize an airhead when and where it wants to operate? For example, how would the United States have dealt with Saddam Hussein had he invaded Saudi Arabia and bombed out or seized all the major airfields?

3. The Iraqis suffered numerous breakdowns even on the march into Kuwait, which should have involved only their best equipment. Soon after they occupied the country, they released television film purportedly showing preparations to withdraw. The film actually showed broken-down vehicles being loaded onto tank transporters (other transporters carried back stolen Kuwaiti cars).

4. It may have been the case more often than might be imagined. The Saracens eventually beat the Christian invaders of the Holy Land largely because they were so much more professional (the Christian princes tended to be more interested in quarrels and in personal honor than in achieving military results). Those who recall the high point of Arabic culture and creativity (e.g., in science) would probably have no difficulty in describing the contemporary Arabic society which had produced the Saracens as much more advanced than contemporary European society. In this sense the Renaissance was partly a reaction to a military shock that had shown that European society was obsolete. There was of course much more to the story, but it is suggestive for the possible future of the Middle East.

5. A soldier will usually have some concept of the force ratios under

which honor or pride requires him to either attack, hold ground, fall back, or surrender. The ratios depend on who he is facing and may be a good measure of the morale factor involved. For example, in World War II a British soldier in the desert would consider the ratios very different when facing the Afrika Korps or the Italian Army. Troops sometimes, to their surprise, find they can fight at radically different ratios (e.g., that they can overcome previously feared opponents). That may have happened with the Arab coalition troops who performed so well at Khafji.

6. This experience was echoed during the air campaign of the Gulf war. Readers will remember a sense of impatience as they heard, day after day, that X sorties had been flown and that the enemy was being hurt in unspecified ways. That was not merely the impatience of bored media executives; it was also very much the American style in reacting to war. We expect movement. In this case, the war could be sustained without obvious movement because there were also no major U.S. losses.

APPENDIX A. GROUND UNITS AND THEIR EQUIPMENT

1. Most adherents of this doctrine believed that the threat or reality of the demonstration attack would stop the war, and therefore that the reality of nuclear war fighting did not have to be faced (as it had been faced in the 1950s). The NATO armies first became interested in tactical nuclear weapons in the 1950s when it became clear that the NATO nations would not field conventional armies large enough to meet Soviet manpower. That was satisfactory only as long as the Soviets could not easily counter NATO tactical nuclear weapons with their own. Once the Soviets began to field their own tactical nuclear weapons in numbers, NATO had to shift to a more conventional stance; flexible response was the result. One major complication in NATO defensive plans for Germany was that large urban concentrations are very close to the old inter-German border. As a consequence, almost any Soviet advance would have caused enormous damage to West Germany. On the other hand, the NATO allies were never very enthusiastic about any preplanned advance to the East, which they feared would provide the Soviets with an excuse to attack. This history survives in modern Western army organizations. The French Army is still built around tactical nuclear weapons (which the French call "pre-strategic"). British armor is less mobile than U.S. because British army strategy is much less oriented toward deep fast thrusts, in accord with much NATO thinking.

2. For example, until the 1970s the Soviets tended to keep the bulk of their tanks well away from the then inter-German border. To mount an attack, they had to transport those tanks to the forward area by rail, aboard special, heavy flat cars. The appearance of large numbers of "war flats" was a sure warning of some forward movement. The sheer time it took to transport the tanks provided NATO with fairly unambiguous war warning. During the 1970s, however, the Soviets began to store their

tanks in forward areas, and that in itself drastically reduced NATO war warning time.

3. There were several instances of coalition vehicles destroyed by U.S. aircraft. The following list is probably incomplete. A Marine Corps LAV was destroyed by a Maverick missile during the battle of Khafji (seven men died). Somewhat later a U.S. Army helicopter destroyed an army vehicle, killing one or two men. On 2 February it was announced that one marine has been killed and two wounded when their convoy was attacked by cluster bombs while returning from an artillery mission. On 16 February an AH-64 hit a Bradley and an M113 with Hellfires (two killed, six wounded). Both British vehicles destroyed were lost to Mavericks launched by A-10s (two Warriors, with nine killed and eleven wounded). The British had two vehicles damaged: a Challenger tank was hit in its gearbox by an A-10 (30-mm cannon fire), and a Scorpion was hit by 25-mm fire from a U.S. Bradley (one killed, three wounded). It seems likely that the Maverick attacks were made by pilots forced to use the Maverick missile seeker as a FLIR (night vision device). It may follow that the identification errors can be attributed to the limited resolution of the seeker (which was not, after all, ever designed as a FLIR). The A-10 has no independent night vision device (a proposal for a night A-10 never gathered sufficient support).

4. The choice to design armies, corps, and divisions so that they can keep moving and fighting over a prolonged period has been characteristic of U.S. practice since the beginning of World War II. U.S. experience at that time was that German divisions could fight had but not for very long, largely because their logistical tail was quite primitive. A smaller number of better-supplied U.S. divisions were quite effective because they did not have to be replaced as they ran out of fuel, food, and ammunition. Much the same thing might be said in comparing the smaller number of NATO divisions with a far larger number of Soviet divisions in Europe. The key question, of course, has been whether the high divisional firepower of the Soviet units could wipe out the U.S. divisions quickly enough that their logistical staying power and mobility do not count.

5. This quote appeared in D. C. Isby and C. Kamps, Jr., *The Armies of NATO's Central Front* (London: Jane's, 1985). The Corps 86 organization given here is from F. Wiener, *The Armies of the NATO Nations: Organization—Concept of War—Weapons and Equipment* (Vienna: Herold, 1987; first updated English-language edition of an earlier German-language book). Division 86 organization is taken from official U.S. Army lists, with some material from the Isby-Kamps book and from other sources.

6. 2d Armored Division was in process of demobilization when the August crisis broke; one of its three brigades had already stood down. In August 1990 it had one brigade in Europe and one in the United States. 1st ("Tiger") Brigade went to 1st Armored Cavalry in place of a National

Guard roundout brigade (155th Armored). 3d Brigade went to 1st Mechanized Division, which had two brigades in the United States and its third forward-deployed in Europe. The European brigade had been scheduled to return to the United States, and it was cannibalized for equipment and trained personnel by units scheduled to remain in Europe. It was therefore not included when the parent division was transferred to the Gulf. In November 1990 three Army National Guard roundout brigades were mobilized, but they were not ultimately deployed to the Gulf: 48th Infantry Brigade (Mechanized) from Georgia, 155th Armored Brigade from Mississippi, and 256th Infantry Brigade from South Carolina. The round-out brigades just were not ready in time (reportedly they would have been available had the war lasted longer). This failure brings into question the earlier decision to cut standing ground forces and to rely on reservists to fill out the formations for combat. It may be possible to revert to full active forces if the total size of the army is cut with the reduction in the European commitment. Note, however, that six National Guard artillery battalions did deploy to the Gulf: Oklahoma 1/158 (MLRS), Kentucky 1/201, West Virginia 1/623, Tennessee 1/181, and Arkansas 1/142 and 2/142. All but the 1/158 were conventional artillery.

7. These figures represented a reduction of one battalion per division. The earlier typical heavy organization provided six mechanized and five armored battalions for a mechanized division in Europe and five mechanized and six armored battalions for an armored division. On the other hand, the number of line companies within the battalion increased by one. The brigades gained support, in line with a West German concept concentrating logistics at the brigade rather than the divisional level.

8. The battalion consists of a headquarters company and four tank companies (each of three platoons [four tanks each]) plus a two-tank headquarters section, for a total of fifty-eight tanks. The battalion headquarters company has two tanks and a cavalry platoon (six M3 Bradley cavalry fighting vehicles), a platoon of six self-propelled heavy mortars, and supporting units. As promulgated in 1986, the breakdown was one Bradley (M2), six cavalry fighting vehicles (M3), six mortar (81-mm) carrier fighting vehicles, six light tracked command posts, and thirteen armored personnel carriers. The battalion also includes seven tracked recovery vehicles, eleven recovery trucks, fifty-four cargo trucks of various sizes, and one high-mobility utility vehicle (HMMWV, equivalent to the old jeep).

9. The battalion consists of a headquarters company, four mechanized infantry companies (each of three platoons [four Bradleys carrying three rifle squads and a command group]), and an antiarmor company (three platoons, each with four M901 improved TOW vehicles and an M113 command vehicle). The headquarters company corresponds to the tank battalion headquarters company, except that it has M2s instead of tanks. As promulgated in 1986, the vehicle breakdown was seven cavalry fighting vehicles (M3s), six mortar carriers (4.2-inch, i.e., 107-mm), eight

command post vehicles, twenty armored personnel carriers, twelve improved TOW (antitank missile) vehicles, and fifty-four Bradleys (M2s). As in the tank battalion, there are seven tracked recovery vehicles. The battalion also includes sixty-four cargo trucks, two recovery trucks (wreckers), and twenty HMMWVs.

10. Each squadron consists of a headquarters troop (including two command tanks), three cavalry troops, and one tank company. Each cavalry troop (company equivalent) has two scout platoons (six M3s each), two tank platoons (four tanks each), a mortar section (two self-propelled mortars), and a headquarters section (including one more tank). The unit thus includes forty-three M1s and thirty-six cavalry fighting vehicles.

11. Other tracked vehicles: eighteen mortar carriers (107-mm), forty-nine cargo carriers (6-ton), forty-eight command posts, and eighty-two armored personnel carriers. The squadron also includes thirty-eight HMMWVs. It has three light and thirty medium armored recovery vehicles and a total of 414 cargo trucks (plus special-purpose types).

12. These figures are for the regiment as defined in 1986. At that time it was conceived as twelve TOW attack helicopters and fourteen advanced attack helicopters (AH-64 Apaches).

13. These data are taken from Isby and Kamps, op. cit. They were compiled before 1985 (and thus before the AH-64 entered service), so numbers of AH-64 helicopters are approximate. Moreover, Wiener, op. cit., gives much higher unit strengths: his airborne division includes a support battalion (two combat support squadrons), two attack helicopter battalions (each including twenty-one AH-1Ss or eighteen AH-64s), and one air cavalry squadron. Wiener's air assault division includes two combat support squadrons (forty-five UH-60s each), one medium helicopter battalion, four attack helicopter battalions (twenty-one AH-1Ss or eighteen AH-64s each), and one air cavalry squadron.

14. The army electronic warfare aircraft were probably RU-21 Guardrails, RV-1D Quick Looks, and EH-60A Quick Fix III. Photographs taken in Saudi Arabia show large numbers of RU-21s, but no reliable figures are available.

15. At the 1985 Canadian Army Trophy competition, M1 crews averaged 10 sec to engage a target, compared to 14 sec for the earlier M60A3; they made 93 percent hits compared to 77 for the earlier tank. In another comparison with the M60, it turned out that M1 gunners did 45 percent better. The new computers are actually much easier to use than their predecessors; the best crews did only 25 percent better with the M1, but the least capable crews did 85 percent better. This performance is probably characteristic of current computer technology. I am indebted to Steven J. Zaloga for these figures.

16. Reconnaissance battalions are nominally subordinated to divisions but are actually directly responsible to the two Fleet Marine Forces (Atlantic and Pacific). Each consists of a headquarters company and three combat companies; a fourth would be added in wartime.

17. Companies are built up from rifle platoons and squads in the usual 3 × 3 way; the squad is thirteen men. The rifle company includes a weapons platoon (mortar squad, machine gun squad, and SMAW squad with, respectively, three 60-mm mortars, six light machine guns, and six SMAW antitank rockets). The weapons company consists of a mortar platoon (81-mm), a heavy machine gun platoon (0.50-cal M2HB and Mk 19 grenade launcher), and an antitank platoon (M47 Dragon). The headquarters company of a marine battalion includes a special sniper unit.

18. Marine tank company composition is changing. At present the 1st and 3d tank battalions are still equipped with the M60; the 2d battalion (reinforced in the Gulf by two reserve companies) is equipped with the M1A1. The M60 battalion has seventeen tanks per company (two HQ plus five for each of three platoons), for a total of seventy tanks, including two for the battalion HQ. The M1A1 tank company is reduced to fourteen tanks (four per platoon plus two HQ), for a total of fifty-eight tanks, including two for the battalion HQ. The planned reorganization, reflecting a reduction in the planned tank purchase from 476 to 221, is to three-company tank battalions with forty-four tanks each. An MPS squadron carries thirty M1A1 tanks. The 1st tank battalion was probably reinforced by reservists in the Gulf, so the actual number of M60s was considerably higher than the nominal seventy.

19. The mechanized guns are organized in three batteries of 155-mm and two of 8-inch.

20. Data on Special Forces composition and operations is from F. Chadwick and M. Caffrey, *Gulf War Fact Book* (Bloomington: GDW, 1991). Their data does not seem to include the navy SEALs, who were certainly active in the war. Chadwick and Caffrey also mention the Air Force Special Operations Force and the army's 75th Infantry Regiment (Ranger). They state that different Special Forces Groups have specific responsibility for different parts of the world: 1st is Far East, 3d is Africa (including North Africa), 5th is Middle East, 7th is Central and South America, and 19th is Europe. There is also a reserve for special contingencies and global response. Generally most of the members of a unit with particular geographical responsibility will speak the local languages. Hence the use of A-Teams as liaison with the Arab forces.

21. Modern British army organization originated in the 1870s, when each regiment was reorganized to provide a battalion for overseas service and a second battalion for home service (including home defense) and also for training. During World War I many regiments raised multiple battalions for combat service. Cutbacks in the overall size of the British army later amalgamated famous regiments and also cut most of them to a single battalion.

22. After World War II, there was a debate within the British army establishment as to whether to form permanent divisions. At present the only British divisions approaching permanency are those in the corps in

Germany (the British Army on the Rhine, or BAOR). In the mid-1960s the three BAOR divisions included a total of two armored brigades and four infantry brigades, plus an attached Canadian infantry brigade (i.e., two brigades per division). At this time brigades consisted of four battalions/regiments (armored was three tank and one mechanized; infantry was one tank and three motorized [i.e., wheeled rather than tracked]). By the early 1970s the armored brigades had shifted to two tank and two mechanized battalions. Each also had its own reconnaissance troop and its own regiment of self-propelled guns. In the mid-1970s the British government ordered a reorganization into four divisions to increase apparent ground firepower. The brigades were abolished, each division being reduced to two armored regiments and three mechanized battalions rather than the earlier four and four. The battalions were too numerous for direct command (they barely conformed to the command span of five rule). Moreover, they were not strong enough to fight independently, particularly after many were drained of their fourth companies to fight in Ulster. The brigades were therefore re-established in 1981–83. They are triangular rather than square, as in the earlier structure. The brigade is preferred as the independent fighting unit largely in order to be able to disperse such units around the battlefield to minimize the possible effect of nuclear attack, yet still be effective in nonnuclear combat. More generally, a larger unit can concentrate more firepower on a nonnuclear battlefield, but it can be devastated by a single nuclear hit and thus makes a more attractive nuclear target. The major armies have, therefore, oscillated between emphasis on brigades and emphasis on divisions and larger units as they have believed more or less firmly in the nuclear (or, equivalently, the chemical) threat. From a British point of view, concentration on the brigade rather than the division made it easier to deploy self-contained units for the very important post-1945 Empire and Commonwealth peacekeeping role; divisions were far too large and unwieldy. The U.S. Marine Corps is built around the MAB/MEB for much the same reason. In the 1970s, when attention within NATO turned toward prolonged conventional battle (and when most Commonwealth obligations lapsed), the British experimented with an army organization built entirely around divisions, within which task forces could be formed.

23. Of these units, only 1st and 4th Armoured Divisions are maintained at full strength in Germany and thus were even candidates for Gulf operations. 3d Armoured Division has two armored brigades (one formerly an experimental airmobile brigade); its infantry brigade is in the United Kingdom. 2d Division is based in the United Kingdom and would protect the corps rear area in wartime. Two of its three infantry brigades would come from the British Territorial Army (reserve force).

24. The French also want to maintain as many divisions as the Germans, despite their smaller population and the financial drains of maintaining nuclear forces and substantial naval forces, neither of which affect Germany.

25. Draftees did serve in Algeria because that was French territory. In 1962 the law was changed to limit draftees to service in France proper (except for volunteers). The FAR has been used in former colonies such as Chad and Mali. It and Foreign Legion units are stationed in Djibouti, in the South Pacific, and in French Guiana.

26. The total reported prewar Saudi fighting vehicle inventory is as follows—tanks: 290 AMX 30s and 258 M60s (158 M60A1s and 100 M60A3s); tank destroyers: 92 AMX 10s, 230 Improved TOW vehicles; armored cars: 250 AMLs, 1,000 V-150 Commandos (also used as armored personnel carriers); armored personnel carriers: 425 AMX 10s (including 201 personnel, 156 command, 24 mortar-carriers, 17 ATAC radar carriers, and 27 hospital), 140 BMR 600s, 154 M3 Panhards, and 1,260 M113s; self-propelled artillery: 93 M109As and 51 AUF 1s (French GCT 155-mm); antiaircraft artillery: 52 AMX 30DCAs, 48 Crotale missiles, 36 Shahine missiles, and 60 M163 Vulcan guns.

27. The composition of the Joint Forces Command is taken from Chadwick and Caffrey, op. cit. The Joint Forces North assault formation composition is from an account of the role of the air liaison officers in the ground campaign, in *Aviation Week and Space Technology*, which is cited in the main text of this book.

28. S. C. Pelletiere and D. V. Johnson III, *Lessons Learned: The Iran-Iraq War* (Carlisle Barracks: U.S. Army War College, 1991). Figures are not available, but the Republican Guard was surely largely Sunni. If, as reported, it was largely manned by ex-college students, Shia among them would have belonged to the urban class most strongly attached to the Ba'ath party.

29. This breakdown is taken from *The GDW Desert Shield Fact Book* (Bloomington: GDW, 1990). Other sources credited Iraq with seven armored and forty infantry divisions, plus twenty commando (special forces) brigades.

30. This account is from the GDW book cited above.

APPENDIX B. AIR UNITS AND THEIR EQUIPMENT

1. Corresponding Pacific Air Forces squadron strengths are twenty-four A-10s, eighteen RF-4Cs, twenty-four F-15s, twenty-four F-16s, and twenty-four F-4E/Gs. Alaskan Air Command strengths are thirty F-15As and twenty-four A-10s. Tactical Air Command (TAC) strengths (squadrons initially deployed to the Gulf): eighteen RF-4s, eighteen F-15A/B/C/Ds (ADTAC) or twenty-four F-15A/B/C/Ds, twenty-three F-16s, eighteen F-111As, twenty-four A-10s, and twenty-four F-4Es. Strategic Air Command (SAC) squadron strengths: eleven FB-111s, sixteen B-1Bs, sixteen B-52Gs, and nineteen B-52Hs. Typically one SAC squadron forms a Bomb Wing at one base.

2. This unit replaced 14C Squadron, whose formation was announced on 23 August 1990. The aircraft originally sent to the Gulf soon had to be replaced due to sand damage to their engine fan cooling blades (the

problem was solved by substituting single-crystal blades, as in the F.3s). 20C Squadron replaced 617(C) Squadron, which also returned to the UK in November 1990. The 31(C) Squadron aircraft plus six new aircraft for Muharraq were the latest Phase 2 version of the Tornado, with radar-absorbent material on wings, fins, and engine inlets, provision for NVGs for their crews, Have Quick 2 secure radios, GPS, and provision for enlarged (495-gallon rather than 330-gallon) drop tanks. The ALARMS missiles sent to the Gulf just before the outbreak of war went to the Tabuk squadron, 20(C). The three squadrons of strike Tornadoes listed here add up to thirty-six aircraft, for a total Tornado force of sixty; another thirty were kept in the area as operational spares.

3. 43 C replaced 11C, which was despatched with the twelve Jaguars in August 1990. It arrived in mid-December. The F.3s used in the Gulf were modified with improved software for their AI.24 radars, an improved Hermes radar warning receiver, radar absorbent material on the wing and fin leading edges and in the engine air intakes, two ALE-40(V) flare dispensers under the rear fuselage, provision for a Phimat chaff pod, and AIM-9M rather than -9L Sidewinders.

4. The twelve aircraft originally flown out to Oman were replaced in October 1990 by Jaguars with uprated engines, Sky Guardian RWRs, and overwing rails for self-defense Sidewinder missiles. Four of these aircraft had reconnaissance pods. They all carried Phimat chaff pods and ALQ-101(V)10 jamming pods. Jaguars normally deliver unguided bombs, but this squadron also had Paveways. The Jaguars do not have their own laser designators, but they have laser receivers and thus can detect targets illuminated either from the ground or by other aircraft.

5. These figures (apart from those for the Su-25s) are taken from *Flight International*, 9–15 January 1991. The squadron numbers are from the 1990/91 edition of the *Military Balance* (London: International Institute for Strategic Studies, 1990).

APPENDIX D. SELECTED MAJOR WEAPONS

1. This is much the same consideration (and much the same language) that applies to tactical nuclear weapons. Two of the coalition partners, the United States and Britain, went so far as to imply that any Iraqi chemical attack would bring nuclear retaliation. One hope may have been to force Saddam Hussein personally to consider each chemical attack. It is known, however, that he had no such direct role during the Iran-Iraq war.

2. This is typical of nuclear weapons practice. For the United States and almost certainly also for the Soviet Union, deployment of tactical nuclear weapons is acceptable only because those weapons cannot easily be fired without opening locks whose codes are held by the central government. This type of procedure carries with it all sorts of problems for nuclear deterrence: if nothing can be fired without permission from Washington, then it pays Moscow to incinerate Washington so as to

disable the U.S. nuclear force. If, however, some key weapons *can* be fired on local initiative, then . . . Saddam is likely to have found local initiative particularly unacceptable, given his general distrust of the Iraqi Army.

3. Newspaper reports of the fighting in the south, against the Shi'ites, claimed that Saddam Hussein ordered his Republican guards to use "cologne" (i.e., gas) against rebels in the Shi'ite holy cities of Karbala and Najaf rather than bombard them (and risk taking the blame for their physical destruction). It is not clear to what extent this was accurate. At the time, the United States threatened severe consequences if Iraq used gas against its own population. In the north, the Kurds claimed that Iraqi helicopters were dropping sulfuric acid on them. It seems unlikely that an Iraqi regime in possession of large stocks of efficient chemical weapons would resort to so crude and inefficient a weapon.

APPENDIX G. NAVAL LOSSES

1. Some of the above claims must be duplicates. CentCom claimed that as of 27 January, total Iraqi naval losses amounted to one oil platform service ship, two patrol boats, one tanker and four unknown presumed destroyed plus four mining vessels, one hovercraft, three patrol boats, and two unknowns known sunk.

2. On 30 January the coalition reported that a total of forty-six Iraqi naval vessels had been sunk or disabled. However, another report at about the same time claimed a total of about sixty.

3. As of 2 February, the coalition claimed eighty-three Iraqi naval craft sunk or damaged to date.

Index

425

The **Naval Institute Press** is the book-publishing arm of the U.S. Naval Institute, a private, nonprofit professional society for members of the sea services and civilians who share an interest in naval and maritime affairs. Established in 1873 at the U.S. Naval Academy in Annapolis, Maryland, where its offices remain today, the Naval Institute has more than 100,000 members worldwide.

Members of the Naval Institute receive the influential monthly magazine *Proceedings* and discounts on fine nautical prints, ship and aircraft photos, and subscriptions to the quarterly *Naval History* magazine. They also have access to the transcripts of the Institute's Oral History Program and get discounted admission to any of the Institute-sponsored seminars regularly offered around the country.

The Naval Institute's book-publishing program, begun in 1898 with basic guides to naval practices, has broadened its scope in recent years to include books of more general interest. Now the Naval Institute Press publishes more than forty new titles each year, ranging from how-to books on boating and navigation to battle histories, biographies, ship and aircraft guides, and novels. Institute members receive discounts on the Press's more than 375 books.

Full-time students are eligible for special half-price membership rates. Life memberships are also available.

For a free catalog describing the Naval Institute Press books currently available, and for further information about U.S. Naval Institute membership, please write to:

Membership & Communications Department
U.S. Naval Institute
Annapolis, Maryland 21402

Or call, toll-free, (800) 233-USNI. In Maryland, call (301) 224-3378.

THE NAVAL INSTITUTE PRESS

DESERT VICTORY

The War for Kuwait

Designed by Pamela L. Schnitter

Set in Electra and Corvinus Skyline
by Maryland Composition Company, Inc.
Glen Burnie, Maryland

Printed on 60-lb. Windsor Offset
by The John D. Lucas Printing Company
Baltimore, Maryland

Bound in Holliston Roxite A (hardback)
by The Maple-Vail Book Manufacturing Group
York, Pennsylvania

ABOUT THE AUTHOR

Norman Friedman is an internationally known defense consultant, analyst, and author. His articles on a wide range of defense subjects appear regularly in journals throughout the world, and he contributes a monthly column on world naval developments to the Naval Institute's *Proceedings* magazine. His more than a dozen books include *The Naval Institute Guide to World Naval Weapons Systems*, a biennial publication. He resides in New York City.